READINGS IN WORLD CIVILIZATIONS

Volume 1: The Great Traditions

Third Edition

KEVIN REILLY

ST. MARTIN'S PRESS / New York

For my friends in the World History Association

Editor: Louise H. Waller
Manager, publishing services: Emily Berleth
Publishing services associate: Kalea Chapman
Project management: Richard Steins
Photo research: Inge King
Cover design: Rod Hernandez
Cover art: Detail of Catalan *Mappamundi* c. 1450, Biblioteca Estense
Modena/Scala

For information, write:
St. Martin's Press, Inc.
175 Fifth Avenue
New York, NY 10010

ISBN: 0-312-09647-X

Acknowledgments

1. Hunters and Gatherers and the Agricultural Revolution

1. From "Civilization and Its Discontents" by Katherine Milton. With permission from
Natural History, March 1992. Copyright © the American Museum of Natural History, 1992.

2. Reprinted by permission of the publishers from *Nisa: The Life and Words of a !Kung
Woman* by Marjorie Shostak. Cambridge, Mass.: Harvard University Press. Copyright ©
1981 by Marjorie Shostak.

3. From Mircea Eliade, *Shamanism: Archaic Techniques of Ecstacy,* translated by Willard R.
Trask, Bollingen Series LXXVI. Copyright © 1964 by Princeton University Press. Reprinted by permission of Princeton University Press.

4. From *The Underside of History: A View of Women through Time* by Elise Boulding. Copyright © 1976 Westview Press. Copyright now held by Elise Boulding.

Acknowledgments and copyrights are continued at the back of the book on pages 354–
356, which constitute an extension of the copyright page.

READINGS IN WORLD CIVILIZATIONS

Volume 1: The Great Traditions

Third Edition

CONTENTS

TOPICAL CONTENTS

GEOGRAPHICAL CONTENTS

Eastern and Southeast Asia

Europe and Russia

India

PREFACE

When I began my teaching career at Rutgers University in the 1960s, there was no course in world history. We taught a course called "Western Civilization" that had developed in American universities between World War I and World War II. It was a course that identified America's fate with that of Europe; the idea of "Europe" or "the West" made more sense to Americans swept up in European wars than it did to many Europeans (who taught their national histories). A course in Western civilization also seemed the appropriate way for an American population largely descended from Europeans to find its roots.

There were problems with this idea from the beginning. One was that it ignored the heritage of Americans whose ancestors came from Africa, Asia, and other parts of the world. Another was that the world was becoming a much smaller place. Transoceanic journeys that formerly took a week or more had been reduced by jet planes to a few hours. Since the 1960s, the importance of the non-European world for Americans has increased even more. Trade with Japan has become larger than that with European countries. More new American immigrants have come from Asia and Latin American than from Europe. The daily newspaper carries more stories concerning the Middle East, Asia, Africa, and Latin America than Europe. The interests of the United States are more global than ever. For these good reasons, an increasing number of colleges and universities (including Rutgers) are now offering courses in global or world history.

Compiling an anthology for use in such introductory world history classes is a task that requires many decisions and that benefits from the input of many friends. The instructor who considers using the result should be apprised of both.

First the decisions. These two volumes are intended for introductory courses. For me, that consideration prescribes a survey format that encompasses all of world history. (The two volumes of this work divide roughly at the year 1500.) It also mandates that the readings be understandable, at least in their essentials, by typical first-year college students.

In nearly every chapter I have included both primary and secondary sources. Primary sources were selected partly to represent "great works" and cultural legacies and partly to provide students with an authentic glimpse of a particular historical time and place. Some readings do both. The epic of Gilgamesh in Volume One, for example, is a "great work" that also opens a window on Sumer. From it students can learn about Sumerian religion, gender roles, and ideas of kingship and also acquire a basis for making important historical comparisons—the Biblical account of the flood is often compared with the flood in Gilgamesh. The selection in Volume Two from Gabriel García Márquez's *One Hundred Years of Solitude*, one of the "great works" of modern literature, releases an explosion of images, characters, settings, and scenes in a magical confection of hypnotic dream and detail that reveals a good deal about Latin America.

Secondary sources were chosen for their capacity to challenge students with information and points of view probably not found in their survey texts, as well as, of course, for their interest and accessibility. Some readings will introduce students to the work of leading modern historians—such as William H. McNeill, Philip Curtin, Natalie Zemon Davis, Alfred W. Crosby, and Jonathan Spence—and perhaps even induce them to read further in the writings of these great scholars. In some cases the selections may lead students to look at additional primary sources beyond what I have been able to include here. In Volume One, for example, S. G. Brandon's "Paul and His Opponents" should encourage students to examine the New Testament letters of Paul with a keener eye. In Volume Two, the secondary readings on "Dependence and Independence" in Asia, Africa, the Middle East, and Latin America will enable students to get more out of their daily newspaper.

For the third edition I have added more interesting primary sources and newer interpretations. I have also tried to make the collection more global (adding selections, for instance, from Southeast Asia) and more universal (for example, with additional selections on women, technology, and on daily life).

I wanted each reading to be able to stand on its own. I know how frustrating it can be to find that a favorite selection or passage has been so condensed as to become almost worthless. Although space considerations have dictated that some abridging be done, I have tried very hard to be as sensitive as possible to this concern.

I also wanted the students *to read the readings*. Therefore the readings are not preceded by lengthy introductions that, in students' minds, may make the selections seem superfluous. For each reading I have provided an introduction that establishes a context but that principally directs students with a series of questions. These questions ask: What is said? What is the evidence? What conclusion or judgment can be drawn? They are intended to aid students in developing critical thinking skills—recall, analysis and evaluation, and self-expression—and to illustrate how historians work.

The historical understanding that, I am hopeful, will develop from the study of these volumes is qualitative. Different students will remember different specifics. All, however, should gain an increased understanding of past civilizations and ways of life and a greater awareness of the connections and contrasts between past and present. My ultimate goal for these two volumes is that they help students to live in a broader world, both temporally and spatially.

Now for the friends. A work like this would not have been possible without many historian friends and colleagues. As president of the World History Association, I have been fortunate in having many people who are both. Many members of the association—too many to name—offered suggestions, read drafts, sent me favorite selections, and in general helped me improve this work. But I am especially indebted to Lynda Shaffer of Tufts University; Stephen Gosch of the University of Wisconsin-Eau Claire; Marc Gilbert of North Georgia College; Jerry Bentley of the University of Hawaii; Ross Dunn of San Diego State; Ray Lorantas of Drexel University; and Ernest Menze of Iona College. Their criticisms and also, of course, the work of an earlier generation of world historians, especially William H. McNeill, Philip Curtin, and Leften Stavrianos, have been invaluable.

I also want to thank my friends and colleagues where I have learned and taught: at Rutgers—Traian Stoianovich, Michael Adas, Allen Howard, Virginia Yans, Robert Rosen (now at UCLA), and Roger Cranse (now at Vermont College of Norwich University); at Princeton—Robert Tignor, Gyan Prakash, and Robert J. Wright; and at Raritan—Brock Haussamen, Bud McKinley, Mark Bezanson, Tom Valasek, and my Humanities colleagues.

Many others have commented, suggested selections, or reviewed the previous edition. Among them are Linda Addo, North Carolina Agriculture and Technical State University; Andrew Clark, University of North Carolina, Wilmington; Eugene Hermitte, Johnson C. Smith University; Ted Kluz, Auburn University, Montgomery; Bogwa Lorence-Kot, California College of Arts and Crafts; William M. McBride, James Madison University; Stephen Morillo, Wabash College; Gary R. Olsen, New Mexico Tech; Patricia O'Malley, Bradford College; V. Padmavathy, University of Wisconsin-La Crosse; and Allen Wittenborn, University of San Diego.

I want to give special thanks to all of the people at St. Martin's Press. Louise Waller, my editor and friend, has been a superb successor to Michael Weber, who helped me create the first edition. The work of Lynette Blevins and Richard Steins was invaluable. And I want to thank Emily Berleth, manager of publishing services of this edition but also my first "agent," for encouraging me to write history some years ago.

And again I thank Pearl for her loving help and support.

KEVIN REILLY

A NOTE ABOUT THE COVER

St. Martin's Press and I have chosen maps for the covers of these volumes that are both historically valuable and, we hope, attractive. On Volume One, courtesy of Biblioteca Estense Modena/Scala, we have reproduced a Catalan world map from about 1450, not one of the most accurate of the period (especially in its drawing of Asia) but one of the more vivid renderings of history geographically, with its inclusion of legendary rulers of Asia and Africa. For Volume Two, Maryland Cartographics produced a "cartogram" in which each country's size is drawn so as to indicate the world population in 1994. Thus, China and India, for example, appear to be quite large on the map, while Russia and Canada are relatively small.

INTRODUCTION

This is a collection of readings from and about the human past. Those that are from the past are usually called *primary sources.* They can be anything from an old parking ticket to an ancient poem. Those that are about the past we call *secondary sources,* interpretations, or just plain "histories." They can be written immediately after the events they describe or centuries later, by professional historians or by other interested parties.

We read primary sources and histories for the same reason: to find out what happened in the past. People have different motivations for finding out about the past. Some people are curious about everything. Some are interested in knowing what it was like to live in a particular time or be a particular kind of person. Some people are interested in how things change, or how the world got to where it is. Some wonder about human variety, trying to figure out how different or similar people have been throughout history. I hope this book will answer all these questions.

The reading selections are what is important in this book. Each reading is preceded by an introduction that poses some questions. These questions are designed to guide your reading and to suggest approaches to the reading. There are no particular ideas or pieces of information that everyone should get from a particular reading. What you learn from a reading depends very much on who you are, what you already know, and how much attention you give it. My hope is that you get as much from each reading as you can. Each reading should affect you in some way. Some you will like more than others, but each should open a world previously closed.

Treat these readings, especially the primary sources, as openings to a lost world. Keep your eyes and ears open. Notice everything you can. But don't worry if you miss a sign, a name, or even the meaning people attach to some things. This is your discovery. In some cases, I have added explanatory notes, but I have tried to keep these to a bare minimum. Ultimately there are never enough explanations. But more important, I do not want my explanations to become the information that is read, remembered, and studied for an exam. The readings should bring you your own insights, discoveries, and questions. Like a good travel guide they should help you see, not tell you what you saw.

READINGS IN WORLD CIVILIZATIONS

Volume 1: The Great Traditions

Third Edition

PART ONE

THE ANCIENT WORLD:
TO 1000 B.C.

Predynastic bird deity, c.3650–3300 B.C. (The Brooklyn Museum)

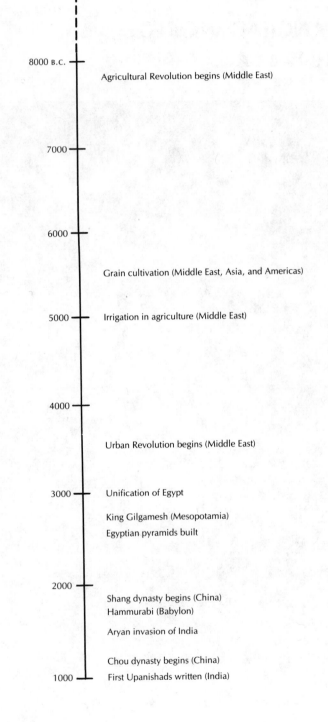

8000 B.C. — Agricultural Revolution begins (Middle East)

7000 —

6000 —

Grain cultivation (Middle East, Asia, and Americas)

5000 — Irrigation in agriculture (Middle East)

4000 —

Urban Revolution begins (Middle East)

3000 — Unification of Egypt

King Gilgamesh (Mesopotamia)

Egyptian pyramids built

2000 —

Shang dynasty begins (China)
Hammurabi (Babylon)

Aryan invasion of India

Chou dynasty begins (China)
1000 — First Upanishads written (India)

CHAPTER ONE

Hunters and Gatherers and the Agricultural Revolution

1. AMAZON HUNTERS AND GATHERERS

Katherine Milton

In this reading Katherine Milton, an anthropologist, discusses her "double life." Half the time she is a college professor in Berkeley and the other half she lives with Indian hunter-gatherers in the Brazilian Amazon. What are the main differences between these two worlds? What does the author say about the importance of possessions in these two worlds? In what ways has the modern world improved the lives of the hunter-gatherers? In what ways has modernity made their lives worse? What do you think of the author's view of her subject?

For more than a decade now, I have led a double life. I spend part of my time in the United States, living in an apartment in Berkeley and teaching anthropology classes at the University of California. The rest of my time is spent in the Amazon Basin, where I live in the company of recently contacted Indian groups, studying their traditional ecology and features of their tropical forest environment. On returning to the United States after one of these extended stays in the jungle, I always experience culture shock as I strive to regain control of my possessions, which I have totally forgotten about.

Usually my first act is to retrieve my dust-covered car, which has languished for some six to eighteen months in a garage. The battery must be charged, and then I must wash and vacuum the car, fill it with gas, and check out its many parts. Once I am mobile, I rush to a large supermarket to stock up on cleaning supplies and food. My first few days are completely taken up with chores; there never seems to be a moment when I am not contemplating some type of home repair or new purchase.

And then there is my body. What a job it is to live up to what is expected of the average American. I must visit the dentist—often more than one kind of dentist—to be sure my teeth are performing at top level. The doctor must be seen for a checkup; my eyes must be examined, glasses and contact lenses adjusted, and so on. I begin to wonder how my friends in Berkeley manage to have any free time at all, since I have fewer possessions than they do—I own no television set, no stereo or compact disk player, no video machine, home computer, food chopper, or any number of other items my friends seem to dote on. I don't even own my apartment.

Plunged back into life in Berkeley, I see myself as a slave of material possessions, and I notice that I deeply resent the time and energy required to maintain them. Nothing could be more different from the life I have been leading with hunter-gatherers deep in the rain forests of Brazil, where people have almost no possessions, and those that they do have are made from local forest materials and are entirely biodegradable.

The groups I have visited live far from any cities, towns, or commercial enterprises. They include the Mayoruna and Maku from Amazonas State; the Arara, Parakana, and Arawete from Pará State; and the Guaja from Maranhão State—peoples so remote and little known that few outside their immediate geographic area have heard of them. Often I am one of the first nonindigenous females many members of the group have ever seen. With my pale skin and hair I am a truly terrifying apparition to younger children, who sometimes scream with fear when they first see me.

All these peoples have been recently contacted: only a few months or, at most, years have passed since the Brazilian Indian Bureau (FUNAI) managed to establish a formal relationship with them. Previously, these groups avoided or were strongly hostile to outsiders, but with contact, they have permitted a few Indian Bureau employees to live with them, to assist them, and at times, protect them in dealings with other Indian groups or members of the wider Brazilian society. Living with these people has given me the chance to see how even modest changes in their traditional lifeways—the introduction of something as innocent in appearance as a metal cooking pot or ax, a box of matches or some salt— can be the thin edge of a wedge that will gradually alter the behavior and ecological practices of an entire society.

These people typically live in small villages of fewer than a hundred inhabitants, in some cases in groups of only fifteen or twenty. Most practice slash-and-burn agriculture on a small scale, complementing crop foods with wild game and fish, forest fruits and nuts, and occasionally, wild honey. For some months life may revolve around the village, but sooner or later every group I have worked with leaves, generally in small parties, and spends weeks or even months traveling through the forest and living on forest products.

Throughout the forest there are paths that the Indians know and have used for generations. They travel mainly when wild forest fruits and nuts are most abundant and game animals are fat, but families or small groups may go on expeditions at other times of year as well. They trek a few miles, make a temporary camp, and then hunt, gather, and eat several meals in the area before moving on to a new site. At certain times of year, many groups relocate to the borders of large rivers, where they obtain turtle eggs or other seasonal river foods.

The accumulation of possessions would be an impediment to this seminomadic life style. Whenever individuals go on a trek, they carry everything they need. Leaving possessions behind in a thatch-and-pole hut, to be retrieved later, is not an option, since the humid climate and voracious insects would quickly destroy them. Great numbers of insects often live inside Indian dwellings, principally jungle cockroaches that hide in the roof thatch by day but come out by the thousands at night. Indians seem oblivious to them, letting them run about on their bodies and even crawl on the food so long as they are not perched on the next bite.

Granted, these are generally soft-bodied, small jungle cockroaches and not the tough, large roaches of our urban areas, but even so, I found it difficult to adjust to them. My frantic efforts to remove cockroaches from my body and clothes were regarded as strange by my Indian hosts. At one site, I resorted to storing my clothing each night in a heavy plastic bag, which I sealed shut and suspended from a piece of plastic fish line tied to a roof pole. Otherwise, at night, the roaches covered my shirt and pants so thoroughly that often the fabric could not be seen. Although the roaches would be gone the next morning, they would leave a musty smell; further, just the idea of wearing garments that I had seen coated with cockroaches gave me a squirmy, unclean feeling.

On the forest treks, the women are invariably the most burdened, something Western observers often find difficult to understand or accept. A woman will walk for hours carrying a toddler, a large palm basket containing fifty or more pounds of animal or plant foods, hammocks, a cooking utensil or two, a machete, and the family pets, such as parrots, monkeys, and young puppies. In all the groups I have observed, the women's legs and feet are deformed by the pigeon-toed walk they adopt to give them added traction and stability on the slippery, narrow forest trails. The feet of adult men turn in only slightly, because men usually carry nothing heavier than a bow and arrows (ostensibly to be free to take advantage of any hunting opportunities).

The most important possession the Indians carry with them, however, is knowledge. There is nothing coded in the genome of an Indian concerning how to make a living in a tropical forest—each individual must become a walking bank of information on the forest landscape, its plants and animals, and their habits and uses. This information must be taught anew to the members of each generation, without the benefit of books, manuals, or educational television. Indians have no stores in which to purchase the things they need for survival. Instead, each individual must learn to collect, manufacture, or produce all the things required for his or her entire lifetime.

Because people differ in their talents, the pool of community information and abilities is far greater than its component parts. Individual men and women have their own areas of expertise, as well as their share of general knowledge. Members of the group know whom to consult for special information on hunting practices, the habits of particular game animals, rituals, tool manufacture, crop varieties, and the like.

Tropical-forest Indians talk incessantly, a characteristic I believe reflects the importance of oral transmission of culture. When I lived with the Maku, I slept in a hammock inside a small communal palm shelter. If a Maku awoke in the middle of the night, he usually began to talk or sing in a very loud voice—apparently without any thought that anyone might object to this behavior. It was considered normal, what you do when you wake up in the middle of the night and aren't sleepy. Others learn, as I did, to sleep through it or, if they aren't sleepy, to listen to it. Vocal expression apparently is expected and tolerated in Maku culture, no matter what the hour, an indication to me of how much it is valued.

Unlike our economic system, in which each person typically tries to secure and control as large a share of the available resources as possible, the hunter-gatherer economic system rests on a set of highly formalized expectations regarding cooperation and sharing. This does not mean hunter-gatherers do not compete with one another for prestige, sexual partners, and the like. But individuals do not amass a surplus. For instance, no hunter fortunate enough to kill a large game animal assumes that all this food is his or belongs only to his immediate family.

Quite the reverse is true: among some forest peoples, the hunter cannot eat game he has killed or is restricted to eating only one specific portion of his kill. Game is cut up and distributed according to defined patterns particular to each group and based in large part on kinship and marriage obligations. A hunter may have amazing luck one day, moderate luck on another, and no luck at all on a third. But he can usually expect to eat meat every day because someone bound to him in this system of reciprocity may well make a kill and share the meat.

Despite the way their culture traditionally eschews possessions, forest-living peoples embrace manufactured goods with amazing enthusiasm. They seem to appreciate instantly the efficacy of a steel machete, ax, or cooking pot. It is love at first sight, and the desire to possess such objects is absolute. There are accounts of Indian groups or individuals who have turned their backs on manufactured trade goods, but such people are the exception.

When Cândido Rondon, the founder of the Indian Protection Service in Brazil, began his pacification efforts in the early 1900s, he used trade goods as bait to attract uncontacted Indians. Pots, machetes, axes, and steel knives were hung from trees or laid along trails that Indians frequented. This practice proved so successful that it is still employed.

Whether they have been formally contacted or not, forest-living groups in the Amazon Basin are probably well aware of steel tools and metal cooking pots. After all, such goods have been in circulation along trade routes in these regions for centuries, and an Indian does not have to have seen a non-Indian in order to acquire them. However, such manufactured goods are likely to be extremely scarce among uncontacted groups. When the Arara Indians were first approached in 1975, they fled their village to escape the pacification party. Examination of their hastily abandoned dwellings showed that stone tools were still being used, but a few steel fragments were also found.

Since they already appreciate the potential utility of manufactured goods, uncontacted Indians are strongly drawn to the new and abundant items offered to lure them from isolation. Once a group has been drawn into the pacification area, all its members are presented with various trade goods—standard gifts include metal cooking pots, salt, matches, machetes, knives, axes, cloth hammocks, T-shirts, and shorts. Not all members of the group get all of these items, but most get at least two or three of them, and in a family, the cumulative mass of new goods can be considerable.

The Indians initially are overwhelmed with delight—this is the honeymoon period when suddenly, from a position in which one or two old metal implements were shared by the entire group, a new situation prevails in which almost every adult individual has some of these wonderful new items. The honeymoon is short-lived, however. Once the Indians have grown accustomed to these new items, the next step is to teach them that these gifts will not be repeated. The Indians are now told that they must work to earn money or must manufacture goods for trade so that they can purchase new items.

Unable to contemplate returning to life without steel axes, the Indians begin to produce extra arrows or blowguns or hunt additional game or weave baskets beyond what they normally need so that this new surplus can be traded. Time that might, in the past, have been used for other tasks—subsistence activities, ceremonial events, or whatever—is now devoted to production of barter goods. In addition, actual settlement patterns may be altered so that the indigenous group is in closer, more immediate contact with sources of manufactured items. Neither of these things, in itself, is necessarily good or bad, but each does alter traditional behavior.

Thus, the newly contacted forest people are rapidly drawn into the wider economic sphere (even into the international economy: for example, the preferred glass beads for personal adornment come from Czechoslovakia). The intrusion of every item—mirrors, cloth, scissors, rice, machetes, axes, pots, bowls, needles, blankets, even bicycles and radios—not only adds to the pressure on individuals to produce trade goods but also disrupts some facet of traditional production.

Anthropologist Paul Henley, who worked with the Panare, a forest-based people in Venezuela, points out that with the introduction of steel tools, particularly axes, indigenous groups suffer a breakdown in the web of cooperative interdependence. In the past, when stone axes were used, various individuals came together and worked communally to fell trees for a new garden. With the introduction of the steel ax, however, one man can clear a garden by himself. As Henley notes, collaboration is no longer mandatory nor particularly frequent.

Indians often begin to cultivate new crops, such as coffee, that they feel can be traded or sold easily. Another is rice, which the Indian Bureau encourages forest peoples to plant because, of course, all "real" Brazilians eat rice every day. Rice is an introduced crop both to Brazil and to forest Indians. Traditional crop foods, the successful cultivation of which has been worked out over generations in the forest environment and which are well suited to the soil conditions in particular regions, may become scarce, with the result that the Indian diet becomes unbalanced.

Indians who traditionally plant manioc as a staple crop may be encouraged to increase the size of their fields and plant more manioc, which can then be transformed into *farinha,* a type of cereal that can be sold in the markets. Larger fields mean more intensive agricultural work and less time to hunt—which also affects the diet. The purchase of a shotgun may temporarily improve hunting returns, but it also tends to eliminate game in the area. In addition, shotgun shells are very expensive in Brazil, costing more than $1 U.S. apiece. Dependence on the shotgun undermines a hunter's skill with traditional hunting weapons, such as blowguns and bows and arrows, as well as the ability required to manufacture them.

Clearing larger areas for fields can also lead to increased risk from diseases such as malaria and leishmanaisis, because cleared areas with standing water of low acidity permit proliferation of disease-bearing mosquitoes and flies. New diseases also appear. Anthropologist-epidemiologist Carlos Coimbra, Jr., for example, has shown that Chagas disease, which is transmitted to humans by trypanosome-carrying assassin bugs, apparently does not yet affect Indian populations in lowland areas of the Amazon Basin. Only when Indians cease their seminomadic way of life and begin to live for prolonged periods in the same dwellings can Chagas-carrying bugs adjust their feeding behavior and begin to depend on human hosts rather than small rodents for their blood meals.

The moment manufactured foods begin to intrude on the indigenous diet, health takes a downward turn. The liberal use of table salt (sodium chloride), one of the first things that Indians are given, is probably no more healthful for them than it is for Westerners. Most Indians do not have table salt; they manufacture small quantities of potassium salts by burning certain types of leaves and collecting the ash. Anthropologist

Darrell Posey reports that the Kayapo Indians of Brazil make salt ash from various palm species and use each type for specific foods.

Sweets and other foods containing refined sugar (sucrose) are also given to Indians, whose wild fruits, according to research by botanists Irene and Herbert Baker, contain primarily other sugars, such as fructose. Indians find that foods containing sucrose taste exceptionally sweet, and they tend to crave them once sampled. While a strong, sugary taste in the natural environment might signal a rare, rich energy source, the indiscriminate consumption of canned foods, candies, and gums containing large amounts of refined sugar contributes to tooth decay and can lead to obesity and even health problems such as diabetes.

Results of dietary change are often difficult to anticipate. Anthropologist Dennis Werner found that the Mekranoti of central Brazil, who did not make pottery, traditionally roasted most of their food. But the introduction of metal cooking pots allowed them to switch to boiled foods. This, in turn, allowed nursing mothers to provide supplemental foods to their infants at an earlier age. Werner found that the average nursing period in the Mekranoti had dropped steadily from 19.7 months prior to 1955 to 16 months in recent years, which corresponded to the period of steady increase in the use of metal cooking pots in the village.

One of the first things the Indian Bureau doctors generally do after contact is try to protect the Indians from the Western diseases that may be communicated to them during their first prolonged interaction with outsiders. The doctors give them immunizations and may also hand out drugs to prevent or eradicate dangerous malarias. Pregnant women, infants, and preadolescents often receive massive doses of antibiotics. Antibiotics and antimalarial drugs, although helpful in some respects, may also have detrimental effects. For example, individuals exposed to antibiotics in utero or when young generally have teeth that are abnormally dark and discolored. Some drugs are reputed to interfere with fertility among women in recently contacted groups. If this lack of fertility combines with a drop in population size due to deaths from new diseases, a population can fall to a precarious low.

Perhaps the most critical disruption suffered by these groups, however, concerns how detailed information on features of the forest environment is diluted and forgotten. This is the pool of shared knowledge that traditionally has been the bedrock, the economic currency, the patrimony of each of these nontechnological forest societies. Manuel Lizarralde, a doctoral student at the University of California, Berkeley, who has done ethnobotanical work with the Bari of Venezuela, reports that in just a single generation there was a staggering loss of information about the identity of forest trees and their uses.

Despite this tale of disruption, disease, and destruction, many of the indigenous forest cultures are proving to be far more resilient than might be expected. The indigenous peoples remaining today in the Amazon Basin are true survivors who have successfully resisted the diseases, explorers, missionaries, soldiers, slave traders, rubber tappers, loggers, gold miners, fur traders, and colonists who have persistently encroached on them during the past five centuries.

Anthropologist Bill Balée, for example, has found that the Ka'apor Indians of Maranhão State, in peaceful contact with outsiders since 1928, still maintain many features of their traditional economy, social organization, and ritual life. He attributes this to the continued integrity of the nuclear family and the persistence of specific ritual duties between husband and wife that prohibit certain foods at different seasons or life stages. Such ritual practices have not only spared red-legged tortoises and other wild resources from being overharvested but have also diffused hunting pressures over a large area, thereby contributing to the persistence of the traditional economy.

Unfortunately, cultural persistence will do indigenous peoples no good if their tropical forest habitat is destroyed. Deforestation is primarily the result of outside influences, such as lumbering, cattle ranching, and colonization, that are permitted by government policies. Some estimates suggest that all remaining tropical forests will be destroyed by the year 2045.

Once the technological roller coaster gets moving, it's hard to jump off or even pause to consider the situation. Some say, so what? We can't all go back to the jungle, we can't all become forest-living Indians. No, we can't. But as I stand in my apartment in Berkeley, listening to my telephone's insistent ring and contemplating my unanswered mail, dusty curtains, dripping faucets, and stacks of newspapers for recycling, I'm not sure we wouldn't be far happier if we could.

2. MEMORIES OF A !KUNG GIRLHOOD

Marjorie Shostak

Marjorie Shostak is a writer and photographer who interviewed Nisa, a 50-year-old !Kung woman, between 1969 and 1971. The !Kung people are hunters and gatherers who live on the fringe of the Kalahari Desert in southern Africa. (The exclamation point at the beginning of !Kung is used to indicate one of the many clicking sounds used in their language.)

How was the childhood of Nisa different from that of young girls in

*other societies? How was it similar? What would be the special challenges
and rewards for a young girl growing up in a hunting-gathering society?*

I remember when my mother was pregnant with Kumsa. I was still small
(about four years old) and I asked, "Mommy, that baby inside you . . .
when that baby is born, will it come out from your bellybutton?" She said,
"No, it won't come out from there. When you give birth, a baby comes
from here." And she pointed to her genitals.

When she gave birth to Kumsa, I wanted the milk she had in her
breasts, and when she nursed him, my eyes watched as the milk spilled
out. I cried all night . . . cried and cried.

Once when my mother was with him and they were lying down asleep,
I took him away from her and put him down on the other side of the hut.
Then I lay down beside her. While she slept I squeezed some milk and
started to nurse, and nursed and nursed and nursed. Maybe she thought
it was him. When she woke and saw me she cried, "Where . . . tell me . . .
what did you do with Kumsa? Where is he?"

I told her he was lying down inside the hut. She grabbed me and
pushed me hard away from her. I lay there and cried. She took Kumsa,
put him down beside her, and insulted me by cursing my genitals.

"Are you crazy? Nisa–Big Genitals, what's the matter with you? What
craziness grabbed you that you took a baby, dropped him somewhere
else, and then lay down beside me and nursed? I thought it was Kumsa."

When my father came home, she told him, "Do you see what kind of
mind your daughter has? Hit her! She almost killed Kumsa. This little
baby, this little thing here, she took from my side and dropped him
somewhere else. I was lying here holding him and fell asleep. She came
and took him away, left him by himself, then lay down where he had
been and nursed. Now, hit her!"

I said, "You're lying! Me . . . daddy, I didn't nurse. Really I didn't. I
don't even want her milk anymore."

He said, "If I ever hear of this again, I'll hit you. Now, don't ever do
that again!"

I said, "Yes, he's my little brother, isn't he? My little baby brother and I
love him. I won't do that again. He can nurse all by himself. Daddy, even
if you're not here, I won't try to steal Mommy's breasts. They belong to
my brother."

We lived and lived, and as I kept growing, I started to carry Kumsa
around on my shoulders. My heart was happy and I started to love him. I
carried him everywhere. I would play with him for a while, and whenever he started to cry, I'd take him over to mother to nurse. Then I'd take
him back with me and we'd play together again.

That was when Kumsa was still little. But once he was older and started
to talk and then to run around, that's when we were mean to each other
all the time. Sometimes we hit each other. Other times I grabbed him and

bit him and said, "Ooooh . . . what is this thing that has such a horrible face and no brains and is so mean? Why is it so mean to me when I'm not doing anything to it?" Then he said, "I'm going to *hit* you!" And I said, "You're just a *baby!* I, *I* am the one who's going to hit *you*. Why are you so miserable to me?" I insulted him and he insulted me and then I insulted him back. We just stayed together and played like that.

Once, when our father came back carrying meat, we both called out, "Ho, ho, Daddy! Ho, ho, Daddy!" But when I heard him say, "Daddy, Daddy," I yelled, "Why are you greeting my father? He's *my* father, isn't he? You can only say, 'Oh, hello Father.' " But he called out, "Ho, ho . . . Daddy!" I said, "Be quiet! Only *I* will greet him. Is he your father? I'm going to hit you!"

We fought and argued until Mother finally stopped us. Then we just sat around while she cooked the meat.

This was also when I used to take food. It happened over all kinds of food—sweet *nin* berries or *klaru* bulbs . . . other times it was mongongo nuts. Sometimes before my mother left to go gathering, she'd leave food inside a leather pouch and hang it high on one of the branches inside the hut.

But as soon as she was gone, I'd take some of whatever food was left in the bag. If it was *klaru*, I'd find the biggest bulbs and take them. I'd hang the bag back on the branch and go sit somewhere to eat them.

One time I sat down in the shade of a tree while my parents gathered food nearby. As soon as they had moved away from me, I climbed the tree where they had left a pouch hanging, full of *klaru*, and took the bulbs.

I had my own little pouch, the one my father had made me, and I took the bulbs and put them in the pouch. Then I climbed down and sat waiting for my parents to return.

They came back. "Nisa, you ate the *klaru!* What do you have to say for yourself?" I said, "Uhn uh, I didn't eat them."

I started to cry. Mother hit me and yelled, "Don't take things. You can't seem to understand! I tell you but you don't listen. Don't your ears hear when I talk to you?"

I said, "Uhn uh. Mommy's been making me feel bad for too long now. She keeps saying I steal things and hits me so that my skin hurts. I'm going to stay with Grandma!"

But when I went to my grandmother, she said, "No, I can't take care of you now. If I try you will be hungry. I am old and just go gathering one day at a time. In the morning I just rest. We would sit together and hunger would kill you. Now go back and sit beside your mother and father."

I said, "No, Daddy will hit me. Mommy will hit me. I want to stay with you."

So I stayed with her. Then one day she said, "I'm going to bring you back to your mother and father." She took me to them, saying, "Today I'm giving Nisa back to you. But isn't there someone here who will take good care of her? You don't just hit a child like this one. She likes food and likes to eat. All of you are lazy and you've just left her so she hasn't grown well. You've killed this child with hunger. Look at her now, how small she still is."

Oh, but my heart was happy! Grandmother was scolding Mother! I had so much happiness in my heart that I laughed and laughed. But then, when Grandmother went home and left me there, I cried and cried.

My father started to yell at me. He didn't hit me. His anger usually came out only from his mouth. "You're so senseless! Don't you realize that after you left, everything felt less important? We wanted you to be with us. Yes, even your mother wanted you and missed you. Today, everything will be all right when you stay with us. Your mother will take you where she goes; the two of you will do things together and go gathering together."

Then when my father dug *klaru* bulbs, I ate them, and when he dug *chon* bulbs, I ate them. I ate everything they gave me, and I wasn't yelled at any more.

Mother and I often went to the bush together. The two of us would walk until we arrived at a place where she collected food. She'd set me down in the shade of a tree and dig roots or gather nuts nearby.

Once I left the tree and went to play in the shade of another tree. I saw a tiny steenbok, one that had just been born, hidden in the grass and among the leaves. It was lying there, its little eye just looking out at me.

I thought, "What should I do?" I shouted, "*Mommy!*" I just stood there and it just lay there looking at me.

Suddenly I knew what to do—I ran at it, trying to grab it. But it jumped up and ran away and I started to chase it. It was running and I was running and it was crying as it ran. Finally, I got very close and put my foot in its way, and it fell down. I grabbed its legs and started to carry it back. It was crying, "Ehn . . . ehn . . . ehn . . ."

Its mother had been close by and when she heard it call, she came running. As soon as I saw her, I started to run again. I wouldn't give it back to its mother!

I called out, "Mommy! Come! Help me with this steenbok! Mommy! The steenbok's mother is coming for me! Run! Come! Take this steenbok from me."

But soon the mother steenbok was no longer following, so I took the baby, held its feet together, and banged it hard against the sand until I killed it. It was no longer crying; it was dead. I felt wonderfully happy. My mother came running and I gave it to her to carry.

The two of us spent the rest of the day walking in the bush. While my mother was gathering, I sat in the shade of a tree, waiting and playing with the dead steenbok. I picked it up. I tried to make it sit up, to open its eyes. I looked at them. After mother had dug enough *sha* roots, we left and returned home.

My father had been out hunting that day and had shot a large steenbok with his arrows. He had skinned it and brought it back hanging on a branch.

"Ho, ho. Daddy killed a steenbok!" I said. "Mommy! Daddy! I'm not going to let anyone have any of *my* steenbok. Now *don't* give it to anyone else. After you cook it, just my little brother and I will eat it, just the two of us."

I remember another time when we were traveling from one place to another and the sun was burning. It was the hot, dry season and there was no water anywhere. The sun was burning! Kumsa had already been born and I was still small.

After we had been walking a long time, my older brother Dau spotted a beehive. We stopped while he and my father chopped open the tree. All of us helped take out the honey. I filled my own little container until it was completely full.

We stayed there, eating the honey, and I found myself getting very thirsty. Then we left and continued to walk, I carrying my honey and my digging stick. Soon the heat began killing us and we were all dying of thirst. I started to cry because I wanted water so badly.

After a while, we stopped and sat down in the shade of a baobab tree. There was still no water anywhere. We just sat in the shade like that.

Finally my father said, "Dau, the rest of the family will stay here under this baobab. But you, take the water containers and get us some water. There's a well not too far away."

Dau collected the empty ostrich eggshell containers and the large clay pot and left. I lay there, already dead from thirst and thought, "If I stay with Mommy and Daddy, I'll surely die of thirst. Why don't I follow my big brother and go drink water with him?"

With that I jumped up and ran after him, crying out, calling to him, following his tracks. But he didn't hear me. I kept running . . . crying and calling out.

Finally, he heard something and turned to see. There I was. "Oh, no!" he said. "Nisa's followed me. What can I do with her now that she's here?" He just stood there and waited for me to catch up. He picked me up and carried me high up on his shoulder, and along we went. He really liked me!

The two of us went on together. We walked and walked and walked and walked. Finally, we reached the well. I ran to the water and drank, and soon my heart was happy again. We filled the water containers, put them in a twine mesh sack, and my brother carried it on his back. Then he took me and put me on his shoulder again.

We walked the long way back until we arrived at the baobab where our parents were sitting. They drank the water. Then they said, "How well our children have done, bringing us this water! We are alive once again!"

We just stayed in the shade of the baobab. Later we left and traveled to another water hole where we settled for a while. My heart was happy . . . eating honey and just living.

We lived there, and after some time passed, we saw the first rain clouds. One came near but just hung in the sky. More rain clouds came over and they too just stood there. Then the rain started to spill itself and it came pouring down.

The rainy season had finally come. The sun rose and set, and the rain spilled itself and fell and kept falling. It fell without ceasing. Soon the water pans were full. And my heart! My heart within me was happy and we lived and ate meat and mongongo nuts. There was more meat and it was all delicious.

And there were caterpillars to eat, those little things that crawl along going "mmm . . . mmmmm . . . mmmmm. . . ." People dug roots and collected nuts and berries and brought home more and more food. There was plenty to eat, and people kept bringing meat back on sticks and hanging it in the trees.

My heart was bursting. I ate lots of food and my tail was wagging, always wagging about like a little dog. I'd laugh with my little tail, laugh with a little donkey's laugh, a tiny thing, that is. I'd throw my tail one way and the other, shouting, "Today I'm going to eat caterpillars . . . *cat-er-pillars!*" Some people gave me meat broth to drink, and others prepared the skins of caterpillars and roasted them for me to eat, and I ate and ate and ate. Then I went to sleep.

But that night, after everyone was dead asleep, I peed right in my sleeping place. In the morning, when everyone got up, I just lay there. The sun rose and had set itself high in the sky, and I was still lying there. I was afraid of people shaming me. Mother said, "Why is Nisa acting like this and refusing to leave her blankets when the sun is sitting up in the sky? Oh . . . she has probably wet herself!"

When I did get up, my heart felt miserable. I thought, "I've peed on myself and now everyone's going to laugh at me." I asked one of my friends, "How come, after I ate all those caterpillars, when I went to sleep I peed in my bed?" Then I thought, "Tonight, when this day is over, I'm going to lie down separate from the others. If I pee in my bed again, won't mother and father hit me?"

When a child sleeps beside her mother, in front, and her father sleeps behind and makes love to her mother, the child watches. Her parents don't fear her, a small child, because even if the child sees, even if she hears, she is unaware of what it is her parents are doing. She is still young and without sense. Perhaps this is the way the child learns. The child is still senseless, without intelligence, and just watches.

If the child is a little boy, when he plays with other children, he plays sex with them and teaches it to himself, just like a baby rooster teaches itself. The little girls also learn it by themselves.

Little boys are the first ones to know its sweetness. Yes, a young girl, while she is still a child, her thoughts don't know it. A boy has a penis, and maybe, while he is still inside his mother's belly, he already knows about sex.

When you are a child you play at nothing things. You build little huts and play. Then you come back to the village and continue to play. If people bother you, you get up and play somewhere else.

Once we left a pool of rain water where we had been playing and went to the little huts we had made. We stayed there and played at being hunters. We went out tracking animals, and when we saw one, we struck it with our make-believe arrows. We took some leaves and hung them over a stick and pretended it was meat. Then we carried it back to our village. When we got back, we stayed there and ate the meat and then the meat was gone. We went out again, found another animal, and killed it.

Sometimes the boys asked if we wanted to play a game with our genitals and the girls said no. We said we didn't want to play that game, but would like to play other games. The boys told us that playing sex was what playing was all about. That's the way we grew up.

When adults talked to me I listened. Once they told me that when a young woman grows up, she takes a husband. When they first talked to me about it, I said: "What? What kind of thing am I that I should take a husband? Me, when I grow up, I won't marry. I'll just lie by myself. If I married a man, what would I think I would be doing it for?"

My father said: "Nisa, I am old. I am your father and I am old; your mother's old, too. When you get married, you will gather food and give it to your husband to eat. He also will do things for you and give you things you can wear. But if you refuse to take a husband, who will give you food to eat? Who will give you things to have? Who will give you things to wear?"

I said to my father and mother, "No. There's no question in my mind—I refuse a husband. I won't take one. Why should I? As I am now, I am still a child and won't marry."

Then I said to Mother, "Why don't you marry the man you want for me and sit him down beside Father? Then you'll have two husbands."

Mother said: "Stop talking nonsense. I'm not going to marry him; you'll marry him. A husband is what I want to give you. Yet you say I should marry him. Why are you playing with me with this talk?"

We just continued to live after that, kept on living and more time passed. One time we went to the village where Old Kantla and his son Tashay were living. My friend Nhuka and I had gone to the water well to get water, and Tashay and his family were there, having just come back from the bush. When Tashay saw me, he decided he wanted to marry me. He called Nhuka over and said, "Nhuka, that young woman, that beautiful young woman . . . what is her name?"

Nhuka told him my name was Nisa, and he said, "That young woman . . . I'm going to tell Mother and Father about her. I'm going to ask them if I can marry her."

The next evening there was a dance at our village, and Tashay and his parents came. We sang and danced into the night. Later his father said, "We have come here, and now that the dancing is finished, I want to speak to you. Give me your child, the child you gave birth to. Give her to me, and I will give her to my son. Yesterday, while we were at the well, he saw your child. When he returned he told me in the name of what he felt that I should come and ask for her today so I could give her to him."

My mother said, "Yes . . . but I didn't give birth to a woman, I bore a child. She doesn't think about marriage, she just doesn't think about the inside of her marriage hut."

Then my father said, "Yes, I also conceived that child, and it is true: She just doesn't think about marriage. When she marries a man, she leaves him and marries another man and leaves him and gets up and marries another man and leaves him. She refuses men completely. There are two men whom she has already refused. So when I look at Nisa today, I say she is not a woman."

Then Tashay's father said, "Yes, I have listened to what you have said. That, of course, is the way of a child; it is a child's custom to do that. She gets married many times until one day she likes one man. Then they stay together. That is a child's way."

They talked about the marriage and agreed to it. In the morning Tashay's parents went back to their camp, and we went to sleep. When the morning was late in the sky, his relatives came back. They stayed around and his parents told my aunt and my mother that they should all start building the marriage hut. They began building it together, and everyone was talking and talking. There were a lot of people there. Then all the young men went and brought Tashay to the hut. They stayed around together near the fire. I was at Mother's hut. They told two of my friends to get me. But I said to myself, "Ooooh . . . I'll just run away."

When they came, they couldn't find me. I was already out in the bush, and I just sat there by the base of a tree. Soon I heard Nhuka call out, "Nisa . . . Nisa . . . my friend . . . there are things there that will bite and kill you. Now leave there and come back here."

They came and brought me back. Then they laid me down inside the hut. I cried and cried, and people told me: "A man is not something that kills you; he is someone who marries you, and becomes like your father or your older brother. He kills animals and gives you things to eat. Even tomorrow he would do that. But because you are crying, when he kills an animal, he will eat it himself and won't give you any. Beads, too. He will get some beads, but he won't give them to you. Why are you afraid of your husband and why are you crying?"

I listened and was quiet. Later Tashay lay down by the mouth of the hut, near the fire, and I was inside. He came in only after he thought I was asleep. Then he lay down and slept. I woke while it was still dark and thought, "How am I going to jump over him? How can I get out and go to Mother's hut?" Then I thought, "This person has married me . . . yes." And, I just lay there. Soon the rain came and beat down and it fell until dawn broke.

In the morning, he got up first and sat by the fire. I was frightened. I was so afraid of him, I just lay there and waited for him to go away before I got up.

We lived together a long time and began to learn to like one another before he slept with me. The first time I didn't refuse. I agreed just a little and he lay with me. But the next morning my insides hurt. I took some leaves and wound them around my waist, but it continued to hurt. Later that day I went with the women to gather mongongo nuts. The whole time I thought "Ooooh . . . what has he done to my insides that they feel this way."

That evening we lay down again. But this time I took a leather strap, held my skin apron tightly against me, tied up my genitals with it, and then tied the strap to the hut's frame. I didn't want him to take me again. The two of us lay there and after a while he started to touch me. When he reached my stomach, he felt the leather strap. He felt around to see what it was. He said, "What is this woman doing? Yesterday she lay with me so nicely when I came to her. Why has she tied up her genitals this way?"

He sat me up and said, "Nisa . . . Nisa . . . what happened? Why are you doing this?" I didn't answer him.

"What are you so afraid of that you tied your genitals?"

I said, "I'm not afraid of anything."

He said, "No, now tell me what you are afraid of. In the name of what you did, I am asking you."

I said, "I refuse because yesterday when you touched me my insides hurt."

He said, "Do you see me as someone who kills people? Am I going to eat you? I am not going to kill you. I have married you and I want to make love to you. Have you seen any man who has married a woman and who just lives with her and doesn't have sex with her?"

I said, "No, I still refuse it! I refuse sex. Yesterday my insides hurt, that's why."

He said, "Mmm. Today you will lie there by yourself. But tomorrow I will take you."

The next day I said to him, "Today I'm going to lie here, and if you take me by force, you will have me. You will have me because today I'm just going to lie here. You are obviously looking for some 'food,' but I don't know if the food I have is food at all, because even if you have some, you won't be full."

I just lay there and he did his work.

We lived and lived, and soon I started to like him. After that I was a grown person and said to myself, "Yes, without doubt, a man sleeps with you. I thought maybe he didn't."

We lived on, and then I loved him and he loved me, and I kept on loving him. When he wanted me I didn't refuse and he just slept with me. I thought, "Why have I been so concerned about my genitals? They are, after all, not so important. So why was I refusing them?"

I thought that and gave myself to him and gave and gave. We lay with one another, and my breasts had grown very large. I had become a woman.

3. HUNTER RELIGION: AN ESKIMO SHAMAN

Mircea Eliade

No one can say what the earliest human religion was, but the first religious specialists may have been the priests or medicine men of hunting-gathering societies. This reading is a description of the work of one such specialist, an Eskimo shaman. Shamans are the healers and spiritual leaders of Arctic hunters throughout Siberia, northeast Asia, and North America.

This selection is an anthropologist's account from 1930, summarized by Mircea Eliade, perhaps the leading twentieth-century student of the history of the world's religions.

Why is the shaman called? What does he do? What role does his audience play? How is this event similar to rituals in other societies? What does this selection suggest to you about the role of religion in hunting and gathering society?

Descent to the abode of Takánakapsâluk, the Mother of the Sea Beasts, is undertaken at an individual's request, sometimes because of illness, sometimes because of bad luck in hunting; only in the latter case is the shaman paid. But it sometimes happens that no game at all is to be found and the village is threatened with famine; then all the villagers gather in the house where the séance is held, and the shaman's ecstatic journey is made in the name of the whole community. Those present must unfasten their belts and laces, and remain silent, their eyes closed. For a time the shaman breathes deeply, in silence, before summoning his helping spirits. When they come the shaman begins to murmur, "The way is made ready for me; the way opens before me!" and the audience answer in chorus: "Let it be so." And now the earth opens, and the shaman struggles for a long time with unknown forces before he finally cries: "Now the way is open." And the audience exclaim in chorus: "Let the way be open before him; let there be way for him." Now, first under the bed, then farther away, under the passage, is heard the cry, "Halala-he-he-he, Halala-he-he-he"; this is the sign that the shaman has set off. The cry grows more and more distant until it is no longer heard.

During this time the audience sing in chorus, their eyes closed, and sometimes the shaman's clothes—which he had taken off before the séance—come to life and start flying about the house, over the heads of the audience. The signs and deep breathing of people long dead are also heard; they are dead shamans come to help their colleague on his dangerous journey. And their signs and their breathing seem to come from very far under water, as if they were sea beasts.

Reaching the bottom of the ocean, the shaman finds himself facing three great stones in constant motion barring his road; he must pass between them at the risk of being crushed. (This is another image of the "strait gate" that forbids access to the plane of higher being to anyone but an "initiate," that is, one who can act like a "spirit.") Successfully passing this obstacle, the shaman follows a path and comes to a sort of bay; on a hill stands Takánakapsâluk's house, made of stone and with a narrow entrance. The shaman hears sea beasts blowing and panting, but does not see them. A dog with bared teeth defends the entrance; the dog is dangerous to anyone who is afraid of it, but the shaman passes over it, and it understands that he is a very powerful magician. (All these obstacles oppose the ordinary shaman, but the really powerful shamans reach the bottom of the sea and the presence of Takánakapsâluk directly, by diving beneath their tent or snow hut, as if slipping through a tube.)

If the goddess is angry with men, a great wall rises before her house. And the shaman has to knock it down with his shoulder. Others say that Takánakapsâluk's house has no roof, so that the goddess can better see men's acts from her place by the fire. All kinds of marine animals are gathered in a pool to the right of the fire, and their cries and breathings are heard. The goddess's hair hangs down over her face and she is dirty and slovenly; this is the effect of men's sins, which have almost made her ill. The shaman must approach her, take her by the shoulder, and comb her hair (for the goddess has no fingers with which to comb herself). Before he can do this, there is another obstacle to be overcome; Takánakapsâluk's father, taking him for a dead man on the way to the land of shades, tries to seize him, but the shaman cries, "I am flesh and blood!" and succeeds in passing.

As he combs Takánakapsâluk's hair, the shaman tells her that men have no more seal. And the goddess answers in the spirit language: "The secret miscarriages of the women and breaches of taboo in eating boiled meat bar the way for the animals." The shaman now has to summon all his powers to appease her anger; finally she opens the pool and sets the animals free. The audience hears their movements at the bottom of the sea, and soon afterward the shaman's gasping breathing, as if he were emerging from the surface of the water. A long silence follows. Finally the shaman speaks: "I have something to say." All answer. "Let us hear, let us hear." And the shaman, in the spirit language, demands the confession of sins. One after another, all confess their miscarriages or their breaches of taboos and repent.

4. WOMEN AND THE AGRICULTURAL REVOLUTION

Elise Boulding

In hunting-gathering society men were usually the hunters and women were the gatherers. As gatherers (or foragers), women were the likely discoverers of plant reproduction. Elise Boulding, a sociologist, shows how the planting of wild einkorn, a grain of the Middle Eastern Fertile Crescent, transformed the lives of women and men.

In what ways was the early discovery of planting "women's work"? To what extent did it increase women's power or prestige? How were the lives of women and children changed by planting?

There is some disagreement about whether the domestication of animals or plants came first. In fact, both were probably happening at the same time. There is evidence from campfire remains as long ago as 20,000 B.C. that women had discovered the food value of einkorn, a kind of wild wheat that grows all through the fertile crescent. An enterprising Oklahoma agronomist, Professor Jack Harlan of the University of Oklahoma, noticed several years ago, on an expedition to eastern Turkey, how thick these stands of wild einkorn grew. He tried harvesting some, and once he had resorted to a nine-thousand-year-old flint sickle blade set in a new wooden handle (he tried to use his bare hands first, with disastrous results), he was able to come away with an excellent harvest. After weighing what he had reaped, he estimated that a single good stand of einkorn would feed a family for a whole year. He also found that the grains had 50 percent more protein than the wheat we use now in North America for bread flour. Einkorn grains are found everywhere on the ancient home-base sites of the fertile crescent, either as roasted hulls in cooking hearths, or as imprints in the mud-and-straw walls of the earliest pre-agriculture huts.

It would be inevitable that grains from sheaves of einkorn carried in from a distant field would drop in well-trodden soil just outside the home base, or perhaps in a nearby pile of refuse. When the band returned the following year to this campsite—perhaps a favorite one, since not all campsites were revisited—there would be a fine stand of einkorn waiting for them right at their doorstep. We might say that the plants taught the women how to cultivate them. Planting, however, was quite a step beyond just leaving some stalks at the site where they were picked, to seed themselves for the next year. There was less reason for deliberate planting as long as bands were primarily nomadic and there was plenty of game to follow. But in time there was a premium on campsites that would have abundant grain and fruit and nuts nearby, and then there was point in scattering extra grain on the ground near the campsite for the next year. Because of the construction of the seed, einkorn easily plants itself, so it was a good plant for initiating humans into agriculture.

Gradually, bands lengthened their stays at their more productive home bases, harvesting what had been "planted" more or less intentionally, and letting the few sheep they had raised from infancy graze on nearby hills. One year there would be such a fine stand of wheat at their favorite home base, and so many sheep ambling about, that a band would decide just to stay for a while, not to move on that year.

If any one band of nomads could have anticipated what lay in store for humankind as a result of that fateful decision (made separately by thousands of little bands over the next ten thousand years), would they after all have moved on? While it may have been a relief not to be on the move, they in fact exchanged a life of relative ease, with enough to eat and few possessions, for a life of hard work, enough to eat, and economic surplus. As Childe says, "a mild acquisitiveness could now take its place among human desires."

Successful nomads have a much easier life than do farmers. Among the !Kung bushmen today, the men hunt about four days a week and the women only need to work two-and-a-half days at gathering to feed their families amply for a week. (At that, meat is a luxury item, and most of the nourishment comes from nuts and roots.) The rest of their time is leisure, to be enjoyed in visiting, creating and carrying out rituals, and just "being."

THE FIRST SETTLEMENTS

For better or worse, the women and the men settled down. They settled in the caves of Belt and Hotu to a prosperous life of farming and herding on the Caspian. They settled in Eynan, Jericho, Jarmo, Beidha, Catal Huyuk, Hacilar, Arpachiyah, and Kherokitia in Cyprus, and in uncounted villages that no archaeologist's shovel has touched. These places were home-base sites first, some going back thousands of years. By 10,000 B.C. Eynan had fifty houses, small stone domes, seven meters in diameter, around a central area with storage pits. This was probably preagricultural, still a hunting and gathering band, but a settled one. The village covered two thousand square meters. Each hut had a hearth, and child and infant burials were found under some of the floors. Three successive layers of fifty stone houses have been found at the same site, so it must have been a remarkably stable site for a settlement.

What was life like, once bands settled down? This was almost from the start a woman's world. She would mark out the fields for planting, because she knew where the grain grew best, and would probably work in the fields together with the other women of the band. There would not be separate fields at first, but as the former nomads shifted from each sleeping in individual huts to building houses for family groups of mother, father, and children, a separate family feeling must have developed and women may have divided the fields by family groups.

Their fire-hardened pointed digging sticks, formerly used in gathering, now became a multipurpose implement for planting and cultivating the soil. At harvest time everyone, including the children, would help bring in the grain. The women also continued to gather fruit and nuts, again with the help of the children. The children watched the sheep and goats, but the women did the milking and cheese making. Ethnologists who have studied both foraging and agricultural societies comment on the change in the way of life for children that comes with agriculture. Whereas in foraging societies they have no responsibilities beyond feeding themselves and learning the hunting and foraging skills they will need, and therefore they have much leisure, it is very common in agricultural societies to put children to work at the age of three, chasing birds from the food plots. Older children watch the animals, and keep them out of the planted areas.

The agriculture practiced by these first women farmers and their children, producing enough food for subsistence only, must be distinguished from that agriculture which developed out of subsistence farming and which produced surpluses and fed nonfarming populations in towns. The first type is commonly called horticulture and is carried out with hand tools only. The second is agriculture proper, and involves intensive cultivation with the use of plow and (where necessary) irrigation. In areas like the hilly flanks of the fertile crescent in the Middle East, horticulture moved fairly rapidly into agriculture as it spread to the fertile plains. As we shall see, trading centers grew into towns and cities needing food from the countryside. Women and children could not unaided produce the necessary surpluses, and by the time the digging stick had turned into an animal-drawn plow, they were no longer the primary workers of the fields.

The simpler form of farming continued in areas where the soil was less fertile, and particularly in the tropical forest areas of Africa. Here soils were quickly exhausted, and each year the village women would enlist the men in helping to clear new fields which were then burned over in the slash-and-burn pattern which helped reconstitute the soils for planting again. The slash-and-burn pattern of horticulture has continued into this century, since it is a highly adaptive technique for meager tropical soils. Where the simple horticultural methods continued to be used, women continued as the primary farmers, always with their children as helpers. In a few of these societies women continued also in the positions of power; these are usually the tribes labeled by ethnologists as matrilocal. Not many tribes have survived into the twentieth century with a matrilocal pattern, however, though traces of matrilineal descent reckoning are not infrequent.

The first women farmers in the Zagreb foothills were very busy. Not only did they tend the fields and do the other chores mentioned above, they also probably built the round stone or mud-brick houses in the first villages. The frequency with which women construct shelters in foraging societies has already been cited.

Women also began to spend more time on making tools and containers. No longer needing to hold the family possessions down to what they could carry, women could luxuriate in being able to choose larger and heavier grinding stones that crushed grain more efficiently. They could make containers to hold food stores that would never have to go on the road. They ground fine stone bowls, made rough baskets, and in the process of lining their baskets with mud accidentally discovered that a mudlined basket placed in the hearth would come out hardened—the first pottery. Sonja Cole suggests that pottery was invented in Khartoum in Africa about 8000 B.C., spreading northwest to the Mediterranean, but the same process probably happened over and over again as people became more sedentary.

The evidence from food remains in these early villages, 10,000 to 6000 B.C., indicates that men were still hunting, to supplement the agriculture and modest domestic herds. This means that they were not around very much. When they were, they probably shared in some of the home-base tasks.

Evidence from some of the earliest village layouts suggests that adults lived in individual huts, women keeping the children with them. Marriage agreements apparently did not at first entail shared living quarters. As the agricultural productivity of the women increased, and the shift was made to dwellings for family units, husband-wife interaction probably became more frequent and family living patterns more complex.

With the accumulation of property, decisions about how it was to be allocated had to be made. The nature of these agreements is hardly to be found in the archaeological record, so we must extrapolate from what we know of the "purest" matrilineal tribes of the recent past.

The senior woman of a family and her daughters and sons formed the property-holding unit for the family. The senior woman's *brother* would be the administrator of the properties. His power, whether over property or in political decision making, would be derivative from his status as brother (usually but not always the oldest) to the senior woman in a family. This role of the brother, so important in present-day matrilineal societies, may not have been very important in the period we are now considering, between 12,000 and 8000 B.C.

CHAPTER TWO

The Urban Revolution in the Near East and North Africa

5. CITY AND CIVILIZATION

Kevin Reilly

This reading is excerpted from a recent history of civilization.

The urban revolution that brought the first cities five thousand years ago also brought the beginnings of civilization. Why do we associate cities with civilization? What were some of the general media of communication that cities created? What does it mean to say that civilization created the "eye" and "I"? How could the city make life impersonal and personal at the same time? What was the importance of class divisions in the first cities? Does modern city life still have the features of the first cities?

The most obvious achievements of the first civilizations are the monuments—the pyramids, temples, palaces, statues, and treasures—that were created for the new ruling class of kings, nobles, priests, and their officials. But civilized life is much more than the capacity to create monuments.

Civilized life is secure life. At the most basic level this means security from the sudden destruction that village communities might suffer. Civilized life gives the feeling of permanence. It offers regularity, stability, order, even routine. Plans can be made. Expectations can be realized. People can be expected to act predictably, according to the rules.

The first cities were able to attain stability with walls that shielded the inhabitants from nomads and armies, with the first codes of law that defined human relationships, with police and officials that enforced the laws, and with institutions that functioned beyond the lives of their particular members. City life offered considerably more permanence and security than village life.

Civilization involves more than security, however. A city that provided only order would be more like a prison than a civilization. The first cities provided something that the best-ordered villages lacked. They provided far greater variety: more races and ethnic groups were speaking more languages, engaged in more occupations, and living a greater variety of life-styles. The abundance of choice, the opportunities for new sensations, new experiences, knowledge—these have always been the appeals of city life. The opportunities for growth and enrichment were far greater than the possibilities of plow-and-pasture life.

Security plus variety equals creativity. At least the possibility of a more creative, expressive life was available in the protected, semipermanent city enclosures which drew, like magnets, foreign traders and diplomats, new ideas about gods and nature, strange foods and customs, and the magicians, ministers, and mercenaries of the king's court. Civilization is the enriched life which this dynamic urban setting permitted and the human creativity and opportunity which it encouraged. At the very least, cities made even the most common slave think and feel a greater range of things than the tightly knit, clannish agricultural village allowed. That was (and still is) the root of innovation and creativity—of civilization itself.

The variety of people and the complexity of city life required new and more general means of communication. The villager knew everyone personally. Cities brought together people who often did not even speak the same language. Not only law codes but written language itself became a way to bridge the many gaps of human variety. Cities invented writing so that strangers could communicate, and so that those communications could become permanent—remembered publicly, officially recorded. Emerson was right when he said that the city lives by memory, but it was the official memory which enabled the city to carry on its business or religion beyond the lifetime of the village elders. Written symbols that everyone could recognize became the basis of laws, invention, education, taxes, accounting, contracts, and obligations. In short, writing and records made it possible for each generation to begin on the shoulders of its ancestors. Village life and knowledge often seemed to start from scratch. Thus, cities cultivated not only memory and the past, but hope and the future as well. City civilizations invented not only history and record keeping but also prophecy and social planning.

Writing was one city invention that made more general communication possible. Money was another. Money made it possible to deal with anyone just as an agreed-upon public language did. Unnecessary in the village climate of mutual obligations, money was essential in the city society of strangers. Such general media of communication as writing and money vastly increased the number of things that could be said and thought, bought and sold. As a consequence, city life was more impersonal than village life, but also more dynamic and more exciting.

THE "EYE" AND "I"

Marshall McLuhan has written that "civilization gave the barbarian an eye for an ear." We might add that civilization also gave an "I" for an "us." City life made the "eye" and the "I" more important than they had been in the village. The invention of writing made knowledge more visual. The eye had to be trained to recognize the minute differences in letters and words. Eyes took in a greater abundance of detail: laws, prices, the strange cloak of the foreigner, the odd type of shoes made by the new craftsman from who-knows-where, the colors of the fruit and vegetable market, elaborate painting in the temple, as well as the written word. In the village one learned by listening. In the city seeing was believing. In the new city courts of law an "eyewitness account" was believed to be more reliable than "hearsay evidence." In some villages even today, the heard and the spoken are thought more reliable than the written and the seen. In the city, even spoken language took on the uniformity and absence of emotion that is unavoidable in the written word. Perhaps emotions themselves became less violent. "Civilized" is always used to mean emotional restraint, control of the more violent passions, and a greater understanding, even tolerance, of the different and foreign.

Perhaps empathy (the capacity to put yourself in someone else's shoes) increased in cities—so full of so many different others that had to be understood. When a Turkish villager was recently asked, "What would you do if you were president of your country?" he stammered: "My God! How can you ask such a thing? How can I . . . I cannot . . . president of Turkey . . . master of the whole world?" He was completely unable to imagine himself as president. It was as removed from his experience as if he were master of the world. Similarly, a Lebanese villager who was asked what he would do if he were editor of a newspaper accused the interviewer of ridiculing him, and frantically waved the interviewer on to another question. Such a life was beyond his comprehension. It was too foreign to imagine. The very variety of city life must have increased the capacity of the lowest commoner to imagine, empathize, sympathize, and criticize.

The oral culture of the village reinforced the accepted by saying and singing it almost monotonously. The elders, the storytellers, and the minstrels must have had a prodigious memory. But their stories changed only gradually and slightly. The spoken word was sacred. To say it differently was to change the truth. The written culture of cities taught "point of *view.*" An urban individual did not have to remember everything. That was done permanently on paper. Knowledge became a recognition of different interpretations and the capacity to look up things. The awareness of variety meant the possibility of criticism, analysis, and an ever-newer synthesis. It is no wonder that the technical and scientific knowledge of cities increased at a geometric rate compared to the knowledge of villages. The multiplication of knowledge was implicit in the city's demand to recognize difference and variety. Civilization has come to mean that ever-expanding body of knowledge and skill. Its finest achievements have been that knowledge, its writing, and its visual art. The city and civilization (like the child) are to be seen and not heard.

It may seem strange to say that the impersonal life of cities contributed greatly to the development of personality—the "I" as well as the "eye." Village life was in a sense much more personal. Everything was taken personally. Villagers deal with each other not as "the blacksmith," "the baker," "that guy who owes me a goat," or "that no good bum." They do not even "deal" with each other. They know each other by name and family. They love, hate, support, and murder each other because of who they are, because of personal feelings, because of personal and family responsibility. They have full, varied relationships with each member of the village. They do not merely buy salt from this person, talk about the weather with this other person, and discuss personal matters with only this other person. They share too much with each other to divide up their relationships in that way.

City life is a life of separated, partial relationships. In a city you do not know about the butcher's life, wife, kids, and problems. You do not care. You are in a hurry. You have too many other things to do. You might discuss the weather—but while he's cutting. You came to buy meat. Many urban relationships are like that. There are many business, trading, or "dealing" relationships because there are simply too many people to know them all as relatives.

The impersonality of city life is a shame in a way. (It makes it easier to get mugged by someone who does not even hate you.) But the luxurious variety of impersonal relationships (at least some of the time) provides the freedom for the individual personality to emerge. Maybe that is why people have often dreamed of leaving family and friends (usually for a city) in the hope of "finding themselves." Certainly, the camaraderie and community of village life had a darker side of surveillance and conformity. When everything was known about everyone, it was difficult for the individual to find his or her individuality. Family ties and village custom were often obstacles to asserting self-identity. The city offered its inhabitants a huge variety of possible relationships and personal identities. The urban inhabitant was freer than his village cousin to choose friends, lovers, associates, occupation, housing, and life-style. The city was full of choices that the village could not afford or condone. The village probably provided more security in being like everyone else and doing what was expected. But the city provided the variety of possibilities that could allow the individual to follow the "inner self " and cultivate inner gardens.

The class divisions of city society made it difficult for commoners to achieve an effective or creative individuality. But the wealthy and powerful—especially the king—were able to develop models of individuality and personality that were revolutionary. No one before had ever achieved such a sense of the self, and the model of the king's power and freedom became a goal for the rest of the society. The luxury, leisure, and opportunity of the king was a revolutionary force. Unlike a village elder, the king could do whatever he wanted. Recognizing that, more and more city inhabitants asked, "Why can't we?" City revolutions have continually extended class privilege and opportunities ever since.

Once a society has achieved a level of abundance, once it can offer the technological means, the educational opportunities, the creative outlets necessary for everyone to lead meaningful, happy, healthy lives, then classes may be a hindrance. Class divisions were, however, a definite stimulus to productivity and creativity in the early city civilizations. The democratic villagers preferred stability to improvement. As a result, their horizons were severely limited. They died early, lived precipitously, and suffered without much hope. The rulers of the first cities discovered the possibilities of leisure, creation, and the good life. They invented heaven and utopia—first for themselves. Only very gradually has the invention of civilization, of human potential, sifted down to those beneath the ruling class. In many cases, luxury, leisure, freedom, and opportunity are still the monopolies of the elite. But once the powerful have exploited the poor enough to establish their own paradise on earth and their own immortality after death, the poor also have broader horizons and plans.

6. INVENTORS AND TECHNOLOGISTS OF PHARAONIC EGYPT

Rashid el-Nadoury and Jean Vercoutter

The authors are modern historians of ancient Egypt. In this reading, they survey a wide variety of ancient Egyptian innovations in the crafts and sciences. According to the authors, the Egyptians excelled in carving, sculpture, cultivation, textiles, glass, papyrus (early paper), shipbuilding, surgery, medicine, mathematics, astronomy, architecture, and engineering. What did the ancient Egyptians contribute to these areas? Which innovations were the most important? What elements of Egyptian society and culture explain these particular successes?

Pharaonic civilization was remarkable for the continuity of its development. To succeeding civilizations of Africa in particular, it bequeathed a legacy whose importance should not be underestimated. It inherited from Neolithic times techniques which were transmitted and enriched in the pre-dynastic period (3500 to 3000 BC) and were subsequently preserved when the historical period was in full flower.

In the crafts, the ancient Egyptians' contribution can be traced in stone, but also in wood, glass, and many other materials.

As early as 3500 BC, the Egyptians, the heirs to the Neolithic period in the Nile valley, used the flint deposits there, especially those at Thebes, to carve instruments of incomparable quality, of which the Gebel-el-Arak Knife is one example among hundreds.

This craftsmanship is also found in the carving of stone vases. Here, too, the technique of the Neolithic period carried on through the pre-dynastic period and the Old Kingdom and continued to the end of ancient Egyptian history. The Egyptian stone-carver used every kind of stone, even the hardest varieties, working with basalt, breccia, diorite, granite, and porphyry as readily as with the softer calcareous alabasters, schists, serpentines and soapstones.

From Egypt, stone-carving techniques later passed to the Mediterranean world. The carvers of Cretan vases must surely have learned their skills, if not in Egypt itself, at least in a milieu that was thoroughly steeped in Egyptian culture like the Syro-Palestinian Corridor. Even the shapes of the vases of the ancient Minoan period betray their Egyptian origins.

The dexterity of the cutters of hard stones passed to the sculptors. This can be seen in the great Egyptian hard stone sculptures, from the diorite Chefren of Cairo to the large black basalt sarcophagi of the Apis bulls. The skill then passed to the sculptors of the Ptolemaic period and later found expression in the statuary of the Roman empire.

The cultivation of flax rapidly led to great ability in hand-spinning and linen making. The latter was known from the start of the Neolithic period and its beginning coincided with the emergence of civilization in the Nile valley. The women spun the linen, doing so with great skill since they frequently handled two spindles simultaneously.

For the Pharaohs, woven fabrics constituted a commodity particularly appreciated abroad. The finest cloth of all, byssus, was woven in the temples and was especially renowned. The Ptolemies supervised the weaving shops and controlled the quality of the manufacture, and their central administration, doubtless following the pattern set by the earlier Pharaohs, organized sales abroad which brought the king huge revenues because of the superior quality of the goods produced by Egyptian weavers. Here we have a graphic example of one of the ways in which the Egyptian legacy was handed down.

Egypt contributed, if not the invention, at least the distribution of glass-making techniques to world civilization. While it is true that Mesopotamia and the civilizations of the Indus were likewise familiar at a very early time with glazing, the technique which is the basis of glass making, there is no evidence to suggest that they spread it abroad.

It is certain that the Egyptians demonstrated their aptitude in the art of glass making in a relatively short time. The presence of glass beads seems to be attested in the pre-dynastic period, although it is not certain that they were deliberately made by the craftsman.

Glass, as such, was known in the fifth dynasty (c. 2500 BC) and began to spread from the time of the New Kingdom (c. 1600). It was then used not only for beads but also for vases in the form of fishes. They were usually polychromatic and always opaque.

Transparent glass made its appearance under Tutankhamen (c. 1300 BC). Starting about 700 BC, Egyptian polychromatic glass vases, in the form called alabaster, spread throughout the Mediterranean area. They were copied by the Phoenicians, who developed their manufacture into an industry.

In the later period, hieroglyphic signs, moulded in coloured glass, were set in wood or stone to make inscriptions. The techniques of the Pharaonic glass makers were handed down to craftsmen of the Hellenistic period who invented blown glass.

Alexandria then became the main centre for the manufacture of glassware, exporting its products as far as China. Aurelius levied a tax on Egyptian glassware imported into Rome. The Meroitic empire later imported some glassware from Alexandria but, above all, adopted its manufacturing techniques and spread them to the upper Nile valley.

One of the most important industries was that of the production of papyrus invented by the ancient Egyptians. No plant played a more significant role in Egypt than papyrus. Its fibres were used for boat making and for caulking, for the wicks of oil lamps, for mats, baskets, ropes and hawsers [anchoring cables].

The hawsers which served to moor the pontoon bridge that Xerxes tried to lay across the Hellespont were made in Egypt out of papyrus fibres. When tied together in bundles, papyrus stems served as pillars in early architecture until classical architects took them as a model for their simple or clustered columns whose capitals were shaped like closed or open flowers. But, above all, papyrus was used to make "papyrus", from which the word "paper" is derived.

Papyrus was made by placing crosswise successive layers of fine strips taken from the stem of the plant which, after pressing and drying, formed a large sheet.

Twenty sheets of papyrus joined together while they were still moist formed a scroll three to six metres in length. Several scrolls could be joined together and reach a length of thirty or forty metres.

It was scrolls of this kind that constituted Egyptian books. They were held in the left hand and unrolled as the reading proceeded. The volumen [roll of parchment] of classical antiquity is a direct heir of this scroll.

Of all the writing materials employed in antiquity, papyrus was certainly the most practical. It was supple and light. Its sole drawback was its fragility. Over a long period it stood up poorly to humidity, and it burnt very easily. It has been estimated that to maintain the inventory of a small Egyptian temple, ten metres of papyrus were required each month.

Provincial notaries, during the Ptolemaic dynasty, used from six to thirteen scrolls or from twenty-five to fifty-seven metres *each day*.

Every large estate and royal palace and all the temples maintained registers, inventories and libraries, which indicates that hundreds of kilometres of papyrus must have existed at that time whereas only a few hundred metres have been rediscovered.

The papyrus used in Egypt from the time of the first dynasty (c. 3000 BC) until the end of the Pharaonic period was later adopted by the Greeks, the Romans, the Copts, the Byzantines, the Aramaeans and the Arabs.

A large part of Greek and Latin literature has come down to us on papyrus. Papyrus was, unquestionably, one of the major legacies bequeathed to civilization by Pharaonic Egypt.

The Egyptian expertise in wood working is brilliantly manifested in their shipbuilding. The necessities of daily life in the Nile valley, where the river is the only convenient thoroughfare, made expert boatmen of the Egyptians from the earliest times.

In 1952, two great pits dug into the rock and covered with huge limestone slabs were discovered along the southern side of the Great Pyramid. In the pits, partially disassembled, but complete with oars, cabins, and rudders, were discovered the very boats used by the Pharaoh Cheops. One of these boats has been removed from the pit and restored. The other one is still waiting to be taken out of its tomb.

Cheops' boat, now in a special museum, has been rebuilt. When found it consisted of 1,224 pieces of wood which had been partially disassembled and stacked in thirteen successive layers in the pit. The boat measures 43.4 metres long, 5.9 metres wide, and has a capacity of about forty tons. The side planks are between thirteen and fourteen centimetres thick. Cheops' boat has no keel, and is flat bottomed and narrow. The most remarkable fact is that it was built without any nails: the pieces of wood are held together solely by the use of tenon and mortise joints.

Beginning with the fifth dynasty, and probably even before, the Egyptians knew how to adapt their ships for ocean-going voyages. The boats of Sahure show that for use at sea the height of the prow and the poop were greatly reduced.

In Cheops' boat, these were raised high above the waterline. This made the ship difficult to manage in the waves of the Mediterranean or the Red Sea. In addition, Egyptian naval engineers lent great solidity to the whole structure by equipping the ship with a torsion-cable passing over the bridge and tying the stern firmly to the bow. This cable also acted as a keel, ensuring the rigidity of the entire structure and reducing the danger of its breaking in the middle.

With these modifications, the Egyptian ship was capable of plying the furthest maritime routes opened up by the Pharaohs, whether on the Mediterranean in the direction of Palestine, Syria, Cyprus and Crete, or on the Red Sea towards the distant country of Punt.

The Pharaonic contribution to science and applied mathematics has left a valuable legacy.

It was, undoubtedly, the knowledge they acquired from mummification that enabled the Egyptians to develop surgical techniques at a very early period in their history. We have quite a good knowledge of Egyptian surgery, in fact, thanks to the Smith Papyrus, a copy of an original which was composed under the Old Kingdom, between 2600 and 2400 BC. This papyrus is virtually a treatise on bone surgery and external pathology. Forty-eight cases are examined systematically.

Several of the treatments indicated in the Smith Papyrus are still used today. Egyptian surgeons knew how to stitch up wounds and to set a fracture using wooden or pasteboard splints. And there were times when the surgeon simply advised that nature should be allowed to take its own course.

Of the cases studied by the Smith Papyrus, the majority concerned superficial lacerations of the skull or face. Others concerned lesions of the bones or joints such as contusions of the cervical or spinal vertebrae, dislocations, perforations of the skull or sternum, and sundry fractures affecting the nose, jaw, collar-bone, humerus, ribs, skull and vertebrae.

Examination of mummies has revealed traces of surgery, such as the jaw dating from the Old Kingdom which has two holes bored to drain an abscess, or the skull fractured by a blow from an axe or sword and successfully reset. There is also evidence of dental work such as fillings done with a mineral cement, and one mummy had a kind of bridge of gold wire joining two shaky teeth.

By its methodical approach, the Smith Papyrus bears testimony to the skill of the surgeons of ancient Egypt, skill which it would be fair to assume was handed on gradually, in Africa as well as in Asia and to classical antiquity, by the doctors who were always attached to Egyptian expeditions to foreign lands.

Moreover, it is known that foreign sovereigns, like the Asian prince of Bakhtan, Bactria, or Cambyses himself, brought in Egyptian doctors, that Hippocrates "had access to the library of the Imhotep temple at Memphis" and that other Greek physicians later followed his example.

Medical knowledge can be considered as one of the most important early scientific contributions of the ancient Egyptians to the history of man. Documents show in detail the titles of Egyptian physicians and their different fields of specialization. In fact the civilizations of the ancient Near East and the classical world recognized the ability and reputation of the ancient Egyptians in medicine and pharmacology.

Among the ailments identified and competently described and treated by Egyptian doctors were gastric disorders, stomach swelling, skin cancer, coryza [head cold], laryngitis, angina pectoris, diabetes, constipation, haemorrhoids, bronchitis, retention and incontinence of urine, Bilharzia and ophthalmia.

The Egyptian doctor treated his patient using suppositories, ointments, syrups, potions, oils, massages, enemas, purges, poultices, and even inhalants whose use the Egyptians taught to the Greeks. The Egyptian pharmacopoeia contained a large variety of medicinal herbs, the names of which, unfortunately, elude translation. Egyptian medicinal techniques and medicines enjoyed great prestige in antiquity, as we know from Herodotus.

The Greek writers Herodotus and Strabo concur in the view that geometry was invented by the Egyptians. The need to calculate the area of the land eroded or added each year by the flooding of the Nile apparently led them to its discovery.

Egyptian geometry, like mathematics, was empirical. In ancient treatises, the task was first and foremost to provide the scribe with a formula that would enable him to find rapidly the area of a field, the volume of grain in a silo or the number of bricks required for a building project. The scribe never applied abstract reasoning to the solution of a particular problem but just provided the practical means in the shape of figures.

Nonetheless, the Egyptians knew perfectly well how to calculate the area of a triangle or a circle, the volume of a cylinder, of a pyramid or a truncated pyramid, and probably that of a hemisphere. Their greatest success was the calculation of the area of a circle. They proceeded by reducing the diameter by one-ninth and squaring the result which was equivalent to assigning a value of 3.1605 to π, which is much more precise than the value 3 given to π by other ancient peoples.

The Egyptian contribution to astronomy must be deduced from practical applications made on the basis of observations. This contribution is however far from insignificant.

The Egyptian calendar year was divided into three seasons of four months, each having thirty days; to these 360 days, five were added at the end of the year. The 365-day calendar year, the most accurate known in antiquity, is at the origin of our own calendar year inasmuch as it served as the basis of the Julian reform (47 BC) and of the Gregorian reform of 1582. Side by side with this civil calendar, the Egyptians also used a religious, lunar calendar and were able to predict the moon's phases with adequate accuracy.

Ever since the Napoleonic expedition to Egypt, Europeans have been struck by the accuracy of the alignment of structures built at the time of the Pharaohs, particularly the pyramids, the four façades of which face the four cardinal points. The Great Pyramids deviate from true North by less than one degree. Such accuracy could have been achieved only by astronomical observation.

The ancient Egyptians applied their mathematical knowledge to the extraction, transportation and positioning of the huge blocks of stone used in their architectural projects. Their tradition of using mud-bricks and various kinds of stone went back to very early times. They first used heavy granite during the beginning of the third millennium before our era. It was used for the flooring of tombs belonging to the first dynasty at Abydos. During the second dynasty they used limestone in constructing the walls of tombs.

A new phase began during the third dynasty. This was a vital development in the history of Egyptian architecture, for it was the construction of the first complete building in stone. This is the step pyramid at Saqqarah, which forms a part of the huge funerary complex of King Zoser.

Imhotep, who was probably the vizier of King Zoser (c. 2580 BC), was the architect who built the ensemble containing the step pyramid where hewn stone was used for the first time. The blocks were small and looked very much like a limestone imitation of the sun-dried brick used earlier in funerary architecture. Similarly, the imbedded columns and the ceiling joists were stone copies of the bundles of plants and beams used in earlier construction. Thus, there is every indication that Egyptian architecture was amongst the first to use hewn stone in coursed work.

Until the Roman conquest, civil architecture continued to use sun-dried bricks even in the building of royal palaces. The outbuildings of Ramses in Thebes and the great Nubian fortresses provide a very good idea of the versatility of this material. It could be used with the utmost refinement, as can be seen from the Palace of Amenhotep IV at Tell el-Amarna with its pavements and ceilings decorated with paintings.

Another contribution in the field of architecture was the creation of the column. This was at first attached to the wall but later became free-standing.

In developing this architectural skill the ancient Egyptian was much influenced by the local environment. For example, in arriving at the idea of a column, he was inspired by his observation of wild plants such as reeds and papyrus.

He cut the capitals of the columns into the shape of lotus flowers, papyrus and other plants, and this was another architectural innovation. The lotus papyrus palm and fluted columns of ancient Egypt were adopted in the architecture of other cultures.

The technical knowledge acquired by the Egyptians in construction and irrigation as the result of digging canals and building dikes or dams manifested itself in other fields allied to architecture.

By 2550 BC, they had sufficient skill to build a dam of hewn stone in a wadi [river] near Cairo. Somewhat later, their engineers cut navigable channels in the rocks of the First Cataract at Aswan. By all evidence, towards 1740 BC, they seem to have succeeded in erecting a barrage on the Nile itself at Semna, in Nubia, to facilitate navigation to the south. And finally, during the same period, they built a ramp parallel to the Second Cataract, over which they slid their boats on the fluid mud of the Nile. The ramp extended over several kilometres, a predecessor of the Greek Diolkos of the Isthmus of Corinth, and ensured that the rapids of the Second Cataract never hindered navigation.

Cultural ties linking Egypt with the African interior existed during the earliest stages of prehistory as well as in historical times. Egyptian civilization under the Pharaohs permeated the neighbouring African cultures.

Comparative studies prove the existence of common cultural elements between black Africa and Egypt, such as the relationship between royalty and natural forces. This is clear from archaeological findings in the former territory of the land of Kush: royal pyramids were built in El-Kurru, Nuri, Gebel Barkal and Meroe. They bear witness to the significance of Egyptian influence in Africa.

Unfortunately, our ignorance of the Meroitic language, and of the extent of the Meroitic empire, prevents us from judging the impact it had on the cultures of ancient Africa as a whole to the east, west and south of the Meroitic empire.

7. THE EPIC OF GILGAMESH

Around 2700 B.C. the Mesopotamian city of Uruk was ruled by a king named Gilgamesh. This epic, however, was written much later—around 2000 B.C. Thus, the epic adds many layers of meaning to what might have originally been a straight historical account. In some ways those extra layers of meaning suggest more about the origins of cities and civilization than a straight history of an early king would.

Notice, for instance, how the king was thought of as part god. The ancient cities gave us our first kings, many of whom must have ruled like gods. Notice also how the conflict between Gilgamesh and Enkidu symbolizes the conflict between the city and the pasture. Ancient cities were continually threatened by the rough nomads of the pasture. The "barbarians" had to be "civilized."

What does the epic tell you about how early city people viewed themselves, their leaders, and the threatening herdsmen? How did they view women? What clues about ancient city life does the epic reveal?

PROLOGUE: GILGAMESH KING IN URUK

I will proclaim to the world the deeds of Gilgamesh. This was the man to whom all things were known; this was the king who knew the countries of the world. He was wise, he saw mysteries and knew secret things, he brought us a tale of the days before the flood. He went on a long journey, was weary, worn-out with labor; returning he rested, he engraved on a stone the whole story.

When the gods created Gilgamesh they gave him a perfect body. Shamash the glorious sun endowed him with beauty, Adad the god of the storm endowed him with courage, the great gods made his beauty perfect, surpassing all others, terrifying like a great wild bull. Two thirds they made him god and one third man.

In Uruk he built walls, a great rampart, and the temple of blessed Eanna for the god of the firmament Anu, and for Ishtar the goddess of love. Look at it still today: the outer wall where the cornice runs, it shines with the brilliance of copper; and the inner wall, it has no equal. Touch the threshold; it is ancient. Approach Eanna the dwelling of Ishtar, our lady of love and war, the like of which no latter-day king, no man alive can equal. Climb upon the wall of Uruk; walk along it, I say; regard the foundation terrace and examine the masonry; is it not burnt brick and good? The seven sages laid the foundations.

THE COMING OF ENKIDU

Gilgamesh went abroad in the world, but he met with none who could withstand his arms till he came to Uruk. But the men of Uruk muttered in their houses, "Gilgamesh sounds the tocsin for his amusement, his arrogance has no bounds by day or night. No son is left with his father, for Gilgamesh takes from all, even the children; yet the king should be a shepherd to his people. His lust leaves no virgin to her lover, neither the warrior's daughter nor the wife of the noble; yet this is the shepherd of the city, wise, comely, and resolute."

The gods heard their lament, the gods of heaven cried to the Lord of Uruk, to Anu the god of Uruk: "A goddess made him, strong as a savage bull, none can withstand his arms. No son is left with his father, for Gilgamesh takes them all; and is this the king, the shepherd of his people? His lust leaves no virgin to her lover, neither the warrior's daughter nor the wife of the noble." When Anu had heard their lamentation the gods cried to Aruru, the goddess of creation, "You made him, O Aruru, now create his equal; let it be as like him as his own reflection, his second self, stormy head for stormy heart. Let them contend together and leave Uruk in quiet."

So the goddess conceived an image in her mind, and it was of the stuff of Anu of the firmament. She dipped her hands in water and pinched off clay, she let it fall in the <u>wilderness</u>, and noble <u>Enkidu</u> was created. There was virtue in him of the god of war, of Ninurta himself. His body was rough; he had long hair like a woman's; it waved like the hair of Nisaba, the goddess of corn. His body was covered with matted hair like Samuqan's, the god of cattle. He was innocent of mankind; he knew nothing of cultivated land.

Enkidu ate grass in the hills with the gazelle and lurked with wild beasts at the water-holes; he had joy of the water with the herds of wild game. But there was a trapper who met him one day face to face at the drinking-hole, for the wild game had entered his territory. On three days he met him face to face, and the trapper was frozen with fear. He went back to his house with the game that he had caught, and he was dumb, be-numbed with terror. His face was altered like that of one who has made a long journey. With awe in his heart he spoke to his father: "Father, there is a man, unlike any other, who comes down from the hills. He is the strongest in the world, he is like an immortal from heaven. He ranges over the hills with wild beasts and eats grass; he ranges through your land and comes down to the wells. I am afraid and dare not go near him. He fills in the pits which I dig and tears up my traps set for the game; he helps the beasts to escape and now they slip through my fingers."

His father opened his mouth and said to the trapper, "My son, in Uruk lives Gilgamesh; no one has ever prevailed against him, he is strong as a star from heaven. Go to Uruk, find Gilgamesh, extol the strength of this wild man. Ask him to give you a harlot, a wanton from the temple of love; return with her, and <u>let her woman's power overpower this man.</u> When next he comes down to drink at the wells she will be there, stripped naked; and when he sees her beckoning he will embrace her, and then the wild beasts will reject him."

So the trapper set out on his journey to Uruk and addressed himself to Gilgamesh saying, "A man unlike any other is roaming now in the pas-tures; he is as strong as a star from heaven and I am afraid to approach him. He helps the wild game to escape; he fills in my pits and pulls up my traps." Gilgamesh said, "Trapper, go back, take with you a harlot, a child of pleasure. At the drinking-hole she will strip, and when he sees her beckoning he will embrace her and the game of the wilderness will surely reject him."

Now the trapper returned, taking the harlot with him. After a three days' journey they came to the drinking-hole, and there they sat down; the harlot and the trapper sat facing one another and waited for the game to come. For the first day and for the second day the two sat waiting, but on the third day the herds came; they came down to drink and Enkidu was with them. The small wild creatures of the plains were glad of the water, and Enkidu with them, who ate grass with the gazelle and was born in the hills; and she saw him, the savage man, come from far-off in the hills. The trapper spoke to her: "There he is. Now, woman, make your breasts bare, have no shame, do not delay but welcome his love. Let him see you naked, let him possess your body. When he comes near uncover yourself and lie with him; teach him, the savage man, your woman's art, for when he murmurs love to you the wild beasts that shared his life in the hills will reject him."

She was not ashamed to take him, she made herself naked and welcomed his eagerness; as he lay on her murmuring love she taught him the woman's art. For six days and seven nights they lay together, for Enkidu had forgotten his home in the hills; but when he was satisfied he went back to the wild beasts. Then, when the gazelle saw him, they bolted away; when the wild creatures saw him they fled. Enkidu would have followed, but his body was bound as though with a cord, his knees gave way when he started to run, his swiftness was gone. And now the wild creatures had all fled away; Enkidu was grown weak, for wisdom was in him, and the thoughts of a man were in his heart. So he returned and sat down at the woman's feet, and listened intently to what she said. "You are wise, Enkidu, and now you have become like a god. Why do you want to run wild with the beasts in the hills? Come with me. I will take you to strong-walled Uruk, to the blessed temple of Ishtar and of Anu, of love and of heaven: there Gilgamesh lives, who is very strong, and like a wild bull he lords it over men."

When she had spoken Enkidu was pleased; he longed for a comrade, for one who would understand his heart. "Come, woman, and take me to that holy temple, to the house of Anu and of Ishtar, and to the place where Gilgamesh lords it over people. I will challenge him boldly, I will cry out aloud in Uruk, 'I am the strongest here, I have come to change the old order, I am he who was born in the hills, I am he who is strongest of all.' "

She said, "Let us go, and let him see your face. I know very well where Gilgamesh is in great Uruk. O Enkidu, there all the people are dressed in their gorgeous robes, every day is holiday, the young men and the girls are wonderful to see. How sweet they smell! All the great ones are roused from their beds. O Enkidu, you who love life, I will show you Gilgamesh, a man of many moods; you shall look at him well in his radiant manhood. His body is perfect in strength and maturity; he never rests by night or day. He is stronger than you, so leave your boasting. Shamash the glorious sun has given favours to Gilgamesh, and Anu of the heavens, and Enlil, and Ea the wise has given him deep understanding. I tell you, even before you have left the wilderness, Gilgamesh will know in his dreams that you are coming."

Now Gilgamesh got up to tell his dream to his mother, Ninsun, one of the wise gods. "Mother, last night I had a dream. I was full of joy, the young heroes were round me and I walked through the night under the stars of the firmament, and one, a meteor of the stuff of Anu, fell down from heaven. I tried to lift it but it proved too heavy. All the people of Uruk came round to see it, the common people jostled and the nobles thronged to kiss its feet; and to me its attraction was like the love of woman. They helped me, I braced my forehead and I raised it with thongs and brought it to you, and you yourself pronounced it my brother."

Then Ninsun, who is well-beloved and wise, said to Gilgamesh, "This star of heaven which descended like a meteor from the sky; which you tried to lift, but found too heavy, when you tried to move it it would not budge, and so you brought it to my feet; I made it for you, a goad and spur, and you were drawn as though to a woman. This is the strong comrade, the one who brings help to his friend in his need. He is the strongest of wild creatures, the stuff of Anu; born in the grass-lands and the wild hills reared him; when you see him you will be glad; you will love him as a woman and he will never forsake you. This is the meaning of the dream."

Gilgamesh said, "Mother, I dreamed a second dream. In the streets of strong-walled Uruk there lay an axe; the shape of it was strange and the people thronged round. I saw it and was glad. I bent down, deeply drawn towards it; I loved it like a woman and wore it at my side." Ninsun answered, "That axe, which you saw, which drew you so powerfully like love of a woman, that is the comrade whom I give you, and he will come in his strength like one of the host of heaven. He is the brave companion who rescues his friend in necessity." Gilgamesh said to his mother, "A friend, a counsellor has come to me from Enlil, and now I shall befriend and counsel him." So Gilgamesh told his dreams; and the harlot retold them to Enkidu.

And now she said to Enkidu, "When I look at you you have become like a god. Why do you yearn to run wild again with the beasts in the hills? Get up from the ground, the bed of a shepherd." He listened to her words with care. It was good advice that she gave. She divided her clothing in two and with the one half she clothed him and with the other herself; and holding his hand she led him like a child to the sheepfolds, into the shepherds' tents. There all the shepherds crowded round to see him, they put down bread in front of him, but Enkidu could only suck the milk of wild animals. He fumbled and gaped, at a loss what to do or how he should eat the bread and drink the strong wine. Then the woman said, "Enkidu, eat bread, it is the staff of life; drink the wine, it is the custom of the land." So he ate till he was full and drank strong wine, seven goblets. He became merry, his heart exulted and his face shone. He rubbed down the matted hair of his body and anointed himself with oil. Enkidu had become a man; but when he had put on man's clothing he appeared like a bridegroom. He took arms to hunt the lion so that the shepherds could rest at night. He caught wolves and lions and the herdsmen lay down in peace; for Enkidu was their watchman, that strong man who had no rival.

He was merry living with the shepherds, till one day lifting his eyes he saw a man approaching. He said to the harlot, "Woman, fetch that man here. Why has he come? I wish to know his name." She went and called the man saying, "Sir, where are you going on this weary journey?" The man answered, saying to Enkidu, "Gilgamesh has gone into the marriage-house and shut out the people. He does strange things in Uruk, the city of great streets. At the roll of the drum work begins for the men, and work for the women. Gilgamesh the king is about to celebrate marriage with the Queen of Love, and he still demands to be first with the bride, the king to be first and the husband to follow, for that was ordained by the gods from his birth, from the time the umbilical cord was cut. But now the drums roll for the choice of the bride and the city groans." At these words Enkidu turned white in the face. "I will go to the place where Gilgamesh lords it over the people, I will challenge him boldly, and I will cry aloud in Uruk, 'I have come to change the old order, for I am the strongest here.' "

Now Enkidu strode in front and the woman followed behind. He entered Uruk, that great market, and all the folk thronged round him where he stood in the street in strong-walled Uruk. The people jostled; speaking of him they said, "He is the spit of Gilgamesh." "He is shorter." "He is bigger of bone." "This is the one who was reared on the milk of wild beasts. His is the greatest strength." The men rejoiced: "Now Gilgamesh has met his match. This great one, this hero whose beauty is like a god, he is a match even for Gilgamesh."

In Uruk the bridal bed was made, fit for the goddess of love. The bride waited for the bridegroom, but in the night Gilgamesh got up and came to the house. Then Enkidu stepped out, he stood in the street and blocked the way. Mighty Gilgamesh came on and Enkidu met him at the gate. He put out his foot and prevented Gilgamesh from entering the house, so they grappled, holding each other like bulls. They broke the doorposts and the walls shook, they snorted like bulls locked together. They shattered the doorposts and the walls shook. Gilgamesh bent his knee with his foot planted on the ground and with a turn Enkidu was thrown. Then immediately his fury died. When Enkidu was thrown he said to Gilgamesh, "There is not another like you in the world. Ninsun, who is as strong as a wild ox in the byre, she was the mother who bore you, and now you are raised above all men, and Enlil has given you the kingship, for your strength surpasses the strength of men." So Enkidu and Gilgamesh embraced and their friendship was sealed.

There are many stories in the Epic of Gilgamesh. *The following story of the flood is one of the most interesting because of its similarity to the later biblical story of the flood in the book of Genesis.*

The speaker is Utnapishtim, who has a story for Gilgamesh. What is the story? What does this story suggest about Sumerian religion? How is the story similar to the biblical one? What accounts for such similarity?

THE STORY OF THE FLOOD

"You know the city Shurrupak, it stands on the banks of Euphrates? That city grew old and the gods that were in it were old. There was Anu, lord of the firmament, their father, and warrior Enlil their counsellor, Ninurta the helper, and Ennugi watcher over canals; and with them also was Ea. In those days the world teemed, the people multiplied, the world bellowed like a wild bull, and the great god was aroused by the clamour. Enlil heard the clamour and he said to the gods in council, 'The uproar of mankind is intolerable and sleep is no longer possible by reason of the babel.' So the gods agreed to exterminate mankind. Enlil did this, but Ea because of his oath warned me in a dream. He whispered their words to my house of reeds, 'Reed-house, reed-house! Wall, O wall, hearken reed-house, wall reflect; O man of Shurrupak, son of Ubara-Tutu; tear down your house and build a boat, abandon possessions and look for life, despise worldly goods and save your soul alive. Tear down your house, I say, and build a boat. These are the measurements of the barque as you shall build her: let her beam equal her length, let her deck be roofed like the vault that covers the abyss; then take up into the boat the seed of all living creatures.'

"When I had understood I said to my lord, 'Behold, what you have commanded I will honour and perform, but how shall I answer the people, the city, the elders?' The Ea opened his mouth and said to me, his servant, 'Tell them this: I have learnt that Enlil is wrathful against me, I dare no longer walk in his land nor live in his city; I will go down to the Gulf to dwell with Ea my lord. But on you he will rain down abundance, rare fish and shy wild-fowl, a rich harvest-tide. In the evening the rider of the storm will bring you wheat in torrents.'

"In the first light of dawn all my household gathered round me, the children brought pitch and the men whatever was necessary. On the fifth day I laid the keel and the ribs, then I made fast the planking. The ground-space was one acre, each side of the deck measured one hundred and twenty cubits, making a square. I built six decks below, seven in all, I divided them into nine sections with bulkheads between. I drove in wedges where needed, I saw to the punt-poles, and laid in supplies. The carriers brought oil in baskets, I poured pitch into the furnace and asphalt and oil; more oil was consumed in caulking, and more again the master of the boat took into his stores. I slaughtered bullocks for the people and every day I killed sheep. I gave the shipwrights wine to drink as though it were river water, raw wine and red wine and oil and white wine. There was feasting then as there is at the time of the New Year's festival; I myself anointed my head. On the seventh day the boat was complete.

"Then was the launching full of difficulty; there was shifting of ballast above and below till two thirds was submerged. I loaded into her all that I had of gold and of living things, my family, my kin, the beast of the field both wild and tame, and all the craftsmen. I sent them on board, for the time that Shamash had ordained was already fulfilled when he said 'In the evening, when the rider of the storm sends down the destroying rain, enter the boat and batten her down.' The time was fulfilled, the evening came, the rider of the storm sent down the rain. I looked out at the weather and it was terrible, so I too boarded the boat and battened her down. All was now complete, the battening and the caulking; so I handed the tiller to Puzur-Amurri the steersman, with the navigation and the care of the whole boat.

"With the first light of dawn a black cloud came from the horizon; it thundered within where Adad, lord of the storm was riding. In front over hill and plain Shullat and Hanish, heralds of the storm, led on. Then the gods of the abyss rose up; Nergal pulled out the dams of the nether waters, Ninurta the war-lord threw down the dykes, and the seven judges of hell, the Annunaki, raised their torches, lighting the land with their livid flame. A stupor of despair went up to heaven when the god of the storm turned daylight to darkness, when he smashed the land like a cup. One whole day the tempest raged, gathering fury as it went, it poured over the people like the tides of battle; a man could not see his brother nor the people be seen from heaven. Even the gods were terrified at the flood, they fled to the highest heaven, the firmament of Anu; they crouched against the walls, cowering like curs. Then Ishtar the sweet-voiced Queen of Heaven cried out like a woman in travail: 'Alas the days of old are turned to dust because I commanded evil; why did I command this evil in the council of all the gods? I commanded wars to destroy the people, but are they not my people, for I brought them forth? Now like the spawn of fish they float in the ocean.' The great gods of heaven and of hell wept, they covered their mouths.

"For six days and six nights the winds blew, torrent and tempest and flood overwhelmed the world, tempest and flood raged together like warring hosts. When the seventh day dawned the storm from the south subsided, the sea grew calm, the flood was stilled; I looked at the face of the world and there was silence, all mankind was turned to clay. The surface of the sea stretched as flat as a roof-top; I opened a hatch and the light fell on my face. Then I bowed low, I sat down and I wept, the tears streamed down my face, for on every side was the waste of water. I looked for land in vain, but fourteen leagues distant there appeared a mountain, and there the boat grounded; on the mountain of Nisir the boat held fast, she held fast and did not budge. One day she held, and a second day on the mountain of Nisir she held fast and did not budge. A third day, and a fourth day she held fast on the mountain and did not budge; a fifth day and a sixth day she held fast on the mountain. When the seventh day dawned I loosed a <u>dove</u> and let her go. She flew away, but finding no resting-place she returned. Then I loosed a swallow, and she flew away but finding no resting-place she returned. I loosed a raven, she saw that the waters had retreated, she ate, she flew around, she cawed, and she did not come back. Then I threw everything open to the four winds, I made a sacrifice and poured out a libation on the mountain top. Seven and again seven cauldrons I set up on their stands, I heaped up wood and cane and cedar and myrtle. When the gods smelled the sweet savour, they gathered like flies over the sacrifice. Then, at last, Ishtar also came, she lifted her necklace with the jewels of heaven that once Anu had made to please her. 'O you gods here present, by the lapis lazuli round my neck I shall remember these days as I remember the jewels of my throat; these last days I shall not forget. Let all the gods gather round the sacrifice, except Enlil. He shall not approach this offering, for without reflection he brought the flood; he consigned my people to destruction.'

"When Enlil had come, when he saw the boat, he was wrath and swelled with anger at the gods, the host of heaven, 'Has any of these mortals escaped? Not one was to have survived the destruction.' Then the god of the wells and canals Ninurta opened his mouth and said to the warrior Enlil, 'Who is there of the gods that devise without Ea? It is Ea alone who knows all things.' Then Ea opened his mouth and spoke to warrior Enlil, 'Wisest of gods, hero Enlil, how could you so senselessly bring down the flood?

> Lay upon the sinner his sin,
> Lay upon the transgressor his transgression,
> Punish him a little when he breaks loose,
> Do not drive him too hard or he perishes;
> Would that a lion had ravaged mankind
> Rather than the flood,
> Would that a wolf had ravaged mankind
> Rather than the flood,
> Would that famine had wasted the world
> Rather than the flood,
> Would that pestilence had wasted mankind
> Rather than the flood.

It was not I that revealed the secret of the gods; the wise man learned it in a dream. Now take your counsel what shall be done with him.'

"Then Enlil went up into the boat, he took me by the hand and my wife and made us enter the boat and kneel down on either side, he standing between us. He touched our foreheads to bless us saying, 'In time past Utnapishtim was a mortal man; henceforth he and his wife shall live in the distance at the mouth of the rivers.' Thus it was that the gods took me and placed me here to live in the distance, at the mouth of the rivers."

8. HAMMURABI'S CODE

The Sumerians were overrun after 2000 B.C. by successive waves of invaders from further up the Euphrates River. Among the most successful of these conquerors were the Babylonians who, under Hammurabi (c. 1792–1750 B.C.), controlled the entire river valley. We remember them for their elaborate code of laws, one of the earliest. It is also the best mirror of their society.

This selection includes only a small fraction of Hammurabi's Code, but it is a fairly representative sample. What do these laws tell us about Babylonian society in the eighteenth century B.C.? To what extent were their legal concerns similar to, or different from, ours today?

THEFT

6. If a man has stolen goods from a temple, or house, he shall be put to death; and he that has received the stolen property from him shall be put to death.

8. If a patrician has stolen ox, sheep, ass, pig, or ship, whether from a temple, or a house, he shall pay thirtyfold. If he be a plebeian, he shall return tenfold. If the thief cannot pay, he shall be put to death.

14. If a man has stolen a child, he shall be put to death.

15. If a man has induced either a male or female slave from the house of a patrician, or plebeian, to leave the city, he shall be put to death.

21. If a man has broken into a house he shall be killed before the breach and buried there.

22. If a man has committed highway robbery and has been caught, that man shall be put to death.

23. If the highwayman has not been caught, the man that has been robbed shall state on oath what he has lost and the city or district governor in whose territory or district the robbery took place shall restore to him what he has lost.

MARRIAGE

128. If a man has taken a wife and has not executed a marriage-contract, that woman is not a wife.

129. If a man's wife be caught lying with another, they shall be strangled and cast into the water. If the wife's husband would save his wife, the king can save his servant.

130. If a man has ravished another's betrothed wife, who is a virgin, while still living in her father's house, and has been caught in the act, that man shall be put to death; the woman shall go free.

131. If a man's wife has been accused by her husband, and has not been caught lying with another, she shall swear her innocence, and return to her house.

138. If a man has divorced his wife, who has not borne him children, he shall pay over to her as much money as was given for her bride-price and the marriage-portion which she brought from her father's house, and so shall divorce her.

139. If there was no bride-price, he shall give her one mina of silver, as a price of divorce.

140. If he be a plebeian, he shall give her one-third of a mina of silver.

148. If a man has married a wife and a disease has seized her, if he is determined to marry a second wife, he shall marry her. He shall not divorce the wife whom the disease has seized. In the home they made together she shall dwell, and he shall maintain her as long as she lives.

149. If that woman was not pleased to stay in her husband's house, he shall pay over to her the marriage-portion which she brought from her father's house, and she shall go away.

153. If a man's wife, for the sake of another, has caused her husband to be killed, that woman shall be impaled.

154. If a man has committed incest with his daughter, that man shall be banished from the city.

155. If a man has betrothed a maiden to his son and his son has known her, and afterward the man has lain in her bosom, and been caught, that man shall be strangled and she shall be cast into the water.

156. If a man has betrothed a maiden to his son, and his son has not known her, and that man has lain in her bosom, he shall pay her half a mina of silver, and shall pay over to her whatever she brought from her father's house, and the husband of her choice shall marry her.

186. If a man has taken a young child to be his son, and after he has taken him, the child discovers his own parents, he shall return to his father's house.

188, 189. If a craftsman has taken a child to bring up and has taught him his handicraft, he shall not be reclaimed. If he has not taught him his handicraft that foster child shall return to his father's house.

ASSAULT

195. If a son has struck his father, his hands shall be cut off.

196. If a man has knocked out the eye of a patrician, his eye shall be knocked out.

197. If he has broken the limb of a patrician, his limb shall be broken.

198. If he has knocked out the eye of a plebeian or has broken the limb of a plebeian's servant, he shall pay one mina of silver.

199. If he has knocked out the eye of a patrician's servant, or broken the limb of a patrician's servant, he shall pay half his value.

200. If a patrician has knocked out the tooth of a man that is his equal, his tooth shall be knocked out.

201. If he has knocked out the tooth of a plebeian, he shall pay one-third of a mina of silver.

LIABILITY

229. If a builder has built a house for a man, and has not made his work sound, and the house he built has fallen, and caused the death of its owner, that builder shall be put to death.

230. If it is the owner's son that is killed, the builder's son shall be put to death.

231. If it is the slave of the owner that is killed, the builder shall give slave for slave to the owner of the house.

232. If he has caused the loss of goods, he shall render back whatever he has destroyed. Moreover, because he did not make sound the house he built, and it fell, at his own cost he shall rebuild the house that fell.

237. If a man has hired a boat and a boatman, and loaded it with corn, wool, oil, or dates, or whatever it be, and the boatman has been careless, and sunk the boat, or lost what is in it, the boatman shall restore the boat which he sank, and whatever he lost that was in it.

238. If a boatman has sunk a man's boat, and has floated it again, he shall pay half its value in silver.

251. If a man's ox be a gorer, and has revealed its evil propensity as a gorer, and he has not blunted its horn, or shut up the ox, and then that ox has gored a free man, and caused his death, the owner shall pay half a mina of silver.

252. If it be a slave that has been killed, he shall pay one-third of a mina of silver.

CHAPTER THREE

The Ancient
Civilizations of Asia

9. INDUS CIVILIZATION
AND THE ARYAN
INVASION

Francis Watson

Ancient Indus civilization, especially that of the two principal cities on the Indus River, Mohenjo-Daro and Harappa, rivaled that of the Middle East after 3000 B.C. It was completely destroyed, however, by the time of the Aryan invasion of about 1500 B.C. Consequently, Indian civilization today owes much more to the Aryan invaders than to the ancient cities of the Indus.

As you read this history of ancient India, note how ancient Indus civilization was similar to, and different from, the civilizations of the ancient Middle East. What were the new elements introduced by the Aryans?

From about 3000 B.C. in about a hundred sites so far uncovered, over a huge area of the Indus plain—almost a thousand miles from north to south—the pottery styles show a startling uniformity. The semi-isolated settlements had been succeeded by something very different: a homogenous realm of villages and townships, with the river as the axis of communication, and with an agricultural surplus sufficient to support two capital cities, more than 350 miles apart: Mohenjo-Daro in the south, Harappa in the north.

Standardization, an ordered society, and ten centuries of relatively stable conditions, are among the surprising features revealed by excavation of these two urban centres. Both made use of vast quantities of baked bricks, presupposing the existence of forests to provide firing fuel. The ground-plans of both were not only similar, but retained through successive phases of rebuilding a common principle, with a raised citadel, or acropolis, on the west, main streets laid out in grid-iron fashion, a network of lanes within each block, the better houses concealed in courtyards, and in both cities a clearly defined labourers' quarter. The great size of the granaries indicates a strong centralized authority, and the water-supply and drainage systems were extremely thorough. "No Indian city," writes

Dr. Kosambi, "possessed anything of the sort until modern times; far too many still lack these amenities."

This civic sophistication sets the Indus civilization apart from its great contemporaries in Sumer and Akkad and Middle Kingdom Egypt. Its written language, which might dispel some of the mystery, remains undeciphered, and has survived only in brief seal-inscriptions apparently concerned with property or commerce. There seem to be no religious dedications, no names of rulers, and so far no dynastic tombs to shed light on a hierarchical system. The terracotta seals, of a type distinct from the Sumerian, are at once enigmatic and suggestive in the frequently consummate quality of their engraved images and in the subjects depicted, which include animals such as the elephant, tiger, rhinoceros and the Indian humped and dewlapped bull—as well as mythical beasts, emblems and figures. A horned deity depicted on some of the seals, seated in yogic posture, with erect phallus and accompanied by wild animals, has been seen as an early prototype of the Hindu god Shiva. The numerous small clay figurines of an earth-goddess, primitive by contrast with the seal-engravings, point to a popular fertility cult; but the absence of monuments, religious or secular, is singular.

At Mohenjo-Daro the enormous stone bath on the citadel mound is presumed to have served ritual ablutions. Other evidence, such as the long conservation of a static pattern of life, has been used to support the argument for a dominant priesthood. All that we really know is that existence at this remote period must have been comfortable for an elite and was certainly highly organized. Humped cattle and buffaloes, goats, sheep and pigs, the camel and the elephant had all been domesticated, though not the horse (which has always, for some reason, presented breeding difficulties in India). The dog, first trained by Paleolithic hunters, left his urban traces at the Indus site of Chanhu-Daro, in footprints chasing those of a cat across the once wet surface of some brickwork. The domestic fowl, one of India's gifts to the world, had by this time been tamed from the jungle-fowl.

Another distinctive Indian product, cotton, was already in use for clothing, as well as wool. Barley and wheat were the chief food crops, and both meat and fish were eaten. Iron was as yet unknown. Copper (probably from Rajasthan east of the Indus) was extensively used for household implements, though some of them were still of stone. Upper-class luxury and advanced craftsmanship were displayed in adornments of gold and silver, ivory, jade, agate, crystal, lapis lazuli and other fine materials; and the absence of large works of art by which to distinguish the Indus culture is compensated, not only by the best of the seals, but by a number of small sculptures—a bronze dancing-girl, a male torso, heads in steatite, and others—each of which has won high admiration in our own day.

There is enough that is unique and indigenous about Harappa and

Mohenjo-Daro to leave the question of influence from or upon the Sumerian culture an open one. Of a flourishing trade between the two there is firm evidence, both by land across the Iranian plateau and by sea from a port near the mouth of the Indus. Hugging the dangerous coastline to reach the Persian Gulf, Indian crews used a "compassbird"—a crow which would fly when released towards the nearest point of land. The story that was later included in the Buddhist *Jatakas* of traders to Babylon using this device—exactly as recorded of Noah in the Bible and of Gilgamesh in the Sumerian epic—is pictorially confirmed on one of the Mesopotamian seals.

Recent excavations have shown the Indus civilization to have been wider in its extent and influence than was previously supposed; and the uniformity of the evidence over an immense area has promoted Sir Mortimer Wheeler to infer "something like an imperial status . . . the vastest political experiment before the Roman Empire." Its mysterious obliteration is thereby rendered all the more intriguing. However the people of the Indus cities met their doom, the Aryans who succeeded them were barbarians in comparison, though their self-given name meant "noble" or "free-born."

THE COMING OF THE ARYANS

From early in the second millennium B.C. the urban cultures of Western Asia were increasingly threatened by that recurrent instrument of history, the hardy nomads of the grasslands of Central Asia. In the words of the Mesopotamian chroniclers, "their onslaught was like a hurricane: a people who had never known a city." The tribes who brought their Aryan languages and their Aryan gods to Iran and India, while a separate wave flowed westwards into Europe, may not have been the sole executioners of the Indus civilization. Mohenjo-Daro in particular provides evidence of trouble and decay over several centuries before 1500 B.C., the date now roughly agreed for the first Aryan immigrations through the passes of the Hindu Kush. But the same site also illustrates, with a huddle of skeletons, the final drama of an overwhelmed defence. There is also, in the collection of Sanskrit hymns called *Rig-Veda*, the earliest product of the Vedic tradition from which, in default of material remains, our knowledge of the next millennium has somehow to be gleaned. Renowned for the beauty of its invocations to the creative spirit of the natural world, this tradition is at the same time positive in the pride of conquest and the concept of racial and religious superiority.

The *Rig-Veda* was not at first committed to writing, but memorized. Almost a quarter of its hymns are addressed to the rain-god Indra, not simply as the seasonal banisher of drought but as the great storm-warrior and wielder of the thunderbolt. Irresistible in strength, gargantuan in appetite, fair-complexioned and bursting with rude vigour, Indra often calls to mind the deified hero of some Norse or Celtic myth. From details of his exploits the horse-drawn chariot of the Aryans, holding a charioteer and a warrior, can be reconstructed as a prime factor of conquest in the plains. The horse, praised in splendid verses in the *Rig-Veda,* must have been as terrifying a novelty to the foe as it was to prove in the Spanish conquest of the Incas in the sixteenth century, but there is little evidence of its use independently of the chariot: effective cavalry had to await the curiously late invention of the stirrup. "Destroyer of Citadels" is one of Indra's epithets, and in the Land of the Seven Rivers (later to be reduced by desiccation to the five which gave the Punjab its name) he assisted an Aryan chief by tearing to pieces "like old clothes" the defending forces of a place called Hariyupiya—surely Harappa? In his capacity as "Releaser of Waters," moreover, Indra is praised for feats suggesting the destruction of the dams now known to have been in use for flood control and irrigation in the basin of the Indus, which by shifting its course had caused Mohenjo-Daro to be rebuilt several times. "On circumstantial evidence," to quote Wheeler again, "Indra stands accused."

The Sanskrit vocabulary is rich in pejorative terms for the appearance, customs and character of the various peoples encountered by the invaders, whether as enemies in pitched battle, peasant communities overrun, cattle-raiders, refugees from defended cities, or wild forest-hunters. Often they were "noseless" or flat-faced demons, and always they were "godless" in their unseemly ways and their indifference to the Aryan pantheon, its rites and sacrifices. From the post-Vedic epics and *Puranas* (miscellaneous sacred texts) such fanciful opprobrium as the description of one-legged aborigines who shaded themselves with a single enormous foot found its way many centuries later, through Pliny and other classical writers, into the travel-lore of medieval Europe.

The generalized name of *dasas,* which began by meaning "enemies" and came to mean "subjects," at all times carried the signification of a darker-skinned race. It would be an over-simplification to suppose that the descendants of the Aryans are found today in the northern half of India and in the higher castes, and the indigenous (Dravidian) strain in the South, in the lower castes and among the tribes. But the persistence of a social prejudice in favour of a light (in matrimonial advertisements "wheaten") complexion cannot be overlooked. In this connection it is often pointed out that the word *varna,* as applied to the four-class system recognized from Vedic times, means "colour" ("caste" comes from the Portuguese and was not used before the sixteenth century). These four classes were of priests (*brahmans*), warriors (*kshatriyas*), peasant farmers (*vaishyas*) and serfs (*shudras*), and in theory the subjugated elements could be admitted into the Aryan system only at the lowest level. The religious sanction for a strict maintenance of the four divisions, however, is either a late Vedic text or, as some think, a subsequent interpolation at a period when miscegenation had gone so far as to threaten the whole system. There is a note almost of desperation in the invocation which lays one more task upon the mighty Indra: "O Indra, find out who is an Aryan and who is a Dasa, and separate them!"

Behind the advancing warriors, agricultural settlement accompanied and gradually gained over pastoral nomadism, in which wealth was at first entirely in cattle. Herds of oxen, sheep and goats gave the Aryans meat (taboos against beef or other flesh were not yet in operation), milk products, and wool for their few garments. The knowledge of cotton cultivation had vanished for the time being with the civilization of their predecessors, but barley and possibly wheat were grown at the first stage of settlement. *Soma*, the unidentified and sanctified potion used in ritual, was one of several intoxicants. Women appear to have had a respected status, and there is no reference to child-marriage. Games, dancing and chariot-races are mentioned in the early Vedas, which also include the lament of an unsuccessful gambler. Musical instruments were developed, and jewellery of some kind came to be worn by the more important Aryans, but no art-objects have survived for comparison either with those found in the Indus culture or with the admired "animal style" produced by the nomads of the Euro-Asian steppes. Their absence might be partly attributed to the burning of their dead by the Indo-Aryans, but simple burial was also practised.

The ways of these vigorous clans and families pushing in from the northwest differed totally from those that had characterized the long-established cities of the Indus valley. In this sense, as has been said, the newcomers were barbarians. But they were not primitive. They had no written language because they needed none, but the feat of memorizing and handing down an increasing body of oral "literature" has to be borne in mind as we peruse it for clues to their life and thought. After the loss of the characters used by the Indus civilization there is no evidence of a script until about the fourth century B.C., a thousand years later, though some use of writing must be presumed from perhaps a couple of centuries earlier. As spoken tongues the sacred and elaborate Sanskrit and the "natural" vernaculars, generally called Prakrit and reflecting a degree of Aryan mingling with the indigenous peoples, existed side by side. Even after Sanskrit was fully mature, however, the priestly ban on the committal of the religious texts to writing was effective for many centuries. The oldest *known* manuscript of the *Rig-Veda* dates from the fifteenth century A.D.—nearly three thousand years after the assumed time of its composition—but the Vedic hymns are used today at Hindu wedding ceremonies, in an astonishing example of continuous tradition.

10. THE VEDAS:
10.1. THE *RIG-VEDA*—
SACRIFICE AS CREATION

Indian Hinduism is rooted in the Vedic Age (1500–600 B.C.), which opened with the Aryan invasion after the disappearance of the ancient Harappa culture. The Vedas are the writings of the priests. They cover a wide variety of religious subjects and concerns: ritual, sacrifice, hymns, healing, incantations, allegories, philosophy, and the problems of everyday life. In general, the earliest Vedas (like the Rig-Veda) are more concerned with the specifics of ritual and sacrifice. They are carefully composed, but reflect the needs and instruction of the priests during the Aryan conquest. The last of the Vedas (like the Upanishads) are in general more philosophical: less concerned with ritual and more speculative.

This first selection is from the Rig-Veda. What happened when Purusha was sacrificed? What is the meaning of this first sacrifice? How does this story support the role of the priests? How does it support the divisions of Indian society?

Thousand-headed Purusha, thousand-eyed, thousand-footed—he having pervaded the earth on all sides, still extends ten fingers beyond it.

Purusha alone is all this—whatever has been and whatever is going to be. Further, he is the lord of immortality and also of what grows for food.

Such is his greatness; greater, indeed, than this is Purusha. All creatures constitute but one quarter of him, his three quarters are the immortal in heaven. . . . Being born, he projected himself behind the earth as also before it.

When the gods performed the sacrifice with Purusha as the oblation [religious offering], then the spring was its clarified butter, the summer the sacrificial fuel, and the autumn the oblation.

The sacrificial victim, namely, Purusha, born at the very beginning, they sprinkled with sacred water upon the sacrificial grass. With him as oblation the gods performed the sacrifice, and also the Sādhyas [a class of semidivine beings] and the rishis [ancient seers].

From that wholly offered sacrificial oblation were born the verses and the sacred chants; from it were born the meters; the sacrificial formula was born from it.

From it horses were born and also those animals who have double rows of teeth; cows were born from it, from it were born goats and sheep.

When they divided Purusha, in how many different portions did they arrange him? What became of his mouth, what of his two arms? What were his two thighs and his two feet called?

His mouth became the brāhman; his two arms were made into the rājanya; his two thighs the vaishyas; from his two feet the shūdra was born.

The moon was born from the mind, from the eye the sun was born; from the mouth Indra and Agni, from the breath the wind was born.

From the navel was the atmosphere created, from the head the heaven issued forth; from the two feet was born the earth and the quarters (the cardinal directions) from the ear. Thus did they fashion the worlds.

Seven were the enclosing sticks in this sacrifice, thrice seven were the fire-sticks made, when the gods, performing the sacrifice, bound down Purusha, the sacrificial victim.

With this sacrificial oblation did the gods offer the sacrifice. These were the first norms (*dharma*) of sacrifice. These greatnesses reached to the sky wherein live the ancient Sādhyas and gods.

10.2. THE UPANISHADS— BRAHMAN AND ATMAN

— dealt more w/ meditation / contemplation

The Upanishads, the "crown" and completion of the Vedic Age, were more philosophical than the earlier Vedas. They treated sacrifice symbolically, preferring meditation, contemplation, and psychological inquiry to the details of a priestly ritual. The numerous gods of the early Vedas were replaced by a single, mysterious Brahman, who was equivalent to each and every interior self (atman).

This selection from the Chandogya Upanishad *begins by comparing the chanting of the Gayatri morning offering with the Brahman. What is meant by this comparison? What is the Brahman? This universal Brahman is identified with the atman, or Spirit. What does this mean? What is the point of this identification?*

Great is the Gayatri, the most sacred verse of the Vedas; but how much greater is the Infinity of Brahman! A quarter of his being is this whole vast universe: the other three quarters are his heaven of Immortality.   (3.12.5)

There is a Light that shines beyond all things on earth, beyond us all, beyond the heavens, beyond the highest, the very highest heavens. This is the Light that shines in our heart.   (3.13.7)

All this universe is in the truth Brahman. He is the beginning and end and life of all. As such, in silence, give unto him adoration.

Man in truth is made of faith. As his faith is in this life, so he becomes in the beyond: with faith and vision let him work.

There is a Spirit that is mind and life, light and truth and vast spaces. He contains all works and desires and all perfumes and all tastes. He enfolds the whole universe, and in silence is loving to all.

This is the Spirit that is in my heart, smaller than a grain of rice, or a grain of barley, or a grain of mustard-seed, or a grain of canary-seed, or the kernel of a grain of canary-seed. This is the Spirit that is in my heart, greater than the earth, greater than the sky, greater than heaven itself, greater than all these worlds.

He contains all works and desires and all perfumes and all tastes. He enfolds the whole universe and in silence is loving to all. This is the Spirit that is in my heart, this is Brahman.

To him I shall come when I go beyond this life. And to him will come he who has faith and doubts not. Thus said Sandilya, thus said Sandilya.   (3.14)

10.3.   THE UPANISHADS— KARMA AND REINCARNATION

The idea of karma, of cause and effect, appropriate consequences, can be found in the earliest Upanishads. Karma meant that the fruits of any thoughts or actions would inevitably be fulfilled. Good karma would be enhanced. Bad karma would lead to more bad karma. The universe was a system of complete justice in which everyone got what they deserved. The idea that the soul might be reborn in another body may have been an even older idea, but in the Upanishads it combined easily with the idea of karma. That a good soul was reborn in a higher life, or a bad soul in a lower, was perhaps a more material, less subtle, version of the justice of karma. The idea of reincarnation, or the transmigration of souls, combined justice and caste.

What effect would these ideas have on people? In what ways would these ideas aid people in gaining a sense of power over their lives? How might these ideas be tools of control? What does "morality" mean in this tradition?

According as one acts, according as one conducts himself, so does he become. The doer of good becomes good. The doer of evil becomes evil. One becomes virtuous by virtuous action, bad by bad action.

But people say: "A person is made not of acts, but of desires only." In reply to this I say: As is his desire, such is his resolve; as is his resolve, such the action he performs; what action (*karma*) he performs, that he procures for himself.

On this point there is this verse:—

> *Where one's mind is attached—the inner self*
> *Goes thereto with action, being attached to it alone.*

> *Obtaining the end of his action,*
> *Whatever he does in this world,*
> *He comes again from that world*
> *To this world of action.*

—So the man who desires.

Now the man who does not desire.—He who is without desire, who is freed from desire, whose desire is satisfied, whose desire is the Soul—his breaths do not depart. Being very Brahman, he goes to Brahman.

Accordingly, those who are of pleasant conduct here—the prospect is, indeed, that they will enter a pleasant womb, either the womb of a Brahman, or the womb of a Kshatriya, or the womb of a Vaishya. But those who are of stinking conduct here—the prospect is, indeed, that they will enter a stinking womb, either the womb of a dog, or the womb of a swine, or the womb of an outcaste (*candāla*).

11. SCIENCE AND CIVILIZATION IN ANCIENT CHINA

Joseph Needham and Colin A. Ronan

The authors of this reading are modern historians of ancient China. They discuss the earliest Chinese (Neolithic) cultures, suggesting interesting contacts with Southeast Asia and North America. They also see major developments in the rise of the Shang dynasty. In what ways was Shang dynasty China different from earlier Chinese society? In what ways were Shang dynasty developments similar to those occurring elsewhere in the world?

China is better provided with original source-material about its past than any other Eastern, and indeed most Western, countries. Unlike, for example, India, where chronology is still very uncertain, with China it is often possible to be certain not only of the year, but even of the month and day as well. A great number of official histories and annals have survived, all written with remarkable lack of bias, but it is an unfortunate fact that only very small parts of them have been translated into European languages. They are very valuable from an economic, political and social point of view, but generally speaking of relatively little use for the history of science. They do indeed provide much astronomical and meteorological information because the heavens were the fundamental basis for computing calendars, and events in them, as well as the weather, were used to foretell the future. But Chinese literary culture was on the whole uninterested in science, and by and large the historian of science has to look elsewhere for his evidence. . . .

CHINESE PRE-HISTORY AND THE SHANG DYNASTY

The first inhabitants on Chinese soil, of whose remains we know, were the race to which 'Peking Man' belonged. *Sinanthropus pekinensis* lived at the beginning or middle of the Pleistocene period, that is around 400,000 B.C., and earlier than Neanderthal Man of Europe and the Mediterranean. There is certain evidence, too, that there was a Neolithic population in China around 12,000 B.C., but after this there is a remarkable gap in continuity; only in Manchuria are all the subsequent prehistoric stages to be found. Then, suddenly, about 2500 B.C., the apparently empty land begins to support a large and busy population. There are hundreds, even thousands, of villages, inhabited by a people tending flocks and having an agricultural economy, acquainted with textiles, carpentry and ceramics. Obviously, extensive archaeological work is needed to throw light on this curious hiatus between the Stone Age and their late Neolithic successors.

The first important culture in China to be revealed by excavations is the Yangshao, which existed in a belt of country running from west to east, and comprising the present provinces of Kansu, Shensi, Shansi, Honan and Shantung. The chief cereal was almost certainly millet and, later, rice, and since neither plant is indigenous to China, the likelihood is that they came from South-East Asia. Bones of dogs, pigs and, later, sheep and cattle, have been found; bones of the horse have been identified too, although this may have been a wild horse of the kind that until recently still existed in Mongolia. The most outstanding characteristic of the Yangshao culture, however, was their painted pottery, made about 2500 B.C. by coiling clay, not by using a potter's wheel.

It is worth noting that at this stage of development, there is evidence for a wide community of culture throughout Northern Asia and Northern America. For instance, an implement to be found throughout the area was a rectangular or semi-lunar knife, quite unlike anything in Europe or the Middle East, but used by Eskimos, Amerindians, Chinese and in Siberia, and this as well as other evidence points to a migration across the Bering Straits. On the other hand, the Chinese themselves developed some characteristic inventions of their own at this time, most notably two types of pottery vessel which seem to be unique, and are of interest to the historian of science in view of the close connection between cooking and chemistry. One was the *li*, a cauldron or pot with three hollow legs which increased the surface area to be heated and so led to greater efficiency. The other was a *tsêng*, a vessel with a perforated bottom that could be stood on top of a *li*, thus making an efficient steam cooking combination, which also had the advantage of allowing more than one foodstuff to be cooked at the same time. When the two were combined into a single form, often with a removable grating, it was called a *hsien* and became more preponderant when bronze replaced pottery. We now know that this led directly later on to the characteristic East Asian apparatus for distillation.

The Yangshao was followed in Honan and Shansi by a later Neolithic culture, the Chhêng-Tzu-Yai or Lung-Shan (archaeological site names). Although still without metal, the people of this culture used a smooth black earthenware of fine texture and high finish, while those of Lung-Shan had domesticated all the animals of the Yangshao including, probably, the horse. There is a possibility, too, that the Lung-Shan knew of wheeled vehicles, although the evidence for this is uncertain. This was also the time at which various inventions appeared, inventions such as the potter's wheel and the use of tamped earth for buildings, long known in the Middle East but new to China.

With the Lung-Shan we reach 1600 B.C. and then, within a century, we come quite suddenly to a mature bronze-age culture, the Shang dynasty.* Most of our knowledge comes from excavations at the capital, Anyang, now in Honan province, and the discovery of the very existence of this dynasty is one of the most romantic in all archaeology. It all began in the late nineteenth century when farmers tilling their fields near Anyang kept turning up curious pieces of bone. Bought up by someone in the village, they were sold to drugstores as 'dragon-bones' for medicine, but not for long as in 1899 some Chinese scholars came across them and realised, with surprise, that the bones were inscribed with very ancient writing; by 1902 their full significance was appreciated. They were nothing less than inscribed oracle-bones, and provided evidence that no one had possessed since the early days of the Han dynasty. At one stroke

*The maturity of Shang bronzes and writing after 1520 B.C. leads some historians to see an earlier, and thus more gradual, development. Some historians date the Shang dynasty from 1766 rather than 1520 B.C. Others believe the legendary Xia (Hsia) dynasty actually existed, from about 2100 to 1520 B.C., and that it developed writing and bronzes at some stage.—Ed.

they pushed back the philology, linguistics and history of China by almost a thousand years, and have made it clear that much of China's hitherto legendary history—the rule of the Yellow Emperor, the work of the Great Engineer Yü, and a host of others—was a reflection of events and practices of times that had been in fact historic. One aspect of this is the question of what script preceded the well-developed writing on the oracle-bones. Recently many signs have been recorded from Neolithic pottery, and these may have been the earliest forms of what afterwards developed into the Chinese characters.

The oracle-bones were used for scapulimancy, a divination technique that involved heating the shoulder-blades of mammals or the shells of turtles with a red-hot poker and discerning the reply of the gods from the shapes and directions of the cracks. It seems to have been a method peculiar to the Anyang area and to have started just a little before the arrival in 1520 B.C. of the Shang dynasty, when the technique was developed. Indeed, the Shang diviners were so well organized that they kept records of their results, possibly as secret dossiers; it is a collection of such records that the Anyang finds have brought to light.

The use of bronze during the Shang dynasty was outstanding. It was employed in all kinds of ways, especially for ritual, military and luxury purposes, for the metal parts of wheeled vehicles, but, interestingly enough, seldom for tools and implements. The high artistic quality and workmanship of Shang bronze ritual vessels is breathtaking and surpasses all later work. Yet the Shang ruled over only a restricted area, perhaps spreading no more than 300 km in any direction from Anyang. Theirs was a feudal society in which matriarchal traces had given place to patriarchal control, where there was family or ancestor worship, and human sacrifice. Slaves were immolated at royal burials, a practice that persisted well into Chou times.

Two other features of the Shang Age are worth noting here. One is the extensive use of bamboo, not least made up into books for writing. Probably similar to the Han books that still survive, bamboo strips were taken and held together by two lines of cords, and it is from these that the character *tshê*, depicting a written book, was derived. Incidentally, it was during Shang times that the Chinese writing brush was introduced, and that pictographs began to be replaced by written characters. The second feature is the use of cowrie shells as a form of currency, an innovation that gave many words expressing 'value' the radical *pei*, which originally meant cowrie shell. Where the cowries came from is still uncertain: the Pacific coast south of the Yangtze estuary seems probable, but their journey to the centre of the Shang civilisation would present a remarkable feat.

PART TWO
THE CLASSICAL WORLD: 1000 B.C. TO A.D. 500

Man and woman, part of a Greek funerary stele, National Museum, Athens (Alinari/Art Resource, NY) .

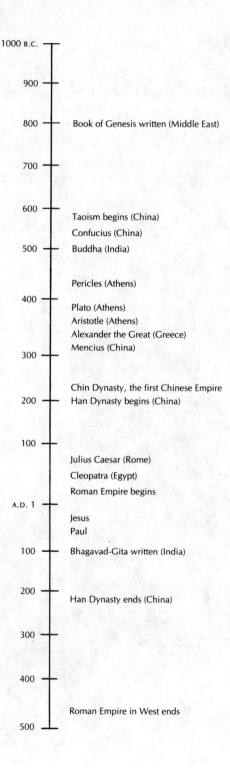

1000 B.C.

900

800 — Book of Genesis written (Middle East)

700

600 — Taoism begins (China)
Confucius (China)
500 — Buddha (India)

Pericles (Athens)
400 — Plato (Athens)
Aristotle (Athens)
Alexander the Great (Greece)
Mencius (China)
300 —

Chin Dynasty, the first Chinese Empire
200 — Han Dynasty begins (China)

100 —

Julius Caesar (Rome)
Cleopatra (Egypt)
Roman Empire begins
A.D. 1 —
Jesus
Paul
100 — Bhagavad-Gita written (India)

200 —
Han Dynasty ends (China)

300 —

400 —

Roman Empire in West ends
500 —

CHAPTER FOUR

Greek Civilization

12. THE DEFINITION OF GREEK CIVILIZATION TO 500 B.C.

William H. McNeill

In this brief excerpt from William H. McNeill's brilliant A World History, *Greek civilization is placed in a broad perspective that includes India and ancient Israel as well as Minoan Crete and Mycenae. McNeill argues that when we compare the experience of the ancient Greeks with that of the Indians or Hebrews, the uniqueness of Greece lies in its political organization into territorial states. What does he mean by that?*

What do you think of this idea? How were the experiences of the Indians, Hebrews, and Greeks similar? How were they different? Or was the Greek experience unusual? Can it still influence us today?

While India worked its way toward the definition of a new and distinctive civilization on one flank of the ancient Middle East, on its other flank another new civilization was also emerging; the Greek. The principal stages of early Greek history closely resemble what we know or can surmise about Indian development. But the end product differed fundamentally. The Greeks put political organization into territorial states above all other bases of human association, and attempted to explain the world and man not in terms of mystic illumination but through laws of nature. Thus despite a similar start, when fierce "tamers of horses"—like those of whom Homer later sang—overran priest-led agricultural societies, the Indian and Greek styles of civilization diverged strikingly by 500 B.C.

MYCENAEAN VIKINGS

One great difference existed from the start. The Aryans of India remained landsmen, whereas the earliest Greek invaders of the Aegean region took readily to the sea, infiltrating Knossos in Minoan Crete and establishing themselves among the Aegean islands as well as on the Greek mainland. The first Greek-speaking rulers of Knossos made very little change in the archaeological remains of Minoan civilization, although they did develop a new script (Linear B), which recorded an archaic form of the Greek language. About 1400 B.C., however, Knossos was destroyed, perhaps by some piratical raid launched from the new-sprung capital at Mycenae on the Greek mainland. For the next two hundred years a series of sea raids—alternating perhaps with more peaceable trade—carried Mycenaean ships to almost all the coasts of the Mediterranean. We know from Egyptian records of three separate attacks launched against Egypt by a coalition of "sea peoples" in which Mycenaean Greeks probably took a minor part. In the year 1190 B.C., however, the Egyptians successfully repelled the last of these ventures, and a remnant of the invading host settled in Palestine to become the Philistines of biblical history. A similar raid (traditionally dated 1184 B.C.) against Troy at the mouth of the Dardanelles became the focus around which Homer's tales of heroism clustered.

THE CITY-STATE

Soon after 1200 B.C. these far-flung enterprises came to an end. A new wave of invaders, Greek-speaking Dorians, came down from the north and overran the centers of Mycenaean power. With the Dorians or very soon after came iron, with all the usual political consequences. Aristo-cratic charioteers, who had controlled war and politics in the days of Mycenae's greatness, were overthrown by wandering tribes of iron-wielding warriors. Such groups were always ready to migrate to any new spot where better cropland or pasture could be found. The Dorian invasions therefore proceeded piecemeal, and involved many secondary displacements of peoples. In particular, refugees from the Greek mainland took ship and established a series of new settlements across the Aegean on the coast of Asia Minor. These regions were subsequently known as Ionia and, further north, Aeolia. For protection against the native inhabitants the Greek settlements clustered on defensible peninsulas and other suitable places on the coast. Since the refugees (like the Hebrews of the Exodus) had no pre-existing pattern of leadership or code of custom to which all unthinkingly subscribed, they had to invent a visible set of laws and system of government to assure effective co-operation in the new settlements. In so doing, they created the earliest Greek city-states.

Moses had faced a similar problem a century or two before, when he led the children of Israel from Egypt into the desert. The legislation with which he organized the Hebrew community in its new environment became the kernel of later Judaism. The self-governing city-states created by Greeks on the coast of Asia Minor had almost as great an importance in world history. For by inventing the city-state or *polis* (hence our word "politics"), the Greeks of Ionia established the prototype from which the whole Western world derived its penchant for political organization into territorially defined sovereign units, i.e., into states. The supremacy of territoriality over all other forms of human association is neither natural nor inevitable, as the Indian caste principle may remind us. Hence, if we Westerners owe our religion to Hebrew refugees from Pharaoh, we also owe our politics to Greek refugees from the Dorians, who had to reorganize and rationalize their traditional society in order to survive in a new and hostile environment just about two centuries after Moses had led his followers out of Egypt into the desert.

Development on the mainland toward supremacy of the polis was slower. Semi-migratory tribes had first to settle permanently on some particular piece of land, and then had to combine with neighbors into a single territorial unit to constitute a polis. The line of evolution is fairly clear. Violence diminished, population grew, land became scarce and fixed farming became the rule. As the population settled down, local chieftains found it convenient to settle disputes by sitting in council under the presidency of a high king. When the full council could not be in session it often seemed desirable to appoint individuals to look after matters of common concern, and to check the king in any attempt he might make to extend his authority. In this fashion magistrates arose, who were appointed for a limited term and entrusted with a delegated and, in course of time, legally defined authority. In some of the emergent city-states the kingship itself became a magistracy; in other cases kingship remained hereditary in a particular family.

13.   THE CONSTITUTION OF ATHENS

Aristotle

The process of establishing political authority based on the territorial state (which McNeill, in the preceding selection, describes as the defining element in Greek and Western politics) was not achieved at a particular moment. Much of Greek history (indeed much of world history since the Greeks) witnessed the struggle of territorial authority over family, blood, and kinship ties.

The process of replacing kinship and tribal alliances with a territorial "politics of place" can, however, be seen in the constitutional reforms attributed to Cleisthenes in 508 B.C. A description of those reforms is contained in a document called The Athenian Constitution, *discovered in Egypt only a hundred years ago and thought to have been written by Aristotle (384–322 B.C.) around 330 B.C.*

Modern scholars doubt that Cleisthenes created the demes (localities). Some existed earlier. But by making the demes the root of political organization, he undoubtedly undercut the power of dominant families. As demes were given real authority, power shifted from "relatives" to "residents." As Cleisthenes also expanded the number of citizens, the deme structure was more "deme-ocratic." Notice also how the constitutional reform combined a sense of local, resident membership with a broader commitment to the entire city-state by tying city, country, and coastal demes together in trittyes (or thirds) of new tribes. Thus members of a single tribe would have not only a local identity, but an Athenian identity that tied their interests to residents of different parts of the Athenian-Attic peninsula. They would identify with their new "tribe" and, thus, with the larger city-state.

Were these new tribes less "tribal" than the old ones? Do you see any evidence of their new artificial character? Aristotle also says that people now took their names from the demes. While this may not have been widespread, what effect would it have on their identities? Elsewhere we learn of another innovation: future generations were to belong to, and take the name of, the deme in which their forebears lived in 508 B.C., not a deme that they themselves might move to during their own lifetimes. What effect would that have on political identity? Finally, was the shift from kinship to territorial identity inevitably more democratic?

[20] The overthrow of the Peisistratid tyranny left the city split into two factions under Isagoras and Cleisthenes respectively. The former, a son of Tisander, had supported the tyrants; the latter was an Alcmaeonid. Cleisthenes, defeated in the political clubs, won over the people by offering citizen rights to the masses. Thereupon Isagoras, who had fallen behind in the race for power, once more invoked the help of his friend Cleomenes and persuaded him to exorcise the pollution, i.e. to expel the Alcmaeonidae, who were believed still to be accursed. Cleisthenes accordingly withdrew from Attica with a small band of adherents, while Cleomenes proceeded to drive out seven hundred Athenian families. The Spartan next attempted to dissolve the Council and to set up Isagoras with three hundred of his supporters as the sovereign authority. The Council, however, resisted; the populace flew to arms; and Cleomenes with Isagoras and all their forces took refuge in the Acropolis, to which the people laid siege and blockaded them for two days. On the third day it was agreed that Cleomenes and his followers should withdraw. Cleisthenes and his fellow exiles were recalled.

The people were now in control, and Cleisthenes, their leader, was recognized as head of the popular party. This was not surprising; for the

Alcmaeonidae were largely responsible for the overthrow of the tyrants, with whom they had been in conflict during most of their rule.

[21] The people, therefore, had every grounds for confidence in Cleisthenes. Accordingly, three years after the destruction of the tyranny, in the archonship of Isagoras, he used his influence as leader of the popular party to carry out a number of reforms. (A) He divided the population into ten tribes instead of the old four. His purpose here was to intermix the members of the tribes so that more persons might have civic rights; and hence the advice "not to notice the tribes" which was tendered to those who would examine the lists of the clans. (B) He increased the membership of the Council from 400 to 500, each tribe now contributing fifty instead of one hundred as before. His reason for not organizing the people into *twelve* tribes was to avoid the necessity of using the existing division into trittyes, which would have meant failing to regroup the population on a satisfactory basis. (C) He divided the country into thirty portions—ten urban and suburban, ten coastal, and ten inland—each containing a certain number of demes. These portions he called trittyes, and assigned three of them by lot to each tribe in such a way that each should have one portion in each of the three localities just mentioned. Furthermore, those who lived in any given deme were to be reckoned fellow demesmen. This arrangement was intended to protect new citizens from being shown up as such by the habitual use of family names. Men were to be officially described by the names of their demes; and it is thus that Athenians still speak of one another. Demes had now supplanted the old naucraries, and Cleisthenes therefore appointed Demarchs whose duties were identical with those of the former Naucrari. He named some of the demes from their localities, and others from their supposed founders; for certain areas no longer corresponded to named localities. On the other hand, he allowed everyone to retain his family and clan and religious rites according to ancestral custom. He also gave the ten tribes names which the Delphic oracle had chosen out of one hundred selected national heroes.

14. THE FUNERAL ORATION OF PERICLES

Thucydides

The most famous statement of Greek loyalty to the city-state is the following account of the funeral speech of Pericles in the classic History of the

Peloponnesian War by the ancient historian Thucydides. The speech com-
memorated the Athenian soldiers who had died in the battle against
Sparta in 431 B.C.

Notice the high value placed on loyalty to Athens and service to the
state. Here is the origin of patriotism. Pericles also insists that Athens is a
democratic city-state. Notice his praise of Athenian freedom as well as
public service. Could there be a conflict between personal freedom and
public service? If so, how would Pericles resolve such a conflict? You
might also notice that Pericles is commending Athenian citizen-soldiers
who died defending not their home but the empire. Could there be a
conflict between Athenian democracy and the ambitions of empire?

Most of those who have spoken here before me have commended the
lawgiver who added this oration to our other funeral customs; it seemed
to them a worthy thing that such an honour should be given at their
burial to the dead who have fallen on the field of battle. But I should
have preferred that, when men's deeds have been brave, they should be
honoured in deed only, and with such an honour as this public funeral,
which you are now witnessing. Then the reputation of many would not
have been imperilled on the eloquence or want of eloquence of one, and
their virtues believed or not as he spoke well or ill. For it is difficult to say
neither too little nor too much; and even moderation is apt not to give
the impression of truthfulness. The friend of the dead who knows the
facts is likely to think that the words of the speaker fall short of his
knowledge and of his wishes; another who is not so well informed, when
he hears of anything which surpasses his own powers, will be envious and
will suspect exaggeration. Mankind are tolerant of the praises of others
as long as each hearer thinks that he can do as well or nearly as well
himself, but, when the speaker rises above him, jealousy is aroused and
he begins to be incredulous. However, since our ancestors have set the
seal of their approval upon the practice, I must obey, and to the utmost
of my power shall endeavour to satisfy the wishes and beliefs of all who
hear me.

I will speak first of our ancestors, for it is right and seemly that now,
when we are lamenting the dead, a tribute should be paid to their
memory. There has never been a time when they did not inhabit this
land, which by their valour they have handed down from generation to
generation, and we have received from them a free state. But if they
were worthy of praise, still more were our fathers, who added to their
inheritance, and after many a struggle transmitted to us their sons this
great empire. And we ourselves assembled here today, who are still
most of us in the vigour of life, have carried the work of improvement
further, and have richly endowed our city with all things, so that she is
sufficient for herself both in peace and war. Of the military exploits by
which our various possessions were acquired, or of the energy with

which we or our fathers drove back the tide of war, Hellenic or Barbarian [non-Greek], I will not speak: for the tale would be long and is familiar to you. But before I praise the dead, I should like to point out by what principles of action we rose to power, and under what institutions and through what manner of life our empire became great. For I conceive that such thoughts are not unsuited to the occasion, and that this numerous assembly of citizens and strangers may profitably listen to them.

Our form of government does not enter into rivalry with the institutions of others. We do not copy our neighbours, but are an example to them. It is true that we are called a democracy, for the administration is in the hands of the many and not of the few. But while the law secures equal justice to all alike in their private disputes, the claim of excellence is also recognised; and when a citizen is in any way distinguished, he is preferred to the public service, not as a matter of privilege, but as the reward of merit. Neither is poverty a bar, but a man may benefit his country whatever be the obscurity of his condition. There is no exclusiveness in our public life, and in our private intercourse we are not suspicious of one another, nor angry with our neighbour if he does what he likes; we do not put on sour looks at him which, though harmless, are not pleasant. While we are thus unconstrained in our private intercourse, a spirit of reverence pervades our public acts; we are prevented from doing wrong by respect for the authorities and for the laws, having an especial regard to those which are ordained for the protection of the injured as well as to those unwritten laws which bring upon the transgressor of them the reprobation of the general sentiment.

And we have not forgotten to provide for our weary spirits many relaxations from toil; we have regular games and sacrifices throughout the year; our homes are beautiful and elegant; and the delight which we daily feel in all these things helps to banish melancholy. Because of the greatness of our city the fruits of the whole earth flow in upon us; so that we enjoy the goods of other countries as freely as of our own.

Then, again, our military training is in many respects superior to that of our adversaries. Our city is thrown open to the world, and we never expel a foreigner or prevent him from seeing or learning anything of which the secret if revealed to an enemy might profit him. We rely not upon management or trickery, but upon our own hearts and hands. And in the matter of education, whereas they from early youth are always undergoing laborious exercises which are to make them brave, we live at ease, and yet are equally ready to face the perils which they face. And here is the proof. The Lacedaemonians come into Attica not by themselves, but with their whole confederacy following; we go alone into a neighbour's country; and although our opponents are fighting for their homes and we on a foreign soil, we have seldom any difficulty in overcoming them. Our enemies have never yet felt our united strength; the care of a navy divides our attention, and on land we are obliged to send our own citizens everywhere. But they, if they meet and defeat a part of our army, are as proud as if they had routed us all, and when defeated they pretend to have been vanquished by us all.

If then we prefer to meet danger with a light heart but without laborious training, and with a courage which is gained by habit and not enforced by law, are we not greatly the gainers? Since we do not anticipate the pain, although, when the hour comes, we can be as brave as those who never allow themselves to rest; and thus too our city is equally admirable in peace and in war. For we are lovers of the beautiful, yet simple in our tastes, and we cultivate the mind without loss of manliness. Wealth we employ, not for talk and ostentation, but when there is a real use for it. To avow poverty with us is no disgrace; the true disgrace is in doing nothing to avoid it. An Athenian citizen does not neglect the state because he takes care of his own household; and even those of us who are engaged in business have a very fair idea of politics. We alone regard a man who takes no interest in public affairs, not as a harmless, but as a useless character; and if few of us are originators, we are all sound judges of policy. The great impediment to action is, in our opinion, not discussion, but the want of that knowledge which is gained by discussion preparatory to action. For we have a peculiar power of thinking before we act and of acting too, whereas other men are courageous from ignorance but hesitate upon reflection. And they are surely to be esteemed the bravest spirits who, having the clearest sense both of the pains and pleasures of life, do not on that account shrink from danger. In doing good, again, we are unlike others; we make our friends by conferring, not by receiving favours. Now he who confers a favour is the firmer friend, because he would fain by kindness keep alive the memory of an obligation; but the recipient is colder in his feelings, because he knows that in requiting another's generosity he will not be winning gratitude but only paying a debt. We alone do good to our neighbours, not upon a calculation of interest, but in the confidence of freedom and in a frank and fearless spirit.

To sum up: I say that Athens is the school of Hellas, and that the individual Athenian in his own person seems to have the power of adapting himself to the most varied forms of action with the utmost versatility and grace. This is no passing and idle word, but truth and fact; and the assertion is verified by the position to which these qualities have raised the state. For in the hour of trial Athens alone among her contemporaries is superior to the report of her. No enemy who comes against her is indignant at the reverses which he sustains at the hands of such a city; no subject complains that his masters are unworthy of him. And we shall assuredly not be without witnesses; there are mighty monuments of our power which will make us the wonder of this and of succeeding ages; we shall not need the praises of Homer or of any other panegyrist whose poetry may please for the moment, although his representation of the facts will not bear the light of day. For we have compelled every land and every sea to open a path for our valour, and have everywhere planted eternal memorials of our friendship and of our enmity. Such is the city of whose sake these men nobly fought and died; they could not bear the thought that she might be taken from them; and every one of us who survive should gladly toil on her behalf.

I have dwelt upon the greatness of Athens because I want to show you that we are contending for a higher prize than those who enjoy none of these privileges, and to establish by manifest proof the merit of these men whom I am now commemorating. Their loftiest praise has been already spoken. For in magnifying the city I have magnified them, and men like them whose virtues made her glorious. And of how few Hellenes can it be said as of them, that their deeds when weighed in the balance have been found equal to their fame! Methinks that a death such as theirs has been given the true measure of a man's worth; it may be the first revelation of his virtues, but is at any rate their final seal. For even those who come short in other ways may justly plead the valour with which they have fought for their country; they have blotted out the evil with the good, and have benefited the state more by their public services than they have injured her by their private actions. None of these men were enervated by wealth or hesitated to resign for pleasures of life, none of them put off the evil day in the hope, natural to poverty, that a man, though poor, may one day become rich. But, deeming that the punishment of their enemies was sweeter than any of these things, and that they could fall in no nobler cause, they determined at the hazard of their lives to be honourably avenged, and to leave the rest. They resigned to hope their unknown chance of happiness; but in the fact of death they resolved to rely upon themselves alone. And when the moment came they were minded to resist and suffer, rather than to fly and save their lives; they ran away from the word of dishonour, but on the battlefield their feet stood fast, and in an instant, at the height of their fortune, they passed away from the scene, not of their fear, but of their glory.

Such was the end of these men; they were worthy of Athens, and the living need not desire to have a more heroic spirit, although they may pray for a less fatal issue. The value of such a spirit is not to be expressed in words. Any one can discourse to you forever about the advantages of a brave defence, which you know already. But instead of listening to him I would have you day by day fix your eyes upon the greatness of Athens, until you become filled with the love of her; and when you are impressed by the spectacle of her glory, reflect that this empire has been acquired by men who knew their duty and had the courage to do it, who in the hour of conflict had the fear of dishonour always present to them, and who, if ever they failed in an enterprise, would not allow their virtues to be lost to their country, but freely gave their lives to her as the fairest offering which they could present at her feast. The sacrifice which they collectively made was individually repaid to them; for they received again each one of himself a praise which grows not old, and the noblest of all sepulchres—I speak not of that in which their remains are laid, but of that in which their glory survives, and is proclaimed always and on every fitting occasion both in word and deed. For the whole earth is the sepulchre of famous men; not only are they commemorated by columns and inscriptions in their own country, but in foreign lands there dwells also an unwritten memorial of them, graven not on stone but in the hearts of men. Make them your examples, and, esteeming courage to be freedom and freedom to be happiness, do not weigh too nicely the perils of war. The unfortunate who has no hope of a change for the better has less reason to throw away his life than the prosperous who, if he survives, is always liable to a change for the worse, and to whom any accidental fall makes the most serious difference. To a man of spirit, cowardice and disaster coming together are far more bitter than death striking him unperceived at a time when he is full of courage and animated by the general hope.

Wherefore I do not now commiserate the parents of the dead who stand here; I would rather comfort them. You know that your life has been passed amid manifold vicissitudes; and that they may be deemed fortunate who have gained most honour, whether an honourable death like theirs, or an honourable sorrow like yours, and whose days have been so ordered that the term of their happiness is likewise the term of their life. I know how hard it is to make you feel this, when the good fortune of others will too often remind you of the gladness which once lightened your hearts. And sorrow is felt at the want of those blessings, not which a man never knew, but which were a part of his life before they were taken from him. Some of you are of an age at which they may hope to have other children, and they ought to bear their sorrow better; not only will the children who may hereafter be born make them forget their own lost ones, but the city will be doubly a gainer. She will not be left desolate, and she will be safer. For a man's counsel cannot have equal weight or worth, when he alone has no children to risk in the general danger. To those of you who have passed their prime, I say: Congratulate yourselves that you have been happy during the greater part of your days; remember that your life of sorrow will not last long, and be comforted by the glory of those who are gone. For the love of honour alone is ever young, and not riches, as some say, but honour is the delight of men when they are old and useless.

To you who are the sons and brothers of the departed, I see that the struggle to emulate them will be an arduous one. For all men praise the dead, and, however pre-eminent your virtue may be, hardly will you be thought, I do not say to equal, but even to approach them. The living have their rivals and detractors, but when a man is out of the way, the honour and good-will which he receives is unalloyed. And, if I am to speak of womanly virtues to those of you who will henceforth be widows, let me sum them up in one short admonition: To a woman not to show more weakness than is natural to her sex is a great glory, and not to be talked about for good or for evil among men.

I have paid the required tribute, in obedience to the law, making use of such fitting words as I had. The tribute of deeds has been paid in part; for the dead have been honourably interred, and it remains only that their children should be maintained at the public charge until they are grown up; this is the solid prize with which, as with a garland, Athens crowns her sons living and dead, after a struggle like theirs. For where the rewards of virtue are greatest, there the noblest citizens are enlisted in the service of the state. And now, when you have duly lamented, everyone his own dead, you may depart.

15. *THE REPUBLIC*

Plato

In the introduction to the funeral oration of Pericles, we suggested that by modern standards Athens was not very democratic. Service to the state, the empire, and (we might add) slavery were its limitations. From the standpoint of many ancient Athenians, however, Athens appeared to be too democratic. They worried that democracy meant the rule of the least capable or the mob. Plato was one of these conservative critics. His famous work, The Republic, *is an extended argument that "justice" is best achieved if the state is ruled by philosophers rather than the demos, or common people. Plato puts this argument in the mouth of Socrates, his teacher.*

The Republic *begins, as do many of the other "dialogues" or discussions, with an account of how the group of friends got together and the discussion began. We might notice here that besides giving us a peek at educated male society in ancient Athens, these introductory discussions are also a testament to how much freedom of thought was enjoyed in the city-state. One might be tempted to argue against Plato that a city which encouraged all citizens to debate legislation in the assembly in democratic fashion also nurtured the wide-ranging intellectual discussions that Plato found so fruitful.*

CHAPTER 1

SOCRATES. I walked down to the Piraeus yesterday with Glaucon, the son of Ariston, to make my prayers to the goddess. As this was the first celebration of her festival, I wished also to see how the ceremony would be conducted. The Thracians, I thought, made as fine a show in the procession as our own people, though they did well enough. The prayers and the spectacle were over, and we were leaving to go back to the city, when from some way off Polemarchus, the son of Cephalus, caught sight of us starting homewards and sent his slave running to ask us to wait for him. The boy caught my garment from behind and gave me the message.

I turned around and asked where his master was.

There, he answered; coming up behind. Please wait.

Very well, said Glaucon; we will.

A minute later Polemarchus joined us, with Glaucon's brother, Adeimantus, and Niceratus, the son of Nicias, and some others who must have been at the procession.

Socrates, said Polemarchus, I do believe you are starting back to town and leaving us.

You have guessed right, I answered.

Well, he said, you see what a large party we are?

I do.

Unless you are more than a match for us, then, you must stay here.

Isn't there another alternative? said I; we might convince you that you must let us go.

How will you convince us, if we refuse to listen?

We cannot, said Glaucon.

Well, we shall refuse; make up your minds to that.

Here Adeimantus interposed: Don't you even know that in the evening there is going to be a torch-race on horseback in honour of the goddess?

On horseback! I exclaimed; that is something new. How will they do it? Are the riders going to race with torches and hand them on to one another?

Just so, said Polemarchus. Besides, there will be a festival lasting all night, which will be worth seeing. We will go out after dinner and look on. We shall find plenty of young men there and we can have a talk. So please stay, and don't disappoint us.

It looks as if we had better stay, said Glaucon.

Well, said I, if you think so, we will.

Accordingly, we went home with Polemarchus.

At the home of Polemarchus, the participants meet a number of other old friends. After the usual greetings and gossip, the discussion begins in response to the question of Socrates: what is justice?

Each of the participants poses an idea of justice that Socrates challenges. Then Socrates outlines an ideal state that would be based on absolute justice. In the following selection he is asked how this ideal could ever come about.

CHAPTER 18

But really, Socrates, Glaucon continued, if you are allowed to go on like this, I am afraid you will forget all about the question you thrust aside some time ago; whether a society so constituted can ever come into existence, and if so, how. No doubt, if it did exist, all manner of good things would come about. I can even add some that you have passed over. Men who acknowledged one another as fathers, sons, or brothers and always used those names among themselves would never desert one another; so they would fight with unequalled bravery. And if their womenfolk went out with them to war, either in the ranks or drawn up in the rear to intimidate the enemy and act as a reserve in case of need, I am sure all this would make them invincible. At home, too, I can see many advantages you have not mentioned. But, since I admit that our commonwealth would have all these merits and any number more, if once it came into existence, you need not describe it in further detail. All we have now to do is to convince ourselves that it can be brought into being and how.

This is a very sudden onslaught, said I; you have no mercy on my shilly-shallying. Perhaps you do not realize that, after I have barely escaped the first two waves, the third, which you are now bringing down upon me, is the most formidable of all. When you have seen what it is like and heard my reply, you will be ready to excuse the very natural fears which made me shrink from putting forward such a paradox for discussion.

The more you talk like that, he said, the less we shall be willing to let you off from telling us how this constitution can come into existence; so you had better waste no more time.

Well, said I, let me begin by reminding you that what brought us to this point was our inquiry into the nature of justice and injustice.

True; but what of that?

Merely this: suppose we do find out what justice is, are we going to demand that a man who is just shall have a character which exactly corresponds in every respect to the ideal of justice? Or shall we be satisfied if he comes as near to the ideal as possible and has in him a larger measure of that quality than the rest of the world?

That will satisfy me.

If so, when we set out to discover the essential nature of justice and injustice and what a perfectly just and a perfectly unjust man would be like, supposing them to exist, our purpose was to use them as ideal patterns: we were to observe the degree of happiness or unhappiness that each exhibited, and to draw the necessary inference that our own destiny would be like that of the one we most resembled. We did not set out to show that these ideals could exist in fact.

That is true.

Then suppose a painter had drawn an ideally beautiful figure complete to the last touch, would you think any the worse of him, if he could not show that a person as beautiful as that could exist?

No, I should not.

Well, we have been constructing in discourse the pattern of an ideal state. Is our theory any the worse, if we cannot prove it possible that a state so organized should be actually founded?

Surely not.

That, then, is the truth of the matter. But if, for your satisfaction, I am to do my best to show under what conditions our ideal would have the best chance of being realized, I must ask you once more to admit that the same principle applies here. Can theory ever be fully realized in practice? Is it not in the nature of things that action should come less close to truth than thought? People may not think so; but do you agree or not?

I do.

Then you must not insist upon my showing that this construction we have traced in thought could be reproduced in fact down to the last detail. You must admit that we shall have found a way to meet your demand for realization, if we can discover how a state might be constituted in the closest accordance with our description. Will not that content you? It would be enough for me.

And for me too.

Then our next attempt, it seems, must be to point out what defect in the working of existing states prevents them from being so organized, and what is the least change that would effect a transformation into this type of government—a single change if possible, or perhaps two; at any rate let us make the changes as few and insignificant as may be.

By all means.

Well, there is one change which, as I believe we can show, would bring about this revolution—not a small change, certainly, nor an easy one, but possible.

What is it?

I have now to confront what we called the third and greatest wave. But I must state my paradox, even though the wave should break in laughter over my head and drown me in ignominy. Now mark what I am going to say.

Go on.

Unless either philosophers become kings in their countries or those who are now called kings and rulers come to be sufficiently inspired with a genuine desire for wisdom; unless, that is to say, political power and philosophy meet together, while the many natures who now go their several ways in the one or the other direction are forcibly debarred from doing so, there can be no rest from troubles, my dear Glaucon, for states, nor yet, as I believe, for all mankind; nor can this commonwealth which we have imagined ever till then see the light of day and grow to its full stature. This it was that I have so long hung back from saying; I knew what a paradox it would be, because it is hard to see that there is no other way of happiness either for the state or for the individual.

Socrates, exclaimed Glaucon, after delivering yourself of such a pronouncement as that, you must expect a whole multitude of by no means contemptible assailants to fling off their coats, snatch up the handiest weapon, and make a rush at you, breathing fire and slaughter. If you cannot find arguments to beat them off and make your escape, you will learn what it means to be the target of scorn and derision.

Well, it was you who got me into this trouble.

Yes, and a good thing too. However, I will not leave you in the lurch. You shall have my friendly encouragement for what it is worth; and perhaps you may find me more complaisant than some would be in answering your questions. With such backing you must try to convince the unbelievers.

I will, now that I have such a powerful ally.

Judging from the reaction of Glaucon, philosophers had no more prestige in ancient Greece than they do in modern America. They were often ridiculed in the popular comedies for their fuzzy impracticality.

By saying that philosophers should be kings, Plato (or Socrates) meant something very different, however. By "philosophers" he meant people with a deeper understanding, more profound wisdom, than that enjoyed by the common people. To explain that difference he turned to a parable of people in a cave whose only experience was the world of shadows, and he compared their understanding with those who had emerged into the light of the real world. This parable, perhaps the most famous in the history of philosophy, seems to undercut all of the claims of Greek democracy.

What is the meaning of the parable of the cave? Isn't Plato right when he suggests that some people only see the shadows? If so, should those people govern?

Perhaps Plato is making a distinction between common sensical knowledge (what everyday experience teaches) and wisdom (the flash of inspiration or enlightenment). If the latter is all that matters, then democratic quibbling is a waste of time. But so may be the carefully reasoned dialogues which Plato, and other Athenians, seem so much to enjoy. Does democracy, after all, mean accepting common sense and even error as preferable to the rule of the wise?

Plato concludes with an additional argument that you might consider.

The value of philosophers as kings, he says, is not only that they know "the truth," but also that they prefer philosophy to government. Thus, they are good rulers because they do not enjoy it. Only those who have nothing better to do seek power for its own sake. Philosophy is something better to do. What do you think of this line of argument?

Next, said I, here is a parable to illustrate the degrees in which our nature may be enlightened or unenlightened. Imagine the condition of men living in a sort of cavernous chamber underground, with an entrance open to the light and a long passage all down the cave. Here they have been from childhood, chained by the leg and also by the neck, so that they cannot move and can see only what is in front of them, because the chains will not let them turn their heads. At some distance higher up is the light of a fire burning behind them; and between the prisoners and the fire is a track with a parapet built along it, like the screen at a puppet-show, which hides the performers while they show their puppets over the top.

I see, said he.

Now behind this parapet imagine persons carrying along various artificial objects, including figures of men and animals in wood or stone or other materials, which project above the parapet. Naturally, some of these persons will be talking, others silent.

It is a strange picture, he said, and a strange sort of prisoners.

Like ourselves, I replied; for in the first place prisoners so confined would have seen nothing of themselves or of one another, except the shadows thrown by the fire-light on the wall of the Cave facing them, would they?

Not if all their lives they had been prevented from moving their heads.

And they would have seen as little of the objects carried past.

Of course.

Now, if they could talk to one another, would they not suppose that their words referred only to those passing shadows which they saw?

Necessarily.

And suppose their prison had an echo from the wall facing them? When one of the people crossing behind them spoke, they could only suppose that the sound came from the shadow passing before their eyes.

No doubt.

In every way, then, such prisoners would recognize as reality nothing but the shadows of those artificial objects.

Inevitably.

Now consider what would happen if their release from the chains and the healing of their unwisdom should come about in this way. Suppose one of them was set free and forced suddenly to stand up, turn his head, and walk with eyes lifted to the light; all these movements would be painful, and he would be too dazzled to make out the objects whose shadows he had been used to see. What do you think he would say, if someone told him that what he had formerly seen was meaningless illusion, but now, being somewhat nearer to reality and turned towards more real objects, he was getting a truer view? Suppose further that he were shown the various objects being carried by and were made to say, in reply to questions, what each of them was. Would he not be perplexed and believe the objects now shown him to be not so real as what he formerly saw?

Yes, not nearly so real.

And if he were forced to look at the firelight itself, would not his eyes ache, so that he would try to escape and turn back to the things which he could see distinctly, convinced that they really were clearer than these other objects now being shown to him?

Yes.

And suppose someone were to drag him away forcibly up the steep and rugged ascent and not let him go until he had hauled him out into the sunlight, would he not suffer pain and vexation at such treatment, and, when he had come out into the light, find his eyes so full of its radiance that he could not see a single one of the things that he was now told were real?

Certainly he would not see them all at once.

He would need, then, to grow accustomed before he could see things in that upper world. At first it would be easiest to make out shadows, and then the images of men and things reflected in water, and later on the things themselves. After that, it would be easier to watch the heavenly bodies and the sky itself by night, looking at the light of the moon and stars rather than the Sun and the Sun's light in the daytime.

Yes, surely.

Last of all, he would be able to look at the Sun and contemplate its nature, not as it appears when reflected in water or any alien medium, but as it is in itself in its own domain.

No doubt.

And now he would begin to draw the conclusion that it is the Sun that produces the seasons and the course of the year and controls everything in the visible world, and moreover is in a way the cause of all that he and his companions used to see.

Clearly he would come at last to that conclusion.

Then if he called to mind his fellow prisoners and what passed for wisdom in his former dwelling-place, he would surely think himself happy in the change and be sorry for them. They may have had a practice of honouring and commending one another, with prizes for the man who had the keenest eye for the passing shadows and the best memory for the order in which they followed or accompanied one another, so that he could make a good guess as to which was going to come next. Would our released prisoner be likely to covet those prizes or to envy the men exalted to honour and power in the Cave? Would he not feel like Homer's Achilles, that he would far sooner "be on earth as a hired servant in the house of a landless man" or endure anything rather than go back to his old beliefs and live in the old way?

Yes, he would prefer any fate to such a life.

Now imagine what would happen if he went down again to take his former seat in the Cave. Coming suddenly out of the sunlight, his eyes would be filled with darkness. He might be required once more to deliver his opinion on those shadows, in competition with the prisoners who had never been released, while his eyesight was still dim and unsteady; and it might take some time to become used to the darkness. They would laugh at him and say that he had gone up only to come back with his sight ruined; it was worth no one's while even to attempt the ascent. If they could lay hands on the man who was trying to set them free and lead them up, they would kill him.

Yes, they would.

Every feature in this parable, my dear Glaucon, is meant to fit our earlier analysis. The prison dwelling corresponds to the region revealed to us through the sense of sight, and the firelight within it to the power of the Sun. The ascent to see the things in the upper world you may take as standing for the upward journey of the soul into the region of the intelligible; then you will be in possession of what I surmise, since that is what you wish to be told. Heaven knows whether it is true; but this, at any rate, is how it appears to me. In the world of knowledge, the last thing to be perceived and only with great difficulty is the essential Form of Goodness. Once it is perceived, the conclusion must follow that, for all things, this is the cause of whatever is right and good; in the visible world it gives birth to light and to the lord of light, while it is itself sovereign in the intelligible world and the parent of intelligence and truth. Without having had a vision of this Form no one can act with wisdom, either in his own life or in matters of state.

So far as I can understand, I share your belief.

Then you may also agree that it is no wonder if those who have reached their height are reluctant to manage the affairs of men. Their souls long to spend all their time in that upper world—naturally enough, if here once more our parable holds true. Nor, again, is it at all strange that one who comes from the contemplation of divine things to the miseries of human life should appear awkward and ridiculous when, with eyes still dazed and not yet accustomed to the darkness, he is compelled, in a law court or elsewhere, to dispute about the shadows of justice or the images that cast those shadows, and to wrangle over the notions of what is right in the minds of men who have never beheld Justice itself.

It is not at all strange.

No; a sensible man will remember that the eyes may be confused in two ways—by a change from light to darkness or from darkness to light;

and he will recognize that the same thing happens to the soul. When he sees it troubled and unable to discern anything clearly, instead of laughing thoughtlessly, he will ask whether, coming from a brighter existence, its unaccustomed vision is obscured by the darkness, in which case he will think its condition enviable and its life a happy one; or whether, emerging from the depths of ignorance, it is dazzled by excess of light. If so, he will rather feel sorry for it; or, if he were inclined to laugh, that would be less ridiculous than to laugh at the soul which has come down from the light.

That is a fair statement.

If this is true, then, we must conclude that education is not what it is said to be by some, who profess to put knowledge into a soul which does not possess it, as if they could put sight into blind eyes. On the contrary, our own account signifies that the soul of every man does possess the power of learning the truth and the organ to see it with; and that, just as one might have to turn the whole body round in order that the eye should see light instead of darkness, so the entire soul must be turned away from this changing world, until its eye can bear to contemplate reality and that supreme splendour which we have called the Good. Hence there may well be an art whose aim would be to effect this very thing, the conversion of the soul, in the readiest way; not to put the power of sight into the soul's eye, which already has it, but to ensure that, instead of looking in the wrong direction, it is turned the way it ought to be.

Yes, it may well be so.

It looks, then, as though wisdom were different from those ordinary virtues, as they are called, which are not far removed from bodily qualities, in that they can be produced by habituation and exercise in a soul which has not possessed them from the first. Wisdom, it seems, is certainly the virtue of some diviner faculty, which never loses its power, though its use for good or harm depends on the direction towards which it is turned. You must have noticed in dishonest men with a reputation for sagacity the shrewd glance of a narrow intelligence piercing the objects to which it is directed. There is nothing wrong with their power of vision, but it has been forced into the service of evil, so that the keener its sight, the more harm it works.

Quite true.

And yet if the growth of a nature like this had been pruned from earliest childhood, cleared of those clinging overgrowths which come of gluttony and all luxurious pleasure and, like leaden weights charged with affinity to this mortal world, hang upon the soul, bending its vision downwards; if, freed from these, the soul were turned round towards true reality, then this same power in these very men would see the truth as keenly as the objects it is turned to now.

Yes, very likely.

Is it not also likely, or indeed certain after what has been said, that a state can never be properly governed either by the uneducated who know nothing of truth or by men who are allowed to spend all their days in the pursuit of culture? The ignorant have no single mark before their eyes at which they must aim in all the conduct of their own lives and of affairs of state; and the others will not engage in action if they can help it, dreaming that, while still alive, they have been translated to the Islands of the Blest.

Quite true.

It is for us, then, as founders of a commonwealth, to bring compulsion to bear on the noblest natures. They must be made to climb the ascent to the vision of Goodness, which we called the highest object of knowledge; and, when they have looked upon it long enough, they must not be allowed, as they now are, to remain on the heights, refusing to come down again to the prisoners or to take any part in their labours and rewards, however much or little these may be worth.

Shall we not be doing them an injustice, if we force on them a worse life than they might have?

You have forgotten again, my friend, that the law is not concerned to make any one class specially happy, but to ensure the welfare of the commonwealth as a whole. By persuasion or constraint it will unite the citizens in harmony, making them share whatever benefits each class can contribute to the common good; and its purpose in forming men of that spirit was not that each should be left to go his own way, but that they should be instrumental in binding the community into one.

True, I had forgotten.

You will see, then, Glaucon, that there will be no real injustice in compelling our philosophers to watch over and care for the other citizens. We can fairly tell them that their compeers in other states may quite reasonably refuse to collaborate: there they have sprung up, like a self-sown plant, in despite of their country's institutions; no one has fostered their growth, and they cannot be expected to show gratitude for a care they have never received. "But," we shall say, "it is not so with you. We have brought you into existence for your country's sake as well as for your own, to be like leaders and king-bees in a hive; you have been better and more thoroughly educated than those others and hence you are more capable of playing your part both as men of thought and as men of action. You must go down, then, each in his turn, to live with the rest and let your eyes grow accustomed to the darkness. You will then see a thousand times better than those who live there always; you will recognize every image for what it is and know what it represents, because you have seen justice, beauty, and goodness in their reality; and so you and we shall find life in our commonwealth no mere dream, as it is in most existing states, where men live fighting one another about shadows and quarrelling for power, as if that were a great prize; whereas in truth government can be at its best and free from dissension only where the destined rulers are least desirous of holding office."

Quite true.

Then will our pupils refuse to listen and to take their turns at sharing in the work of the community, though they may live together for most of their time in a purer air?

No; it is a fair demand, and they are fair-minded men. No doubt, unlike any ruler of the present day, they will think of holding power as an unavoidable necessity.

Yes, my friend; for the truth is that you can have a well-governed society only if you can discover for your future rulers a better way of life than being in office; then only will power be in the hands of men who are rich, not in gold, but in the wealth that brings happiness, a good and wise life. All goes wrong when, starved for lack of anything good in their own lives, men turn to public affairs hoping to snatch from thence the happiness they hunger for. They set about fighting for power, and this internecine conflict ruins them and their country. The life of true philosophy is the only one that looks down upon offices of state; and access to power must be confined to men who are not in love with it; otherwise rivals will start fighting. So whom else can you compel to undertake the guardianship of the commonwealth, if not those who, besides understanding best the principles of government, enjoy a nobler life than the politician's and look for rewards of a different kind?

There is indeed no other choice.

CHAPTER FIVE

Hellenistic and Roman Civilization

16. HELLENISTIC RELIGION: HEALING OF ASCLEPIUS

In classical Greek civilization (especially in the "golden age" of the fifth century) Greek religion was highly mythological and civic-minded. In most city-states important temples were dedicated to the guardian deities of the city—Athena in Athens, Hera in Argos, Apollo in Corinth, for instance. But the citizens of all cities worshipped all gods of Greek mythology, and there were special cults for many gods, such as the mother goddess Demeter, Artemis the goddess of the hunt, Aphrodite the goddess of love, and Zeus, the king of the gods who presided on Mount Olympus, to name just a few. In some cities, there was also a temple to the god Asclepius, the god of healing. The comic playwright of the Athenian golden age, Aristophanes, wrote a play, The Plutus, *which shows us an Asclepion (temple to Asclepius). We see food offerings, a purifying bath, priests mixing potions, and healing snakes.*

While Asclepius was worshipped in the classical age, he became more popular in the Hellenistic period (after the death of Alexander the Great). This may have been because civic religions were less powerful or because people felt a greater need for spiritual and personal healing. In any case, Asclepions had become elaborate complexes with baths, a gymnasium, and often a theater and sanitarium.

The following description of the worship of Asclepius comes from the second century A.D. The author, Aelius Aristides, had visited the great Asclepion in Pergamum in search of healing. What kinds of religious acts and ideas does he describe? What does this religion suggest about Hellenistic society?

(30) One of the two ministers in the temple was named Philadelphus. He had the same dream that I had one night, with only the slightest variations. Philadelphus dreamed—at least I remember this much—that in the sacred theater were a number of men clad all in white who had come to visit the god. In their midst stood I, and delivered a panegyric in honor of the god [Asclepius], in which, among other things, I told how he had often intervened in my course of life. Only recently he had ordained that I should drink vermouth [wormwood] in thin vinegar, in

order to be relieved of my complaint. He [Philadelphus] also told me of a sacred stairway, if I rightly remember, and of an epiphany of the god and his wondrous deeds.

(31) This is what Philadelphus dreamed. What happened to me was as follows: I dreamed that I stood in the entrance to the sanctuary, where also some other people were gathered, as at the time of the sacrifice for purification; they wore white garments and were otherwise festively garbed. Then I spoke about the god and named him, among other things, Distributor of Destiny, since he assigns to men their fate. The expression came to me out of my own personal experience. Then I told about the potion of wormwood, which had somehow been revealed [to me]. The revelation was unquestionable, just as in a thousand other instances the epiphany of the god was felt with absolute certainty. (32) You have a sense of contact with him, and are aware of his arrival in a state of mind intermediate between sleep and waking; you try to look up and are afraid to, lest before you see him he shall have vanished; you sharpen your ears and listen, half in dream and half awake; your hair stands up, tears of joy roll down, a proud kind of modesty fills your breast. How can anyone really describe this experience in words? If one belongs to the initiated, he will know about it and recognize it. . . .

(34) When morning came, following this vision, I called in the physician Theodotus, and when he came I told him about the dream. Its divine character astonished him, but he did not know what to do about it, since it was winter and my bodily weakness somewhat alarmed him; for I had already been in bed for months. (35) It seemed to us desirable to call in the sacristan Asklepiacus, in whose house I was then living; I was used to telling him most of my dreams. The sacristan came, but before we could say a word he began speaking [as follows]: "I have just come from my colleague"—he meant Philadelphus—"who had sent for me; for last night he had a wonderful dream, which had to do with you." And so Asklepiacus related what Philadelphus had dreamed; and Philadelphus himself, whom we called in, related the same things. Since the dreams agreed, we applied the remedy and I drank more of it than anyone had ever drunk before, and on the following day, at the god's direction, an equal quantity. The relief it brought me and the good it did me simply cannot be described. (36) . . . Many other things of the same kind took place both before this and afterward and showed [me] the same kind of help. . . .

(74) It was during the spring equinox, when in honor of the god people were accustomed to smear themselves with mud; but I was unable to do so, unless he gave me some sign of command. So I hesitated, though I remember that it was a nice warm day. A few days later there came a storm; the north wind swept across the sky, thick black clouds gathered, and it was winter once more. Such was the weather when he now commanded me to smear myself with mud from the sacred spring

and to wash there. I was surprised, since the ground and the air were so cold, to find myself eager to go to the spring and [to discover] that the water really helped to warm me. That was only the beginning of miracles! (75) The following night he ordered me again to smear myself with mud, in the same way, and then to run around the temple three times; the north wind was indescribably fierce, and the cold was increasing; one could not find a garment thick enough to protect him from it—it went right through and stabbed one in the side like a knife. (76) Some of my companions decided to help me by going along, though they were under no obligation to do so, and by performing [the same rite] with me. So I smeared myself and ran, and let the north wind thoroughly blow me about, and finally came to the spring and washed myself off. As for my two companions, one of them soon turned back, while another fell into convulsions and had to be hurriedly carried into a bath, and got warm again only with the greatest difficulty. The next day was a real spring day. (77) But when winter temperature returned, with frost and ice-cold wind, he [the god] bade me take mud and put it on me, then sit in the court of the sacred gymnasium and call upon Zeus, the highest and best of gods; and there were many persons who saw me do this. . . .

17.   WOMEN AND MEN:
17.1.   A ROMAN HUSBAND'S EULOGY TO HIS WIFE, 1ST CENTURY B.C.

This is part of a long eulogy for the wife of a Roman who evidently had both friends and enemies in high places. The mourning husband refers to both public and personal crises in the lives of the couple. Notice the references to money, wills, and the power of husbands and fathers. What did this Roman seem to love about his wife? What seems to have been her feelings toward him? Would you hear anything like these sentiments in a funeral eulogy to a wife today?

. . . You became an orphan suddenly before the day of our wedding, when both your parents were murdered together in the solitude of the countryside. It was mainly due to your efforts that the death of your parents was not left unavenged. For I had left for Macedonia, and your sister's husband Cluvius had gone to the Province of Africa.

So strenuously did you perform your filial duty by your insistent demands and your pursuit of justice that we could not have done more if we had been present. But these merits you have in common with that most virtuous lady your sister.

While you were engaged in these things, having secured the punishment of the guilty, you immediately left your own house in order to guard your modesty and you came to my mother's house, where you awaited my return. Then pressure was brought to bear on you and your sister to accept the view that your father's will, by which you and I were heirs, had been invalidated by his having contracted a *coemptio** with his wife. If that was the case, then you together with all your father's property would necessarily come under the guardianship of those who pursued the matter; your sister would be left without any share at all of that inheritance, since she had been transferred to the *potestas* [power] of Cluvius. How you reacted to this, with what presence of mind you offered resistance, I know full well, although I was absent.

You defended our common cause by asserting the truth, namely, that the will had not in fact been broken, so that we should both keep the property, instead of your getting all of it alone. It was your firm decision that you would defend your father's written word; you would do this anyhow, you declared, by sharing your inheritance with your sister, if you were unable to uphold the validity of the will. And you maintained that you would not come under the state of legal guardianship, since there was no such right against you in law, for there was no proof that your father belonged to any *gens* that could by law compel you to do this. For even assuming that your father's will had become void, those who prosecuted had no such right since they did not belong to the same *gens*.

They gave way before your firm resolution and did not pursue the matter any further. Thus you on your own brought to a successful conclusion the defence you took up of your duty to your father, your devotion to your sister, and your faithfulness towards me.

Marriages as long as ours are rare, marriages that are ended by death and not broken by divorce. For we were fortunate enough to see our marriage last without disharmony for fully 40 years. I wish that our long union had come to its final end through something that had befallen me instead of you; it would have been more just if I as the older partner had had to yield to fate through such an event.

Why should I mention your domestic virtues: your loyalty, obedience, affability, reasonableness, industry in working wool, religion without superstition, sobriety of attire, modesty of appearance? Why dwell on your love for your relatives, your devotion to your family? You have shown the same attention to my mother as you did to your own parents, and

---

*A kind of Roman marriage in which the bride technically sells her rights to a husband or guardian.

have taken care to secure an equally peaceful life for her as you did for your own people, and you have innumerable other merits in common with all married women who care for their good name. It is your very own virtues that I am asserting, and very few women have encountered comparable circumstances to make them endure such sufferings and perform such deeds. Providentially Fate has made such hard tests rare for women.

We have preserved all the property you inherited from your parents under common custody, for you were not concerned to make your own what you had given to me without any restriction. We divided our duties in such a way that I had the guardianship of your property and you had the care of mine. Concerning this side of our relationship I pass over much, in case I should take a share myself in what is properly yours. May it be enough for me to have said this much to indicate how you felt and thought.

Your generosity you have manifested to many friends and particularly to your beloved relatives. On this point someone might mention with praise other women, but the only equal you have had has been your sister. For you brought up your female relations who deserved such kindness in your own houses with us. You also prepared marriage-portions for them so that they could obtain marriages worthy of your family. The dowries you had decided upon Cluvius and I by common accord took upon ourselves to pay, and since we approved of your generosity we did not wish that you should let your own patrimony suffer diminution but substituted our own money and gave our own estates as dowries. I have mentioned this not from a wish to commend ourselves but to make clear that it was a point of honour for us to execute with our means what you had conceived in a spirit of generous family affection.

A number of other benefits of yours I have preferred not to mention . . . (*several lines missing*)

You provided abundantly for my needs during my flight and gave me the means for a dignified manner of living, when you took all the gold and jewellery from your own body and sent it to me and over and over again enriched me in my absence with servants, money and provisions, showing great ingenuity in deceiving the guards posted by our adversaries.

You begged for my life when I was abroad—it was your courage that urged you to this step—and because of your entreaties I was shielded by the clemency of those against whom you marshalled your words. But whatever you said was always said with undaunted courage.

Meanwhile when a troop of men collected by Milo, whose house I had acquired through purchase when he was in exile, tried to profit by the opportunities provided by the civil war and break into our house to plunder, you beat them back successfully and were able to defend our home. (*About 12 lines missing*)

. . . exist . . . that I was brought back to my country by him (Caesar Augustus), for if you had not, by taking care for my safety, provided what he could save, he would have promised his support in vain. Thus I owe my life no less to your devotion than to Caesar.

Why should I now hold up to view our intimate and secret plans and private conversations: how I was saved by your good advice when I was roused by startling reports to meet sudden and imminent dangers; how you did not allow me imprudently to tempt providence by an overbold step but prepared a safe hiding-place for me, when I had given up my ambitious designs, choosing as partners in your plans to save me your sister and her husband Cluvius, all of you taking the same risk? There would be no end, if I tried to go into all this. It is enough for me and for you that I was hidden and my life was saved.

But I must say that the bitterest thing that happened to me in my life befell me through what happened to you. When thanks to the kindness and judgment of the absent Caesar Augustus I had been restored to my country as a citizen, Marcus Lepidus, his colleague, who was present, was confronted with your request concerning my recall, and you lay prostrate at his feet, and you were not only not raised up but were dragged away and carried off brutally like a slave. But although your body was full of bruises, your spirit was unbroken and you kept reminding him of Caesar's edict with its expression of pleasure at my reinstatement, and although you had to listen to insulting words and suffer cruel wounds, you pronounced the words of the edict in a loud voice, so that it should be known who was the cause of my deadly perils. This matter was soon to prove harmful for him.

What could have been more effective than the virtue you displayed? You managed to give Caesar an opportunity to display his clemency and not only to preserve my life but also to brand Lepidus' insolent cruelty by your admirable endurance.

But why go on? Let me cut my speech short. My words should and can be brief, lest by dwelling on your great deeds I treat them unworthily. In gratitude for your great services towards me let me display before the eyes of all men my public acknowledgment that you saved my life.

When peace had been restored throughout the world and the lawful political order re-established, we began to enjoy quiet and happy times. It is true that we did wish to have children, who had for a long time been denied to us by an envious fate. If it had pleased Fortune to continue to be favourable to us as she was wont to be, what would have been lacking for either of us? But Fortune took a different course, and our hopes were sinking. The courses you considered and the steps you attempted to take because of this would perhaps be remarkable and praiseworthy in some other women, but in you they are nothing to wonder at when compared to your great qualities and I will not go into them.

When you despaired of your ability to bear children and grieved over my childlessness, you became anxious lest by retaining you in marriage I might lose all hope of having children and be distressed for that reason. So you proposed a divorce outright and offered to yield our house free to another woman's fertility. Your intention was in fact that you yourself, relying on our well-known conformity of sentiment, would search out and provide for me a wife who was worthy and suitable for me, and you declared that you would regard future children as joint and as though your own, and that you would not effect a separation of our property which had hitherto been held in common, but that it would still be under my control and, if I wished so, under your administration: nothing would be kept apart by you, nothing separate, and you would thereafter take upon yourself the duties and the loyalty of a sister and a mother-in-law.

I must admit that I flared up so that I almost lost control of myself; so horrified was I by what you tried to do that I found it difficult to retrieve my composure. To think that separation should be considered between us before fate had so ordained, to think that you had been able to conceive in your mind the idea that you might cease to be my wife while I was still alive, although you had been utterly faithful to me when I was exiled and practically dead!

What desire, what need to have children could I have had that was so great that I should have broken faith for that reason and changed certainty for uncertainty? But no more about this! You remained with me as my wife, for I could not have given in to you without disgrace for me and unhappiness for both of us.

But on your part, what could have been more worthy of commemoration and praise than your efforts in devotion to my interests: when I could not have children from yourself, you wanted me to have them through your good offices, and since you despaired of bearing children, to provide me with offspring by my marriage to another woman.

Would that the life-span of each of us had allowed our marriage to continue until I, as the older partner, had been borne to the grave—that would have been more just—and you had performed for me the last rites, and that I had died leaving you still alive and that I had had you as a daughter to myself in place of my childlessness.

Fate decreed that you should precede me. You bequeathed me sorrow through my longing for you and left me a miserable man without children to comfort me. I on my part will, however, bend my way of thinking and feeling to your judgments and be guided by your admonitions.

But all your opinions and instructions should give precedence to the praise you have won so that this praise will be a consolation for me and I will not feel too much the loss of what I have consecrated to immortality to be remembered for ever.

What you have achieved in your life will not be lost to me. The thought of your fame gives me strength of mind and from your actions I draw instruction so that I shall be able to resist Fortune. Fortune did not rob me of everything since it permitted your memory to be glorified by praise. But along with you I have lost the tranquility of my existence. When I recall how you used to foresee and ward off the dangers that threatened me, I break down under my calamity and cannot hold steadfastly by my promise.

Natural sorrow wrests away my power of self-control and I am overwhelmed by sorrow. I am tormented by two emotions: grief and fear—and I do not stand firm against either. When I go back in thought to my previous misfortunes and when I envisage what the future may have in store for me, fixing my eyes on your glory does not give me strength to bear my sorrow with patience. Rather I seem to be destined to long mourning.

The conclusions of my speech will be that you deserved everything but that it did not fall to my lot to give you everything as I ought; your last wishes I have regarded as law; whatever it will be in my power to do in addition, I shall do.

I pray that your Di Manes will grant you rest and protection.

17.2.   CLEOPATRA

Plutarch

Cleopatra, Queen of Egypt, lover of Julius Caesar and, later, Mark Antony, is one of the great romantic figures of history. Married, in the Egyptian custom, to her brother Ptolemy XII, she met and married Caesar (who was also married) while still young and bore him a son. In this section from Life of Mark Antony, *the Roman biographer Plutarch tells of Cleopatra's spectacular appearance before Mark Antony in Tarsus, Cilicia (now southern Turkey), at the age of 28 in 41* B.C. *On their marriage in 37* B.C., *Mark Antony recognized their two children and gave Cleopatra large parts of Syria, Palestine, and the Phoenician coast to govern on behalf of Rome. But in 31–30* B.C. *Mark Antony and Cleopatra were defeated by Octavian, marking the end of the Roman Republic. To avoid capture, Cleopatra had herself bitten by an asp, a poisonous snake. What can you tell about Cleopatra from Plutarch's account?*

[Caesar and Pompey knew Cleopatra when she was] still a girl, and ignorant of the world, but it was a different matter in the case of Antony, because she was ready to meet him when she had reached the time of life when women are most beautiful and have full understanding. So she prepared for him many gifts and money and adornment, of a magnitude appropriate to her great wealth and prosperous kingdom, but she put most of her hopes in her own personal magical arts and charms.

Although she had received many letters from Antony and his friends asking her to come to meet him [in Cilicia], she took his summons so lightly and laughed at it, that she sailed up the Cydnus river in a barge with a gilded stern, with purple sails outstretched, pulled by silver oars in time to piping accompanied by fifes and lyres. She herself lay under a gold-embroidered awning, got up like Aphrodite in a painting, with slaves dressed as Erotes fanning her on either side. Likewise the prettiest slave-women, dressed like Nereids and Graces, were at the tillers and the ropes. Remarkable perfumes from many censers surrounded them. People followed after Cleopatra on both sides of the river, and others came downstream from the city to see the sight. When finally the entire crowd in the marketplace had disappeared, Antony was left sitting on the tribunal by himself, and word got round that Aphrodite was leading a festival procession to Dionysus for the benefit of Asia.

Antony sent messengers inviting her to dinner. She insisted instead that he come to her. Because he wished to show his readiness to accept her invitation and his friendship, he obeyed her summons and came. The preparations she had made for him were indescribable, and he was particularly struck by the number of lights. Many are said to have been lowered and lit up at the same time, ordered and arranged in such intricate relationships with one another, and patterns, some in squares, some in circles, so that it was a sight among the most noteworthy and beautiful.

The next day he invited her in return, and he considered it a matter of honour to exceed the magnificence and care of her entertainment, but when he was outdone and vanquished by her in both respects, he was the first to make fun of himself for his bombast and rusticity. Cleopatra saw the soldierly and common nature of Antony's jokes, and she used the same soldier's humour towards him in a relaxed and confident manner. For (as they say) it was not because her beauty in itself was so striking that it stunned the onlooker, but the inescapable impression produced by daily contact with her: the attractiveness in the persuasiveness of her talk, and the character that surrounded her conversation was stimulating. It was a pleasure to hear the sound of her voice, and she tuned her tongue like a many-stringed instrument expertly to whatever language she chose, and only used interpreters to talk to a few foreigners; usually she gave responses by herself, as in the case of Ethiopians, Troglodytes, Hebrews, Arabs, Syrians, Medes, Parthians, and she is said to have learned the languages of many other peoples, although her predecessors on the throne did not bother to learn Egyptian, and some had even forgotten how to speak the Macedonian dialect.

She took such hold over Antony, that while his wife Fulvia was carrying on the war in Rome against Octavian on his behalf, and the Parthian army had been gathered in Mesopotamia (the general of that Army,

Labienus was now being addressed by the generals of the King of Persia as Commander of the Parthians) and was about to invade Syria, Antony was carried off by Cleopatra to Alexandria, and amused himself there with the pastimes of a boy on holiday and games, and spent and luxuriated away that (as Antiphon says) most precious of commodities, time . . .

Cleopatra used not (as Plato says) the four kinds of flattery, but many, and whether Antony was in a serious or playful mood she could always produce some new pleasure or charm, and she kept watch over him and neither by day or night let him out of her sight. She played dice with him and hunted with him and watched him exercising with his weapons, and she roamed around and wandered about with him at night when he stood at people's doors and windows and made fun of the people inside, dressed in a slave-woman's outfit; for he also attempted to dress up like a slave.

He returned from these expeditions having been mocked in return, and often beaten, although most people suspected who he was. But the Alexandrians got pleasure from his irreverence and accompanied it with good timing and good taste, enjoying his humour and saying that he showed his tragic face to the Romans and his comic one to them.

Although it would be a waste of time to catalogue all of his amusements, one time he went fishing and had the misfortune not to catch anything while Cleopatra was present. So he ordered the fisherman secretly to dive underneath and attach fish that had already been caught to his hooks, but Cleopatra was not fooled after she saw him pull up two or three. She pretended to be amazed and told her friends and invited them to come as observers on the next day. After a large audience had gathered on the fishing boats and Antony had lowered his line, Cleopatra told one of her slaves to get in ahead of the others and attach a salted fish from the Black Sea to his hook. When Antony thought he had caught something he pulled it up, and when (as might be expected) loud laughter followed, she said, 'General, leave the fishing rod to us, the rulers of the Pharos and Canopus; your game is cities and kingdoms and countries.'

18.   THE ROMAN EMPIRE IN THE YEAR ONE

M. I. Finley

The Year One, this modern historian reminds us, was not a Roman date but a Christian one. And even if it was not the correct date for the beginning of

Christianity, it was very close to the beginning of the Roman Empire (twenty-seven years after Octavian became the Emperor Augustus).

What was it like to be a Roman in this period of the early empire? What was it like to be a colonial subject? What were the accomplishments of Augustus? What were his failures? How did Roman rule come into conflict with the Jews? What, if anything, began in the Year One?

Decisive years, like decisive battles, are an old favourite with historians. Some—1492, 1776, 1914—are pretty obvious: knowledgeable contemporaries could not have escaped the feeling that something big was up, even though they could not have foreseen all the consequences. More often, however, great historical processes begin altogether invisibly, and only much later, looking back, is it possible to pin the critical date down. Such a year is the Year One. Indeed, of all the great years in history it is the oddest because no one alive at the time, or for centuries thereafter, had any idea that this was the Year One at all. If they ever used such a date, they would have meant by it the year in which the world was created, not what we mean by A.D. 1.

How, for example, was a birth certificate, a marriage contract, a business agreement, dated in the Year One? There is no single answer to such a question, since for most of the purposes of ordinary living, local dates were used. In Rome a contract would be dated "in the consulship of C. Caesar son of Augustus and L. Aemilius Paullus son of Paullus." Elsewhere there were regnal years, or years of local officials, or of priesthoods. This may look like chaos to us, habituated as we are to a continuous, fixed calendar in use more or less all over the world, but it worked well enough. Only the learned were troubled, the men who wanted an exact answer to the question "How long ago?" or who wished to synchronize events in Greek and Roman history. A number of systems had been invented for their use. In Rome scholars commonly dated events from the legendary foundation of the city by Romulus in the year we call 753 B.C.; in Greece they used four-year units, Olympiads, beginning with the first Olympic Games in 776 B.C. In those two systems the Year One was, respectively, 754 A.U.C. (*ab urbe condita*) and the first year of the 195th Olympiad. No system was official: every scholar and historian was free to choose whichever he preferred, singly or in combination.

It is therefore hardly surprising that it took the Christians a long time to think up and introduce a scheme of their own. The honour goes to an eastern Greek-speaking monk, Dionysius Exiguus, who lived in Rome in the first half of the sixth century. He calculated that Christ was born in 754 A.U.C., called that the first "year of our Lord," *anno Domini*, and counted everything that preceded it as so many years *ante Christum*, "before Christ." His calculation was slightly inaccurate. The only real evidence is in two of the four Gospels, and unfortunately that is conflicting and irreconcilable. If Matthew is right in the way he dates the flight into Egypt, then Jesus was born in or shortly before the last year of the reign of King Herod the Great, who died in 4 B.C. But if Luke is right in linking the Nativity with a census—"And all went to enrol themselves, everyone to his own city"—then the date must be A.D. 6 or even 7. On neither account is A.D. 1 possible. Nevertheless, Dionysius's chronological scheme spread gradually, first in the west, more slowly in the east, until it achieved near universality. The Year One—whatever it really was— became a great year, for many the greatest year in all history.

If A.D. 6 is the right date, then Jesus was born in the newly established Roman province of Judaea. In that year the Romans deposed Herod's son Archelaus, took over Judaea, and sent in Syria's governor, Quirinius, with instructions to conduct the first census there. Galilee, on the other hand, was allowed to continue under the family of Herod for another generation. This rather confusing political situation was not untypical of districts on the eastern frontier of the Roman empire, where imperial policy fluctuated between backing local client-kings and ruling directly. After all, Palestine was a long way from Rome. Problems much nearer home were pressing: large forces were just then occupied with trying to incorporate the German territory between the Rhine and the Elbe. They were wiped out in A.D. 9 in a treacherous ambush by Arminius (Hermann), a German chieftain who had earlier served in the Roman auxiliary forces and been rewarded with Roman citizenship. That disaster in the Teutoburg Forest effectively settled the northern frontier of the empire on the Rhine-Danube line, subject to various later adjustments, including the conquest of Britain. The western frontier was the Atlantic Ocean; the southern was the Atlas Mountains, the Sahara, and the cataracts [steep rapids] of the Nile—though parts of northern Africa had the same shifting political history as Judaea.

The Roman Empire was an empire in the strictest possible sense. The "Roman people"—that is, Roman citizens who were concentrated very largely in Rome and central or northern Italy—ruled all the rest as subjects. The empire outside Italy was divided into what were called *provinciae*, which were not provinces in the way Ontario is now a province of Canada, but rather colonies in the way India or Nigeria were British colonies before they obtained their independence. The total area of the empire in A.D. 2 was nearly 1,250,000 square miles, the population perhaps 60,000,000. Whether anyone, in or out of government, actually knew the latter figure is much to be doubted. Although censuses were taken, they were irregular, and they came at different times in different provinces. Their sole purpose was to bring the tax rolls up to date: the tax collector, along with the soldier, was the most obvious and ubiquitous link between the provinces and Rome.

Rome had begun to acquire provinces as far back as the third century B.C., and the process never stopped until the second century of the Christian Era. Imperial expansion usually looks deceptive in its motivation because defence and strategy can so plausibly be adduced as the excuse: the farther the frontiers are extended, the farther the menaces—real or imaginary—are pushed back. But in antiquity in general, and among the Romans in particular, there seems to have been much less effort than in modern times to disguise or deny the open exploitation of empire. Whatever the reasons piously given for their conquest and incorporation in each individual instance, the right to profit directly from conquered lands was freely recognized. That meant not only taxes—in goods, services and money—for the state, but often great personal income, legal or illegal, for high officials and members of the tax-farming corporations. It was also in the interests of Rome that her empire be pacific and orderly, as well as reasonably well administered locally. To achieve the latter aim she depended chiefly on the local ruling classes, for she lacked the manpower to do otherwise, and they normally played the part assigned to them as a pro-Roman counter-weight in what could well have become a rebellious situation.

From the days when Rome first began to expand, her rulers had also adopted a policy of as much non-interference as possible in social and cultural institutions, although not so much from a broad theory or principle of toleration as from the much more elementary consideration, Why bother? Rome had no "mission"—that myth was imposed retrospectively much later. She wished to rule successfully, and it was repeatedly demonstrated to her that minimum interference paid off—even though the Roman provincial governor retained virtually absolute power and did not hesitate to use it when he felt the need, including the imposition of the death penalty. Under normal conditions the upshot was that in their daily lives very large numbers of people were touched lightly indeed by Roman rule. That was particularly true in the eastern parts of the empire which had a high civilization of their own long before the Romans came. These areas remained very diverse, both among themselves and from the west—about as diverse as they had been in their days of independence. The calendar is fairly symptomatic, language even more so. Latin was of course the official language of the Roman state. But it was not the language spoken in the east or even in some western regions such as Sicily and Libya. There the ruling classes and the intellectuals tended to speak and write and think in Greek, the rest in their native tongues—in some places Greek, in others Aramaic or Egyptian or whatever. Educated Romans were more or less fluent in Greek, but their counterparts in the eastern provinces rarely troubled to know Latin equally well. When Josephus—Joseph ben Matthias, member of a Jewish priestly family, highly educated, born and bred in Judaea—wrote his *Jewish War*, a pro-Roman eyewitness acount of the Roman capture of rebel Jerusalem and the destruction of the Temple in A.D. 70, his first version was in Aramaic, his second in Greek.

Josephus was a Pharisee, for whom the villains among his own people were the Zealots, who stirred up and led the revolt against Rome. His favourite word for the rebels is "bandits," so that bandits, Zealots, and lower classes are virtually synonymous in his books. The mighty Romans needed four years to quell the Jewish uprising—precisely because social revolt, the desire for independence and sectarian religious conflict were closely intertwined. This was an age of lavish living among relatively few men at one end of the scale, and extreme poverty among the many at the other end. The Gargantuan banquet given by the freedman Trimalchio in the *Satyricon* of Petronius is funny in the way it exaggerates; the account caricatures, but it does not invent out of whole cloth. The wealth of Herod the Great was a subject for never-ending comment by Josephus. But the linen weavers of Tarsus, skilled free craftsmen whose products were sought after throughout the empire, could never afford the small fees charged for the acquisition of local citizenship in their own city.

Outside Judaea serious revolt was rare, for whatever reason. There was much unhappiness and much grumbling, but it takes more than that to make a lasting mark on the record: history tends to be the history of the winners, with the losers assigned the passive, largely unvoiced, faceless role of the people on whom the winners operated. Romans in the Year One were able to contemplate their position with much satisfaction. Not only were they the rulers of what they chose to believe was the civilized world, but they had emerged successfully from a long, desperately violent, and dangerous period of civil war. The republican machinery of government, led by the exclusive, oligarchical Senate—which had sent victorious Roman armies east, west, north and south and had carved out the greatest empire yet known—had broken down badly by the end of the second century B.C. Various attempts to mend it had failed, until Julius Caesar's great-nephew and adopted son, Octavian, finally replaced the old system by a monarchy—although the explicit terminology of kingship was carefully avoided and a republican façade reconstructed, with Senate, popular assembly, consuls, praetors and so on. But a façade is just that: its function is to conceal the reality behind it. In January of 27 B.C. the Senate formally ratified the position Octavian had won by arms and conferred on him a new name, Augustus, by which he has been known ever since. At the same time a euphemistic title was chosen for him, Princeps—before this a common Latin word which the dictionary defines as "the first, chief, principal, most distinguished person," hence lacking any of the undesirable overtones of *rex* (king). He was also Imperator, a military title he used often because it affirmed his special relationship with the base and guarantee of his power: the army, roughly half of it Roman citizens in the legions, the other half auxiliaries recruited chiefly in the less Romanized provinces.

Twenty-seven years later Augustus was firmly in control of an empire which he had considerably enlarged. Small stirrings of anti-monarchical sentiment were crushed, all lingering misunderstandings about the real nature of his rule removed. In 2 B.C. he had been given the title *pater patriae*, Father of the Nation, which recalled to Roman citizens the despotic authority of the Roman *pater* at least as much as paternal benevolence. He lived on to A.D. 14, with only one new honour to look forward to: his formal deification upon his death (like Julius Caesar before him). As important as these titular acquisitions were his open manoeuvrings to establish a royal dynasty: Augustus and no one else was going to choose his successor, and in the process he trampled on some of the most deeply rooted of Roman traditions. In 4 B.C. the Senate decreed that his two grandsons (and sons by adoption), Gaius and Lucius, should be designated consuls at the age of fifteen and that they should actually assume office when they were twenty. Each was entitled "Princeps of the Youth." This rigmarole was pure crown-princedom. In the Year One, Gaius, having become twenty, was duly elected consul along with his sister's husband, L. Aemilius Paullus. Then Augustus's luck ran out: Lucius died the next year, Gaius in A.D. 4. The sick, aging emperor proceeded to adopt Tiberius who eventually succeeded him.

That Tiberius was able to take over smoothly and peacefully is a measure of the full extent of Augustus's success. Historians commonly and rightly call Augustus the "architect of the Roman Empire." In the days when imperialism was still a virtue and Roman imperialism the accepted model, he was regularly referred to with unmixed adulation. The pendulum has now swung back, though less for some, perhaps, than for others—E. M. Forster calls Augustus "one of the most odious of the world's successful men." It is hard to imagine anyone today reading without discomfort these lines[1]:

> And here, here is the man, the promised one you know of—
> Caesar Augustus, son of a god, destined to rule
> Where Saturn ruled of old in Latium, and there
> Bring back the age of gold: his empire shall expand
> Past Garamants and Indians to a land beyond the zodiac.

Virgil and Horace were the towering figures in the literary circle patronized by one of Augustus's closest and richest friends, Maecenas. (It was not for nothing that the very name of Maecenas became a common word in the languages of Europe.) Augustus thought of everything: public opinion was not to be neglected any more than finance, dynastic arrangements, food supply, or the army. Even the coinage was harnessed. When he was given the title *pater patriae*, for example, his chief mint, at Lugdunum (Lyons), began to issue silver coins carrying his

---

1. From *The Aeneid of Virgil,* edited and translated by C. Day Lewis (London: The Hogarth Press, 1952; New York: Doubleday, Anchor Books ed., 1953).

portrait with the legend *pater patriae* on the obverse; on the reverse were his two young grandsons in togas, with emblems of priesthood and the legend, "Gaius and Lucius Caesar, sons [by adoption] of Augustus, consuls-designate, *principes* of the youth." Coins circulate rapidly, and public response was not slow. Poets picked up the theme; so did individuals and communities in dedicatory inscriptions on monuments.

Yet it would be a mistake to speak cynically of prostituted art. Neither Virgil nor Horace, who died in 19 and 8 B.C., respectively, nor the historian Livy, who in the Year One was still writing away on his vast epic history of Rome, had been bought in any real sense. Horace was the son of a rich ex-slave, while Virgil and Livy came from the propertied middle classes of northern Italy. These classes had suffered heavily in the civil wars, but now there was peace again—the *pax Augusta*—and great hope for the future, both for Rome and for the empire. With renewed greatness would come moral regeneration. This last was a favourite theme of Augustus, expressed in a stream of legislation designed to curb excessively wasteful personal living, licentiousness and depravity in the upper classes. They were to be called back, these upper classes—not to the freedom and power they had had in the Republic, but to responsible participation in the army and the civil administration under the Princeps. Augustus himself, according to his Roman biographer Suetonius, listened to poetry recitals and readings from history, and he even enjoyed them "provided they were serious and the author of the first rank."

Moral crusades are never easy to judge: standards, motives and realities are too much like icebergs. Certainly the visible part of contemporary behaviour looked rotten enough, even allowing for differences between ancient and modern values. The banishment at different times for sexual depravity of Augustus's daughter and granddaughter is proof enough. A number of men of high rank were exiled with the former as her accomplices; the husband of the latter, L. Aemilius Paullus (who had been the second consul in the Year One), was executed. There is thus something altogether mysterious about both affairs. There is no particular reason to whitewash either of the Julias, but it is hard to avoid the implication that dynastic palace plotting was a more important element in the picture. Conspiracy was henceforth endemic in the empire, and it is not unimportant that it touched the heart of the regime as early as the reign of the founder himself.

One of the younger Julia's co-victims was the poet Ovid, sent off to Tomi (now Constanța) on the Black Sea, where he was forced to live out the remaining ten years of his life, grumbling, whining, and begging in the most toadying terms for a reprieve which never came. In a sense Ovid sums up in his own career the great paradox of the Rome of his day. What had he done to warrant such severe punishment? As far as we know, nothing—or at worst something trifling. But ten years earlier he had written the *Art of Love,* and throughout his brilliant career—he was enormously popular—he belonged to a circle of poets and intellectuals who gave only lip service to the glories of the new reign while they exulted in their own individuality and, sin of sins, in the delights of love when the Emperor was demanding moral regeneration. The *pax Augusta* was enforced by a military despotism; the literary renaissance was expected to stay pretty much in line; the rule of law could be broken at the ruler's whim.

It was not the brutality that disturbed anyone. The list of Augustus's massive philanthropies, which he himself compiled for posthumous publication, included the sponsorship of eight monster exhibitions in which about ten thousand gladiators fought, the largest number on record. These were now the most popular type of public show in the empire. If the theatre was the characteristic secular building of classical Greek civilization, the amphitheatre was its Roman counterpart. What critics of the imperial system (the few whose voices we hear) attacked was not its brutality but the arbitrariness and the sycophancy it bred, the inevitable conspiratorial atmosphere.

Yet there *was* a great cultural renaissance under Augustus. And there was peace throughout the empire most of the time, peace without political freedom as the Greeks had once understood it, even without freedom in the more limited sense men had experienced in republican Rome, but more continuous peace than the Mediterranean world had perhaps ever known. The Roman and Italian response is well documented in literature and sculptured monuments, and is not hard to understand. But what of the "provincials," the subjects, and particularly what of the great mass of them who were not local magnates supporting Rome in return for benefits received? Part of the answer, for the east in particular, is that they began to worship Augustus as Saviour, Benefactor and God Manifest (Epiphanes), just as they had deified a succession of Ptolemies, Seleucids, and other rulers in the preceding centuries. Among the Romans themselves divinity had to wait until his death; in the meantime only his genius or *daemon*, the immortal spirit within him, could have an altar. But the east, with a different tradition, built temples to Augustus the god.

This ruler-cult should neither be underestimated nor misunderstood. It was cult in the strict sense, difficult as that may be to grasp today. At the same time it did not prove the existence of widespread popular enthusiasm for the ruler as a person, or of anything more positive than a recognition of the facts of life. Power had to be worshipped, that was self-evident: the power of natural forces, Fate or Fortune, the many gods and goddesses in their multiple attributes, and the great power on earth. To do otherwise was stupid and brought certain punishment, even though rewards for proper veneration were unfortunately far from guaranteed, at least in this life. In so one-sided a relationship, in a world in which there was little hope of material success for the majority of the free population (let alone the slaves), and in which the earthly power was now pretty close to despotism, fear rather than love was often the dominating emotion behind worship, at best fear and love together. Religion became increasingly centered on salvation in the next world, whereas it had once been chiefly concerned with life in this one.

However complicated the psychology, emperor worship was a binding force in the empire. The first manifestations were more or less spontaneous, but it would be naïve to imagine that Augustus or his advisers and successors were unaware of the value of the institution. Particularly zealous to foster it were the petty tyrants and client-kings who depended on Roman arms for their very existence, among them King Herod of Judaea (who also, significantly, introduced the amphitheatre and gladiators into his realm). Herod thereby set off a delayed chain reaction with the most far-reaching consequences. Where there were already many gods, to add the emperor to the pantheon was easy. The polytheistic religions of the eastern Mediterranean had been adding, combining, and altering their divinities and their rituals for millennia. A small minority of intellectuals rationalized the system into one or another kind of universal religion, in which the individual gods and their cults were all manifestations of one God. Everyone else was more literal-minded, with a take-it-or-leave-it approach that permitted one to pick and choose. It was physically impossible for anyone to participate in the observances of all the divinities. A policy of *laissez faire* prevailed, provided only that no one blasphemed against anyone else's gods and that cult did not become entangled with political opposition or create an excessive amount of vicious public immorality.

The Jews stood apart. Many now lived outside Judaea: there were particularly large communities in Egypt and elsewhere in North Africa, smaller ones in Asia Minor and in Rome itself. In the Diaspora they had become very much Hellenized: parts of the Old Testament had been translated into Greek by the middle of the third century B.C. because few could any longer understand Hebrew. In Palestine, by contrast, Hellenization had been relatively negligible, restricted to small aristocratic circles and to certain districts. Yet wherever they were, Greek and other external influences left untouched the fundamental commandments:

> Thou shalt have no other gods before me. Thou shalt not make unto thee any graven image. . . . Thou shalt not bow down thyself to them, nor serve them: for I the Lord thy God am a jealous God.

Once before, in the second century B.C., there had been grave trouble over this question, when the Jews under the leadership of the Maccabees had rebelled successfully against Antiochus IV Epiphanes, the Greek ruler of Syria and Babylonia. Now Herod was trying to repeat the same sacrilege. There was an outcry and he quickly backed down, in time to avoid civil war but not an abortive attempt to assassinate him.

In the next generations the Romans were thus faced with a strange and to them distasteful and even unintelligible situation, with a people who would not play the rules of the game as they were understood by everyone else, who worshipped one God, an exclusive, jealous God. Opposition to emperor worship was to the Romans not so much a religious issue as a political offence, *contumacia*, insubordination, civil disobedience. Augustus and Tiberius made no attempt to force matters with the Jews, and under their immediate successors official policy was inconsistent. But Roman officials in the provinces, and the local populations, for reasons of their own, were far less tolerant and cautious; there were flare-ups against the Jews, ostensibly over imperial statues, in Egypt as well as in Palestine. The Jews themselves were right to be nervous about it. Jewish "extremists" played on these fears, and on social unrest, till finally they brought about the great revolt which the emperor Vespasian and his son Titus smashed in A.D. 70.

It is this complicated combination of motives and circumstances that explains why Jewish nationalism emerged and rebelled whereas Egyptian or Syrian or Greek did not, though widespread poverty, imperial taxation, and similar factors were equally present in these other areas. Economic misery and social unrest had long been turning people to religious salvation as the only promise for the future. In this instance religion drove men to political action (as druidism may also have done in Gaul in A.D. 21). To put the whole burden of explanation on emperor worship would be wrong: religious exclusiveness and alienness, in a world which otherwise found room for all varieties of cult and belief, bred misunderstanding, dislike, wild rumours, irrational hate, mob violence. It cannot be doubted that the destruction of Jerusalem was a popular measure, on the whole, with other peoples of the empire. Imperial Rome triumphed for the moment, only to discover that she was faced with the same problem under a new name, Christianity—a religion which was just as fiercely monotheistic and exclusive as Judaism, and even more dynamic in its proselytizing zeal. "Render unto Caesar the things that are Caesar's" did not extend to worship of Caesar for Christians any more than for the Jews.

Of course there were no Christians in the Year One. Not even a hundred or two hundred years later could anyone have foreseen how radically the balance was going to shift, that the invincible Roman Empire would turn out to be transitory while the still negligible Christian sect would one day bid for universality. To emperors and ordinary non-Christians alike, Christianity was a nuisance and no more. Early in the second century, Pliny the Younger, governor of the province of Bithynia, wrote to the emperor Trajan for advice on how to deal with men and women denounced to him for being Christians. "I have never participated in interrogations of Christians," was his significant opening remark, and his long letter confirms his ignorance on the subject. To test persons accused, he continued, he required them to call upon the gods, to sacrifice before the imperial statue and to revile the name of Christ—"none of which things, it is said, genuine Christians can be induced to do." Trajan in reply agreed that Christians must be punished, but "they should not be hunted out." Roman emperors never took so casual a view of problems they regarded as really serious.

Trajan, incidentally, was the last Roman expansionist. He conquered Dacia, roughly modern Transylvania in the loop of the lower Danube, and created a new province there. Then he embarked on an absurd campaign against the Parthian empire, the heirs of the Persians east of the Euphrates River. He had fleeting success, but Hadrian—who followed him on the throne—immediately and unavoidably gave up the new eastern gains. All in all, the frontiers of the Year One were not far from the absolute limits of the Roman world, except for adjustments, a few conquests, and the final elimination of client-kingdoms as in Judaea. Roman contacts through trade were something else again. Luxury goods moved back and forth across vast distances, and with the products some information and more misinformation. Even though silk came overland from China (the middlemen living in what is now Chinese Turkestan), it may safely be doubted if anyone within the Roman Empire had ever heard of the early Han dynasty or that it was about to come to an end just then (actually in A.D. 8). Trade with India and even Ceylon was more direct and on a considerably larger scale, chiefly by sea from Egypt. Indo-Roman trading stations existed as far away as Pondicherry; there was a drain of Roman coins to India and still farther east. Yet the knowledge of Indian life and civilization scattered in Roman literature is thin and unreliable, showing little advance over the reports brought back from the campaigns of Alexander the Great several centuries earlier. Similarly, there was trans-Sahara trade, especially for ivory, but almost total ignorance of the African continent below the desert.

The peoples the Romans knew best were of course their neighbours, the Armenians and Parthians immediately to the east, and, more important, the Germans beyond the Rhine and Danube. The latter were illiterate, organized in loose tribal federations rather than in more advanced political systems, and constantly on the move, both because their relatively primitive agricultural techniques exhausted the soil rapidly and because from time to time they were driven by invaders, such as the later Huns, who swept across the eastern and central European plains. Germans and Romans were in constant contact, sometimes hostile but more often neutral or even friendly, exchanging goods and occasionally ideas. It is hardly surprising that these less-advanced peoples envied the superior Roman material standards and tried to share them, which meant trying to come into the empire.

Whatever the cultural influences going out—and they are visible in such far-flung places as Taxila in the Punjab, or among the Celts of

Britain—it is easy (and sometimes too tempting) to exaggerate the reverse process, except in religion. Astrology from Babylon, the god Mithras, and the old Zoroastrian dual principle of Light and Darkness from Persia spread rapidly through the empire. Again one must not exaggerate; apart from these examples, the great matrix of religious innovation was *within* the empire, in its eastern regions: Egypt, Syria and Palestine, Asia Minor. And, of course, in the end the triumphant contribution from that area in this period was Christianity.

All this outruns the Year One by centuries, and it must be confessed that it was a decisive year only by convention, thanks to the slight error committed by Dionysius Exiguus. Nevertheless, the victory of Augustus and the birth of Christ between them marked out paths for the future, the impact of which cannot possibly be overstated. It is a commonplace to say that European civilization (and therefore American, too) has three roots, Greek, Roman and Judaeo-Christian. But it has become a commonplace because it is so obviously true. The Romanization of western Europe, for which the Augustan imperial settlement was essential, was one factor that eventually made the idea of Europe possible. The eastern half of the empire was fundamentally not Romanized, and in the end it broke away, from Rome and from Europe; but it produced and exported to Europe a second binding factor, a common and exclusive religion. These were not the only factors in subsequent European history, to be sure. In history, unlike biology, one must not ask too much of roots. They cannot explain everything. It is enough to understand how deep down they go and what they have contributed.

CHAPTER SIX

Judeo-Christian Tradition

19. THE BIBLE

The world "Bible" has different meanings for Jews and Christians. Jews use the word to mean just the Judaic writings that were composed between about 900 and 165 B.C., mainly in Hebrew, with some Aramaic. Christians use the word "Bible" to refer to both these writings (which they call the Old Testament) and the writings about Jesus and the early Christian church (the New Testament) that were written between about A.D. 50 and 100 in Greek, based in part on earlier Aramaic sources.

The Hebrew Bible is a rich collection of laws, history, poems, and prophecy. It reflects the life of a tribe of Hebrews, descended from a patriarch named Abraham, who may have left the ancient Mesopotamian city of Ur around 2000 B.C. These Hebrews were a nomadic, pastoral people (see Psalm 23), who practiced animal sacrifice (see Leviticus). Their wanderings took them across the Fertile Crescent to Egypt, which they fled about 1300 B.C. to settle in Canaan, or Palestine, where they built a kingdom (later divided) after 1000 B.C. around the city of Jerusalem.

Sometime between 2000 and 165 B.C., the Hebrews developed a radically different religion from that of their neighbors. The most striking element of this religion was its belief in one god (monotheism). This belief might be called the core message of the Bible. As such, it rings out from the first line of the first book, Genesis. The idea of a single creator God, not just a tribal ancestor or nature spirit, was unique. It meant the possibility of a single human story, and this is the story Genesis sets out to tell. Monotheism also implied a belief that the world was orderly and good. How are these ideas presented in Genesis? What does Genesis say about the relationship between God and humans? What is the relationship in Genesis between humans and nature?

Some scholars have suggested that we have two creation accounts here, a philosophical, "priestly" account written about 650 B.C. in 1:1 to 2:3, followed by an older, legendary, "storytelling" account written about 850 B.C. starting at 2:4. Do you see any evidence for this idea? How does the tone or meaning of Genesis change after 2:4? What does Genesis tell you about women in Hebrew society? What else does it tell you about the Hebrews?

All biblical selections are from the King James Version.

GENESIS

1

1 In the beginning God created the heaven and the earth. 2 And the earth was without form, and void; and darkness was upon the face of the deep. And the Spirit of God moved upon the face of the waters. 3 And God said, Let there be light: and there was light. 4 And God saw the light, and it was good: and God divided the light from the darkness. 5 And God called the light Day, and the darkness he called Night. And the evening and the morning were the first day.

6 And God said, Let there be a firmament in the midst of the waters, and let it divide the waters from the waters. 7 And God made the firmament, and divided the waters which were under the firmament from the waters which were above the firmament: and it was so. 8 And God called the firmament Heaven. And the evening and the morning were the second day.

9 And God said, Let the waters under the heaven be gathered together unto one place, and let the dry land appear: and it was so. 10 And God called the dry land Earth; and the gathering together of the water called he Seas: and God saw it was good. 11 And God said, Let the earth bring forth grass, the herb yielding seed, and the fruit tree yielding fruit after his kind, whose seed is in itself, upon the earth: and it was so. 12 And the earth brought forth grass, and herb yielding seed after his kind, and the tree yielding fruit, whose seed was in itself, after his kind: and God saw it was good. 13 And the evening and the morning were the third day.

14 And God said, Let there be lights in the firmament of the heaven to divide the day from the night; and let them be for signs, and for seasons, and for days, and years: 15 And let them be for lights in the firmament of the heaven to give light upon the earth: and it was so. 16 And God made two great lights; the greater light to rule the day, and the lesser light to rule the night: he made the stars also. 17 And God set them in the firmament of the heaven to give light upon the earth, 18 And to rule over the day and over the night, and to divide the light from the darkness: and God saw that it was good. 19 And the evening and the morning were the fourth day.

20 And God said, Let the waters bring forth abundantly the moving creatures that hath life, and fowl that may fly above the earth in the open firmament of heaven. 21 And God created great whales, and every living creature that moveth, which the waters brought forth abundantly, after their kind, and every winged fowl after his kind: and God saw that it was good. 22 And God blessed them, saying, Be fruitful, and multiply, and fill the waters in the seas, and let fowl multiply in the earth. 23 And the evening and the morning were the fifth day.

24 And God said, Let the earth bring forth the living creature after his

kind, cattle, and creeping thing, and beast of the earth after his kind: and it was so. 25 And God made the beast of the earth after his kind, and cattle after their kind, and every thing that creepeth upon the earth after his kind: and God saw that it was good.

26 And God said, Let us make man in our image, after our likeness: and let them have dominion over the fish of the sea, and over the fowl of the air, and over the cattle, and over all the earth, and over every creeping thing that creepeth upon the earth. 27 So God created man in his own image, in the image of God created he him: male and female created he them. 28 And God blessed them, and God said unto them, Be fruitful, and multiply, and replenish the earth, and subdue it: and have dominion over the fish of the sea, and over the fowl of the air, and over every living thing that moveth upon the earth.

29 And God said, Behold, I have given you every herb bearing seed, which is upon the face of all the earth, and every tree, in which is the fruit of a tree yielding seed; to you it shall be for meat. 30 And to every beast of the earth, and to every fowl of the air, and to every thing that creepeth upon the earth, wherein there is life, I have given every green herb for meat: and it was so. 31 And God saw every thing that he had made, and, behold, it was very good. And the evening and the morning were the sixth day.

2

1 Thus the heavens and the earth were finished, and all the host of them. 2 And on the seventh day God ended his work which he had made; and he rested on the seventh day from all his work which he had made. 3 And God blessed the seventh day, and sanctified it: because that in it he had rested from all his work which God created and made.

4 These are the generations of the heavens and of the earth when they were created, in the day that the Lord God made the earth and the heavens. 5 And every plant of the field before it was in the earth, and every herb of the field before it grew: for the Lord God had not caused it to rain upon the earth, and there was not a man to till the ground. 6 But there went up a mist from the earth, and watered the whole face of the ground. 7 And the Lord God formed man of the dust of the ground, and breathed into his nostrils the breath of life; and man became a living soul.

8 And the Lord God planted a garden eastward in Eden; and there he put the man whom he had formed. 9 And out of the ground made the Lord God to grow every tree that is pleasant to the sight, and good for food; and the tree of life also in the midst of the garden, and the tree of knowledge of good and evil. 10 And a river went out of Eden to water the garden; and from thence it was parted, and became into four heads. 11 The name of the first is Pison: that is it which compasseth the whole land of Havilah, where there is gold; 12 And the gold of the land is good:

there is bdellium and the onyx stone. 13 And the name of the second river is Gihon: the same is it that compasseth the whole land of Ethiopia. 14 And the name of the third river is Hiddekel: that is it which goeth toward the east of Assyria. And the fourth river is Euphrates. 15 And the Lord God took the man, and put him into the garden of Eden to dress it and to keep it. 16 And the Lord God commanded the man, saying, Of every tree of the garden thou mayest freely eat: 17 But of the tree of the knowledge of good and evil, thou shalt not eat of it: for in the day that thou eatest thereof thou shalt surely die.

18 And the Lord God said, It is not good that the man should be alone; I will make him a help meet for him. 19 And out of the ground the Lord God formed every beast of the field, and every fowl of the air; and brought them unto Adam to see what he would call them: and whatsoever Adam called every living creature, that was the name thereof. 20 And Adam gave names to all cattle, and to the fowl of the air, and to every beast of the field; but for Adam there was not found a help meet for him. 21 And the Lord God caused a deep sleep to fall upon Adam, and he slept; and he took one of his ribs, and closed up the flesh instead thereof. 22 And the rib, which the Lord God had taken from man, made he a woman, and brought her unto the man. 23 And Adam said, This is now bone of my bones, and flesh of my flesh: she shall be called Woman, because she was taken out of man. 24 Therefore shall a man leave his father and his mother, and shall cleave unto his wife: and they shall be one flesh. 25 And they were both naked, the man and his wife, and were not ashamed.

Genesis is both a history of the world and a history of Abraham's tribe. Thus, it accounts for how the God of Abraham is the Creator of the world. According to this account (Gen. 17:1–14), God made a special covenant (or agreement) with Abraham. What was the nature of this covenant? What does this account tell you about Hebrew society?

17

1 And when Abram was ninety years old and nine, the Lord appeared to Abram, and said unto him, I am the Almighty God; walk before me, and be thou perfect. 2 And I will make my covenant between me and thee, and will multiply thee exceedingly. 3 And Abram fell on his face: and God talked with him, saying, 4 As for me, behold, my covenant is with thee, and thou shalt be a father of many nations. 5 Neither shall thy name any more be called Abram, but thy name shall be Abraham; for a father of many nations I have made thee. 6 And I will make thee exceeding fruitful, and I will make nations of thee, and kings shall come out of thee. 7 And I will establish my covenant between me and thee and thy

seed after thee in their generations, for an everlasting covenant, to be a God unto thee and to thy seed after thee. 8 And I will give unto thee, and to thy seed after thee, the land wherein thou art a stranger, all the land of Canaan, for an everlasting possession; and I will be their God. 9 And God said unto Abraham, Thou shalt keep my covenant therefore, thou, and thy seed after thee in their generations. 10 This is my covenant, which he shall keep, between me and you and thy seed after thee; Every man child among you shall be circumcised. 11 And ye shall circumcise the flesh of your foreskin; and it shall be a token of the covenant betwixt me and you. 12 And he that is eight days old shall be circumcised among you, every man child in your generations, he that is born in the house, or bought with money of any stranger, which is not of thy seed. 13 He that is born in thy house, and he that is bought with thy money, must needs be circumcised: and my covenant shall be in your flesh for an everlasting covenant. 14 And the uncircumcised man child whose flesh of his fore-skin is not circumcised, that soul shall be cut off from his people; he hath broken my covenant.

In the following selection from Exodus, the second book of the Bible, God has just led his "chosen people" out of bondage in Egypt. He renews the covenant with all of the "children of Israel." (Israel, also called Jacob, was the son of Isaac and grandson of Abraham.) Then God revealed his law, beginning with the Ten Commandments. What does this selection suggest about Hebrew society? What do you think the Hebrews expected to gain by following the covenant?

EXODUS

19

1 In the third month, when the children of Israel were gone forth out of the land of Egypt, the same day came they into the wilderness of Sinai. 2 For they were departed from Rephidim, and were come to the desert of Sinai, and had pitched in the wilderness; and there Israel camped before the mount. 3 And Moses went up unto God, and the Lord called unto him out of the mountain, saying, Thus shalt thou say to the house of Jacob, and tell the children of Israel; 4 Ye have seen what I did unto the Egyptians, and how I bare you on eagles' wings, and brought you unto myself. 5 Now therefore, if ye will obey my voice indeed, and keep my covenant, then ye shall be a peculiar treasure unto me above all people: for all the earth is mine: 6 And ye shall be unto me a kingdom of priests, and a holy nation. These are the words which thou shalt speak unto the children of Israel.

7 And Moses came and called for the elders of the people, and laid

before their faces all these words which the Lord commanded him. 8 And all the people answered together, and said, All that the Lord hath spoken we will do. And Moses returned the words of the people unto the Lord. 9 And the Lord said unto Moses, Lo, I come unto thee in a thick cloud, that the people may hear when I speak with thee, and believe thee for ever. And Moses told the words of the people unto the Lord.

20

1 And God spake all these words, saying,

2 I am the Lord thy God, which have brought thee out of the land of Egypt, out of the house of bondage. 3 Thou shalt have no other gods before me.

4 Thou shalt not make unto thee any graven image, or any likeness of any thing that is in heaven above, or that is in the earth beneath, or that is in the water under the earth: 5 Thou shalt not bow down thyself to them, nor serve them: for I the Lord thy God am a jealous God, visiting the iniquity of the fathers upon the children unto the third and fourth generation of them that hate me; 6 And showing mercy unto thousands of them that love me, and keep my commandments.

7 Thou shalt not take the name of the Lord thy God in vain: for the Lord will not hold him guiltless that taketh his name in vain.

8 Remember the sabbath day, to keep it holy. 9 Six days shalt thou labor, and do all thy work: 10 But the seventh day is the sabbath of the Lord thy God: in it thou shalt not do any work, thou, nor thy son, nor thy daughter, nor thy manservant, nor thy maidservant, nor thy cattle, nor thy stranger that is within thy gates: 11 For in six days the Lord made heaven and earth, the sea, and all that in them is, and rested the seventh day: wherefore the Lord blessed the sabbath day, and hallowed it.

12 Honor thy father and thy mother: that thy days may be long upon the land which the Lord thy God giveth thee.

13 Thou shalt not kill.

14 Thou shalt not commit adultery.

15 Thou shalt not steal.

16 Thou shalt not bear false witness against thy neighbor.

17 Thou shalt not covet thy neighbor's house; thou shalt not covet thy neighbor's wife, nor his manservant, nor his maidservant, nor his ox, nor his ass, nor any thing that is thy neighbor's.

18 And all the people saw the thunderings, and the lightnings, and the noise of the trumpet, and the mountain smoking: and when the people saw it, they removed, and stood afar off.

The high moral tone of the Ten Commandments contrasts with the elaborate directions for animal sacrifice in Leviticus, a brief selection of which follows. Do these passages from Leviticus represent a different cultural stage in Hebrew history? Would you expect animal sacrifice to have increased or decreased in importance as the moral law developed?

LEVITICUS

1

1 And the Lord called unto Moses, and spake unto him out of the tabernacle of the congregation, saying, 2 Speak unto the children of Israel, and say unto them, If any man of you bring an offering unto the Lord, ye shall bring your offering of the cattle, even of the herd, and of the flock.

3 If his offering be a burnt sacrifice of the herd, let him offer a male without blemish: he shall offer it of his own voluntary will at the door of the tabernacle of the congregation before the Lord. 4 And he shall put his hand upon the head of the burnt offering; and it shall be accepted for him to make atonement for him. 5 And he shall kill the bullock before the Lord: and the priests, Aaron's sons, shall bring the blood, and sprinkle the blood round about upon the altar that is by the door of the tabernacle of the congregation. 6 And he shall flay the burnt offering, and cut it into his pieces. 7 And the sons of Aaron the priest shall put fire upon the altar, and lay the wood in order upon the fire: 8 And the priests, Aaron's sons, shall lay the parts, the head, and the fat, in order upon the wood that is on the fire which is upon the altar: 9 But his inwards and his legs shall he wash in water: and the priest shall burn all on the altar, to be a burnt sacrifice, an offering made by fire, of a sweet savor unto the Lord.

Psalm 23, which follows, is attributed to King David, who ruled around 1000 B.C. It points backward in time to a day when the Hebrews were still shepherds. Who but shepherds would declare their Lord is "a shepherd"? What would farmers call their god? What would be the metaphor for a city god? Psalm 23 also points forward to a belief in a "for ever." You may have noticed that there has been no mention of an afterlife in the writings so far. Why?

PSALM 23

1 The Lord is my shepherd; I shall not want.

2 He maketh me to lie down in green pastures: He leadeth me beside the still waters.

3 He restoreth my soul: He leadeth me in the paths of righteousness for his name's sake.

4 Yea, though I walk through the valley of the shadow of death, I will fear no evil: for thou art with me; Thy rod and thy staff they comfort me.

5 Thou preparest a table before me in the presence of mine enemies: Thou anointest my head with oil; my cup runneth over.

6 Surely goodness and mercy shall follow me all the days of my life: And I will dwell in the house of the Lord for ever.

After the kingdoms of Israel and Judah were conquered, a new breed of Jewish thinkers, called prophets, tried to show how God had intended the conquest of His people as punishment for their transgressions. In the process these prophets reshaped God's message in significant ways. Instead of animal sacrifice or even ritual and law, they urged piety (religious feeling) and justice. One of the most eloquent of these prophets was Amos. This selection is Amos 5:21–24. How are these ideas different from those of Leviticus?

AMOS

5

21 I hate, I despise your feast days, and I will not delight in your solemn assemblies.

22 Though you offer me burnt offerings and your meat offerings, I will not accept them: neither will I regard the peace offerings of your fat beasts.

23 Take thou away from me the noise of thy songs; for I will not hear the melody of thy viols.

24 But let judgment run down as waters, and righteousness as a mighty stream.

The last of the prophets was the author of the book of Daniel, written about 165 B.C. The author presents himself as a Daniel taken to Babylon in the sixth century B.C. In this way, he is able to present Hebrew history from 600 to 165 B.C. as if from the eye of God, divinely preordained. Seen in this light, the Babylonian, Median, Persian, and Greek conquests of the Jews take on a providential meaning. They are not unexpected disasters but part of a larger divine plan. Events seemed to be moving to history's ultimate struggle. The end would come not only to the Kingdom of Israel, Daniel declares, but to all earthly kingdoms. There would be a final catastrophe for Jew and Gentile alike, a Last Judgment and a new dawn.

This is the first explicit mention in the Bible of an end to history and an afterlife, central ideas in Christianity. Daniel predicted the apocalypse, the end of the world. When would the end come? The first answer is after "time, times, and a half." Then he alludes to "the time that the daily sacrifice shall be taken away, and the abomination that maketh desolate set up." This refers to the desecration of the Hebrew temple in Jerusalem by the Syrian king Antiochus Epiphanes in 168 B.C. When will the end come? Now Daniel is specific: 1,290 days after the desecration by Antiochus. That would be 164 B.C., which is why we know the book was written in 165 B.C. Why does the next line say, in effect, "Blessed are those who wait 1,335 days"?

How is this selection from Daniel different from the other Bible selections you have read? In what ways is it similar? What function did this prophetic literature serve? Does it still today?

DANIEL

12

1 And at that time shall Michael stand up, the great prince which standeth for the children of thy people: and there shall be a time of trouble, such as never was since there was a nation even to that same time: and at that time thy people shall be delivered, every one that shall be found written in the book. 2 And many of them that sleep in the dust of the earth shall awake, some to everlasting life, and some to shame and everlasting contempt. 3 And they that be wise shall shine as the brightness of the firmament; and they that turn many to righteousness, as the stars for ever and ever. 4 But thou, O Daniel, shut up the words, and seal the book, even to the time of the end: many shall run to and fro, and knowledge shall be increased.

5 Then I Daniel looked, and, behold, there stood other two, the one on this side of the bank of the river, and the other on that side of the bank of the river. 6 And one said to the man clothed in linen, which was upon the waters of the river, How long shall it be to the end of these wonders? 7 And I heard the man clothed in linen, which was upon the waters of the river, when he held up his right hand and his left hand unto heaven, and swore by him that liveth for ever, that it shall be for a time, times, and a half; and when he shall have accomplished to scatter the power of the holy people, all of these things shall be finished.

8 And I heard, but I understood not: then said I, O my Lord, what shall be the end of these things? 9 And he said, Go thy way, Daniel: for the words are closed up and sealed till the time of the end. 10 Many shall be purified, and made white, and tried; but the wicked shall do wickedly: and none of the wicked shall understand; but the wise shall understand.

11 And from the time that the daily sacrifice shall be taken away, and the abomination that maketh desolate set up, there shall be a thousand two hundred and ninety days. 12 Blessed is he that waiteth, and cometh to the thousand three hundred and five and thirty days. 13 But go thou thy way till the end be: for thou shalt rest, and stand in thy lot at the end of the days.

Jesus was a Jew, familiar with the Bible, including the book of Daniel. Some Jews, like the Essenes whom we have come to know through the Dead Sea Scrolls, prepared for God's ending of a world polluted by Roman occupation in the same way that Daniel urged preparation in his time. The New Testament Gospels of Mark and Matthew show Jesus following the footsteps of John the Baptist, who taught preparation for the end. Matthew put John's role this way (Matt: 3:1–2):

> *In those days came John the Baptist, preaching in the wilderness of Judea, And saying, Repent Ye: for the kingdom of heaven is at hand.*

Jesus is also quoted as preaching that the end of the world is at hand. But the author of Matthew (written about A.D. 70) quotes Jesus giving two very different, perhaps contradictory, messages. One is that people should immediately repent because the end is at hand. The other is that there will be plenty of time before the end comes. Find these different messages in the following selection (Matt. 24). How do you account for these differences? Is it possible that one of these messages is closer to the actual sayings of Jesus and the other was added later? Would the followers of Jesus be more likely to add the urgent message or the long-term view? Why?

MATTHEW

24

1 And Jesus went out, and departed from the temple: and his disciples came to him for to show him the buildings of the temple. 2 And Jesus said unto them, See ye not all these things? verily I say unto You, There shall not be left here one stone upon another, that shall not be thrown down. 3 And as he sat upon the mount of Olives, the disciples came unto him privately, saying, Tell us, when shall these things be? and what shall be the sign of thy coming, and of the end of the world? 4 And Jesus answered and said unto them, Take heed that no man deceive you. 5 For many shall come in my name, saying, I am Christ; and shall deceive many. 6 And ye shall hear of wars and rumors of wars: see that ye be not troubled: for all these things must come to pass, but the end is not yet.

7 For nation shall rise against nation, and kingdom against kingdom: and there shall be famines, and pestilences, and earthquakes, in divers places. 8 All these are the beginning of sorrows. 9 Then shall they deliver you up to be afflicted, and shall kill you: and ye shall be hated of all nations for my name's sake. 10 And then shall many be offended, and shall betray one another, and shall hate one another. 11 And many false prophets shall rise, and shall deceive many. 12 And because iniquity shall abound, the love of many shall wax cold. 13 But he that shall endure unto the end, the same shall be saved. 14 And this gospel of the kingdom shall be preached in all the world for a witness unto all nations; and then shall the end come.

15 When ye therefore shall see the abomination of desolation, spoken of by Daniel the prophet, stand in the holy place (whoso readeth, let him understand), 16 Then let them which be in Judea flee into the mountains: 17 Let him which is on the housetop not come down to take any thing out of his house: 18 Neither let him which is in the field return back to take his clothes. 19 And woe unto them that are with child, and to them that give suck in those days! 20 But pray ye that your flight be not in the winter, neither on the sabbath day: 21 For then shall be great tribulation, such as was not since the beginning of the world to this time, no, nor ever shall be. 22 And except those days should be shortened, there should no flesh be saved: but for the elect's sake those days shall be shortened. 23 Then if any man shall say unto you, Lo, here is Christ, or there; believe it not. 24 For there shall arise false Christs, and false prophets, and shall show great signs and wonders; insomuch that, if it were possible, they shall deceive the very elect. 25 Behold, I have told you before. 26 Wherefore if they shall say unto you, Behold, he is in the desert; go not forth: behold he is in the secret chambers; believe it not. 27 For as the lightning cometh out of the east, and shineth even unto the west; so shall also the coming of the Son of man be. 28 For wheresoever the carcass is, there will the eagles be gathered together.

29 Immediately after the tribulation of those days shall the sun be darkened, and the moon shall not give her light, and the stars shall fall from heaven, and the powers of the heavens shall be shaken: 30 And then shall appear the sign of the Son of man in heaven: and then shall all the tribes of the earth mourn, and they shall see the Son of man coming in the clouds of heaven with power and great glory. 31 And he shall send his angels with a great sound of a trumpet, and they shall gather together his elect from the four winds, from one end of heaven to the other. 32 Now learn a parable of the fig tree; When his branch is yet tender, and putteth forth leaves, ye know that summer is nigh: 33 So likewise ye, when ye shall see all these things, know that it is near, even at the doors. 34 Verily I say unto you, This generation shall not pass, till all these things be fulfilled. 35 Heaven and earth shall pass away, but my words shall not pass away.

36 But of that day and hour knoweth no man, no, not the angels of heaven, but my Father only. 37 But as the days of Noe [Noah] were, so shall also the coming of the Son of man be. 38 For as in the days that were before the flood they were eating and drinking, marrying and giving in marriage, until the day that Noe entered into the ark, 39 And knew not until the flood came, and took them all away; so shall also the coming of the Son of man be. 40 Then shall two be in the field; the one shall be taken, and the other left. 41 Two women shall be grinding at the mill; the one shall be taken, and the other left.

20. PAUL AND HIS OPPONENTS

S. G. Brandon

Paul's idea that Jesus was the savior of mankind was seriously challenged by the disciples of Jesus in Jerusalem. That is the thesis of this essay by S. G. Brandon, a professor of comparative religion at Manchester University and author of a number of books on Jesus. In fact, Brandon says, the victory of Paul's interpretation of Jesus as the son of God rather than a Jewish Messiah was quite accidental. Who were Paul's opponents? Why did Paul have such a difficult time convincing them? How did Paul's view of Jesus eventually win out? What difference did that make?

Whoever turns the pages of that collection of ancient Christian writings called the New Testament must surely conclude that Paul was the apostle par excellence of the early church. For no less than thirteen separate items of that collection are entitled "Epistles of Paul," whereas to no other apostle are more than two letters assigned. And that is not all: not only do the writings of Paul comprise a quarter of the whole content of the New Testament: the larger part of the Acts of the Apostles, which sets out to record the early history of the Christian faith, is devoted to recounting his career.

But this impression of the primacy of Paul, both as a leader and a teacher in the early church, is strangely belied by the internal evidence of Paul's own writings. When we read many of these documents, we at once sense an atmosphere of great tension. Paul often appears profoundly concerned with what he regards as the pernicious influence of certain opponents who operate among his own converts; he sometimes uses the fiercest invective against them, but in a curiously oblique way, never naming them.

Herein lies one of the fundamental problems that beset our understanding of the origins of Christianity. How is it that Paul's own letters are so full of bitter controversy, yet the space given to his letters in the New Testament, as well as the evidence of the Acts, so signally attest his pre-eminence as the great leader and exponent of the faith, a position that is also abundantly confirmed in later Christian tradition?

An attempt to answer this question takes us into the intricate study of one of the most crucial episodes in the history of mankind. It is a field, too, where in recent years many new evaluations of traditional views have been taking place. The attempt is worth making, for it will afford an insight into the dramatic clash of two powerful personalities with whom lay the future of one of the world's greatest religions.

It is necessary at the outset to appreciate the nature of our chief sources of information about Paul and his career. His own writings, of course, are of primary importance; but since they mostly comprise letters dealing with specific situations among the Christian communities that he had founded in various places in the Roman Empire, their interpretation is no easy task. Paul rarely outlines the situation with which he is dealing, because it was obviously well known to his readers; consequently we are obliged to reconstruct the issue from passing references and allusions. Moreover, it must be remembered that the Epistles are essentially ex parte accounts of the basic conflict; we have no documents giving us the case of Paul's opponents, and our chief information about it must be inferred from Paul's own statements.

The Acts of the Apostles constitutes our secondary source of information. When it was written, some four decades separated it from the events it records; in the interval the destruction of Jerusalem by the Romans in A.D. 70 had decisively altered the internal situation of the church. The Acts, moreover, is clearly motivated by an apologetic purpose; it is concerned with tracing the triumphant spread of Christianity from its beginnings in Jerusalem to its establishment in Rome, the metropolis of the world. Thus it gives an idealized picture of the past, passing lightly over the conflicts and representing the leading figures as amicably disposed to each other. However, the evidence of the Acts can be of great value when carefully interpreted, and it does supply us with two precious facts about Paul: that he was a Hellenized Jew, being a native of the Cilician city of Tarsus, and that he enjoyed the privilege of Roman citizenship.

Both our sources are clear on one point of basic significance: Paul had never been an original disciple of Jesus but had joined the church sometime after the Crucifixion. Another important point on which the sources agree is that Paul was not converted to the new faith by the original community of disciples living in Jerusalem. His independence of the Jerusalem Christians at this crucial stage in his career was a matter of supreme importance to Paul, and it provides the key to the role that he was destined to play in the development of the new faith. Paul gives us his own account of the events that led up to his conversion in a context of great significance. He is writing to his converts in Galatia, who are in danger of being won over by his opponents, and he seeks to prove to them the greater authority of his own teaching. The passage is from Epistle to the Galatians (1:11–20).

> For I make known to you, brethren, as touching the gospel which was preached by me, that it is not after man. For neither did I receive it from man, nor was I taught it, but *it came to me* through revelation of Jesus Christ. For ye have heard of my manner of life in time past in the Jews' religion, how that beyond measure I persecuted the Church of God, and made havoc of it. And I advanced in the Jews' religion beyond many of mine own age among my countrymen, being more exceedingly zealous for the tradition of my fathers. But when it was the good pleasure of God, who separated me, *even* from my mother's womb, and called me through his grace, to reveal his Son in me, that I might preach him among the Gentiles; immediately I conferred not with flesh and blood. Neither went I up to Jerusalem to them which were apostles before me: but I went away in Arabia; and again I returned unto Damascus. Then after three years I went up to Jerusalem to visit Cephas, and tarried with him fifteen days. But other of the apostles saw I none, save James the Lord's brother. Now touching the things which I write unto you, behold, before God, I lie not.

The implications of this passage are immense. It informs us about three vital aspects of Paul's position. To defend his own teaching to his converts against that of his opponents Paul asserts that he had not derived it from any human source and, in particular, that he did not owe it to the original apostles at Jerusalem. This teaching, moreover, he claimed had been communicated to him directly by God for the express purpose of revealing "his Son in me, that I might preach him among the Gentiles." In other words, Paul maintains that his teaching was especially designed to be intelligible to those who were not Jews. He therefore admits by implication that his teaching differed from the tradition of the original apostles of Jerusalem, and he defends its novelty by claiming for it a direct divine origin.

We begin to perceive, then, the outlines of a truly amazing situation in the Christian church within some two decades of the Crucifixion. Paul is anxious to assert his independence of the Jerusalem apostles and to explain that his teaching has been divinely revealed for the Gentiles. Since he evidently had to defend his teaching against certain opponents, it becomes necessary to attempt to identify these opponents and the cause of their hostility to Paul.

In two separate writings Paul refers to these opponents and their rival teaching in very remarkable terms. In his Galatian letter (1:6–9) he writes in admonition to his converts:

I marvel that ye are so quickly removing from him that called you in the grace of Christ unto a different gospel; which is not another *gospel:* only there are some that trouble you, and would pervert the gospel of Christ. But though we, or an angel from heaven, should preach any gospel other than that we preached unto you, let him be anathema. As we have said before so say I now again: If any man preacheth unto you any gospel other than that which ye received, let him be anathema.

The extraordinary language used here is paralleled in another passage, which occurs in the Second Epistle to the Corinthians (11:3–6). A situation had apparently developed among his converts in the Greek city of Corinth similar to that with which Paul sought to deal in Galatia. He writes:

But I fear lest by any means, as the serpent beguiled Eve in his craftiness, your minds should be corrupted from the simplicity and the purity that is toward Christ. For if he that cometh preacheth another Jesus, whom we did not preach, or if ye received a different spirit, which he did not receive, or a different gospel, which ye did not accept, ye do well to bear with *him.* For I reckon that I am not a whit behind the very chiefest apostles. But though I be rude in speech, yet *am* I not in knowledge; nay, in everything we have made *it* manifest among all men to you-ward.

Paul's language in both these passages is as amazing as it is significant. Paul does in fact attest to the presence in the Church of two rival interpretations of the faith. For the references to "another Jesus" and "a different gospel" must mean that Paul's opponents were teaching a different version of the meaning of the person and roles of Jesus from Paul's version.

But who *were* these opponents? Obviously they were not some obscure sect of heretics; otherwise Paul would surely have repudiated them with all that vehemence of utterance of which he was capable. Clearly they were men who could operate effectively enough within Paul's own mission-field to cause him profound concern. But, curiously, Paul never explicitly names them or questions their authority. He does, however, give a clue to their identity in the latter of the passages just quoted, when he significantly adds, after referring to this rival teaching, "I reckon that I am not a whit behind the very chiefest apostles." In view of the facts just considered, and of Paul's concern to assert his independence of the Jerusalem apostles, there can indeed be little doubt that those opponents who taught "another Jesus" were either the leaders of the church in Jerusalem or their emissaries. In his Galatian epistle, describing a later visit to Jerusalem, Paul gives more details of these leaders. They formed a kind of triumvirate of what he calls *stuloi* (pillars); their names are James, Cephas, and John. The order in which these names are given is significant. James was certainly the leader; he precedes Cephas, i.e., Peter, who had apparently been the leader of the apostles during the lifetime of Jesus. The fact that James was the brother of Jesus (Galatians 1:19) probably accounts, at least in part, for this preeminence. But a mystery seems to surround this James. According to the Gospels, he had not been an original disciple—indeed he had actually been unsympathetic to Jesus. The Acts is strangely silent about his antecedents; it represents him suddenly, without explanation, as the head of the church of Jerusalem. How he ousted Peter from the leadership of the new movement remains a veiled episode in the Christian documents. His blood relationship to Jesus obviously gave him great prestige, but it is evident that he was also a man of strong character and ability. In his Galatian letter Paul tells of a dispute at Antioch over whether Jewish Christians might eat with Gentile believers; Peter, who had agreed with Paul on the matter, had later withdrawn on the arrival of emissaries from James—surely a significant act of submission.

It was, then, the teaching of the Jerusalem church, presided over by James, from which Paul differed and against which he tacitly directs his innuendo by describing it as a "different gospel" that taught "another Jesus." But how did this Jerusalem gospel differ so radically from that of Paul? In brief, since it is certain that the Jerusalem Christians continued to worship in the Temple at Jerusalem and to practice the ritual customs of Judaism, it is evident that they did not regard their faith in Jesus as inconsistent with Jewish orthodoxy or as separating them from their national religion. To them Jesus was the promised Messiah of Israel. His death by crucifixion was a problem, since there was no expectation that the Messiah should die—rather he was to be the mighty champion who would free Israel from subjugation to a heathen conqueror. But Jesus' death could be explained as a martyr's death for Israel at the hands of the Romans. And it was believed that God had raised him from this death, so that he might soon return with supernatural power to "restore the kingdom to Israel." Such, then, was the "gospel" of the Jerusalem Christians, it was conceived essentially in terms of Jewish thought, and it was calculated to emphasize and maintain that claim to a unique spiritual status and destiny that characterized Judaism. According to the evidence of the Acts, a considerable number of priests and Pharisees had, significantly, been won to the new movement.

If such was the "gospel of Jerusalem," what was Paul's version of the new faith? It would seem that before his conversion Paul was scandalized by the new movement because it taught "a crucified Messiah." On his conversion, whatever the true nature of that mysterious episode may be, Paul became convinced that the crucified Jesus was alive and of divine status. But he still had to explain to himself the apparent scandal of the Crucifixion. It was at this point, so it would seem, that Paul came to differ fundamentally from the Jerusalem Christians and to assert his original independence of them. To him the death of Jesus could not be just a martyr's death for Israel; it must have some more profound and universal meaning. It was in his attempt to interpret this meaning that Paul surely drew, though unconsciously, on his Hellenistic background.

This Hellenistic background teemed with religious cults and esoteric philosophies that promised salvation of various kinds. Consciously Paul would have vigorously rejected them as the service of false gods or "philosophy and vain deceit." But he could not have escaped their influence, since they reflected the aspirations and fears of contemporary Greco-Roman society and provided the current religious vocabulary. Two ideas of key importance that these cults and philosophies severally enshrined and propagated were those of the savior-god and of the fallen state of man. The classic pattern of the savior-god was afforded by the ancient Egyptian deity Osiris. The initiates of his mysteries believed that he had once died and risen again to life and that by ritual assimilation with him they too could win immortal life. The various esoteric philosophies that can be described as Gnostic taught that each human being was compounded of an immortal soul imprisoned in a physical body. This unhappy condition was due to an original fall of the soul from its abode of light and bliss and its involvement in matter. By thus becoming incarnated in this world the soul had also become subject to the demonic powers that inhabited the planets and controlled the world. From this state of perdition it could be rescued by acquiring a proper knowledge (gnosis) of its nature; emancipated from its involvement in matter, it would ascend through the celestial spheres to its original home.

Such ideas were foreign to orthodox Judaism. Hence it is significant that Paul, seeking to interpret the meaning of the Crucifixion, does so in terms that presuppose that mankind is enslaved by demonic powers, from whom they are redeemed through the death and resurrection of a divine savior. Thus he writes: "So we also, when we were children, were held in bondage under the *stoicheia* of the world. But when the fulness of the time came, God sent forth his Son, born of a woman, born under the law, that he might redeem them which were under the law, that we might receive the adoption of sons." The word *stoicheia*, which the Revised Standard Version translates as "elemental spirits," means in this context the demonic powers that were identified with the astral phenomena. Consequently Paul here envisages the human situation as one of subjection to these demonic powers until redemption is won by the incarnated Son of God. Paul clearly regards the crucifixion of Jesus as achieving this redemption, but of the way in which this was achieved he is not clear. Sometimes he invokes the concepts of the Jewish sacrificial cultus, thereby implying that the death of Jesus was a sacrifice; but who demanded it and to whom it was made, he is not explicit. A more coherent conception, which links up with the thought of the Galatian passage just quoted, is found in his First Epistle to the Corinthians (2:7–8): "But we speak God's wisdom in mystery, *even* the *wisdom* that hath been hidden, which God foreordained before the *aeons* unto our glory; which none of the *archontes* of this *aeon* knoweth; for had they known it, they would not have crucified the Lord of glory." In this passage Paul professes to explain the Crucifixion as an event, arranged for in a divine plan conceived before the *aeons*, whereby the *archontes* of this *aeon* were led, unwittingly, to crucify a supernatural being called "the Lord of glory." Since "*archontes* of this *aeon*" is in effect an alternative designation for the demonic powers described as the *stoicheia* in the Galatian letter, a further phase of Paul's interpretation of the death of Jesus can be discerned. In other words, the hold that the demonic powers had over mankind was broken when they were deceived into crucifying the "Lord of glory."

By employing ideas and terminology current in the Greco-Roman world, Paul thus fashioned an interpretation, intelligible to his Gentile converts, of a movement that was in origin and essence Jewish. But that was not all. Whereas the rite of circumcision was the form of initiation into the spiritual privileges of Judaism, baptism was adopted as the means of entry into the church of Christ. Paul's explanation of it is also indicative of the milieu of syncretistic faith and practice upon which he drew. He writes to the Christians in Rome:

> Or are ye ignorant that all we who were baptized into Christ Jesus were baptized into his death? We were buried therefore with him through baptism into death: that like as Christ was raised from the dead through the glory of the Father, so we also might walk in newness of life. For if we have become united with *him* by the likeness of his death, we shall be also *by the likeness of* his resurrection.

In other words, according to Paul, in baptism the neophyte was ritually assimilated to Christ in his death in order to be one with him in his resurrection. When Paul wrote, for nearly three thousand years in Egypt resurrection from death had been sought by ritual assimilation with the dying-rising god Osiris.

Such, then, was the gospel with which Paul believed that he had been divinely entrusted for preaching to the Gentiles. In effect it replaced the presentation of Jesus as the Messiah of Israel by that of Jesus as the divine savior of mankind; and it presupposed that all men, whether Jew or Gentile, were equally in need of the same kind of salvation.

Such a gospel diverged fundamentally from the teaching of the Jerusalem Christians, and it was obnoxious to them. For not only did it equate the Jew with the Gentile, thereby robbing the former of his cherished sense of spiritual superiority; it made the Messiah of Israel into the savior of those heathen who had done him to death and who daily opposed his people.

When the Jerusalem leaders understood the nature and implications of Paul's teaching, they set about opposing it. They were in a strong position to do this: whereas they could repudiate Paul as a latecomer to the faith, he could not openly challenge their authority as the original disciples and eyewitnesses of Jesus. Accordingly they sent out their emissaries among Paul's converts, asserting that theirs was the original and authentic version of the faith.

As his letters eloquently attest, the activities of these Jerusalem emissaries seriously threatened Paul's position, undermining his authority with his converts and causing them to accept a "different gospel" and "another Jesus." The situation eventually became so serious that Paul resolved to go to Jerusalem in an attempt to negotiate some *modus vivendi* with the authorities there. He sought to strengthen his case by taking with him a delegation of his Gentile converts and a considerable sum of money, which he had collected from his churches for the support of the mother church of Jerusalem. Paul seems to have known that a visit to Jerusalem might be dangerous for him, and according to the narrative of the Acts, he received several divine warnings of impending danger. To have persisted in going against such advice surely attests that he felt the need to achieve an understanding with the Jerusalem leaders was urgent.

The outcome of the visit is recorded in Acts 21; its testimony must be evaluated in terms of that apologetic purpose that, as we have already noticed, inspires the work.

Paul was received by James in the presence of the elders of the Jerusalem church and is represented as reporting on the success of his work among the Gentiles. Paul's coming to Jerusalem must clearly have embarrassed the Christians there, and James comes quickly to the point about the matter.

> Thou seest, brother, how many thousands there are among the Jews of them that have believed; and they are all zealous for the law; and they have been informed concerning thee, that thou teachest all the Jews which are among the Gentiles to forsake Moses, telling them not to circumcise their children, neither to walk after the customs. What is it therefore? They will certainly hear that thou art come.

The accusation was in fact a calumny, but it represented a plausible deduction from the logic of Paul's teaching. Reference to it by James was an astute move to solve the difficulty that Paul's visit had created. Accordingly he proposes a test of Paul's Jewish orthodoxy:

> Do therefore this that we say to thee: We have four men which have a vow on them; these take, and purify thyself with them; and be at charges for them,

that they may shave their heads: and all shall know that there is no truth in the things whereof they have been informed concerning thee; but that thou thyself also walkest orderly, keeping the law.

Paul was placed in a dilemma. James had shrewdly detected the weakness of his position, in that while the logic of his teaching negated the peculiar spiritual claims of Judaism, he still endeavored himself to remain an orthodox Jew. Now James challenged him to give a public demonstration of his orthodoxy, for the ceremony in which Paul should take part, i.e., the discharge of the so-called Nazarite vow, was performed in the Temple. To refuse the test was tantamount to a declaration of apostasy from his native faith: but to accept it was to admit the validity of Judaism on the order of the Jerusalem church.

Paul felt obliged to submit, but the sequel was disastrous to his cause. While performing the rites in the Temple courts, he was set upon by a Jewish mob and only rescued from death by the intervention of the Roman guard from the nearby fortress of the Antonia. To escape subsequent trial and certain condemnation by the Jewish authorities, Paul invoked his right as a Roman citizen to be tried before the imperial tribunal. After recording his survival from shipwreck en route to Rome, the narrative of the Acts finally leaves Paul a prisoner there. What was his ultimate fate is unrecorded. According to ancient tradition he suffered martyrdom in Rome, and there is much reason for thinking that his appeal to Caesar did not prove successful.

The arrest of Paul probably took place in the year 55, and from that date he seems to have been removed from personal contact with his converts. What, then, was the fate of his work?

It would seem reasonable to conjecture, since Paul had previously felt his position to be gravely threatened by the Jerusalem Christians, that after his arrest the defeat of his cause was inevitable. His converts would have been left defenseless against the propaganda of the Jerusalem emissaries. That this did actually happen seems to be confirmed by the prophecy that is attributed to Paul when he took his farewell of the elders of the church of Ephesus: the prophecy is recorded by the author of Acts, who knew what had happened:

I know that after my departure grievous wolves shall enter in among you, not sparing the flock; and from among your own selves shall men arise, speaking perverse things to draw away the disciples after them.

If this situation had continued, without doubt Paul's interpretation of Christianity would have perished, and the faith evoked by Jesus would have remained but the belief of a small messianic sect within the fold of Judaism. But this was not to be. In the year 66 the Jewish nationalists raised the standard of revolt against Roman rule in Judaea. After four years of bitter warfare, the Jewish state was overthrown, Jerusalem ruined and its Temple destroyed. In the course of that cataclysm the Christian church of Jerusalem disappeared.

In consequence of these tremendous events the future of Christianity was completely changed. The hold of the mother church of Jerusalem was broken, and the Gentile churches were left to work out their own destiny. This signal overthrow of Jewish Christianity led, understandably, to a rehabilitation of Paul's reputation as the great exponent of the faith. When the author of Acts wrote his story of the beginnings of the Church, magnifying the part played by Paul, others were searching for Paul's writings as the inspired teaching of a revered master and saint. Eventually the *Corpus Paulinum* was formed, becoming one of the earliest components of the New Testament, but bearing also within it evidence both of the eclipse and the rehabilitation of Paul in the mind of the Church. For the formation of Christian theology this rehabilitation was definitive. From Paul's teaching has stemmed the foundational doctrine of Christianity; namely, the incarnation of the Son of God, in the person of Jesus of Nazareth, to be the savior of mankind.

21. THE SIGNIFICANCE OF CHRISTMAS

Ernest Jones

Ernest Jones is known as the student, friend, and biographer of Sigmund Freud and as an important psychologist himself. In this essay he brings a rich background in the classics, a knowledge of anthropology, and Freudian psychological theory to bear on an important and interesting question. Why, according to Jones, did Christianity succeed over Mithraism and other popular religions of the Roman Empire? What elements of popular pagan culture and human psychological need did Christianity satisfy most effectively?

To ask why we keep Christmas is to ask a good question, i.e., one which one does not usually ask because of taking something for granted. Yet a moment's reflection will show that there is much worth in asking the question. To begin with, we might wonder why Christmas is the only one of the Christian religious festivals that makes any appeal to people who are not Christians. If someone becomes a sceptic or atheist he is apt to lose interest in the important Christian dates; he is likely to forget what ideas are commemorated by the words Epiphany, Whitsun, Advent or Palm Sunday; Eastertide loses its emotional significance and becomes merely a spring holiday. But Christmas commonly retains as much meaning as ever. And the same is often true of people with other religions who live in contact with Christians. I remember when crossing to America a couple of years ago in December finding that nearly half of the passengers were American Jews rushing through in order to be "home for Christmas"; and no doubt the same observation could be made in any other year. There must therefore be something in the idea of Christmas that appeals to far more than interest in the date, or even the fact, of Christ's birth.

Perhaps we ought to begin further back in our inquiry and raise the question of why mankind keeps festivals at all on particular dates. It was Sir Isaac Newton, in 1730, who first drew attention to the astronomical associations of Christmas and other festivals. Many years ago General Furlong, the distinguished anthropologist, in his famous *Rivers of Life,* took the trouble to collect the dates of festivals in all parts of the world and to construct a curve indicating the times of year in which they most often occurred. The curve revealed the unmistakable fact that by far the greatest number of festivals was held at one or other of the four cardinal points in the earth's journey round the sun. The most favoured times are those of the summer and winter solstice, towards the end of June and December respectively, when the sun begins to wane or wax, when the days begin to shorten or lengthen. The times of year next in favour are those of the spring or autumn equinox, towards the end of March or of September. There can be little doubt that man has always tended, sometimes even consciously so, to associate his aspirations and emotions with these fundamental changes relating to the source of all life, the sun. It is well known how extensively the idea of the sun has permeated the religions of the world, He being the most visible and striking emblem of both the life-giving and the life-destroying forces of the universe.

We can further divide the innumerable religious festivals of the world into two broad groups, happy and unhappy ones or—to speak more accurately—into cheerful and solemn ones. There are festivals of celebration, of rejoicing; there are occasions of sheer merriment and they have at times passed over into bacchanalian orgies. Christmas plainly belongs to this group. On the other hand there are festivals which mark man's periodic need to search his heart, to make a serious review of his position in the Universe or to question his purpose in life and take a strict account with himself. The former group indicate moods of easy conscience, the latter of uneasy conscience.

To get back to the particular festival of Christmas. Before trying to ascertain what it stands for it is necessary to know something of its historical background. Literally, of course, it signifies the dates of Christ's birthday. But actually we have no knowledge of what time of the year that fell in, and even the year itself is uncertain, so there must have been some other reason for choosing a particular day on which to celebrate it. In spite of hints in the New Testament that the birth took place at the beginning of the Jewish New Year, i.e., at about the time of the autumn equinox, there was in early Christian times a number of sects who proclaimed the spring equinox as the most suitable date. Most Christians, however, seem at first to have regarded the matter of His physical birth as too mundane or even desecrating a thought to dwell on; in A.D. 245, for instance, Origen declared it to be a sin even to think of celebrating the birthday of Christ "as if he were a King Pharaoh." They confined their attention to the date when the Holy Spirit took possession of Him; that was His real Divine birth. This moment they regarded as the occasion of His baptism, and to commemorate it they chose the date of 6th January, now called Epiphany. We do not know why they chose that date, but it was one when many festivals were held in the Ancient World—probably on astronomical grounds, it being the first day on which the morning hours begin to lengthen. Epiphany and Baptism were for many centuries closely associated. By the fourth century the date of 6th January was universally accepted in the Eastern World as the time to celebrate the birth of Christ, whether the human or the divine one, and, in the oldest Christian nation (the Armenian), that is still the date adhered to.

The theological controversies on the nature of Christ decided, however, that His divinity began at birth, so that attention was directed there. Discarding some earlier forgeries we can say that the first authentic date when Christmas Day was recorded in connection with the physical birth of Christ was A.D. 354. The matter seems to have been settled in A.D. 329 at a Council known by the name of Dionysius the Little. In A.D. 400 an Imperical rescript ordered all theatres to be closed on that day (as well as at Epiphany and Easter), and in the course of the fifth century 25th December was firmly established in both East and West as the proper time to celebrate the anniversary of Christ.

The reasons why the festival was established at all, and why that particular date was selected for the purpose, are both interesting and complex. A Syrian writer of the period (a Christian) is quoted for the following frank description of the motives. "The reason why the fathers transferred the celebration of 6th January to 25th December was this. It was a custom of the heathen to celebrate on the same 25th December the birthday of the Sun, at which they kindled lights in token of festivity. In these solemnities and festivities the Christians also took part. Accordingly when the doctors of the Church perceived that the Christians had a leaning to this festival, they took counsel and resolved that the true Nativity should be solemnized on that day." The political reason had of course to be defined by the Church, and both St. Augustine and the Pope Leo the Great found it necessary to rebuke Christians for still associating Christmas with the rebirth of the Sun. The fact remains that the date had already been established in innumerable pagan religions in just this sense. The 25th of December was the birthday of many a Persian, Phoenician, Egyptian, and even Teutonic Sun-God. And the decision was in line with the general syncretizing activities of the Church in the early centuries when it was combating paganism: it cannot be coincidence that—to quote a few examples—the date of Easter coincides with the similar celebration of the Phrygian god Attis (so popular in Rome) at the vernal equinox; that the festival of the Assumption of the Virgin in August has replaced the festival of the goddess Diana; the festival of St. George in April has replaced the ancient festival of the goddess Pales (one which the Romans later combined with that of Dea Roma); that the festival of St. John the Baptist in June has succeeded to the water festivals of Adonis in midsummer; that the feast of All Souls in November continues the Keltic Feast of the Dead at that time (the beginning of their New Year), and so on.

The matter was, however, a good deal more complex than the Syrian writer supposed, and can be elucidated only by considering the life-and-death struggle that Christianity was going through in the first three or four centuries in Rome. When faith in the orthodox Roman religion began to wane a number of competing Oriental ones crowded in to secure the succession, one of which was the Christian one. The general characteristic of them was the theme of a young Saviour-God who dies, either periodically or once for all, and thereby assures the eternal salvation (from the wrath of the Almighty) of those who believe in him. The series included Attis, Osiris, Adonis, Mithra, and Jesus himself. With all of them except the last two mentioned the belief in a powerful Mother goddess, whose help secured the reassuring Resurrection of the dying God, played an important part. And it was just those two that were ahead in the struggle for general acceptance, the only two, incidentally, in which the young God died only once and afterwards reigned in heaven. There is little doubt that Mithraism, the religion especially of the army, was the most dangerous rival to Christianity, and the issue of the conflict between the two faiths appears for a time to have hung in the balance. There was much similarity in their beliefs, rituals and moral aspirations: virginity, baptism, holy communion, purity, etc. But Mithraism had one serious weakness, on which the Christians seized and thereby ensured their ultimate success. Its attitude and beliefs were exclusively masculine. In its ritual the young God took up the challenge of the wrathful father, slew him and reigned in his stead, whereas in Christianity he submits in a more feminine fashion to the will of the Father and by sacrificing himself assuages His wrath. Consistently with this solution Mithraism made the conflict one entirely between two males; there was no feminine element, no goddess, in its theology, and women were excluded from its worship. Christianity here saw its chance and incorporated from the other religions the element that had been missing in both itself and Mithraism.

Isis, Cybele, Rhea, Astarte and the rest began a new lease of life. Mary, who had been little but the necessary vehicle for the begetting of a son, was rapidly raised in status and from being the Mother of God was given in the fourth century the exalted title of Queen of Heaven. Her virginal conception, the usual belief then attaching to the birth of heroes and gods, had long been established. From then on the increasing Mariolatry demanded that more attention be paid, not only to her intercessory and saving powers, but especially her maternal role. Mother and Infant, resembling Isis and Horus, began to play a more central part in Christianity, and it still does in Roman Catholicism, so that the circumstances of the birth, including its date and the appropriate festival, assumed a cardinal importance. One might even wonder whether Christianity would have survived had it not instituted the festival of Christmas with all that it signified!

In the crisis the Roman Christians would not have been long in doubt about choosing the actual date. It was indeed dictated by the situation. In the Julian calendar 25th December was reckoned as the winter solstice and hence as the Nativity of the Sun when the day begins to lengthen and the power of the sun to increase. In Eastern countries the pagan celebrants of the Nativity had retired to inner shrines or caves, from which at midnight they issued with cries of "The Virgin has brought forth! The light is waxing!" The Egyptians even represented the new-born sun by the image of an infant which on his birthday, the winter solstice, they exhibited to the worshippers. The Virgin who thus bore a son on that day was of course the great Oriental Mother-Goddess, who had many forms and names in different countries. Mithra after conquering the sun had become a Sun-God himself with the title of Solus Invictus, and his festival, the Mithrakana, was appropriately celebrated on 25th December. If, therefore, the Christians had to compete with such a formidable rival they had to assert that it was *their* God who had been born on that significant date, and surely of a Heavenly Virgin.

From the vast importance of the sun in earlier days one might suppose that man was anxiously concerned lest he might fail them, since it was evident that without his heat and light life could not go on. This might occasionally have been so, to judge by the anxiety displayed during an eclipse and the human efforts (tom-toms, etc.) made to assist him in his fight with the monster apparently swallowing him. But I am persuaded that the case was really otherwise, and that the sun was on the contrary much more a source of security. One must remember that, in the East particularly, celestial phenomena were observed with astonishing accuracy, and that the motions of the stars and planets were known in great detail; astronomy was in fact the first of the sciences. Those people knew perfectly well that the sun would wax after 25th December just as surely as he would wane before then and that day would infallibly follow night. Uncertain human happenings could therefore be referred to his activities as a means of obtaining reassurance. We still say, as an expression of the utmost certainty, "It is sure as the sun will rise tomorrow." The sun, therefore, belonged to the external absolutes of the universe, like God, and human uncertainties that could be brought into association with him, or better still identification, would to that extent be dispelled.

Comparative anthropology has clearly shown that man has always tended to identify the changes in the sun's apparent powers with the most vital of his own activities. The waxing young sun of spring brings times for confident rejoicing which culminate in the mad triumph of Midsummer Eve, the German's Johannisnacht. Then the bonfires shoot upward and proclaim the apothegm of human and divine power. How wise were the Fathers of the Revolution to choose the beginning of July to declare their independence and thus provide a whole nation with the opportunity of perpetuating man's delight in the crackling of fire at that time of the year! On the other hand, the diminishing strength of the sun arouses by association the deep fears man always nurses of his own failing powers, of impotence, old age, and death—with the terrors of what may follow this. The re-birth of the sun, therefore, has often been the greatest reassurance he can receive of eternal hope, always provided—and that was vital—that he was identified with the Deity. That a God, however powerful, should periodically (most often annually), die, to be constantly re-born, is the central theme of many religions. It is fitting that this re-birth should take place on what, according to Bede, the pagan Anglo-Saxons called "Mother-Night," i.e., Christmas Eve, the date from which their new year commenced. The Sun and the God may die, but they will surely be eternally re-born, so all is well.

The most natural expression of the re-birth idea is the association with a newborn babe, and to Christians it is the birth of the babe Jesus that is the central emblem of all that Christmas stands for. In the Roman Catholic Church, in particular, there is no moment of the year in which the Madonna and Babe are more adored; they can occupy the centre of interest to the exclusion of all other theological preoccupations. In Catholic countries Christmas is little else; the more mundane accompaniments and ceremonies of Northern Christmases are postponed to another date.

The feeling, however, that Christmas is in some deep sense a pagan festival has evinced itself with a strange persistence throughout the ages. The Western Church was responsible for its incorporation in the Christian religion, and the Eastern Church for long protested against what they regarded as a pagan innovation. Behind this word "pagan" surely lies the idea of Mother-Goddess worship, the attraction of which so often seduced the patriarchal monotheistic Hebrews and indeed the Christian Church itself. It is perhaps fundamentally what Protestantism protested against, following the Hebrew prophets. Our own Puritans have felt very strongly on the matter, and an Act of Parliament in 1644 forbade the celebration of Christmas as being a heathen festival, until the Merry

Monarch once more sanctioned it. To this day many Protestant sects, notably in Scotland, look distinctly askance at Christmas as being something alien to the pure faith. Ever since the Reformation this attitude of suspicion has connected Christmas with what has often been called the "paganism" of the Roman Catholic Church. An amusing example is recorded of a fanatical member of Parliament moving that, in order to eliminate any association with the Mass, the word itself be purified by being changed to Christ-tide; by way of answer, however, he was exhorted to initiate the change by altering his own name from Thomas Massey Massey to Thotide Tidey Tidey!

To return to the concept of the sacrificial God. It is probably that this was preceded by the custom of sacrificing a king from time to time, either when he grew old or even, as Frazer has expounded in his *Golden Bough,* annually.

However much such a king may have acquiesced in the proceeding, sharing the belief of his people that it would accrue to the good of the community, it was inevitable that he should also feel some objection to it; so it was not surprising that an alternative procedure should be sought for. Two were found. One was to displace his majesty to the skies in the form either of a God like Adonis or an actual Sun-God. That the Sun should decline almost to death every year and then arise refreshed in his glory and strength was a solution satisfying to all concerned and was a relatively innocent form of regicide (i.e., parricide). The other, and perhaps more obvious, solution was to provide a substitute, a mock king. Here we touch on the vast theme of the scapegoat in mythology. In Babylonia, for example, the king originally had to die at the end of his year's rule, ostensibly so as to go and help the God Marduk in his periodical struggle with the monsters of chaos in the regions below, but after a time a criminal was set up for a few days as a "mock king" and then executed in the king's stead. The periodical rebellion against authority (ultimately the Father) implied in the ceremony is attested by the general license of the rejoicings and by the curious reversal of slaves and masters so characteristic of the Roman Saturnalia (15th December to 1st January) and before that the Persian Sacaea and the Babylonian Zagmuk festivals. Relics of the mock king idea have persisted into historical times. In the early centuries of our era the Roman soldiers stationed in the Balkans had the custom of choosing by lot one of their number to preside over the Saturnalia as king of the revels. After he was feted and boisterously paid court to he had to complete his career by standing at the altar and killing himself. St. Dasius is said to have achieved his fame (and martyrdom) by refusing to play this part on the ground of its being a pagan custom. In parts of central Europe a troupe of masqueraders are still headed by a "fool" or "wild man" who leads their carol singing, but with less lethal results than formerly. In the Middle Ages the "Feast of Fools" was similarly presided over by someone who was given the various titles of "Lord of Misrule," "Abbot of Unreason," "King of the Bean," etc., and who reigned from All Hallows' Eve till Christmas. His position was abrogated in Scotland by Act of Parliament in 1555. A mock service was held in the Church, with an imitation Mass, robes were worn inside out and music sheets held upside down—a general reversal very reminiscent of the Satanic Black Mass and like that indicating a violent reaction against divine authority. The only trace left of it all nowadays is the license of kissing anyone encountered under the mistletoe, as part of the jollification of a Merry Christmas.

Perhaps the last emblem of the sacrificed god or king was the ceremony of the boar's head at the Christmas banquet, thus turning it into a totemistic feast. For the boar, sacred to the God Frey in the north and to others in the East, is one of the patriarchal symbols in the unconscious; in his parricidal ritual Mithra slew sometimes a bull, sometimes a boar. And he was treated as a royal personage, his entry to the banqueting hall being preceded by a flourish of trumpets and similar rituals. In the Balkans and in Scandinavia cakes or loaves in the form of a pig are still sold at Christmas, reminding the anthropologist how long the impulse to cannibalistic parricide persists in the folklore of the people.

The many other constituents of the Christmas festival accord with its significance as just described. Some date from Rome, but more have been added as Christianity advanced northward and in doing so incorporated preexisting customs and rituals. Some of them have just been mentioned. Others are the Yule log, cut down by a young man and burned ceremoniously to rekindle the sun; holly and evergreens to show that there is still life in nature; the Christmas tree, which was added only in the seventeenth century but which has an ancient tradition from the days of tree worship (may trees, etc.); the Christmas candles which replace the old Feast of Lights. All life will surely be somehow renewed and one need not fear extinction.

It is hard to determine how and when Christmas became so predominantly the children's festival it now is—at least in Northern countries. The birth of a babe is, it is true, its central feature, and in this connection it is interesting that to receive a present—which is what Christmas means to children—is in the unconscious mind always associated with the idea of the birth of a baby—the primordial gift *par excellence*. Oddly enough, in Catholic countries this custom is usually postponed to 1st January, such as with the French *étrennes* on the *jour de l'an*. The giver, Father Christmas—evidently Father Time himself—has in the past century got fused with the figure of St. Nicholas, the Archbishop of Myra, the children's saint, famous for his habit of giving presents; and Santa Klaus—the American corruption of the Dutch Colonists' San Nicolaas—is now his accepted name in all English-speaking countries. In Germany he was identified, as Knecht Rupprecht, with Odin himself, the god who sacrificed himself by hanging on a tree, his side pierced by a spear, for nine days; and so St. Nicholas wears his broad-brimmed hat and rides his white horse. In Holland hay has to be put out for the white horse on 6th December, St. Nicholas' own Day; on this day also Perchta, the companion of Odin, comes to inspect households to see if they have been properly managed.

Historically expressed, the festival of Christmas is thus a fusion of many strains of pagan customs and beliefs, but one which Christianity has inspired with a fresh spiritual significance. Psychologically it represents the ideal of resolving all family discord in a happy reunion, and to this it owes its perennial attraction. These two points of view are seen to be identical when one remembers that the ultimate significance of all religions is the attempted solution on a cosmic stage of the loves and hatreds that take their source in the complicated relations of children and parents.

CHAPTER SEVEN

Indian Civilization

22. THE *BHAGAVAD-GITA*

The Bhagavad-Gita is the best-known work in Hindu religious literature. It is part of a larger epic called the Mahabharata, *a story of two feuding families that may have had its origins in the Aryan invasion of 1500 B.C. The Bhagavad-Gita is a philosophical interlude that interrupts the story just before the great battle between the two families. It poses some fundamental questions about the nature of life, death, and proper religious behavior. It begins as the leader of one of the battling armies, Arjuna, asks why he should fight his friends and relatives on the other side. The answer comes from none other than the god Krishna, who has taken the form of Arjuna's charioteer.*

What is Krishna's answer? What will happen to the people Arjuna kills? What will happen to Arjuna? What would happen to Arjuna if he refused to fight the battle? What does this selection tell you about Hindu ideas of life, death, and the self?

LORD KRISHNA

You grieve for those beyond grief,
and you speak words of insight;
but learned men do not grieve
for the dead or the living.

Never have I not existed,
nor you, nor these kings;
and never in the future
shall we cease to exist.

Just as the embodied self
enters childhood, youth, and old age,
so does it enter another body;
this does not confound a steadfast man.

Contacts with matter make us feel
heat and cold, pleasure and pain.

Arjuna, you must learn to endure
fleeting things—they come and go!

When these cannot torment a man,
when suffering and joy are equal
for him and he has courage,
he is fit for immortality.

Nothing of nonbeing comes to be,
nor does being cease to exist;   ,
the boundary between these two
is seen by men who see reality.

Indestructible is the presence
that pervades all this;
no one can destroy
this unchanging reality.

Our bodies are known to end,
but the embodied self is enduring,
indestructible, and immeasurable;
therefore, Arjuna, fight the battle!

He who thinks this self a killer
and he who thinks it killed,
both fail to understand;
it does not kill, nor is it killed.

It is not born,
it does not die;
having been,
it will never not be;
unborn, enduring,
constant, and primordial,
it is not killed   — soul lives; soul is 'recycled'
when the body is killed.

Arjuna, when a man knows the self .
to be indestructible, enduring, unborn,
unchanging, how does he kill
or cause anyone to kill?

As a man discards
worn-out clothes
to put on new

and different ones,
so the embodied self
discards
its worn-out bodies
to take on other new ones.

Weapons do not cut it,
fire does not burn it,
waters do not wet it,
wind does not wither it.

It cannot be cut or burned;
it cannot be wet or withered;
it is enduring, all-pervasive,
fixed, immovable, and timeless.

It is called unmanifest,
inconceivable, and immutable;
since you know that to be so,
you should not grieve!

If you think of its birth
and death as ever-recurring,
then too, Great Warrior,
you have no cause to grieve!

Death is certain for anyone born,
and birth is certain for the dead;
since the cycle is inevitable,
you have no cause to grieve!

Creatures are unmanifest in origin,
manifest in the midst of life,
and unmanifest again in the end.
Since this is so, why do you lament!

Rarely someone
sees it,
rarely another
speaks it,
rarely anyone
hears it—
even hearing it,
no one really knows it.

The self embodied in the body
of every being is indestructible;
you have no cause to grieve
for all these creatures, Arjuna!

Look to your own duty;
do not tremble before it;
nothing is better for a warrior
than a battle of sacred duty.

The doors of heaven open
for warriors who rejoice
to have a battle like this
thrust on them by chance.

If you fail to wage this war
of sacred duty,
you will abandon your own duty
and fame only to gain evil.

People will tell
of your undying shame,
and for a man of honor
shame is worse than death.

> *In this next passage from the* Bhagavad-Gita, *Krishna reveals a deeper meaning to his message to Arjuna. Not only must Arjuna act like a warrior because that is his caste, but he must also act without regard to the consequences of his action. What does Krishna seem to mean by this? How does one do "nothing at all even when he engages in action"? In what sense is this advice "religious"?*

Abandoning attachment to fruits
of action, always content, independent,
he does nothing at all
even when he engages in action.

He incurs no guilt if he has no hope,
restrains his thought and himself,
abandons possessions,
and performs actions with his body only.

Content with whatever comes by chance,
beyond dualities, free from envy,
impartial to failure and success,
he is not bound even when he acts.

When a man is unattached and free,
his reason deep in knowledge,
acting only in sacrifice,
his action is wholly dissolved.

When devoted men sacrifice
to other deities with faith,
they sacrifice to me, Arjuna,
however aberrant the rites.

I am the enjoyer
and the lord of all sacrifices;
they do not know me in reality,
and so they fail.

Votaries of the gods go to the gods,
ancestor-worshippers go to the ancestors,
those who propitiate ghosts go to them,
and my worshippers go to me.

The leaf or flower or fruit or water
that he offers with devotion,
I take from the man of self-restraint
in response to his devotion.

Whatever you do—what you take,
what you offer, what you give,
what penances you perform—
do as an offering to me, Arjuna!

You will be freed from the bonds of action,
from the fruit of fortune and misfortune;
armed with the discipline of renunciation,
your self liberated, you will join me.

I am impartial to all creatures,
and no one is hateful or dear to me;
but men devoted to me are in me,
and I am within them.

If he is devoted solely to me,
even a violent criminal
must be deemed a man of virtue,
for his resolve is right.

His spirit quickens to sacred duty,
and he finds eternal peace;
Arjuna, know that no one
devoted to me is lost.

If they rely on me, Arjuna,
women, commoners, men of low rank,
even men born in the womb of evil,
reach the highest way.

How easy it is then for holy priests
and devoted royal sages—
in this transient world of sorrow,
devote yourself to me!

Keep me in your mind and devotion,
sacrifice to me, bow to me,
discipline your self toward me,
and you will reach me!

23.   BUDDHISM:
23.1. GOTAMA'S DISCOVERY

One of the traditional stories told about the Buddha (who grew up in northern India around 500 B.C.) is the following account of how he discovered old age, sickness, and death. According to the story, at the birth of the Buddha wise men predicted that he would be either a prince like his father or a wandering hermit. His father tried to ensure the first result by keeping him content within the palace and unaware of human suffering. Eventually, however, the young prince decided to see the world beyond the palace gates. the saw pain.

What did he see? What did it mean to him? What did it mean to the later Buddhists who told this story? What important idea of Buddhism did it contain? In what ways were these ideas similar to, or different from, the ideas that Prince Gotama (Gautama) Siddhartha (later the Buddha) learned when reciting the Vedas and the Gita?

Now the young lord Gotama, when many days had passed by, bade his charioteer make ready the state carriages, saying: "Get ready the carriages, good charioteer, and let us go through the park to inspect the pleasaunce" [a recreation place attached to a mansion—Ed.]. "Yes, my lord," replied the charioteer, and harnessed the state carriages and sent word to Gotama: "The carriages are ready, my lord; do now what you deem fit." Then Gotama mounted a state carriage and drove out in state into the park.

Now the young lord saw, as he was driving to the park, an aged man as bent as a roof gable, decrepit, leaning on a staff, tottering as he walked, afflicted and long past his prime. And seeing him Gotama said: "That man, good charioteer, what has he done, that his hair is not like that of other men, nor his body?"

"He is what is called an aged man, my lord."

"But why is he called aged?"

"He is called aged, my lord, because he has not much longer to live."

"But then, good charioteer, am I too subject to old age, one who has not got past old age?"

"You, my lord, and we too, we all are of a kind to grow old; we have not got past old age."

"Why then, good charioteer, enough of the park for today. Drive me back hence to my rooms."

"Yea, my lord," answered the charioteer, and drove him back. And he, going to his rooms, sat brooding sorrowful and depressed, thinking, "Shame then verily be upon this thing called birth, since to one born old age shows itself like that!"

Thereupon the rāja sent for the charioteer and asked him: "Well, good charioteer, did the boy take pleasure in the park? Was he pleased with it?"

"No, my lord, he was not."

"What then did he see on his drive?"

(And the Charioteer told the rāja all.)

Then the rāja thought thus: We must not have Gotama declining to rule. We must not have him going forth from the house into the homeless state. We must not let what the brāhman soothsayers spoke of come true.

So, that these things might not come to pass, he let the youth be still more surrounded by sensuous pleasures. And thus Gotama continued to live amidst the pleasures of sense.

Now after many days had passed by, the young lord again bade his charioteer make ready and drove forth as once before. . . .

And Gotama saw, as he was driving to the park, a sick man, suffering and very ill, fallen and weltering in his own water, by some being lifted up, by others being dressed. Seeing this, Gotama asked: "That man, good charioteer, what has he done that his eyes are not like others' eyes, nor his voice like the voice of other men?"

"He is what is called ill, my lord."

"But what is meant by ill?"

"It means, my lord, that he will hardly recover from his illness."

"But am I too, then, good charioteer, subject to fall ill; have I not got out of reach of illness?"

"You, my lord, and we too, we are all subject to fall ill; we have not got beyond the reach of illness."

"Why then, good charioteer, enough of the park for today. Drive me back hence to my rooms." "Yea, my lord," answered the charioteer, and drove him back. And he, going to his rooms, sat brooding sorrowful and depressed, thinking: Shame then verily be upon this thing called birth, since to one born decay shows itself like that, disease shows itself like that.

Thereupon the rāja sent for the charioteer and asked him: "Well, good charioteer, did the young lord take pleasure in the park and was he pleased with it?"

"No, my lord, he was not."

"What did he see then on his drive?"

(And the charioteer told the rāja all.)

Then the rāja thought thus: We must not have Gotama declining to rule; we must not have him going forth from the house to the homeless state; we must not let what the brāhman soothsayers spoke of come true.

So, that these things might not come to pass, he let the young man be still more abundantly surrounded by sensuous pleasures. And thus Gotama continued to live amidst the pleasures of sense.

Now once again, after many days . . . the young lord Gotama . . . drove forth.

And he saw, as he was driving to the park, a great concourse of people clad in garments of different colours constructing a funeral pyre. And seeing this he asked his charioteer: "Why now are all those people come together in garments of different colours, and making that pile?"

"It is because someone, my lord, has ended his days."

"Then drive the carriage close to him who has ended his days."

"Yea, my lord," answered the charioteer, and did so. And Gotama saw the corpse of him who had ended his days and asked: "What, good charioteer, is ending one's days?"

"It means, my lord, that neither mother, nor father, nor other kinsfolk will now see him, nor will he see them."

"But am I too then subject to death, have I not got beyond reach of death? Will neither the rāja, nor the ranee, nor any other of my kin see me more, or shall I again see them?"

"You, my lord, and we too, we are all subject to death; we have not passed beyond the reach of death. Neither the rāja, nor the ranee, nor any other of your kin will see you any more, nor will you see them."

"Why then, good charioteer, enough of the park for today. Drive me back hence to my rooms."

"Yea, my lord," replied the charioteer, and drove him back.

And he, going to his rooms, sat brooding sorrowful and depressed, thinking: Shame verily be upon this thing called birth, since to one born the decay of life, since disease, since death shows itself like that!

Thereupon the rāja questioned the charioteer as before and as before let Gotama be still more surrounded by sensuous enjoyment. And thus he continued to live amidst the pleasures of sense.

Now once again, after many days . . . the lord Gotama . . . drove forth.

And he saw, as he was driving to the park, a shaven-headed man, a recluse, wearing the yellow robe. And seeing him he asked the charioteer, "That man, good charioteer, what has he done that his head is unlike other men's heads and his clothes too are unlike those of others?"

"That is what they call a recluse, because, my lord, he is one who has gone forth."

"What is that, 'to have gone forth'?"

"To have gone forth, my lord, means being thorough in the religious life, thorough in the peaceful life, thorough in good action, thorough in meritorious conduct, thorough in harmlessness, thorough in kindness to all creatures."

"Excellent indeed, friend charioteer, is what they call a recluse, since so thorough is his conduct in all those respects, wherefore drive me up to that forthgone man."

"Yea, my lord," replied the charioteer and drove up to the recluse. Then Gotama addressed him, saying, "You master, what have you done that your head is not as other men's heads, nor your clothes as those of other men?"

"I, my lord, am one who has gone forth."

"What, master, does that mean?"

"It means, my lord, being thorough in the religious life, thorough in the peaceful life, thorough in good actions, thorough in meritorious conduct, thorough in harmlessness, thorough in kindness to all creatures."

"Excellently indeed, master, are you said to have gone forth since so thorough is your conduct in all those respects." Then the lord Gotama bade his charioteer, saying: "Come then, good charioteer, do you take the carriage and drive it back hence to my rooms. But I will even here cut off my hair, and don the yellow robe, and go forth from the house into the homeless state."

"Yea, my lord," replied the charioteer, and drove back. But the prince Gotama, there and then cutting off his hair and donning the yellow robe, went forth from the house into the homeless state.

Now at Kapilavatthu, the rāja's seat, a great number of persons, some eighty-four thousand souls, heard of what prince Gotama had done and thought: Surely this is no ordinary religious rule, this is no common going forth, in that prince Gotama himself has had his head shaved and has donned the yellow robe and has gone forth from the house into the homeless state. If prince Gotama has done this, why then should not we also? And they all had their heads shaved and donned the yellow robes; and in imitation of the Bodhisat [Buddha] they went forth from the house into the homeless state. So the Bodhisat went forth from the house into the homeless state. So the Bodhisat went up on his rounds through the villages, towns and cities accompanied by that multitude.

Now there arose in the mind of Gotama the Bodhisat, when he was meditating in seclusion, this thought: That indeed is not suitable for me that I should live beset. 'Twere better were I to dwell alone, far from the crowd.

So after a time he dwelt alone, away from the crowd. Those eighty-four thousand recluses went one way, and the Bodhisat went another way.

Now there arose in the mind of Gotama the Bodhisat, when he had gone to his place and was meditating in seclusion, this thought: Verily, this world has fallen upon trouble—one is born, and grows old, and dies, and falls from one state, and springs up in another. And from the suffering, moreover, no one knows of any way to escape, even from decay and death. O, when shall a way of escape from this suffering be made known—from decay and from death?

23.2. THE BUDDHA'S FIRST SERMON

This is said to be the Buddha's first sermon, delivered shortly after he achieved enlightenment. It contains the essence of Buddhist thought: the four noble truths, the eightfold path, and the middle way. The middle way is the path between the extremes of the pursuit of pleasure and the pursuit of pain. It is defined by an eightfold path, an eight-step path to a peaceful mind (right concentration). The four noble truths might be summarized as the following:

1. *Life is sorrow.*
2. *Sorrow is the result of selfish desire.*
3. *Selfish desire can be destroyed.*
4. *It can be destroyed by following the eightfold path.*

*at do these ideas mean? What was considered the value of a "middle
ay"? In what ways did the eightfold path offer a spiritual discipline?
/hat answers did the four noble truths provide?*

is I have heard. Once the Lord was at Vṝānasī, at the deer park called
Iwipatana. There he addressed the five monks:

There are two ends not to be served by a wanderer. What are these
two? The pursuit of desires and of the pleasure which springs from
desire, which is base, common, leading to rebirth, ignoble, and unprofitable; and the pursuit of pain and hardship, which is grievous, ignoble,
and unprofitable. The Middle Way of the Tathāgata avoids both these
ends. It is enlightened, it brings clear vision, it makes for wisdom, and
leads to peace, insight, enlightenment, and Nirvāna. What is the Middle
Way? . . . It is the Noble Eightfold Path—Right Views, Right Resolve,
Right Speech, Right Conduct, Right Livelihood, Right Effort, Right
Mindfulness, and Right Concentration. This is the Middle Way. . . .

And this is the Noble Truth of Sorrow. Birth is sorrow, age is sorrow,
disease is sorrow, death is sorrow; contact with the unpleasant is sorrow,
separation from the pleasant is sorrow, every wish unfulfilled is sorrow—
in short all the five components of individuality are sorrow.

And this is the Noble Truth of the Arising of Sorrow. It arises from
craving, which leads to rebirth, which brings delight and passion, and
seeks pleasure now here, now there—the craving for sensual pleasure,
the craving for continued life, the craving for power.

And this is the Noble Truth of the Stopping of Sorrow. It is the complete stopping of that craving, so that no passion remains, leaving it,
being emancipated from it, being released from it, giving no place to it.

And this is the Noble Truth of the Way which Leads to the Stopping of
Sorrow. It is the Noble Eightfold Path—Right Views, Right Resolve,
Right Speech, Right Conduct, Right Livelihood, Right Effort, Right
Mindfulness, and Right Concentration.

23.3. THE STORY OF ISIDĀSĪ, A BUDDHIST NUN

*Buddhism, like Christianity, was a monastic religion. One of its ideals was
the renunciation of the everyday world in favor of a life of poverty and
devotion in a monastery. There were mendicant (begging) nuns as well as
monks in Buddhism.*

In this selection a Buddhist nun, Isidāsī, explains why she became a

mendicant nun. How was she rejected by three husbands? Why did she
decide to become a nun? What were her previous lives? What did they
have to do with her decision to renounce the world? What does Isidāsī's
story say about Buddhist ideas of karma and reincarnation?

In the city of Pātaliputta, treasured
on earth for its glorious flowers,
there were two mendicant nuns
of the Buddha's own Sakya clan.
One was Isidāsī, the other was Bodhī,
both of them morally pure,
skilled in meditation, wise,
and freed from painful vices.
They begged alms, ate their food,
washed their bowls,
and found a secret place
to rest and share their stories.

"You're still beautiful, Isidāsī.
Your youth hasn't faded.
What vision of evil drove you
to renounce the world?"
In that secret place she told her tale
to teach the truth of Buddha's way.
Isidāsī said to Bodhī,
"Hear why I am a mendicant nun:

In the great city of Ujjenī
my father was a merchant of high repute.
I was his only daughter,
deeply loved and pampered.
A wealthy merchant sent noblemen
from the city of Sāketa
to arrange a marriage, and my father
gave me to be his son's wife.
Day and night I humbled myself
to honor my in-laws—
my training made me bow
my head down at their feet.
When I saw my husband's
sisters and brothers
I cringed and crept away
to free my seat for them.
I kept fresh-cooked food and drink
and spiced pickles ready

to serve their demands.
I woke early every morning
to scrub my hands and feet
before I crossed the threshold
to beg my husband's blessing.
Like a slave girl,
I took combs and scented oils
and my mirror
to groom him.
I cooked his rice gruel,
I washed his bowl,
I waited on this husband
like a mother doting on her son.
Though I was diligent and humble,
meticulous and virtuous
in serving him,
my husband despised me.
He begged his parents,
'Give me your leave.
I must go away. I will not stay
in this house with Isidāsī!'
'Don't speak this way, son!
Isidāsī is intelligent and wise,
diligent, meticulous.
Doesn't she please you, son?'
'She does me no harm,
but I will not stay with Isidāsī.
I detest her! Enough!
Give me leave, I must go away.'
My husband's parents heard
his words and questioned me,
'How did you offend him?
Confide what really happened.'
'I committed no offense or harm
or ever answered his cruel words.
I don't know what I did
to make this husband hate me.'
They took me back
to my father's house.
'To keep our precious son
we sacrifice this goddess.'

Then my father married me
into another wealthy house.
The second merchant took me

for half the first bride price.
I lived in that house
for barely a month,
serving him like a slave
until he sent me back.
Then my father snared an ascetic
begging for alms; he said,
'Be my daughter's husband!
Throw away your robe and pot!'
He stayed for two weeks
before he told my father,
'Give me my robe and pot and cup!
I'll beg for alms again.'
My parents and my family
beseeched him,
'What have we neglected?
Quickly, name your every want!'
He answered, 'I only want
enough to feed myself.
I will not stay in this house
with Isidāsī!'
They dismissed him and he left.
I brooded in my solitude:
'I'll tell them I'm going to die
unless I become a mendicant nun.'
And the great nun Jinadattā
came begging alms
at my father's house—she was
disciplined, wise, morally pure.
I rose when I saw her
and gave her my seat,
bowed at her feet
and offered her a meal.
I served her fresh-cooked food
and drink and spiced pickles.
When she had eaten, I said,
'Lady, I want to be a nun.'
My father argued, 'My child,
you may follow the Buddha's way
by giving food and drink
to holy men and brahmin priests.'
I pleaded in tears,
begging his blessing,
'I must destroy
the evil I have done!'

My father blessed me then,
'Attain enlightenment
and the Buddha's way
that leads to liberation!'
I bid farewell to my parents
and became a mendicant nun.
After only seven days
I reached the triple wisdom.
I know my former seven births
that ripened into this one.
I'll recount them.
Listen carefully!

In the city of Ekakaccha
I was a wealthy goldsmith,
intoxicated by youth's wine,
seducing other men's wives.
I died and boiled in hell
for some time; tormented,
I rose from my tortures
and entered a monkey's belly.
Seven days after my birth
the troop's leader castrated me;
this was the fruit
of seducing other men's wives.
Then I died again,
spent time in the forest of Sindh,
and entered the belly
of a wild, blind, lame goat.
I suffered twelve years
as a worm-ridden, sickly,
castrated goat
for seducing other men's wives.
When I died again, I was born
to a cattle-trader's cow,
a calf the color of coppery lac [resin],
castrated in the twelfth month.
I pulled a plough and cart,
wretched, blind, and sickly,
for seducing other men's wives.
I died again on the road
to be born an androgyne
in a slave girl's house
for seducing other men's wives.
At thirty I died and was born

a female in a carter's family,
out-caste, indigent, enslaved
by money-lenders' loans.
A caravan trader claiming
interest on a loan
dragged me screaming
from my family.
When I was sixteen
the son of this merchant
noticed my maiden youth
and took me.
He had another wife
who was moral and virtuous,
in love with her husband.
I sowed discord with her.
The fruit of seven former lives
made three husbands scorn me,
though I served them like a slave—
I have ended all this now.

CHAPTER EIGHT

Chinese Civilization

24. THE *ANALECTS* OF CONFUCIUS

Not much is known about the life of Confucius. He was born about 551 B.C., orphaned at an early age, became a minor official and teacher and then traveled widely to give advice to princes. He died in 479 B.C. at the age of 70. His teachings are not religious, but they are very moral. He seems to have believed that the moral life was the most worthy goal one could have. The ideal moral character for Confucius was "the gentleman." The most important virtue of the gentleman is jen (humanity or benevolence). He must also demonstrate chung (doing his best) and shu (knowing what other people want). These are highly social ideals. Confucianism became the moral code of Chinese culture for thousands of years. Whether practiced or honored in the breach, interpreted in various ways, enshrined as official orthodoxy, or sometimes vilified, probably no set of ideas has influenced so many people in the history of the world.

What kind of people are these ideas likely to produce? Are there certain groups in society who would find these ideas more appealing? In what ways are these ideas different from those which you have been taught in your own moral education? What, if anything, do these ideas of morality have to do with religion?

ON EDUCATION

II,15 The Master said, " 'He who learns but does not think, is lost.' He who thinks but does not learn is in great danger."

II,17 The Master said, "Yu, shall I teach you what knowledge is? When you know a thing, to recognize that you know it, and when you do not know a thing, to recognize that you do not know it. That is knowledge."

VII,1 The Master said, "I have 'transmitted what was taught to me without making up anything of my own.' I have been faithful to and loved the Ancients. In these respects, I make bold to think, not even our old P'eng can have excelled me."

VII,2 The Master said, "I have listened in silence and noted what was said. I have never grown tired of learning nor wearied of teaching others what I have learnt. These at least are merits which I can confidently claim."

XIII,9 When the Master was going to Wei, Jan Ch'iu drove him. The Master said, "What a dense population!" Jan Ch'iu said, "When the people have multiplied, what next should be done for them?" The Master said, "Enrich them." Jan Ch'iu said, "When one has enriched them, what next should be done for them?" The Master said, "Instruct them."

XV,35 The Master said, "When it comes to Goodness one need not avoid competing with one's teacher."

ON GOODNESS

I,3 The Master said, " 'Clever talk and a pretentious manner' are seldom found in the Good."

I,6 The Master said, "A young man's duty is to behave well to his parents at home and to his elders abroad, to be cautious in giving promises and punctual in keeping them, to have kindly feelings towards everyone, but seek the intimacy of the Good. If, when all that is done, he has any energy to spare, then let him study the polite arts."

IV,3,4 Of the adage, "Only a Good Man knows how to like people, knows how to dislike them," the Master said, "He whose heart is in the smallest degree set upon Goodness will dislike no one."

VII,15 The Master said, "He who seeks only coarse food to eat, water to drink and bent arm for pillow, will without looking for it find happiness to boot. Any thought of accepting wealth and rank by means that I know to be wrong is as remote from me as the clouds that float above."

XII,2 Jan Yung asked about Goodness. The Master said, "Behave when away from home as though you were in the presence of an important guest. Deal with the common people as though you were officiating at an important sacrifice. Do not do to others what you would not like yourself. Then there will be no feelings of opposition to you, whether it is the affairs of a State that you are handling or the affairs of a Family."

XV,23 Tzu-kung asked saying, "Is there any single saying that one can act upon all day and every day?" The Master said, "Perhaps the saying about consideration: 'Never do to others what you would not like them to do to you.' "

ON THE GENTLEMAN

II,13 Tzu-kung asked about the true gentleman. The Master said, "He does not preach what he practices till he has practiced what he preaches."

III,7 The Master said, "Gentlemen never compete. You will say that in archery they do so. But even then they bow and make way for one another when they are going up to the archery-ground, when they are coming down and at the subsequent drinking bout. Thus even when competing, they still remain gentlemen."

IV,5 "Wealth and rank are what every man desires; but if they can only be retained to the detriment of the Way he professes, he must relinquish them. Poverty and obscurity are what every man detests; but if they can only be avoided to the detriment of the Way he professes, he must accept them. The gentleman who ever parts company with Goodness does not fulfill that name. Never for a moment does a gentleman quit the way of Goodness. He is never so harried but that he cleaves to this; never so tottering but that he cleaves to this."

IV,16 The Master said, "A gentleman takes as much trouble to discover what is right as lesser men take to discover what will pay."

VI,25 The Master said, "A gentleman who is widely versed in letters and at the same time knows how to submit his learning to the restraints of ritual is not likely, I think, to go far wrong."

VIII,2 . . . The Master said, "When gentlemen deal generously with their own kin, the common people are incited to Goodness. When old dependents are not discarded, the common people will not be fickle."

IX,13 The Master wanted to settle among the Nine Wild Tribes of the East. Someone said, "I am afraid you would find it hard to put up with their lack of refinement." The Master said, "Were a true gentleman to settle among them there would soon be no trouble about lack of refinement."

XII,16 The Master said, "The gentleman calls attention to the good points in others; he does not call attention to their defects. The small man does just the reverse of this."

XV,18 The Master said, "A gentleman is distressed by his own lack of capacity; he is never distressed at the failure of others to recognize his merits."

XV,20 The Master said, " 'The demands that a gentleman makes are upon himself; those that a small man makes are upon others.' "

XV,21 The Master said, "A gentleman is proud, but not quarrelsome, allies himself with individuals, but not with parties."

X,6 A gentleman does not wear facings of purple or mauve, nor in undress does he use pink or roan. In hot weather he wears an unlined gown of fine thread loosely woven, but puts on an outside garment before going out-of-doors. With a black robe he wears black lambskin; with a robe of undyed silk, fawn. With a yellow robe, fox fur. On his undress robe the fur cuffs are long; but the right is shorter than the left. His bedclothes must be half as long again as a man's height. The thicker kinds of fox and badger are for home wear. Except when in mourning, he wears all his girdle-ornaments. Apart from his Court apron, all his skirts are wider at the bottom than at the waist. Lambskin dyed black and a hat of dark-dyed silk must not be worn when making visits of condolence. At the Announcement of the New Moon he must go to Court in full Court dress.

ON FILIAL PIETY

II,5 Meng I Tzu asked about the treatment of parents. The Master said, "Never disobey!" When Fan Ch'ih was driving his carriage for him, the Master said, "Meng asked me about the treatment of parents and I said, 'Never disobey!' " Fan Ch'ih said, "In what sense did you mean it?" The Master said, "While they are alive, serve them according to ritual. When they die, bury them according to ritual and sacrifice to them according to ritual."

II,7 Tzu-yu asked about the treatment of parents. The Master said, " 'Filial sons' nowadays are people who see to it that their parents get enough to eat. But even dogs and horses are cared for to that extent. If there is no feeling of respect, wherein lies the difference?"

ON RITUAL AND MUSIC

III,3 The Master said, "A man who is not Good, what can he have to do with ritual? A man who is not Good, what can he have to do with music?"

III,4 Lin Fang asked for some main principles in connexion with ritual. The Master said, "A very big question. In ritual at large it is a safe rule always to be too sparing rather than too lavish; and in the particular case of mourning-rites, they should be dictated by grief rather than by fear."

VIII,2 The Master said, "Courtesy not bounded by the prescriptions of ritual becomes tiresome. Caution not bounded by the prescriptions of ritual becomes timidity, daring becomes turbulence, inflexibility becomes harshness."

VIII,8 The Master said, "Let a man be first incited by the *Songs*, then given a firm footing by the study of ritual, and finally perfected by music."

ON GOVERNMENT BY MORAL FORCE

I,5 The Master said, "A country of a thousand war-chariots cannot be administered unless the ruler attends strictly to business, punctually observes his promises, is economical in expenditure, shows affection toward his subjects in general, and uses the labour of the peasantry only at the proper times of year."

II,3 The Master said, "Govern the people by regulations, keep order among them by chastisements, and they will flee from you, and lose all self-respect. Govern them by moral force, keep order among them by ritual and they will keep their self-respect and come to you of their own accord."

XII,11 Duke Ching of Ch'i asked Master K'ung about government, Master K'ung replied saying, "Let the prince be a prince, the minister a minister, the father a father and the son a son." The Duke said, "How true! For indeed when the prince is not a prince, the minister not a minister, the father not a father, the son not a son, one may have a dish of millet in front of one and yet not know if one will live to eat it."

XII,19 Chi L'ang-tzu asked Master K'ung about government, saying, "Suppose I were to slay those who have not the Way in order to help on those who have the Way, what would you think of it?" Master K'ung replied saying, "You are there to rule, not to slay. If you desire what is good, the people will at once be good. The essence of the gentleman is that of wind; the essence of small people is that of grass. And when a wind passes over the grass, it cannot choose but bend."

XIII,6 The Master said, "If the ruler himself is upright, all will go well even though he does not give orders. But if he himself is not upright, even though he gives orders, they will not be obeyed."

XIII,10 The Master said, "If only someone were to make use of me, even for a single year, I could do a great deal; and in three years I could finish off the whole work."

XIII,11 The Master said, " 'Only if the right sort of people had charge of a country for a hundred years would it become really possible to stop cruelty and do away with slaughter.' How true the saying is!"

ON PUBLIC OPINION

II,19 Duke Ai asked, "What can I do in order to get the support of the common people?" Master K'ung replied, "If you 'raise up the straight and set them on top of the crooked,' the commoners will support you. But if you raise the crooked and set them on top of the straight, the commoners will not support you."

II,20 Chi L'ang-tzu asked whether there were any form of encouragement by which he could induce the common people to be respectful and loyal. The Master said, "Approach them with dignity, and they will respect you. Show piety towards your parents and kindness toward your children, and they will be loyal to you. Promote those who are worthy, train those who are incompetent; that is the best form of encouragement."

XII,7 Tzu-kung asked about government. The Master said, "Sufficient food, sufficient weapons, and the confidence of the common people." Tzu-kung said, "Suppose you had no choice but to dispense with one of these three, which would you forgo?" The Master said, "Weapons." Tzu-kung said, "Suppose you were forced to dispense with one of the two that were left, which would you forgo?" The Master said, "Food. For from of old death has been the lot of all men; but a people that no longer trusts its rulers is lost indeed."

ON RELIGION

III,11 Someone asked for an explanation of the Ancestral Sacrifice. The Master said, "I do not know. Anyone who knew the explanation could deal with all things under Heaven as easily as I lay this here"; and he laid his finger upon the palm of his hand.

V,12 Tzu-kung said, "Our Master's views concerning culture and the outward insignia of goodness, we are permitted to hear; but about Man's nature and the ways of Heaven he will not tell us anything at all."

VII,20 The Master never talked of prodigies, feats of strength, disorders or spirits.

VII,34 When the Master was very ill, Tzu-lu asked leave to perform the Rite of Expiation. The Master said, "Is there such a thing?" Tzu-lu answered saying, "There is. In one of the Dirges it says, 'We performed rites of expiation for you, calling upon the sky-spirits above and the earth-spirits below.'" The Master said, "My expiation began long ago!"

XI,11 Tzu-lu asked how one should serve ghosts and spirits. The Master said, "Till you have learnt to serve men, how can you serve ghosts?" Tzu-lu then ventured upon a question about the dead. The Master said, "Till you know about the living, how are you to know about the dead?"

25. CONFUCIANISM: *THE MENCIUS*

Mencius

Confucianism is more than the writings of Confucius. It is a tradition that includes the thought of many of his followers as well. Second only to Confucius is Mencius, who lived during the fourth century B.C. In opposition to those who urged political manipulation, Mencius directed Confucians toward a more optimistic view of human nature and a richer regard for the rewards of benevolence.

What is Mencius's reason for saying that human nature is fundamentally good? What is benevolence? Are people born benevolent, or do they have to develop it? How is this philosophy different from Buddhism?

6. Mencius said, "No man is devoid of a heart sensitive to the suffering of others. Such a sensitive heart was possessed by the Former Kings and this manifested itself in compassionate government. With such a sensitive heart behind compassionate government, it was as easy to rule the Empire as rolling it on your palm.

"My reason for saying that no man is devoid of a heart sensitive to the suffering of others is this. Suppose a man were, all of a sudden, to see a young child on the verge of falling into a well. He would certainly be moved to compassion, not because he wanted to get in the good graces of the parents, nor because he wished to win the praise of his fellow villagers or friends, nor yet because he disliked the cry of the child. From this it can be seen that whoever is devoid of the heart of compassion is not human, whoever is devoid of the heart of shame is not human, whoever is devoid of the heart of courtesy and modesty is not human, and whoever is devoid of the heart of right and wrong is not human. The heart of compassion is the germ of benevolence; the heart of shame, of dutifulness; the heart of courtesy and modesty, of observance of the rites; the heart of right and wrong, of wisdom. Man has these four germs just as he has four limbs. For a man possessing these four germs to deny his own potentialities is for him to cripple himself; for him to deny the potentialities of his prince is for him to cripple his prince. If a man is able to develop all these four germs that he possesses, it will be like a fire starting up or a spring coming through. When these are fully developed, he can take under this protection the whole realm within the Four Seas, but if he fails to develop them, he will not be able even to serve his parents."

7. Mencius said, "Is the maker of arrows really more unfeeling than the maker of armour? He is afraid lest he should fail to harm people, whereas the maker of armour is afraid lest he should fail to protect them. The case is similar with the sorcerer-doctor and the coffin-maker. For this reason one cannot be too careful in the choice of one's calling.

"Confucius said, "The best neighbourhood is where benevolence is to be found. Not to live in such a neighbourhood when one has the choice cannot by any means be considered wise." Benevolence is the high honour bestowed by Heaven and the peaceful abode of man. Not to be benevolent when nothing stands in the way is to show a lack of wisdom. A man neither benevolent nor wise, devoid of courtesy and dutifulness, is a slave. A slave ashamed of serving is like a maker of bows ashamed of making bows, or a maker of arrows ashamed of making arrows. If one is ashamed, there is no better remedy than to practice benevolence. Benevolence is like archery: an archer makes sure his stance is correct before letting fly the arrow, and if he fails to hit the mark, he does not hold it against his victor. He simply seeks the cause within himself."

26. TAOISM:
THE *TAO TE CHING*

Lao Tzu

When Indian missionaries brought Buddhism to China, they initially met strong resistance from Confucianism. A selection in the next chapter will reveal some of the points of disagreement between Buddhism and Confucianism.

Eventually the Buddhists were successful by using the language of a very different Chinese philosophical tradition, Taoism. Lao Tzu may or may not have been an actual contemporary of Confucius, but the Tao Te Ching was written around the sixth century B.C. and Taoism remained an alternative vision to the dominant Confucianism. In what ways are the ideas expressed in the Tao Te Ching different from those of Confucianism? Might a person easily follow both Confucianism and Taoism, or would these philosophies appeal to different people? Compared to Confucianism, are the Taoist ideas more "religious"? Which set of ideas do you find more appealing? Why?

CHAPTER 1

The Way that can be told of is not an Unvarying Way;
The names that can be named are not unvarying names.
It was from the Nameless that Heaven and Earth sprang;
The named is but the mother that rears the ten thousand creatures,
    each after its kind.
Truly, "Only he that rids himself forever of desire can see the Secret
    Essences";
He that has never rid himself of desire can see only the Outcomes.
These two things issued from the same mould, but nevertheless are
    different in name.
This "same mould" we can but call the Mystery.
Or rather the "Darker than any Mystery,"
The Doorway whence issued all Secret Essences.

CHAPTER II

It is because everyone under Heaven recognizes beauty as beauty, that
    the idea of ugliness exists.
And equally if everyone recognized virtue as virtue, this would merely
    create fresh conceptions of wickedness.
For truly "Being and Not-being grow out of one another;
Difficult and easy complete one another.
Long and short test one another;
High and low determine one another.
The sounds of instrument and voice give harmony to one another.
Front and back give sequence to one another."
Therefore the Sage relies on actionless activity,
Carries on wordless teaching,
But the myriad creatures are worked upon by him; he does not disown
    them.
He rears them, but does not lay claim to them,
Controls them, but does not lean upon them,
Achieves his aim, but does not call attention to what he does;
And for the very reason that he does not call attention to what he does
He is not ejected from fruition of what he has done.

CHAPTER III

Oppof Con.

If we stop looking for "persons of superior morality" (*hsien*) to put in
power, there will be no more jealousies among the people.
    If we cease to set store by products that are hard to get, there will be no
more thieves. If the people never see such things as excite desire, their
hearts will remain placid and undisturbed.
    Therefore the Sage rules

> By emptying their hearts
> And filling their bellies,
> Weakening their intelligence
> And toughening their sinews
> Ever striving to make the people knowledgeless and desireless.

Indeed he sees to it that if there be any who have knowledge, they dare not
interfere. Yet through his actionless activity all things are duly regulated.

CHAPTER IV

The Way is like an empty vessel
That yet may be drawn from

Without ever needing to be filled.
It is bottomless; the very progenitor of all things in the world.
In it all sharpness is blunted,
All tangles untied,
All glare tempered,
All dust smoothed.
It is like a deep pool that never dries.
Was it too the child of something else? We cannot tell.
But as a substanceless image it existed before the Ancestor.

CHAPTER VIII

The highest good is like that of water. The goodness of water is that it benefits the ten thousand creatures; yet itself does not scramble, but is content with the places that all men disdain. It is this that makes water so near to the Way.

And if men think the ground the best place for building a house upon,
If among thoughts they value those that are profound,
If in friendship they value gentleness,
In words, truth; in government, good order;
In deeds, effectiveness; in actions, timeliness—
In each case it is because they prefer what does not lead to strife,
And therefore does not go amiss.

CHAPTER IX

Stretch a bow to the very full,
And you will wish you had stopped in time;
Temper a sword-edge to its very sharpest,
And you will find it soon grows dull.
When bronze and jade fill your hall
It can no longer be guarded.
Wealth and place breed insolence
That brings ruin in its train.
When your work is done, then withdraw!
Such is Heaven's Way.

CHAPTER XI

We put thirty spokes together and call it a wheel;
But it is on the space where there is nothing that the utility of the wheel depends.

We turn clay to make a vessel;
But it is on the space where there is nothing that the utility of the vessel
depends.
We pierce doors and windows to make a house;
And it is on these spaces where there is nothing that the utility of the
house depends.
Therefore just as we take advantage of what is, we should recognize
the utility of what is not.

CHAPTER XII

The five colours confuse the eye,
The five sounds dull the ear,
The five tastes spoil the palate.
Excess of hunting and chasing
Makes minds go mad.
Products that are hard to get
Impede their owner's movements.
Therefore the Sage
Considers the belly not the eye.
Truly, "he rejects that but takes this."

CHAPTER XVIII

It was when the Great Way declined
That human kindness and morality arose;
It was when intelligence and knowledge appeared
That the Great Artifice began.
It was when the six near ones were no longer at peace
That there was talk of "dutiful sons";
Nor till fatherland was dark with strife
Did we hear of "loyal slaves."

CHAPTER XIX

Banish wisdom, discard knowledge,
And the people will be benefited a hundredfold.
Banish human kindness, discard morality,
And the people will be dutiful and compassionate.
Banish skill, discard profit,
And thieves and robbers will disappear.

If when these three things are done they find life too plain and
    unadorned,
Then let them have accessories;
Give them Simplicity to look at, the Uncarved Block to hold,
Give them selflessness and fewness of desires.

PART THREE
THE TRADITIONAL
WORLD: 500 TO 1500

Wooden head of Buddha, Japan, 12th century (Bettmann Archive)

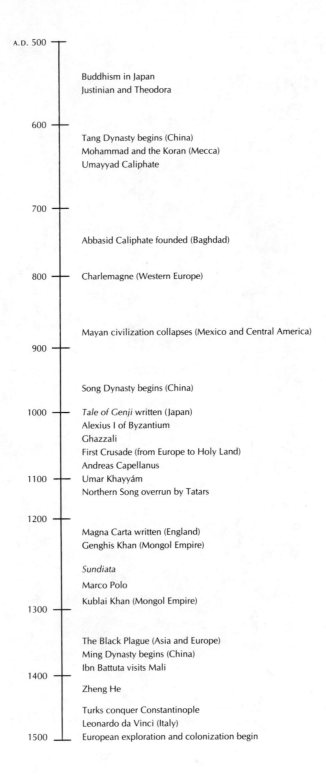

A.D. 500 —

Buddhism in Japan
Justinian and Theodora

600 —

Tang Dynasty begins (China)
Mohammad and the Koran (Mecca)
Umayyad Caliphate

700 —

Abbasid Caliphate founded (Baghdad)

800 —

Charlemagne (Western Europe)

Mayan civilization collapses (Mexico and Central America)

900 —

Song Dynasty begins (China)

1000 —

Tale of Genji written (Japan)
Alexius I of Byzantium
Ghazzali
First Crusade (from Europe to Holy Land)
Andreas Capellanus

1100 —

Umar Khayyám
Northern Song overrun by Tatars

1200 —

Magna Carta written (England)
Genghis Khan (Mongol Empire)

Sundiata

Marco Polo

Kublai Khan (Mongol Empire)

1300 —

The Black Plague (Asia and Europe)
Ming Dynasty begins (China)
Ibn Battuta visits Mali

1400 —

Zheng He

Turks conquer Constantinople
Leonardo da Vinci (Italy)

1500 —

European exploration and colonization begin

CHAPTER NINE

Hindu-Buddhist Civilization

27. HINDUISM AND BUDDHISM IN SOUTHEAST ASIA

John F. Cady

In this selection, John F. Cady, a modern historian of Southeast Asia, discusses the differing appeal of Mahayana and Theravada (or Hinayana) Buddhism. While Mahayana Buddhism passed easily into China, the older tradition, Theravada Buddhism, spread through Southeast Asia (modern Myanmar [Burma], Cambodia, Laos, and Thailand, but not Vietnam). The cultures of Southeast Asia were also heavily influenced by Hinduism. In fact, we might speak of the "Indianization" of Southeast Asia as a general phenomenon. India, especially in the Gupta Age (c. A.D. 320–550) was the cultural center of southern Asia and the Buddhist monastery at Nalanda in India remained the educational center into the seventh century.

What were the differing appeals of Theravada and Mahayana Buddhism in Southeast Asia? Why did Hinduism appeal to different groups than Buddhism? How did Indian culture influence or change the indigenous cultures of Southeast Asia?

HINDUISM AS IT AFFECTED SOUTHEAST ASIA

Hinduism as a cultural system was far too complex and deeply rooted in the context of India itself to be capable of transfer to Southeast Asia in any complete way. It included many sects and many philosophical systems; its religious values were relative to time and place, to a person's social level, and also to his intellectual and spiritual capacity to discern. Its cohesion in India derived from tenacity of social custom and from the organized caste structure in particular. Hinduism was thus a religious accumulation derived from all periods of India's history; primitive cults of fertility, hero reverence, and sun worship were combined with Aryan governmental practices and overlaid with an elaborate system of philosophical speculation. Hinduism countenanced almost every level of religious belief from crude animism to metaphysical monism.

Hinduism could be transferred, therefore, only in a selective way. Sophisticated Indians affirmed the mystical principle that the phenomenal world was illusion (*maya*) and that the ultimate reality of all life was Brahma, the indestructible soul of the universe. Failure to realize the soul's potential identity with the absolute essence (through mystical and ascetic exercises) bound an individual to phenomenal existence in a physical body through an endless series of rebirths. Persons of inferior spiritual capacities conceived their relative levels of truth in more tangible symbols. Moral and social duties in India thus varied according to caste status, itself determined by karma, or the law of deeds, which derived its character from previous existences. Neither the full philosophical implications of Brahmanism nor the full scope of the caste system proved capable of transference to Southeast Asian people. Southeast Asia's matrilineal tradition also rejected for the most part the severe restraints imposed by Hinduism upon women, such as seclusion, suttee, and child marriage.

For persons unable to grasp the truth of Brahma, the Hindu pantheon provided two rival gods, each capable of theoretical embodiment in many variant forms. Śiva [Shiva], the destroyer, personified the principle of attrition, the malevolent or destructive aspects of time which devours all, neither compassionate nor forgiving. His wives, especially Parvati and Kālī, assumed the role of the universal mother. The *linga*, or phallic symbol, was widely employed. During the development of Hinduism in India, Śiva worship absorbed a large number of pre-Aryan spirit cults. It did the same in Southeast Asia, where an easy accommodation was made to indigenous animistic worship of the godlings of forest, rivers, and mountains and of the earth goddess of fertility and to various expressions of supernatural malevolence.

The second god, Vishnu, and his favorite wife, Lakshmi, represented the more optimistic principles of restoration and prosperity. Krishna and Rama, the heroes of the *Bhagavad Gita* (*Song of the Blessed One*) and of the *Ramayana* epic respectively, were conceived as incarnations of Vishnu. Rama represented ideal kingship, and his wife, Sita, represented the highest pattern of motherhood. For various reasons, Vishnu found less wide acceptance than Śiva among the peoples of Southeast Asia. Cult practices appropriate to both gods were nevertheless widely copied. Images of Śiva and Vishnu, whether used in India or in Southeast Asia, could be symbolic intellectual principles to the sophisticated and at the same time crude idols to the simpler folk. In the Hinduized states, the divine rulers were frequently represented as *avatars* (reincarnations) of either Śiva or Vishnu.

Three other religio-political principles borrowed from Hindu culture were widely appropriated in Southeast Asia, often in combination. The first of these was derived from the idea that magical astrological forces emanating from the cardinal points of the compass and from heavenly bodies determined the destiny of individuals and states. Indian cosmology identified Mount Meru, the abode of the gods, as the cosmic center of the universe (Jambudvipa), around which the sun, moon, and stars revolved. Mount Meru was allegedly protected by eight guardian gods and surrounded by seven concentric rings of mountains and eight ocean belts separating it from the four man-inhabited islands located at the cardinal points of the compass. The city of the gods occupied the mountain's central summit. Buddhist as well as Hindu countries in Southeast Asia demanded as an important requirement for stable governmental authority the location of the royal palace at the exact center of the universe, magically determined by learned astrologers. The divine authority of Southeast Asian rulers was thus derived not only from their status as divine reincarnations but also in large measure from their occupancy of a palace conceived as a mundane Mount Meru.

Buddhist rulers as well as Hindu princes frequently identified themselves as agents or reincarnations of the ancient storm god Indra (derived from Rudra, the Aryan god of sky and storm), representing kingly authority and power. Thus the Pyu capital at Old Prome (Śrikshetra) was allegedly built by Indra. Its gates, each protected by a sacrificed guardian spirit, numbered thirty-two, a multiple of eight and four, and the thirty-two provinces of the Pyu state plus the capital corresponded to the thirty-three gods, including Indra, who were supposed to reside on Mount Meru. Preoccupation with the numbers four, eight, sixteen, and thirty-two as attributes of the famous Mount Meru was a persistent legacy of all Southeast Asian courts. The same symbolism for kingly authority has been identifed in the fourteenth-century Pegu state of the Mons. Burma's coronation building at Pagan was designated "Indra's palace," and around the enthroned Burmese king eight Brahman priests served as specialists in cosmologic magic and acted as counterparts of the eight guardian gods of Mount Meru. The royal regalia—crown, sword, and white umbrella—also symbolized magical authority under the Indian tradition of royalty. Kings of Burma and Thailand normally had a palace of four walls, with gates in multiples of fours, plus four major queens, four chief ministers, and four assistant ministers.

A third symbol of royalty was the multiple-headed Naga snake, traditional god of the soil. The fabulous role of the Naga spirit was to combine the magical resources of soil fertility with the royal principle of ownership and sovereignty over the land. In peninsular Southeast Asia it was widely applied and identified immediately with the indigenous fertility god of the soil. Kings often attributed their credentials as rulers to the alleged marriage of an ancestor with the beauteous daughter of the Naga snake. The royal symbol of the Naga's head has been long used in Thailand and Cambodia, and somewhat less frequently in Burma.

INDIAN BUDDHISM IN ITS VARIANT FORMS

Buddhism appeared in India during the sixth century B.C. as part of a protest against the presumptuous claims of Brahman priestly superiority and the degrading implications of caste. It was associated with the teachings and personality of Gautama, a Kshatriya-caste prince of the minor Indian state of Oudh. In revulsion against the brutality of warfare and suppression, Gautama left his throne and his family and became an ascetic and mendicant. His Buddhahood, or enlightenment, provided a new interpretation of life and destiny. It was based on characteristic Hindu premises of maya [illusion] and karma, but the new faith emphasized moral principles of conduct as affording an escape from the otherwise endless and burdensome gyrations of the wheel of existence.

Gautama's message was for ordinary men. It afforded a practical moral approach to life, not dependent on spells or priestly magic. Life's suffering, he affirmed, stemmed from desire, which could be conquered by following the meritful eightfold path of right belief, aspiration, speech, action, honest livelihood, sustained mental exertion, alertness, and serenity. Buddhist teachings provided the inspiration for the splendid reign of Emperor Asoka in the third century B.C., and they became the basis of much of the ethical appeal which India's culture later held out to leading peoples of Southeast Asia.

In its original interpretations, Buddhism placed everyone on his own, with no possibility of borrowed merit. It condemned outright as sinful or criminal such deeds as stealing, deceit, adultery, murder, and drinking of intoxicants. Buddhism accepted much Hindu legend, mythology, and folklore. It affirmed the principle of the sacredness of all life with its corollary obligation of *ahinsa*, noninjury to men and animals. The Buddhist goal of Nirvana, a merging with the absolute essence, thus ending life's cycle of suffering existences, corresponded to the Hindu principle of Brahma, except that the Buddhist path to the goal was one of righteous living, serenity, and peace, theoretically available to all men. By implication, Buddhism rejected priestly magic and the elaborate Hindu pantheon of the gods, but it was not dogmatic and was therefore subject to reinterpretation. It was missionary in spirit, not because it presumed to set forth any final or exclusive statement of truth, but rather because its message was broadly humanitarian and its appeal intended for all stations and races of men.

Some indication of the spirit and teachings of orthodox Indian Buddhism as it developed at the famous Nalanda monastery in the Ganges Valley can be gleaned from the writings of the Chinese pilgrim I-Ching, who visited the place during the last quarter of the 600s. The monastery at the time housed three thousand monks and had two hundred villages assigned to its support. The recluse-scholars were free of administrative responsibilities and of concern for providing food and clothing needs.

According to I-Ching, Buddhism favored forest-contemplation over the "noisy pursuit of fame and profit" and also deprecated land cultivation, which carried the hazards of taking the lives of creatures living in the soil. Drinking water must be strained, not to purify it for human consumption, but to avoid the possible sin of swallowing live organisms present in the water. The monks were nevertheless permitted to accept pieces of silken cloth presented to them, since, in I-Ching's view, there was really no point in being over-meticulous about the sin of taking the life of the silkworm. The Buddhist view was lugubrious but not hopeless:

> Life here below . . . is but a dungeon for beings who have gone astray but look eagerly for the shore of Nirvana, which is the open gate of enlightenment and quietude. The ship of the Law should be manned ready for the sea of suffering, and the lamp of wisdom should be held up during the long period of darkness. . . . Each individual must himself be responsible for the results of his own practices, whether good or bad.

The variant form of Buddhism called Mahayana (greater vehicle) developed to its full expression in the middle Ganges area during Gupta times. It succeeded by the mid-seventh century in entirely supplanting in India the simpler Hinayana, or Theravada (teacher's), sect, only to succumb itself to Hinduism in time. The Mahayana system included three innovations which were important in strengthening its impact on Southeast Asia. In the first place, it posited the not unreasonable proposition that Gautama was only the most recent of a long series of Enlightened Ones and that other Buddhas would doubtless follow him. It also affirmed the possibility of the transference of merit of Buddhist saints about to enter into Nirvana, who generously elected to endure life's suffering a little longer in order to help struggling brethren along the path. They drew aid, as it were, from a kind of Buddhist treasure of grace. A third idea closely associated with the other two established the Bodhisattva status of near divinity for a meritful ruler who could be presumed to qualify as an emergent Buddha. This idea was perennially popular with the rulers of Buddhist countries of Southeast Asia, who frequently aspired to the pretensions of Bodhisattva status as a kind of substitute for royal divinity denied to them as a reincarnation (avatar) of Śiva, Vishnu, or Indra. Mahayana Buddhism in Southeast Asia frequently degenerated into corrupted and magical forms. In Java and Cambodia in particular, Buddhist courts found the transition fairly easy back to Śiva or Vishnu worship as providing a more effective religious sanction to the authority of the divine ruler.

In its acceptability to the peoples of Southeast Asia Buddhism was strong where Hinduism was weak, and vice versa. As a revealed faith repudiating caste and race, Buddhism could be transmitted by Indian missionary devotees and also by Southeast Asian converts and pilgrims.

It was also a trader's religion. Hinduism, on the other hand, could be transmitted only by high-caste immigrants, Kshatriya or Brahman. Hinduism buttressed royal authority through the system of divine kingship, synthetically achieved by priestly intervention. Apart from the indispensable services of Brahman advisers at coronations, they assisted the rulers as clerks and scribes, as astrologers and numerologists, and also in the development of larger-scale systems of administration, revenue, and military operation. Buddhism, by contrast, could contribute little to political authority or government, except insofar as kings might choose to exploit the Bodhisattva principle. On the other hand, Hinduism was unable to attract the degree of popular acceptance so widely accorded to the more democratic Buddhist faith. Caste was not transferable in its full sense to the peoples of Southeast Asia. Lacking popular roots, the Hindu cult was dependent on royal favor and therefore on the vagaries of rulership, such as war, economic disaster, or governmental decay. Although remnants of the Hindu cultural impact long survived in many areas of Southeast Asia, the vitality of Śiva and Vishnu worship ebbed away not long after direct cultural contact was lost with sources in India.

THE PROCESS OF INDIANIZATION

The several attempted explanations of the process of Indianization in the various regions of Southeast Asia vary rather widely. They agree only in the conclusions that it was accomplished by peaceful and nonpolitical means, that Indian culture was ingratiating and assimilable in terms of indigenous traditions, and that it proved particularly attractive to local ruling princes.

Whereas Hinduization was mainly an aristocratic process, Buddhism involved cultural transfer at popular levels. Pilgrimages of Southeast Asian monks and scholars to Indian mainland monasteries and, in the case of the Hinayana sect, to Ceylon were commonplace. Endowed hostelries were established periodically at convenient points in India such as Negapatam and Nalanda for the care and entertainment of such pilgrims. Southeast Asian Buddhist scholars trained in India or Ceylon could be called back home to fill prominent posts at court or in monasteries. The vogue of Buddhism in early Southeast Asia coincided with the visits of large numbers of such pilgrims to India in Gupta and post-Gupta times. It is more than likely that the vast majority of the hundreds of Buddhist scholars whom the Chinese pilgrim I-Ching found studying at Śrivijaya during his visits from 671 to 695 were indigenous Malays or Javanese. It is also highly probable that some Southeast Asian students visiting India may have advanced Brahman pretensions when they returned.

SOUTHEAST ASIAN APPROPRIATION OF INDIAN CULTURE

Several final questions concern the thoroughness of the Indianizing process. Did Hinduism and Buddhism overwhelm the indigenous culture patterns, or were they merely an accretion added as a veneer to the traditional systems? Did contributions from India provide Southeast Asia with a cultural base from which further progress was possible?

The broad cultural gaps between cosmopolitan port cities dependent for food on imported grain, the court-oriented capitals with their Indianized atmosphere and their highly articulate symbolization of political authority, and the rural villages producing food and forest products under traditional social and religious patterns were never completely closed. The History of the region, in fact, drew its dynamics from just such contrasting situations. The alien trader vied with the local potentate; rulers who were bent on personal glorification and monument construction were forced in time to come to terms with a people wincing under heavy tax and *corvée* exactions (unpaid labor in lieu of taxes, particularly for road construction—Ed.) and the burdens of warfare. Even so, the impact of Indian culture was massively impressive down to the time of its diminution in the late thirteenth century. It demonstrated its genius for incorporating local deities and religious practices, reinterpreting them as variants of the great Vedic tradition. Thus, indigenous traditions concerned with worship of the lord of the mountain became part of the Devaraja cult, with Śiva as lord of the mountain and the ruler as an emanation of Śiva. The process generated in time a measure of cultural homogeneity, a kind of synthesis developed from a profusion of crude animistic practices reinterpreted on a higher level.

28. BUDDHISM IN CHINA: *THE DISPOSITION OF ERROR*

The Disposition of Error appears to be a defense of Buddhism, written to refute some of the charges against the new religion from India by Confucians and other Chinese. While the author and date of composition are uncertain, we know that this kind of tract was common in China under the Southern Dynasties (A.D. 420–589).

What kind of objections to Buddhism did Chinese Confucians have? How did the Buddhists answer these objections? Was Buddhism fundamentally "un-Chinese"?

WHY IS BUDDHISM NOT MENTIONED IN THE CHINESE CLASSICS?

The questioner said: If the way of the Buddha is the greatest and most venerable of ways, why did Yao, Shun, the Duke of Chou, and Confucius not practice it? In the seven Classics one sees no mention of it. You, sir, are fond of the *Book of Odes* and the *Book of History,* and you take pleasure in rites and music. Why, then, do you love the way of the Buddha and rejoice in outlandish arts? Can they exceed the Classics and commentaries and beautify the accomplishments of the sages? Permit me the liberty, sir, of advising you to reject them.

Mou Tzu[1] said: All written works need not necessarily be the words of Confucius, and all medicine does not necessarily consist of the formulae of [the famous physician] P'ien-ch'üeh. What accords with principle is to be followed, what heals the sick is good. The gentleman-scholar draws widely on all forms of good, and thereby benefits his character. Tzu-kung [a disciple of Confucius] said, "Did the Master have a permanent teacher?" Yao served Yin Shou, Shun served Wu-ch'eng, the Duke of Chou learned from Lü Wang, and Confucius learned from Lao Tzu. And none of these teachers is mentioned in the seven Classics. Although these four teachers were sages, to compare them to the Buddha would be like comparing a white deer to a unicorn, or a swallow to a phoenix. Yao, Shun, the Duke of Chou, and Confucius learned even from such teachers as these. How much less, then, may one reject the Buddha, whose distinguishing marks are extraordinary and whose superhuman powers know no bounds! How may one reject him and refuse to learn from him? The records and teachings of the Five Classics do not contain everything. Even if the Buddha is not mentioned in them, what occasion is there for suspicion?

WHY DO BUDDHIST MONKS DO INJURY TO THEIR BODIES?

The questioner said: The *Classic of Filial Piety* says, "Our torso, limbs, hair, and skin we receive from our fathers and mothers. We dare not do them injury." When Tseng Tzu was about to die, he bared his hands and feet.[2] But now the monks shave their heads. How this violates the sayings of the sages and is out of keeping with the way of the filially pious! . . .

---

1. A Chinese Buddhist.
2. To show he had preserved them intact from all harm.

Mou Tzu said: . . . Confucius has said, "He with whom one may follow a course is not necessarily he with whom one may weigh its merits." This is what is meant by doing what is best at the time. Furthermore, the *Classic of Filial Piety* says, "The kings of yore possessed the ultimate virtue and the essential Way." T'ai-po cut his hair short and tattooed his body, thus following of his own accord the customs of Wu and Yüeh and going against the spirit of the "torso, limbs, hair, and skin" passage.[3] And yet Confucius praised him, saying that his might well be called the ultimate virtue.

WHY DO MONKS NOT MARRY?

The questioner said: Now of felicities there is none greater than the continuation of one's line, of unfilial conduct there is none worse than childlessness. The monks forsake wife and children, reject property and wealth. Some do not marry all their lives. How opposed this conduct is to felicity and filial piety! . . .

Mou Tzu said: . . . Wives, children, and property are the luxuries of the world, but simple living and inaction are the wonders of the Way. Lao Tzu has said, "Of reputation and life, which is dearer? Of life and property, which is worth more?" . . . Hsü Yu and Ch'ao-fu dwelt in a tree. Po I and Shu Ch'i starved in Shou-yang, but Confucius praised their worth, saying, "They sought to act in accordance with humanity and they succeeded in acting so." One does not hear of their being ill-spoken of because they were childless and propertyless. The monk practices the Way and substitutes that for the pleasures of disporting himself in the world. He accumulates goodness and wisdom in exchange for the joys of wife and children.

DEATH AND REBIRTH

The questioner said: The Buddhists say that after a man dies he will be reborn. I do not believe in the truth of these words. . . .

Mou Tzu said: . . . The spirit never perishes. Only the body decays. The body is like the roots and leaves of the five grains, the spirit is like the seeds and kernels of the five grains. When the roots and leaves come forth they inevitably die. But do the seeds and kernels perish? Only the body of one who has achieved the Way perishes. . . .

Someone said: If one follows the Way one dies. If one does not follow the Way one dies. What difference is there?

---

3. Uncle of King Wen of the Chou who retired to the barbarian land of Wu and cut his hair and tattooed his body in barbarian fashion, thus yielding his claim to the throne to King Wen.

Mou Tzu said: You are the sort of person who, having not a single day of goodness, yet seeks a lifetime of fame. If one has the Way, even if one dies one's soul goes to an abode of happiness. If one does not have the Way, when one is dead one's soul suffers misfortune.

WHY SHOULD A CHINESE ALLOW HIMSELF TO BE INFLUENCED BY INDIAN WAYS?

The questioner said: Confucius said, "The barbarians with a ruler are not so good as the Chinese without one." Mencius criticized Ch'en Hsiang for rejecting his own education to adopt the ways of [the foreign teacher] Hsü Hsing, saying, "I have heard of using what is Chinese to change what is barbarian, but I have never heard of using what is barbarian to change what is Chinese." You, sir, at the age of twenty learned the way of Yao, Shun, Confucius, and the Duke of Chou. But now you have rejected them, and instead have taken up the arts of the barbarians. Is this not a great error?

Mou Tzu said: . . . What Confucius said was meant to rectify the way of the world, and what Mencius said was meant to deplore one-sidedness. Of old, when Confucius was thinking of taking residence among the nine barbarian nations, he said, "If a gentleman-scholar dwells in their midst, what baseness can there be among them?" . . . The Commentary says, "The north polar star is in the center of heaven and to the north of man." From this one can see that the land of China is not necessarily situated under the center of heaven. According to the Buddhist scriptures, above, below, and all around, all beings containing blood belong to the Buddha-clan. Therefore I revere and study these scriptures. Why should I reject the Way of Yao, Shun, Confucius, and the Duke of Chou? Gold and jade do not harm each other, crystal and amber do not cheapen each other. You say that another is in error when it is you yourself who err.

WHY MUST A MONK RENOUNCE WORLDLY PLEASURES?

The questioner said: Of those who live in the world, there is none who does not love wealth and position and hate poverty and baseness, none who does not enjoy pleasure and idleness and shrink from labor and fatigue. . . . But now the monks wear red cloth, they eat one meal a day, they bottle up the six emotions, and thus they live out their lives. What value is there in such an existence?

Mou Tzu said: Wealth and rank are what man desires, but if he cannot obtain them in a moral way, he should not enjoy them. Poverty and meanness are what man hates, but if he can only avoid them by departing from the Way, he should not avoid them. Lao Tzu has said, "The five colors make men's eyes blind, the five sounds make men's ears deaf, the five flavors dull the palate, chasing about and hunting make men's minds mad, possessions difficult to acquire bring men's conduct to an impasse. The sage acts for his belly, not for his eyes." Can these words possibly be vain? Liu-hsia Hui would not exchange his way of life for the rank of the three highest princes of the realm. Tuan-kan Mu would not exchange his for the wealth of Prince Wen of Wei. . . . All of them followed their ideals, and cared for nothing more. Is there no value in such an existence?

WHY DOES MOU TZU SUPPORT HIS CONTENTIONS FROM SECULAR RATHER THAN BUDDHIST LITERATURE?

The questioner said: You, sir, say that the scriptures are like the rivers and the sea, their phrases like brocade and embroidery. Why, then, do you not draw on the Buddhist scriptures to answer my question? Why instead do you refer to the books of *Odes* and *History,* joining together things that are different to make them appear the same?

Mou Tzu said: . . . I have quoted those things, sir, which I knew you would understand. Had I preached the words of the Buddhist scriptures or discussed the essence of non-action, it would have been like speaking to a blind man of the five colors or playing the five sounds to a deaf man.

DOES BUDDHISM HAVE NO RECIPE FOR IMMORTALITY?

The questioner said: The Taoists say that Yao, Shun, the Duke of Chou, and Confucius and his seventy-two disciples did not die, but became immortals. The Buddhists say that men must all die, and that none can escape. What does this mean?

Mou Tzu said: Talk of immortality is superstitious and unfounded; it is not the word of the sages. Lao Tzu says, "Even Heaven and earth cannot be eternal. How much the less can man!" Confucius says, "The wise man leaves the world, but humanity and filial piety last forever." I have observed the six arts and examined the commentaries and records. According to them, Yao died, Shun had his [death place at] Mount Ts'ang-wu, Yü has his tomb on K'uai-chi, Po I and Shu Ch'i have their grave in Shou-yang. King Wen died before he could chastise Chou, King Wu died without waiting for King Ch'eng to grow up. We read of the

Duke of Chou that he was reburied, and of Confucius that [shortly before his death] he dreamed of two pillars. [As for the disciples of Confucius], Po-yü died before his father, of Tzu Lu it is said that his flesh was chopped up and pickled.

29. THE INTRODUCTION OF BUDDHISM INTO JAPAN: THE *CHRONICLES OF JAPAN (NIHONGI)*

The Chronicles of Japan (Nihongi) *is one of the oldest primary sources for Japanese history. Written in Chinese in A.D. 720 by Japanese in the court of the reigning Yamato family, it is a valuable source of information about Japan in the sixth century.*

The following two selections, the first from the year 538 and the second from 584, concern the introduction of Buddhism. How was Buddhism first introduced into Japan? What seems to have been the initial appeal of the new religion? How was the fate of the new religion determined? What seems to have happened between 538 and 584?

[A.D. 538], Winter, 10th month. King Syong of Paekche[1] sent [two envoys] with a present to the Emperor of an image of [the Buddha] in gold and copper, several flags and umbrellas, and a number of volumes of Sutras. Separately he presented a memorial in which he lauded the merit of diffusing abroad religious worship, saying:—"This doctrine is amongst all doctrines the most excellent. But it is hard to explain, and hard to comprehend. Even the Duke of Chou and Confucius had not attained to a knowledge of it. This doctrine can create religious merit and retribution [karma] without measure and without bounds, and so lead on to a full appreciation of the highest wisdom. Imagine a man in possession of treasures to his heart's content, so that he might satisfy all his wishes in proportion as he used them. Thus it is with the treasure of this wonderful doctrine. Every prayer is fulfilled and naught is wanting. Moreover, from distant India it has extended hither to the three [kingdoms of Korea], where there are none who do not receive it with reverence as it is preached to them.

---

1. Paekche was one of the three main Korean kingdoms.

"Thy servant, therefore, Syong, King of Paekche, has humbly des-
patched a retainer to transmit it to the Imperial Country [of Japan], and
to diffuse it abroad throughout the home provinces, so as to fulfil the
recorded saying of Buddha: 'My law shall spread to the East.' "

This day the Emperor, having heard to the end, leaped for joy, and
gave command to the envoys, saying:—"Never from former days until
now have we had the opportunity of listening to so wonderful a doctrine.
We are unable, however, to decide of ourselves." Accordingly he in-
quired of his ministers one after another, saying:—"The countenance of
this Buddha which has been presented by the Western frontier state is of
a severe dignity, such as we have never at all seen before. Ought it to be
worshipped or not?" The Oho-omi [chief of the Soga clan] addressed the
Emperor, saying:—"All the Western frontier lands without exception do
it worship. Shall [our land of] Yamato alone refuse to do so?" [The chiefs
of the Mononobe and Nakatomi clans] addressed the Emperor jointly,
saying:—"Those who have ruled the Empire in this our state have always
made it their care to worship in spring, summer, autumn, and winter the
180 [Shinto] gods of heaven and earth, and the gods of the land and of
grain. If just at this time we were to worship in their stead foreign deities,
it may be feared that we should incur the wrath of our national gods."

The Emperor said:—"Let [the image] be given to [the Oho-omi], who
has shown his willingness to take it, and, as an experiment, make him to
worship it."

The Oho-omi knelt down and received it with joy. He enthroned it in
his house at Oharida, where he diligently carried out the rites of retire-
ment from the world, and on that score purified his house at Muku-hara
and made it a temple. After this a pestilence was rife in the land, from
which the people died prematurely. As time went on it became worse and
worse, and there was no remedy. [The chiefs of the Mononobe and
Nakatomi clans] addressed the Emperor jointly, saying:—"It was because
thy servants' advice on a former day was not approved that the people
are dying thus of disease. If thou dost now retrace thy steps before
matters have gone too far, joy will surely be the result! It will be well
promptly to fling it away, and diligently to seek happiness in the future."

The Emperor said:—"Let it be done as you advise." Accordingly officials took the image of Buddha and abandoned it to the current of the
Canal of Naniha. They also set fire to the Temple, and burnt it so that
nothing was left. Hereupon, there being in the heavens neither clouds nor
wind, a sudden conflagration consumed the Great Hall (of the Palace).

[A.D. 584], Autumn, 9th month. [A man] who had come from Paekche
had a stone image of [the Bodhisattva] and an image of Buddha. This
year [a Soga clansman named] Mumako Sukune, having asked for these
two Buddhist images, sent [three retainers] in all directions to search out
persons who practised Buddhism. Upon this he only found in the prov-

ince of Harima a man [of Korean origin], who from a Buddhist priest had become a layman again. So the Oho-omi made him teacher, and caused him to receive [three young women] into religion . . . Mumako Sukune, still in accordance with the Law of Buddha, reverenced the three nuns, and gave orders to provide them with food and clothing. He erected a Buddhist temple on the east side of his dwelling, in which he enshrined the stone image of [the Bodhisattva]. He insisted on the three nuns holding a general meeting to partake of [a vegetarian meal]. At this time [the father of one of the nuns] found a Buddhist relic on [top of] the food, and presented it to Mumako Sukune. Mumako Sukune, by way of experiment, took the relic, and placing it on the middle of a block of iron, beat it with an iron sledgehammer, which he flourished aloft. The block and the sledgehammer were shattered to atoms, but the relic could not be crushed. Then the relic was cast into water, where it floated on the water or sank as one desired. In consequence of this, Mumako Sukune held faith in Buddhism and practised it unremittingly. [He] built another Buddhist temple at his house in Ishikaha. From this arose the beginning of Buddhism.

CHAPTER TEN

East Asian Civilizations

30. THE CHINESE CIVIL SERVICE EXAM SYSTEM

Ichisada Miyazaki

The Chinese civil service examination system originated fourteen hundred years ago, making it by far the first in the world. As a device for ensuring government by the brightest young men, regardless of class or social standing, it may also be viewed as one of the world's earliest democratic systems. It was not perfect. Like democratic systems in the West only two hundred years ago, it excluded women. The system also put enormous pressure on young boys of ambitious families.

This selection consists of two passages from a book by a noted modern Japanese historian of China. The first passage concerns the elaborate early preparations for the exams.

What did young boys have to learn? In what ways was their education different from your own? What effects did the examination system have on the goals and values of young people?

PREPARING FOR THE EXAMINATIONS

Competition for a chance to take the civil service examinations began, if we may be allowed to exaggerate only a little, even before birth. On the back of many a woman's copper mirror the five-character formula "Five Sons Pass the Examinations" expressed her heart's desire to bear five successful sons. Girls, since they could not take the examinations and become officials but merely ran up dowry expenses, were no asset to a family; a man who had no sons was considered to be childless. People said that thieves warned each other not to enter a household with five or more girls because there would be nothing to steal in it. The luckless parents of girls hoped to make up for such misfortune in the generation of their grandchildren by sending their daughters into marriage equipped with those auspicious mirrors.

Prenatal care began as soon as a woman was known to be pregnant. She had to be very careful then, because her conduct was thought to have an influence on the unborn child, and everything she did had to be right. She had to sit erect, with her seat and pillows arranged in exactly the proper way, to sleep without carelessly pillowing her head on an arm, to abstain from strange foods, and so on. She had to be careful to avoid unpleasant colors, and she spent her leisure listening to poetry and the classics being read aloud. These preparations were thought to lead to the birth of an unusually gifted boy.

If, indeed, a boy was born the whole family rejoiced, but if a girl arrived everyone was dejected. On the third day after her birth it was the custom to place a girl on the floor beneath her bed, and to make her grasp a tile and a pebble so that even then she would begin to form a lifelong habit of submission and an acquaintance with hardship. In contrast, in early times when a boy was born arrows were shot from an exorcising bow in the four directions of the compass and straight up and down. In later times, when literary accomplishments had become more important than the martial arts, this practice was replaced by the custom of scattering coins for servants and others to pick up as gifts. Frequently the words "First-place Graduate" were cast on those coins, to signify the highest dreams of the family and indeed of the entire clan.

It was thought best for a boy to start upon his studies as early as possible. From the very beginning he was instructed almost entirely in the classics, since mathematics could be left to merchants, while science and technology were relegated to the working class. A potential grand official must study the Four Books, the Five Classics, and other Confucian works, and, further, he must know how to compose poems and write essays. For the most part, questions in civil service examinations did not go beyond these areas of competence.

When he was just a little more than three years old, a boy's education began at home, under the supervision of his mother or some other suitable person. Even at this early stage the child's home environment exerted a great effect upon his development. In cultivated families, where books were stacked high against the walls, the baby sitter taught the boy his first characters while playing. As far as possible these were characters written with only a few strokes.

First a character was written in outline with red ink on a single sheet of paper. Then the boy was made to fill it in with black ink. Finally he himself had to write each character. At this stage there was no special need for him to know the meanings of the characters.

After he had learned in this way to hold the brush and to write a number of characters, he usually started on the *Primer of One Thousand Characters.* This is a poem that begins:

Heaven is dark, earth is yellow,
The universe vast and boundless . . .

It consists of a total of two hundred and fifty lines, and since no character is repeated, it provided the student with a foundation of a thousand basic ideograms.

Upon completing the *Primer,* a very bright boy, who could memorize one thing after another without difficulty, would go on to a history text called *Meng Ch'iu (The Beginner's Search)* and then proceed to the Four Books and the Five Classics normally studied in school. If rumors of such a prodigy reached the capital, a special "tough examination" was held, but often such a precocious boy merely served as a plaything for adults and did not accomplish much in later life. Youth examinations were popular during the Sung dynasty, but declined and finally were eliminated when people realized how much harm they did to the boys.

Formal education began at about seven years of age (or eight, counting in Chinese style). Boys from families that could afford the expense were sent to a temple, village, communal, or private school staffed by former officials who had lost their positions, or by old scholars who had repeatedly failed the examinations as the years slipped by. Sons of rich men and powerful officials often were taught at home by a family tutor in an elegant small room located in a detached building, which stood in a courtyard planted with trees and shrubs, in order to create an atmosphere conducive to study.

A class usually consisted of eight or nine students. Instruction centered on the Four Books, beginning with the *Analects,* and the process of learning was almost entirely a matter of sheer memorization. With their books open before them, the students would parrot the teacher, phrase by phrase, as he read out the text. Inattentive students, or those who amused themselves by playing with toys hidden in their sleeves, would be scolded by the teacher or hit on the palms and thighs with his fan-shaped "warning ruler." The high regard for discipline was reflected in the saying, "If education is not strict, it shows that the teacher is lazy."

Students who had learned how to read a passage would return to their seats and review what they had just been taught. After reciting it a hundred times, fifty times while looking at the book and fifty with the book face down, even the least gifted would have memorized it. At first the boys were given twenty to thirty characters a day, but as they became more experienced they memorized one, two, or several hundred each day. In order not to force a student beyond his capacity, a boy who could memorize four hundred characters would be assigned no more than two hundred. Otherwise he might become so distressed as to end by detesting his studies.

Along with the literary curriculum, the boys were taught proper conduct, such as when to use honorific terms, how to bow to superiors and to equals, and so forth—although from a modern point of view their training in deportment may seem somewhat defective, as is suggested by the incident concerning a high-ranking Chinese diplomat in the late Ch'ing dynasty who startled Westerners by blowing his nose with his fingers at a public ceremony.

It was usual for a boy to enter school at the age of eight and to complete the general classical education at fifteen. The heart of the curriculum was the classics. If we count the number of characters in the classics that the boys were required to learn by heart, we get the following figures:

Analects	11,705
Mencius	34,685
Book of Changes	24,107
Book of Documents	25,700
Book of Poetry	39,234
Book of Rites	99,010
Tso Chuan	196,845

The total number of characters a student had to learn, then, was 431,286.

The *Great Learning* and the *Doctrine of the Mean,* which together with the *Analects* and the *Mencius* constitute the Four Books, are not counted separately, since they are included in the *Book of Rites.* And, of course, those were not 431,286 *different* characters: most of the ideographs would have been used many times in the several texts. Even so, the task of having to memorize textual material amounting to more than 400,000 characters is enough to make one reel. They required exactly six years of memorizing, at the rate of two hundred characters a day.

After the students had memorized a book, they read commentaries, which often were several times the length of the original text, and practiced answering questions involving passages selected as examination topics. On top of all this, other classical, historical, and literary works had to be scanned, and some literary works had to be examined carefully, since the students were required to write poems and essays modeled upon them. Anyone not very vigorous mentally might well become sick of it all halfway through the course.

Moreover, the boys were at an age when the urge to play is strongest, and they suffered bitterly when they were confined all day in a classroom as though under detention. Parents and teachers, therefore, supported a lad, urging him on to "become a great man!" From ancient times, many poems were composed on the theme, "If you study while young, you will get ahead." The Sung emperor Chen-tsung wrote such a one:

To enrich your family, no need to buy good land:
Books hold a thousand measures of grain.
For an easy life, no need to build a mansion:
In books are found houses of gold.

Going out, be not vexed at absence of followers:
In books, carriages and horses form a crowd.
Marrying, be not vexed by lack of a good go-between:
In books there are girls and faces of jade.
A boy who wants to become a somebody
Devotes himself to the classics, faces the window, and reads.

In later times this poem was criticized because it tempted students with the promise of beautiful women and riches, but that was the very reason it was effective.

Nonetheless, in all times and places students find shortcuts to learning. Despite repeated official and private injunctions to study the Four Books and Five Classics honestly, rapid-study methods were devised with the sole purpose of preparing candidates for the examinations. Because not very many places in the classics were suitable as subjects for examination questions, similar passages and problems were often repeated. Aware of this, publishers compiled collections of examination answers, and a candidate who, relying on these compilations, guessed successfully during the course of his own examinations could obtain a good rating without having worked very hard. But if he guessed wrong he faced unmitigated disaster because, unprepared, he would have submitted so bad a paper that the officials could only shake their heads and fail him. Reports from perturbed officials caused the government to issue frequent prohibitions of the publication of such collections of model answers, but since it was a profitable business with a steady demand, ways of issuing them surreptitiously were arranged, and time and again the prohibitions rapidly became mere empty formalities.

AN EVALUATION OF THE EXAMINATION SYSTEM

Did the examination system serve a useful purpose? . . .

The purpose of instituting the examinations, some fourteen hundred years ago under the Sui rulers, was to strike a blow against government by the hereditary aristocracy, which had prevailed until then, and to establish in its place an imperial autocracy. The period of disunion lasting from the third to the sixth century was the golden age of the Chinese aristocracy: during that time it controlled political offices in central and local governments. . . .

The important point in China, as in Japan, was that the power of the aristocracy seriously constrained the emperor's power to appoint officials. He could not employ men simply on the basis of their ability, since any imperial initiative to depart from the traditional personnel policy evoked a sharp counterattack from the aristocratic officials. This was the situation when the Sui emperor, exploiting the fact that he had reestablished order and that his authority was at its height, ended the power of the aristocracy to become officials merely by virtue of family status. He achieved this revolution when he enacted the examination system (and provided that only its graduates were to be considered qualified to hold government office), kept at hand a reserve of such officials, and made it a rule to use only them to fill vacancies in central and local government as they occurred. This was the origin of the examination system.

The Sui dynasty was soon replaced by the T'ang, which for the most part continued the policies of its predecessor. Actually, as the T'ang was in the process of winning control over China, a new group of aristocrats appeared who hoped to transmit their privileges to their descendants. To deal with this problem the emperor used the examination system and favored its *chin-shih* [highest degree winner—Ed.] trying to place them in important posts so that he could run the government as he wished. The consequence was strife between the aristocrats and the *chin-shih,* with the contest gradually turning in favor of the latter. Since those who gained office simply through their parentage were not highly regarded, either by the imperial government or by society at large, career-minded aristocrats, too, seem to have found it necessary to enter officialdom through the examination system. Their acceptance of this hard fact meant a real defeat for the aristocracy.

The T'ang can be regarded as a period of transition from the aristocratic government inherited from the time of the Six Dynasties to the purely bureaucratic government of future regimes. The examination system made a large contribution to what was certainly a great advance for China's society, and in this respect its immense significance in Chinese history cannot be denied. Furthermore, that change was begun fourteen hundred years ago, at about the time when in Europe the feudal system had scarcely been formed. In comparison, the examination system was immeasurably progressive, containing as it did a superb idea the equal of which could not be found anywhere else in the world at that time.

This is not to say that the T'ang examination system was without defects. First, the number of those who passed through it was extremely small. In part this was an inevitable result of the limited diffusion of China's literary culture at a time when printing had not yet become practical and hand-copied books were still both rare and expensive, thus restricting the number of men able to pursue scholarly studies. Furthermore, because the historical and economic roots of the new bureaucratic system were still shallow, matters did not always go smoothly and sometimes there were harsh factional conflicts among officials. The development of those conflicts indicates that they were caused by the examination system itself and constituted a second serious defect.

As has been indicated, a master-disciple relationship between the examiner and the men he passed was established, much like that between a political leader and his henchmen, while the men who passed the examination in the same year considered one another as classmates and helped one another forever after. When such combinations became too strong, factions were born.

These two defects of the examination system were eliminated during the Sung regime. For one thing, the number of men who were granted degrees suddenly rose, indicating a similar rise in the number of candidates. This was made possible by the increase in productive power and the consequent accumulation of wealth, which was the underlying reason that Chinese society changed so greatly from the T'ang period to the Sung. A new class appeared in China, comparable to the bourgeoisie in early modern Europe. In China this newly risen class concentrated hard on scholarship, and with the custom of this group, publishers prospered mightily. The classic books of Buddhism and Confucianism were printed; the collected writings of contemporaries and their discourses and essays on current topics were published; and the government issued an official gazette, so that in a sense China entered upon an age of mass communications. As a result learning was so widespread that candidates for the examinations came from virtually every part of the land, and the government could freely pick the best among them to form a reserve of officials.

In the Sung dynasty the system of conducting the examinations every three years was established. Since about three hundred men were selected each time, the government obtained an average of one hundred men a year who were qualified for the highest government positions. Thus the most important positions in government were occupied by *chin-shih,* and no longer were there conflicts between men who differed in their preparatory backgrounds, such as those between *chin-shih* and non–*chin-shih* that had arisen in the T'ang period.

Another improvement made during the Sung period was the establishment of the palace examination as the apex of the normal examination sequence. Under the T'ang emperors the conduct of the examinations was completely entrusted to officials, but this does not mean that emperors neglected them, because they were held by imperial order. It even happened that Empress Wu (r. 684–705) herself conducted the examinations in an attempt to win popularity. . . .

The position of the emperor in the political system changed greatly from T'ang times to Sung. No longer did the emperor consult on matters of high state policy with two or three great ministers deep in the interior of the palace, far removed from actual administrators. Now he was an autocrat, directly supervising all important departments of government and giving instructions about every aspect of government. Even minor matters of personnel needed imperial sanction. Now the emperor resembled the pivot of a fan, without which the various ribs of government would fall apart and be scattered. The creation of the palace examination as the final examination, given directly under the emperor's personal supervision, went hand in hand with this change in his function in the nation's political machinery and was a necessary step in the strengthening of imperial autocracy.

Thus, the examination system changed, along with Chinese society as a whole. Created to meet an essential need, it changed in response to that society's demand. It was most effective in those early stages when, first in the T'ang period, it was used by the emperor to suppress the power of the aristocracy, and then later, in the Sung period, when the cooperation of young officials with the *chin-shih* was essential for the establishment of imperial autocracy. Therefore, in the early Sung years *chin-shih* enjoyed very rapid promotion; this was especially true of the first-place *chin-shih*, not a few of whom rose to the position of chief councilor in fewer than ten years.

31.   A WIFE'S COLLECTION
Li Ch'ing-chao

In this document written in 1132 as the Northern Song empire of China was being overrun by the Chin Tatars, Li Ch'ing-chao tells the story of a collection of books and artworks that she and her husband had collected in their youth. What does the story tell you about the domestic life of a husband and wife in Song China? How does the significance of the collection change over the course of their lives? What was the point of this story?

In 1101, in the first year of the Chien-chung Reign, I came as a bride to the Chao household. At that time my father was a division head in the Ministry of Rites, and my father-in-law, later Grand Councilor, was an executive in the Ministry of Personnel. My husband was then twenty-one and a student in the Imperial Academy. In those days both families, the Chaos and the Lis, were not well-to-do and were always frugal. On the first and fifteenth day of every month, my husband would get a short vacation from the Academy: he would "pawn some clothes" for five hundred cash and go to the market at Hsiang-kuo Temple, where he would buy fruit and rubbings of inscriptions. When he brought these home, we would sit facing one another, rolling them out before us, examining and munching. And we thought ourselves persons of the age of Ko-t'ien. . . .* When, two years later, he went to take up a post, we lived on rice and vegetables, dressed in common cloth; but he would search out the most remote spots and out-of-the-way places to fulfill his interest in the world's most ancient writings and unusual characters. When his father, the Grand Councilor, was in office, various friends and relations held positions in the Imperial Libraries; there one might find many ancient poems omitted from the *Book of Songs,* unofficial histories, and writings never before seen, works hidden in walls and recovered from tombs. He would work hard at copying such things, drawing ever more pleasure from the activity, until he was unable to stop himself. Later, if he happened to see a work of painting or calligraphy by some person of ancient or modern times, or unusual vessels of the Three Dynasties of high antiquity, he would still pawn our clothes to buy them. I recall that in the Ch'ung-ning Reign a man came with a painting of peonies by Hsü Hsi and asked twenty thousand cash for it. In those days twenty thousand cash was a hard sum to raise, even for children of the nobility. We kept it with us a few days, and having thought of no plan by which we could purchase it, we returned it. For several days afterward husband and wife faced one another in deep depression.

Later we lived privately at home for ten years, gathering what we could here and there to have enough for food and clothing. Afterward, my husband governed two commanderies in succession, and he used up all his salary on "lead and wooden tablets" [for scholarly work]. Whenever he got a book, we would collate it with other editions and make corrections together, repair it, and label it with the correct title. When he got hold of a piece of calligraphy, a painting, a goblet, or a tripod, we would go over it at our leisure, pointing out faults and flaws, setting for our nightly limit the time it took one candle to burn down. Thus our collection came to surpass all others in fineness of paper and the perfection of the characters.

I happen to have an excellent memory, and every evening after we finished eating, we would sit in the hall called "Return Home" and make tea. Pointing to the heaps of books and histories, we would guess on which line of which page in which chapter of which book a certain passage could be found. Success in guessing determined who got to drink his or her tea first. Whenever I got it right, I would raise the teacup, laughing so hard that the tea would spill in my lap, and I would get up, not having been able to drink anything at all. I would have been glad to grow old in such a world. Thus, even though we were living in anxiety, hardship, and poverty, our wills were not broken.

When the book collection was complete, we set up a library in "Return Home" hall, with huge bookcases where the books were catalogued in

---

*A mythic golden age.—Ed.

sequence. There we put the books. Whenever I wanted to read, I would ask for the key, make a note in the ledger, then take out the books. If one of them was a bit damaged or soiled, it would be our responsibility to repair the spot and copy it out in a neat hand. There was no longer the same ease and casualness as before. This was an attempt to gain convenience which led instead to nervousness and anxiety. I couldn't bear it. And I began to plan how to do away with more than one meat in our meals, how to do away with all finery in my dress; for my hair there were no ornaments of bright pearls or kingfisher feathers; the household had no implements for gilding or embroidery. Whenever we would come upon a history or the work of a major writer, if there was nothing wrong with the printing and no errors in the edition, we would buy it on the spot to have as a second copy. His family had always specialized in *The Book of Changes* and the *Tso chuan,* so the collection of works in those two traditions was most perfect and complete. Books lay ranged on tables and desks, scattered on top of one another on pillows and bedding. This was what took our fancy and what occupied our minds, what drew our eyes and what our spirits inclined to; and our joy was greater than the pleasure others had in dancing girls, dogs, and horses. . . .

In 1126, the first year of the Ching-k'ang Reign, my husband was governing Tse-ch'uan when we heard that the Chin Tartars were moving against the capital. He was in a daze, realizing that all those full trunks and overflowing chests, which he regarded so lovingly and mournfully, would surely soon be his possessions no longer. In the third month of spring in 1127, the first year of the Chien-yen Reign, we hurried south for the funeral of his mother. Since we could not take the overabundance of our possessions with us, we first gave up the bulky printed volumes, the albums of paintings, and the most cumbersome of the vessels. Thus we reduced the size of the collection several times, and still we had fifteen cartloads of books. When we reached Tung-hai, it took a string of boats to ferry them all across the Huai, and again across the Yangtse to Chien-k'ang. In our old mansion in Ch'ing-chou we still had more than ten rooms of books and various items locked away, and we planned to have them all brought by boat the next year. But in the twelfth month Chin forces sacked Ch'ing-chou, and those ten or so rooms I spoke of were all reduced to ashes.

The next autumn, the ninth month of 1128, my husband took charge of Chien-k'ang Prefecture but relinquished the position in the spring of the following year. Again we put everything in boats and went up to Wu-hu and Ku-shu, intending to take up lodging on the River Kan. That summer in the fifth month we had reached Ch'ih-yang. At that point an imperial decree arrived, ordering my husband to take charge of Hu-chou, and before he assumed that office, to proceed to an audience with the Emperor. Therefore he had the household stop at Ch'ih-yang from which he would go off alone to answer the summons. On the thirteenth day of the sixth month he set off to carry out his duty. He had the boats pulled up onto the shore, and he sat there on the bank, in summer clothes with his headband set high on his forehead, his spirit like a tiger's, his eyes gleaming as though they would shoot into a person, while he gazed toward the boats and took his leave. I was in a terrible state of mind. I shouted to him, "If I hear the city is in danger, what should I do?" He answered from afar, his hands on his hips: "Follow the crowd. If you can't do otherwise, abandon the household goods first, then the clothes, then the books and scrolls, then the old bronzes—but carry the sacrificial vessels for the ancestral temple yourself; live or die with them; don't give *them* up." With this he galloped off on his horse.

As he was hurrying on his journey, he suffered sunstroke from the intense heat, and by the time he reached imperial headquarters, he had contracted a malarial fever. At the end of the seventh month I received a letter that he was lying sick. I was much alarmed, considering my husband's excitable nature and how nothing had been able to prevent the illness deteriorating into fever; his temperature might rise even higher, and in that case he would have to take chilled medicines; then the sickness would really be something to be worried about. Thereupon I set out by boat and in one day and night traveled three hundred leagues. At the point when I arrived he was taking large doses of ch'ai-hu and yellow ch'in; he had a recurring fever with dysentery, and the illness appeared terminal. I was weeping, and in such a desperate situation I could not bring myself to ask him what was to be done after his death. On the eighteenth day of the eighth month he could no longer get up; he took his brush and wrote a poem; when he finished, he passed away, with no thought at all for the future provision of his family. . . .

When the funeral was over I had nowhere to go. His Majesty had already sent the palace ladies elsewhere, and I heard that crossings of the Yangtse were to be prohibited. At the time I still had twenty thousand *chüan* of books, two thousand copies of inscriptions on metal and stone with colophons, table service and mats enough to entertain a hundred guests, along with other possessions equaling those already mentioned. I also grew very sick, to the point that my only vital sign was a rasping breath. The situation was getting more serious every day. I thought of my husband's brother-in-law, an executive in the Ministry of War on garrison duty in Hung-chou, and I dispatched two former employees of my husband to go ahead to my brother-in-law, taking the baggage. That winter in the twelfth month Chin invaders sacked Hung-chou and all was lost. Those books which, as I said, took a string of boats to ferry across the Yangtse were scattered into clouds of smoke. What remained were a few light scrolls and calligraphy pieces; manuscript copies of the collections of Li Po, Tu Fu, Han Yü, and Liu Tsung-yüan; a copy of *A New*

Account of Tales of the World (Shih-shuo hsin-yü); a copy of *Discourses on Salt and Iron (Yen-t'ieh lun);* a few dozen rubbings of stone inscriptions from the Han and T'ang; ten or so ancient tripods and cauldrons; a few boxes of Southern T'ang manuscript editions—all of which I happened to have had removed to my chambers to pass the time during my illness—now a solitary pile of leftovers.

Since I could no longer go upriver, and since the movements of the invaders were unfathomable, I went to stay with my younger brother Li Hang, a reviser of edicts. By the time I reached T'ai-chou, the governor of the place had already fled. Proceeding on to Shan through Mu-chou, we left the clothing and linen behind. Hurrying to Yellow Cliff, we hired a boat to take us toward the sea, following the fleeing court. The court halted a while in Chang-an, then we followed the imperial barge on the sea route to Wen-chou and Yüeh-chou. In the twelfth month of the fourth year of the Chien-yen Reign, early in 1131, all the officials of the government were released from their posts. We went to Ch'ü-chou, and then in the third month of spring, now the first year of the Shao-hsing Reign (1131), we returned to Yüeh-chou, and in 1132, back again to Hang-chou.

When my husband had been gravely ill, a certain academician, Chang Fei-ch'ing, had visited him with a jade pot—actually it wasn't really jade but *min*, a stone like jade. I have no idea who started the story, but there was a false rumor that they had been discussing presenting it to the Chin as a tribute gift. I also learned that someone had made formal charges in the matter. I was terrified and dared say nothing, but I took all the bronze vessels and such things in the household and was about to turn them over to the imperial court. But by the time I reached Yüeh-chou, the court had already gone on to Ssu-ming. I didn't dare keep these things in the household any longer, so I sent them along with the manuscript books to Shan. Later, when the imperial army was rounding up defeated enemy troops, I heard that these had all been taken into the household of General Li. That "solitary pile of leftovers" of which I spoke had now been reduced by about fifty or sixty percent. All that remained were six or so baskets of books, painting, ink, and inkstones that I hadn't been able to part with. I always kept these under my bed and opened them only with my own hands.

At K'uai-chi I chose lodging in a cottage belonging to a local named Chung. Suddenly one night someone made off with five of the baskets through a hole in the wall. I was terribly upset and offered a substantial reward to get them back. Two days later Chung Fu-hao next door produced eighteen of the scrolls and asked for a reward. By that I knew the thief was not far away. I tried every means I could, but I still couldn't get hold of the rest. I have now found out that they were all purchased at a low price by the Circuit Fiscal Supervisor, Wu Yüeh. Now seventy or eighty percent of that "solitary pile of leftovers" is gone. I still have a few volumes from three or so sets, none complete, and some very ordinary pieces of calligraphy, but I still treasure them as if I were protecting my own head—how foolish I am!

Nowadays, when I chance to look over these books, it's like meeting old friends. And I recall when my husband was in the hall called "Calm Governance" in Lai-chou: he had first finished binding the volumes, making title slips of rue leaves to keep out insects and tie-ribbons of pale blue silk, binding ten *chüan* into one volume. Every day in the evening when the office clerks would go home, he would do editorial collations on two *chüan* and write a colophon for one inscription. . . .

Of those two thousand items, colophons were written on five hundred and two. It is so sad—today the ink of his writing seems still fresh, yet the trees by his grave have grown to an armspan in girth. . . .

Long ago when the city of Chiang-ling fell, Hsiao Yi, Emperor Yüan of the Liang, did not regret the fall of his kingdom, yet destroyed his books and printings [unwilling to see them fall into the hands of his conquerors]. When his capital Chiang-tu was sacked, Yang Kuang, Emperor Yang of the Sui, wasn't concerned with his own death, only with recovering his books [his spirit overturning the boat in which they were being transported so that he could have his library in the land of the dead]. It must be that the passions of human nature cannot be forgotten, even standing between life and death. Or maybe it is Heaven's will that beings as insignificant as ourselves are not fit to enjoy these superb things. Or it might be that the dead too have consciousness, and they still treasure such things, give them their devoted attention, unwilling to leave them in the world of the living. How hard they are to obtain and how easy to lose!

From the time I was eighteen [two years younger than Lu Chi when he wrote the "Poetic Exposition on Literature"] until now at the age of fifty-two [two years after the age at which Ch'u Po-yü realized the error of his earlier life]—a span of thirty years—how much calamity, how much gain and loss I have witnessed! When there is possession, there must be lack of possession; when there is a gathering together, there must be a dissolution—that is the constant principle of things. Someone loses a bow; someone else happens to find a bow—what's worth noticing in that? The reason why I have so minutely recorded this story from beginning to end is to serve as a warning for scholars and collectors in later generations.

Written this second year of the Shao-hsing Reign (1132), the eighth month, first day.

Li Ch'ing-chao

32.   STREET LIFE
IN HANGCHOW

Jacques Gernet

Hangchow in 1275, at the end of the Song dynasty, on the eve of the Mongol invasion, was the largest and richest city in the world. Rarely are we able to get a glimpse of the daily lives of the ordinary people in a city like Hangchow. But Hangchow was different. The city that Marco Polo wrote home about was described by many other visitors and residents as well. The abundance of sources has allowed the historian Jacques Gernet to paint a vivid canvas.

Who were the ordinary people of Hangchow? What were their lives like? How were the poor protected and cared for?

THE COMMON PEOPLE IN URBAN SURROUNDINGS

The concentration of wealth in the towns and the poverty in the country-side combined to promote a constant influx of peasants into the great urban centres. They quickly adapted to urban life, and it was they who formed the greater part of the population of Hangchow. Their numbers increased year by year until the phenomenon began to take on the aspect of a catastrophe. The existence of large towns in thirteenth-century China is in itself concrete proof of the malady from which the economy was suffering. Their overpopulation reflects the artificial overdevelopment of commercial activity and the immoderate growth of the luxury trades at the expense of the production of basic necessities.

All the ordinary people of Hangchow—whether poor devils who slaved all day long to satisfy the demands of their masters or employers, or porters, prostitutes, petty tradesmen with stalls set up at street corners, entertainers, pickpockets, thieves and beggars—had one thing in common: they had nothing to depend on for their living but the strength of their muscles or the sharpness of their wits. They had endless stores of patience and of courage, of guile and cunning. The struggle was hard, because while capital was scarce and brought in a big return to its possessors, labour, on the contrary, was superabundant and wages always low.

The effect of the abundance and cheapness of labour was to produce an extraordinary degree of specialization. This was almost a kind of luxury not at all in keeping with the level of wealth and of techniques reached in China at that time. The labour market was remarkably well-organized thanks to the guilds, who acted as employment exchanges. It was to them that both employers and employees applied, since no transaction was ever carried through without recourse to an intermediary (and it is probable that the guilds did not permit independent practice of any trade). It was through the heads of the guilds that merchants and members of the upper classes in Hangchow were able to procure managers for pawnshops and shops for selling rice wine, for restaurants and pharmacies, or stewards for private mansions, gardeners, secretaries, accountants, cooks, specialists for heating and lighting. Some of these employment agencies even offered, on a short-term basis no doubt, concubines, dancers, young boy-singers (pederasty, let us note, was common and accepted), embroiderers, chair-porters, and escorts for people of rank proposing to travel, either in order to return to their native province or to make a tour for their education, or for officials travelling to take up their posts.

The wealth of the great families and of the *nouveau riche* merchants acted like a magnet to all the masses of poor people; most of the lower classes were either servants in the houses of or suppliers to the demands of the rich. Imperial princes, high- and middle-grade officials, wealthy shipowners, owners of huge landed fortunes, all maintained a crowd of dependents in their vast town houses or luxurious country estates. It was a sign of social success to keep a large establishment, and even newly enriched courtesans were accompanied by a retinue of servants, according to Marco Polo. The wealthiest families, particularly the princes, had their own artisans: jewellers, sculptors in ivory, embroiderers. . . . They also had their own private militia, and the staff of a great family was divided among various service departments. They were known in Hangchow as "the four services and the six offices." The four services consisted of the servants in charge of furnishings (chairs, tables, curtains, blinds, mats, hangings, screens, paintings and scrolls of calligraphy); those in charge of alcoholic liquors and teas; those in charge of the table-furnishings for banquets and the masters of ceremony who led in the guests and attended to the sending out of invitations and to the ceremonies at marriages and funerals; and those in charge of the kitchen and the kitchen staff. The six offices had tasks that were more precise and more limited; the decoration of dishes ready for serving, the purchase of fruits, the purchase of snacks for accompanying drinks, lighting, the purchase of incense and perfumes and of medicines, the heating, cleaning and decorating of the rooms.

This large staff of domestic servants did not, however, by any means complete the number of persons employed in the great houses. There was, at a higher level, a whole bevy of people, not strictly servants, who were maintained on a permanent or a temporary basis by the great families in virtue of their social talents or special gifts: tutors, tellers of tales ancient and modern, chanters of poetry, zither players, chess players, horsemen, painters of orchids, literary men, copyists, bibliophiles. There were others who gave exhibitions of cockfighting or pigeon fighting, who could imitate animal noises, train performing insects, pose amusing riddles, or who were experts in hanging paintings or arranging flowers for interior decoration, or who served as go-between with fashionable courtesans and undertook to deliver notes to them.

The people who depended on the wealthy families for their living certainly formed one of the largest groups among the lower classes because dozens of people were employed by the great houses in various capacities. On the other hand, the number of people employed in the workshops, pork-butchers' shops, restaurants, tea-houses and luxury-trade shops was confined to as few hands as possible. But the relationship between all these people and their masters or employers was everywhere the same: a paternalistic attitude on the part of the master, and one of respect and submission on the part of the servants or employees. The latter formed part of the family, and sometimes served from father to son in the same houses. Their complete economic dependence together with the persistence of the old family system provides an explanation for the strength of this bond. There were no big factories nor yards in Hangchow, and almost the only revolts of any kind were those which broke out in the provinces, either among the peasants or in the big industrial concerns, both public and private, such as the salt-wells in Szechwan, where a large number of poverty-stricken people were employed.

As for the guilds, they were too numerous and too varied to allow their influence to be felt. There was no consciousness among the lower classes of their unity vis-à-vis the rich. Not only an indefatigable zeal, but complete devotion as well was expected of servants and employees. Their slightest faults were severely punished, and the State gave every assistance towards maintaining the requisite sense of duty and obligation. The law provided sanctions for any deviation from the traditional relationship between master and servant. Moreover, heads of families and owners of shops and workshops were usually careful to ensure that their dependents had no cause for revolt. They refrained from any crying injustice, saw to it that they amassed some savings, and did their best to arrange marriages for them. These dependents, although they were early to rise and late to bed and constantly at the beck and call of their masters or of the chief steward or shop manager, had one great advantage over the peasant: a relative security of livelihood. A particular advantage attendant upon being a servant in a rich family was the certainty of finding a wife among the domestic staff of his master, and this was one of the main incitements to acceptance of this particular form of servitude.

All those who did not belong to the comparatively fortunate class of servants and employees and who had therefore not succeeded in linking their fortunes with those of a master or employer, lived for the most part from hand to mouth. They occupied a lower level in the stratification of the lower classes. Among them were the heavy labourers: navvies, water-carriers, scavengers, etc., they, too, with their guilds—for what trade was without one? One tends to imagine these thirteenth-century coolies as having the same characteristics as their modern counterparts: faces marked by a life of toil, thin as an ascetic, yet full of humour. Also to be included are the numberless pedlars of various types who went about the streets shouldering their poles, or set themselves up at street corners or in the markets: vendors of tea who could be seen going their rounds at night on the Imperial Way or from door to door in the poorer districts, and who were favourites with the gossips because they knew all the tid-bits of the neighbourhood; sellers of toys, of cooked food, hot-water pedlars squatting at the doorways of bathing establishments, horoscope pedlars, physiognomists, soothsayers, sellers of sugarcane from which one sucked the juice, of honeycomb, of jujubes, or of sweets for children: little figures, animals, birds, flowers and fruits fashioned out of sugar made from soya beans, sugarcane, barley or sesame. Each had his special street cry, if he did not simply attract the attention of customers by beating on a piece of wood or metal.

Some of them worked in the pay of shopkeepers, and there were even some concerns which used only pedlars for selling their goods, pedlars "poor and honest," in the words of an inhabitant, who went at dawn to collect their merchandise from shops known as "factory workshops." At the end of the day they brought back the money they had earned, and were given a commission of ten percent. The products sold by these poor wretches were ready-cooked dishes carried in a series of small boxes which could be packed away inside each other, sweets, and a fumigating product for getting rid of mosquitoes. All such people, whether working on their own account or in the pay of some shopkeeper or artisan, only just managed to scrape a living from the little cash they earned on their unwearying rounds. No doubt many of them were recent arrivals from the country.

People engaged in popular entertainment were innumerable: actors of little comic or historical scenes, storytellers, puppeteers or producers of Chinese shadow-plays, jugglers, acrobats, tightrope walkers, exhibitors of wild animals, etc. They gave their shows in the "pleasure grounds," covered bazaars of a kind situated in the markets and at the approaches to bridges and frequented by all classes of society.

Some of them came in from the country on feast days and could be seen "on the bridges and in the streets, trailing their children along with them"; others drew crowds by displaying stupendous muscular strength, and to the roll of a drum lifted iron weights, wooden beams or blocks of stone. Sometimes these were old soldiers, such as the Strong Man at one time celebrated in Ch'ang-an (Si-an) under the T'ang, who had this proud device tattooed on his arms: "Alive, I fear not the governor of the capital; dead, I fear not the king of the infernal regions." It is quite remarkable how large a number of the lower class in Hangchow were occupied in the popular entertainment industry. However, the show people only put on their best turns during the times of the great annual festivals when business in the town had a sudden burst of feverish activity that went on day and night without stopping.

Prostitution was very widespread in Hangchow. In Cambaluc, the Mongol capital, the walls of which were slightly further to the north than those of present-day Peking (vestiges of them are still to be seen today), Marco Polo had been struck by the large number of prostitutes in this cosmopolitan city. "And again I tell you another thing," he says, "that inside the town dare live no sinful woman . . . but . . . they all live outside in the suburbs. And you may know that there is so great a multitude of them for the foreigners that no man could believe it, for I dare tell you in truth that they are quite twenty thousand who all serve men for money, and they all find a living. . . . Then you can see if there is great abundance of people in Cambaluc since the worldly women there are as many as I have told."

The Mongols, stricter in morals than the Southern Chinese, had relegated the prostitutes to the districts outside the walls of their capital. In Hangchow, however, prostitution had infiltrated everywhere. There was hardly a single public place, tavern, restaurant, hotel, market, "pleasure ground," square or bridge where one did not encounter dozens of ladies of the town. A contemporary gives a list of the districts and addresses where low-class prostitutes were to be found in large numbers together. There were also brothels: "singing-girl houses" and taverns, which had for sign a bamboo shade over the light at the entrance.

It is difficult to assess the social status of the prostitutes in Hangchow. They must, actually, have formed a cross-section of urban society. The humble origins and poverty of many of them points to their inclusion among the lower classes. But all degrees of poverty and wealth were to be found among them. Some, like the geishas of ancient Japan, were celebrated as courtesans, and having got rich quick, lived in luxury of the most exotic kind and only consorted with people of the upper classes. Their names have been preserved by contemporaries. Talented singers and musicians, they were invited to the banquets held by high officials or noble families. A fashionable marriage was not complete unless "singing-girls" were included in the celebrations. The most celebrated ones were even invited to the court to play before the Emperor on the evening of the 15th of the first moon, the feast of lanterns. They played, seated, on the zither or on the *p'i-p'a*, a kind of guitar of Central Asian origin, or sang standing up, accompanying their song with sinuous movements of the body. A description of a singing-girl runs: "Her face is the colour of peaches, her lips are like cherries, her fingers delicate as jade, her eyes brilliant and bewitching, and her body sways as she sings."

Some courtesans were frequented by the gilded youth of Hangchow and by the students from the big colleges. The State taverns, which were run in connection with the big storehouses of alcoholic liquor, had their own singing-girls whose names were kept on special lists. Each of these taverns also kept several dozen official courtesans of whom a list was supplied to the regular customer. But the most celebrated of them usually stayed confined to their apartments and were only on view to important visitors. The *entrée* to these taverns was theoretically reserved for the students of the big colleges in Hangchow (the National University, the Imperial Academy and the Military Academy) but wealthy young men had access as well.

Here is what Marco Polo has to say about prostitution in Hangchow:

> Certain of the streets are occupied by the women of the town, who are in such number that I dare not say what it is. They are found not only in the vicinity of the market places, where usually a quarter is assigned to them, but all over the city. They exhibit themselves splendidly attired and abundantly perfumed, in finely garnished houses, with trains of waiting women. These women are extremely accomplished in all the arts of allurement, and readily adapt their conversation to all sorts of persons, insomuch that strangers who have once tasted their attractions seem to get so bewitched, and are so taken with their blandishments and their fascinating ways that they never can get these out of their heads. Hence it comes to pass that when they return home they say they have been to Kinsay or the City of Heaven, and their only desire is to get back thither as soon as possible.

This description obviously only applies to those wealthy singing-girls who had been able to emancipate themselves from all forms of protection. A Chinese author of the end of the thirteenth century tells us how one of them succeeded in attaining wealth and fame. She was a native of Suchow, a town to the north of Hangchow celebrated for its beautiful women. A petty official who came of a very rich family had heard of her charms and went by boat to Suchow to make her conquest. The gift of a sumptuous wardrobe of clothes, and handsome presents to her domestics, brought no results: the young lady was well aware of the wealth of her admirer. She did not yield until he had presented her with five hundred pounds of silver and a hundred rolls of silk. In six months the unfortunate young man had squandered several million cash, but the fame and fortune of the lady were assured. The gilded youth of Kiangsu besieged her doors. Her house, although small, was extremely luxurious. It lacked nothing: pavilions, summer-houses, belvederes, flower-gardens and artificial lakes. The floors were carpeted with brocade, the walls covered with hangings woven with gold thread, the beds decked with priceless covers. The domestic staff ran to more than ten servants and musicians. As for the ornaments and vases in gold, silver and jade, the paintings and the calligraphy scrolls, all were chosen with the most exquisite taste. At her death, the Lady Hsü Lan was buried on Tiger Hill, the burial place for people of high rank, and a student at the College composed her epitaph.

Successes of this kind were exceptional. The majority of the singing-girls, even those who lived in comparatively easy circumstances, did not succeed in emancipating themselves entirely from some kind of protection. Even if they did not actually live in one of the "singing-girl houses," they remained attached to certain taverns or restaurants whose proprietors no doubt found it advantageous to round out their income by allowing singing-girls to entertain customers in their courtyards. In the best teahouses in the city there were no singing-girls. But they were to be found, upstairs, in five teahouses on the Imperial Way. However, according to a contemporary, these were noisy places with a bad name where decent people did not venture to go.

As for the singing-girls of the lowest category, they were to be found by the dozen in the markets and near the bridges in the poorer districts. Their musical training seems to have been scanty. They were not usually called "singing-girls" or "artistes," but simply "flowers."

A word should be said here about male prostitution, which appears to have been a phenomenon peculiar to the big cities in the Sung period. Already in Kaifeng at the beginning of the twelfth century the existence of certain inverts who prostituted their charms is noted. They simpered, used cosmetics, decked themselves up, sang and danced just as their feminine counterparts did. During the years 1111–17 an imperial decree authorized their arrest and imposed a punishment of a hundred strokes of the rod. A reward of fifty strings of cash was promised to anyone catching one of them or making a deposition or denunciation. But finding out such prostitutes, while difficult enough in Kaifeng, was still more difficult in Hangchow, where the population was both numerous and more fluid. Doubtless also there was far greater tolerance after the court had moved south. So a considerable number of inverts were to be found in Hangchow, probably several hundred, who had no other means of support but prostitution. Better organized than the singing-girls, being a more homogenous group, they had their special haunt outside the ramparts, near the New Gate.

The dregs of the population consisted of thieves, ruffians, swindlers and beggars, all grouped into guilds. There were criminal gangs. A small troop of them would block the streets and rob the citizens in full daylight, in spite of being pitilessly hunted down by the city police. Others, experts in housebreaking, slipped into wealthy houses through holes made in brick walls or in bamboo partitions and took boxes of valuables. There were "daylight robbers," selling bogus wares: imitation silk clothing made of paper, lumps of lead or copper that looked like ingots of silver or gold, drugs which were nothing but earth and sawdust. A contemporary is unable to restrain his admiration: "The cunning of these people is extraordinary." Sneak-thieves threaded among the crowds in the markets and the lanes snatching purses and necklaces. Swindlers hid their reprehensible activities behind attractive offers that seemed socially advantageous. There were "services" which, owing to supposed influence in high places, undertook to procure for their clients appointments, promotions, court favours, success in legal proceedings or in commercial transactions. Others, bearing the name of "Beautiful Ladies Service," dealt in the sale of gay ladies as concubines, while yet others specialized in lotteries and gambling. Theft and fraud could not be entirely suppressed in a town containing such a large conglomeration of people. Marco Polo may be correct when he declares that "the city was so safe that the doors of the houses and shops and stores full of all very dear merchandise often stayed open at night as by day," but his account is only valid for the period of the Mongol occupation, when the police in the city must have been reinforced.

The number of paupers, beggars, thieves, country girls turned prostitutes, and poor devils living from hand to mouth by peddling worthless wares—sleeping anywhere they could find, nearly dying of cold and hunger—probably varied sharply from year to year and from month to month. The least rise in the price of rice was enough to double or triple the number of those who had to live by their wits in Hangchow. The great mass of humanity that filled the city of Hangchow to overflowing was sometimes subjected to violent shocks, and the resulting sudden increase in poverty and starvation became a matter of concern to the State. The frequency of such crises made it necessary to take precautionary measures. The court and the prefecture decided to make distributions of rice and cash at times when there was heavy snow or extreme cold, or following upon big fires, summer floods and autumn droughts. Thus, after the excessive rains in the Hangchow region in 1223, there was a famine in the town in the 3rd moon of the following year (about April), and the government had to distribute aid.

The great official ceremonies and the great annual festivals were also made the occasion for distributions to the poor: "At times when prayers for fine weather or for rain are offered by the Emperor and his ministers, when snow falls or when there are lucky omens, on the occasion of the birth of a prince or on the Emperor's birthday, when there is an eclipse of the sun, or excessive rains, or intense cold, when the townspeople are in want or when the grand rites of the Sacred Palace are celebrated or ceremonies of congratulations offered to the Emperor are performed—at all these times, an imperial notice is published announcing the gift of 200,000 strings in paper money for the army and the same for the common people."

Those in want could also look to private charity. To enhance their prestige, officials on being newly appointed or promoted would distribute cash to the poor. . . . [T]he rich shipowners who lived on Phoenix

Hill in the south side of the town devoted a part of their immense fortunes to works of charity. But that was not all. Buddhism had, from the fifth century, introduced and developed in China various charitable institutions (hospitals, almshouses, dispensaries, centres for the distribution of aid to the poor) which were supported by the income derived from the land with which they had been endowed. Following upon the widespread confiscation of property belonging to Buddhist communities in 845, the almshouses and hospitals had been taken over by the public authorities. On moving to Hangchow, the court had established there a big dispensary which distributed drugs through seventy branch dispensaries scattered all about the urban area, and we have seen how the medicaments, which were supposed to be sold at a third of their price to the people of the town, were actually misappropriated by the employees and officials serving in these dispensaries. But other charitable institutions were run with greater honesty: hospitals for the aged and the penniless, orphanages for foundlings, free funerals and public cemeteries for the poor, homes for the infirm. This last institution still existed at the beginning of the Mongol occupation, if Marco Polo is to be believed: "If in the daytime," he says, "they find any poor cripple unable to work for his livelihood, they take him to one of the hospitals, of which there are many, founded by the ancient kings, and endowed with great revenues. Or if he be capable of work they oblige him to take up some trade."

33. CHINA, TECHNOLOGY, AND CHANGE

Lynda Norene Shaffer

In this selection a modern historian of China cautions against judging Chinese history by later events in Europe. What was the impact of printing, the compass, and gunpowder in Europe? What was the earlier impact of these inventions in China? To what extent were Chinese and European effects similar? To what extent were they different?

Francis Bacon (1561–1626), an early advocate of the empirical method, upon which the scientific revolution was based, attributed Western Europe's early modern take-off to three things in particular: printing, the compass, and gunpowder. Bacon had no idea where these things had come from, but historians now know that all three were invented in China. Since, unlike Europe, China did not take off onto a path leading from the scientific to the Industrial Revolution, some historians are now asking why these inventions were so revolutionary in Western Europe and, apparently, so unrevolutionary in China.

In fact, the question has been posed by none other than Joseph Needham, the foremost English-language scholar of Chinese science and technology. It is only because of Needham's work that the Western academic community has become aware that until Europe's take-off, China was the unrivaled world leader in technological development. That is why it is so disturbing that Needham himself has posed this apparent puzzle. The English-speaking academic world relies upon him and repeats him; soon this question and the vision of China that it implies will become dogma. Traditional China will take on supersociety qualities—able to contain the power of printing, to rein in the potential of the compass, even to muffle the blast of gunpowder.

The impact of these inventions on Western Europe is well known. Printing not only eliminated much of the opportunity for human copying errors, it also encouraged the production of more copies of old books and an increasing number of new books. As written material became both cheaper and more easily available, intellectual activity increased. Printing would eventually be held responsible, at least in part, for the spread of classical humanism and other ideas from the Renaissance. It is also said to have stimulated the Protestant Reformation, which urged a return to the Bible as the primary religious authority.

The introduction of gunpowder in Europe made castles and other medieval fortifications obsolete (since it could be used to blow holes in their walls) and thus helped to liberate Western Europe from feudal aristocratic power. As an aid to navigation the compass facilitated the Portuguese- and Spanish-sponsored voyages that led to Atlantic Europe's sole possession of the Western Hemisphere, as well as the Portuguese circumnavigation of Africa, which opened up the first all-sea route from Western Europe to the long-established ports of East Africa and Asia.

Needham's question can thus be understood to mean, Why didn't China use gunpowder to destroy feudal walls? Why didn't China use the compass to cross the Pacific and discover America, or to find an all-sea route to Western Europe? Why didn't China undergo a Renaissance or Reformation? The implication is that even though China possessed these technologies, it did not change much. Essentially Needham's question is asking, What was wrong with China?

Actually, there was nothing wrong with China. China was changed fundamentally by these inventions. But in order to see the changes, one must abandon the search for peculiarly European events in Chinese history, and look instead at China itself before and after these breakthroughs.

To begin, one should note that China possessed all three of these technologies by the latter part of the Tang dynasty (618–906)—between four and six hundred years before they appeared in Europe. And it was during just that time, from about 850, when the Tang dynasty began to falter, until 960, when the Song dynasty (960–1279) was established, that China underwent fundamental changes in all spheres. In fact, historians are now beginning to use the term *revolution* when referring to technological and commercial changes that culminated in the Song dynasty, in the same way that they refer to the changes in eighteenth- and nineteenth-century England as the Industrial Revolution. And the word might well be applied to other sorts of changes in China during this period.

For example, the Tang dynasty elite was aristocratic, but that of the Song was not. No one has ever considered whether the invention of gunpowder contributed to the demise of China's aristocrats, which occurred between 750 and 960, shortly after its invention. Gunpowder may, indeed, have been a factor although it is unlikely that its importance lay in blowing up feudal walls. Tang China enjoyed such internal peace that its aristocratic lineages did not engage in castle-building of the sort typical in Europe. Thus, China did not have many feudal fortifications to blow up.

The only wall of significance in this respect was the Great Wall, which was designed to keep steppe nomads from invading China. In fact, gunpowder may have played a role in blowing holes in this wall, for the Chinese could not monopolize the terrible new weapon, and their nomadic enemies to the north soon learned to use it against them. The Song dynasty ultimately fell to the Mongols, the most formidable force ever to emerge from the Eurasian steppe. Gunpowder may have had a profound effect on China—exposing a united empire to foreign invasion and terrible devastation—but an effect quite opposite to the one it had on Western Europe.

On the other hand, the impact of printing on China was in some ways very similar to its later impact on Europe. For example, printing contributed to a rebirth of classical (that is, preceding the third century A.D.) Confucian learning, helping to revive a fundamentally humanistic outlook that had been pushed aside for several centuries.

After the fall of the Han dynasty (206 B.C.–A.D. 220), Confucianism had lost much of its credibility as a world view, and it eventually lost its central place in the scholarly world. It was replaced by Buddhism, which had come from India. Buddhists believed that much human pain and confusion resulted from the pursuit of illusory pleasures and dubious ambitions: enlightenment and, ultimately, salvation would come from a progressive disengagement from the real world, which they also believed to be illusory. This point of view dominated Chinese intellectual life until the ninth century. Thus the academic and intellectual comeback of classical Confucianism was in essence a return to a more optimistic literature that affirmed the world as humans had made it.

The resurgence of Confucianism within the scholarly community was due to many factors, but printing was certainly one of the most important. Although it was invented by Buddhist monks in China, and at first benefited Buddhism, by the middle of the tenth century, printers were turning out innumerable copies of the classical Confucian corpus. This return of scholars to classical learning was part of a more general movement that shared not only its humanistic features with the later Western European Renaissance, but certain artistic trends as well.

Furthermore, the Protestant Reformation in Western Europe was in some ways reminiscent of the emergence and eventual triumph of Neo-Confucian philosophy. Although the roots of Neo-Confucianism can be found in the ninth century, the man who created what would become its most orthodox synthesis was Zhu Xi (Chu Hsi, 1130–1200). Neo-Confucianism was significantly different from classical Confucianism, for it had undergone an intellectual (and political) confrontation with Buddhism and had emerged profoundly changed. It is of the utmost importance to understand that not only was Neo-Confucianism new, it was also heresy, even during Zhu Xi's lifetime. It did not triumph until the thirteenth century, and it was not until 1313 (when Mongol conquerors ruled China) that Zhu Xi's commentaries on the classics became the single authoritative text against which all academic opinion was judged.

In the same way that Protestantism emerged out of a confrontation with the Roman Catholic establishment and asserted the individual Christian's autonomy, Neo-Confucianism emerged as a critique of Buddhist ideas that had taken hold in China, and it asserted an individual moral capacity totally unrelated to the ascetic practices and prayers of the Buddhist priesthood. In the twelfth century Neo-Confucianists lifted the work of Mencius (Meng Zi, 370–290 B.C.) out of obscurity and assigned it a place in the corpus second only to that of the *Analects of Confucius*. Many facets of Mencius appealed to the Neo-Confucianists, but one of the most important was his argument that humans by nature are fundamentally good. Within the context of the Song dynasty, this was an assertion that morality could be pursued through an engagement in human affairs, and that the Buddhist monks' withdrawal from life's mainstream did not bestow upon them any special virtue.

The importance of these philosophical developments notwithstanding, printing probably had its greatest impact on the Chinese political system. The origin of the civil service examination system in China can be traced back to the Han dynasty, but in the Song dynasty government-administered examinations became the most important route to political power in China. For almost a thousand years (except the early period of Mongol rule), China was governed by men who had come to power simply because they had done exceedingly well in examinations on the Neo-Confucian canon. At any one time thousands of students were studying for the exams, and thousands of inexpensive books were required. Without printing, such a system would not have been possible.

The development of this alternative to aristocratic rule was one of the most radical changes in world history. Since the examinations were ultimately open to 98 percent of all males (actors were one of the few groups excluded), it was the most democratic system in the world prior to the development of representative democracy and popular suffrage in Western Europe in the eighteenth and nineteenth centuries. (There were some small-scale systems, such as the classical Greek city-states, which might be considered more democratic, but nothing comparable in size to Song China or even the modern nation-states of Europe.)

Finally we come to the compass. Suffice it to say that during the Song dynasty, China developed the world's largest and most technologically sophisticated merchant marine and navy. By the fifteenth century its ships were sailing from the north Pacific to the east coast of Africa. They could have made the arduous journey around the tip of Africa and on into Portuguese ports; however, they had no reason to do so. Although the Western European economy was prospering, it offered nothing that China could not acquire much closer to home at much less cost. In particular, wool, Western Europe's most important export, could easily be obtained along China's northern frontier.

Certainly, the Portuguese and the Spanish did not make their unprecedented voyages out of idle curiosity. They were trying to go to the Spice Islands, in what is now Indonesia, in order to acquire the most valuable commercial items of the time. In the fifteenth century these islands were the world's sole suppliers of the fine spices, such as cloves, nutmeg, and mace, as well as a source for the more generally available pepper. It was this spice market that lured Columbus westward from Spain and drew Vasco Da Gama around Africa and across the Indian Ocean.

After the invention of the compass, China also wanted to go to the Spice Islands and, in fact, did go, regularly—but Chinese ships did not have to go around the world to get there. The Atlantic nations of Western Europe, on the other hand, had to buy spices from Venice (which controlled the Mediterranean trade routes) or from other Italian city-states; or they had to find a new way to the Spice Islands. It was necessity that mothered those revolutionary routes that ultimately changed the world.

Gunpowder, printing, the compass—clearly these three inventions changed China as much as they changed Europe. And it should come as no surprise that changes wrought in China between the eighth and tenth centuries were different from changes wrought in Western Europe between the thirteenth and fifteenth centuries. It would, of course, be unfair and ahistorical to imply that something was wrong with Western Europe because the technologies appeared there later. It is equally unfair to ask why the Chinese did not accidentally bump into the Western

Hemisphere while sailing east across the Pacific to find the wool markets of Spain.

34. JAPAN:
THE TALE OF GENJI
Lady Murasaki Shikibu

The Tale of Genji is, by most measures, the world's first novel. It was written by Murasaki Shikibu, a woman at the Japanese court, probably in the first decade after the year 1000. While Japanese men were still using a dated form of Chinese for official documents, women like Lady Murasaki were fashioning the Japanese language into an effective and contempo-rary medium of communication. As ladies of the court, they also had the leisure and experience for writing intriguing, richly evocative stories. This novel is about Prince Genji, an attractive, talented, and sensitive son of the emperor, and his loves.

This selection tells of one of Prince Genji's many flirtations. It is proba-bly of greater interest to us, however, for the light it sheds on the imperial court in the Heian Period (794–1185) in Japanese history. Notice the lux-ury of surroundings and the elaborate cultivation of sentiments enjoyed by the court nobility. Notice the immediate role of dance, music, and poetry in their lives. How was their idea of a "good time" different from your own? What might account for the difference? In what ways were the relationships of men and women similar to, or different from, others you are aware of?

About the twentieth day of the second month the Emperor gave a Chi-nese banquet under the great cherry-tree of the Southern Court. Both Fujitsubo and the Heir Apparent were to be there. Kokiden, although she knew that the mere presence of the Empress was sufficient to spoil her pleasure, could not bring herself to forego so delightful an entertain-ment. After some promise of rain the day turned out magnificent; and in full sunshine, with the birds singing in every tree, the guests (royal princes, noblemen and professional poets alike) were handed the rhyme words which the Emperor had drawn by lot, and set to work to compose their poems. It was with a clear and ringing voice that Genji read out the word "Spring" which he had received as the rhyme-sound of his poem. Next came To no Chujo who, feeling that all eyes were upon him and determined to impress himself favourably on his audience, moved with the greatest possible elegance and grace; and when on receiving his rhyme he announced his name, rank, and titles, he took great pains to speak pleasantly as well as audibly. Many of the other gentlemen were rather nervous and looked quite pale as they came forward, yet they acquitted themselves well enough. But the professional poets, particularly owing to the high standard of accomplishment which the Emperor's and Heir Apparent's lively interest in Chinese poetry had at that time diffused through the Court, were very ill at ease; as they crossed the long space of the garden on their way to receive their rhymes they felt utterly helpless. A simple Chinese verse is surely not much to ask of a professional poet; but they all wore an expression of the deepest gloom. One expects elderly scholars to be somewhat odd in their movements and behaviour, and it was amusing to see the lively concern with which the Emperor watched their various but always uncouth and erratic methods of approaching the Throne. Needless to say a great deal of music had been arranged for. Towards dusk the delightful dance known as the Warbling of Spring Nightingales was performed, and when it was over the Heir Apparent, remembering the Festival of Red Leaves, placed a wreath on Genji's head and pressed him so urgently that it was impossible for him to refuse. Rising to his feet he danced very quietly a fragment of the sleeve-turning passage in the Wave Dance. In a few moments he was seated again, but even into this brief extract from a long dance he managed to import an unrivalled charm and grace. Even his father-in-law who was not in the best of humour with him was deeply moved and found himself wiping away a tear.

"And why have we not seen To no Chujo?" said the Heir Apparent. Whereupon Chujo danced the Park of Willow Flowers, giving a far more complete performance than Genji, for no doubt he knew that he would be called upon and had taken trouble to prepare his dance. It was a great success and the Emperor presented him with a cloak, which everyone said was a most unusual honour. After this the other young noblemen who were present danced in no particular order, but it was now so dark that it was impossible to discriminate between their performances.

Then the poems were opened and read aloud. The reading of Genji's verses was continually interrupted by loud murmurs of applause. Even the professional poets were deeply impressed, and it may well be imagined with what pride the Emperor, to whom at times Genji was a source of consolation and delight, watched him upon such an occasion as this. Fujitsubo, when she allowed herself to glance in his direction, marvelled that even Kokiden could find it in her heart to hate him. "It is because he is fond of me; there can be no other reason," she decided at last, and the verse, "Were I but a common mortal who now am gazing at the beauty of this flower, from its sweet petals not long should I withhold the dew of love," framed itself on her lips, though she dared not utter it aloud.

It was now very late and the banquet was over. The guests had scattered. The Empress and the Heir Apparent had both returned to the Palace—all was still. The moon had risen very bright and clear, and Genji, heated with wine, could not bear to quit so lovely a scene. The people at the Palace were probably all plunged in a heavy sleep. On such a night it was not impossible that some careless person might have left some door unfastened, some shutter unbarred. Cautiously and stealthily he crept towards Fujitsubo's apartments and inspected them. Every bolt was fast. He sighed; here there was evidently nothing to be done. He was passing the loggia of Kokiden's palace when he noted that the shutters of the third arch were not drawn. After the banquet Kokiden herself had gone straight to the Emperor's rooms. There did not seem to be anyone about. A door leading from the loggia into the house was standing open, but he could hear no sound within. "It is under just such circumstances as this that one is apt to drift into compromising situations," thought Genji. Nevertheless he climbed quietly on to the balustrade and peeped. Everyone must be asleep. But no; a very agreeable young voice with an intonation which was certainly not that of any waiting-woman or common person was softly humming the last two lines of the *Oborozuki-yo.*[1] Was not the voice coming towards him? It seemed so, and stretching out his hand he suddenly found that he was grasping a lady's sleeve. "Oh, how you frightened me!" she cried. "Who is it?" "Do not be alarmed," he whispered. "That both of us were not content to miss the beauty of this departing night is proof more clear than the half-clouded moon that we were meant to meet," and as he recited the words he took her gently by the hand and led her into the house, closing the door behind them. Her surprised and puzzled air fascinated him. "There is someone there," she whispered tremulously, pointing to the inner room. "Child," he answered, "I am allowed to go wherever I please and if you send for your friends they will only tell you that I have every right to be here. But if you will stay quietly here . . ." It was Genji. She knew his voice and the discovery somewhat reassured her. She thought his conduct rather strange, but she was determined that he should not think her prudish or stiff. And so because he on his side was still somewhat excited after the doings of the evening, while she was far too young and pliant to offer any serious resistance, he soon got his own way with her.

Suddenly they saw to their discomfiture that dawn was creeping into the sky. She looked, thought Genji, as though many disquieting reflections were crowding into her mind. "Tell me your name" he said. "How can I write you unless you do? Surely this is not going to be our only meeting?" She answered with a poem in which she said that names are of this world only and he would not care to know hers if he were resolved that their love should last till worlds to come. It was a mere quip and

---

1. A famous poem by Oye no Chisato (ninth century): "What so lovely as a night when the moon though dimly clouded is never wholly lost to sight!"

Genji, amused at her quickness, answered, "You are quite right. It was a mistake on my part to ask." And he recited the poem: "While still I seek to find on which blade dwells the dew, a great wind shakes the grasses of the level land." "If you did not repent of this meeting," he continued, "you would surely tell me who you are. I do not believe that you want . . ." But here he was interrupted by the noise of people stirring in the next room. There was a great bustle and it was clear that they would soon be starting out to fetch Princess Kokiden back from the palace. There was just time to exchange fans in token of their new friendship before Genji was forced to fly precipitately from the room. In his own apartments he found many of his gentlemen waiting for him. Some were awake, and these nudged one another when he entered the room as though to say, "Will he never cease these disreputable excursions?" But discretion forbad them to show that they had seen him and they all pretended to be fast asleep. Genji too lay down, but he could not rest. He tried to recall the features of the lady with whom he had just spent so agreeable a time. Certainly she must be one of Kokiden's sisters. Perhaps the fifth or sixth daughter, both of whom were still unmarried. The handsomest of them (or so he had always heard) were Prince Sochi's wife and the fourth daughter, the one with whom To no Chujo got on so badly. It would really be rather amusing if it did turn out to be Chujo's wife. The sixth was shortly to be married to the Heir Apparent. How tiresome if it were she! But at present he could think of no way to make sure. She had not behaved at all as though she did not want to see him again. Why then had she refused to give him any chance of communicating with her? In fact he worried about the matter so much and turned it over in his mind with such endless persistency that it soon became evident he had fallen deeply in love with her. Nevertheless no sooner did the recollection of Fujitsubo's serious and reticent demeanour come back to his mind than he realized how incomparably more she meant to him than this light-hearted lady.

That day the after-banquet kept him occupied till late at night. At the Emperor's command he performed on the thirteen-stringed zithern and had an even greater success than with his dancing on the day before. At dawn Fujitsubo retired to the Emperor's rooms. Disappointed in his hope that the lady of last night would somewhere or somehow make her appearance on the scene, he sent for Yoshikiyo and Koremitsu with whom all his secrets were shared and bade them keep watch upon the lady's family. When he returned next day from duty at the Palace they reported that they had just witnessed the departure of several coaches which had been drawn up under shelter in the Courtyard of the Watch. "Among a group of persons who seemed to be the domestic attendants of those for whom the coaches were waiting two gentlemen came threading their way in a great hurry. These we recognized as Shii no Shosho and Uchuben, so there is little doubt that the carriages belonged to Princess Kokiden. For the rest we noted that the ladies were by no means ill-looking and that the whole party drove away in three carriages." Genji's heart beat fast. But he was no nearer than before to finding out which of the sisters it had been. Supposing her father, the Minister of the Right, should hear anything of this, what a to-do there would be! It would indeed mean his absolute ruin. It was a pity that while he was about it he did not stay with her till it was a little lighter. But there it was! He did not know her face, but yet he was determined to recognize her. How? He lay on his bed devising and rejecting endless schemes. Murasaki too must be growing impatient. Days had passed since he had visited her and he remembered with tenderness how low-spirited she became when he was not able to be with her. But in a moment his thoughts had returned to the unknown lady. He still had her fan. It was a folding fan with ribs of hinoki-wood and tassels tied in a splice-knot. One side was covered with silverleaf on which was painted a dim moon, giving the impression of a moon reflected in water. It was a device which he had seen many times before, but it had agreeable associations for him, and continuing the metaphor of the "grass on the moor" which she had used in her poem, he wrote on the fan—"Has mortal man ever puzzled his head with such a question before as to ask where the moon goes to when she leaves the sky at dawn?" And he put the fan safely away. It was on his conscience that he had not for a long while been to the Great Hall; but fearing that Murasaki too might be feeling very unhappy, he first went home to give her her lessons. Every day she was improving not only in looks, but also in amiability of character. The beauty of her disposition was indeed quite out of the common. The idea that so perfect a nature was in his hands, to train and cultivate as he thought best, was very attractive to Genji. It might however have been objected that to receive all her education from a young man is likely to make a girl somewhat forward in her manner.

First there was a great deal to tell about what happened at the Court entertainments of the last few days. Then followed her music lesson, and already it was time to go. "Oh, why must he always go away so soon?" she wondered sadly, but by now she was so used to it that she no longer fretted as she had done a little while ago.

At the Great Hall he could, as usual, scarcely get a word out of Aoi. The moment that he sat idle a thousand doubts and puzzles began to revolve in his mind. He took up his zithern and began to sing:

Not softlier pillowed is my head
That rests by thine, unloving bride,
Than were those jagged stones my bed
Through which the falls of Nuki stride.

At this moment Aoi's father came by and began to discuss the unusual success of the recent festivities. "Old as I am," he said—"and I may say that I have lived to see four illustrious sovereigns occupy the Throne, I have never taken part in a banquet which produced verses so spirited or dancing and music so admirably performed. Talent of every description seems at present to exist in abundance; but it is creditable to those in authority that they knew how to make good use of it. For my part I enjoyed myself so much that had I but been a few years younger I would positively have joined in the dancing!" "No special steps were taken to discover the musicians," answered Genji. "We merely used those who were known to the government in one part of the country and another as capable performers. If I may say so, it was Chujo's Willow Dance that made the deepest impression and is likely always to be remembered as a remarkable performance. But if you, Sir, had indeed honoured us, a new lustre would have been added to my Father's reign." Aoi's brothers now arrived and leaning against the balustrade gave a little concert, their various instruments blending delightfully.

Fugitive as their meeting had been, it had sufficed to plunge the lady whose identity Prince Genji was now seeking to establish into the depths of despair; for in the fourth month she was to become the Heir Apparent's wife. Turmoil filled her brain. Why had not Genji visited her again? He must surely know whose daughter she was. But how should he know which daughter? Besides, her sister Kokiden's house was not a place where, save under very strange circumstances, he was likely to feel at all at his ease. And so she waited in great impatience and distress; but of Genji there was no news.

About the twentieth day of the third month her father, the Minister of the Right, held an archery meeting in which most of the young noblemen and princes were present. It was followed by a wistaria feast. The cherry blossom was for the most part over, but two trees, which the Minister seemed somehow to have persuaded to flower later than all the rest, were still an enchanting sight. He had had his house rebuilt only a short time ago when celebrating the initiation of his granddaughters, the children of Kokiden. It was now a magnificent building and not a thing in it but was of the very latest fashion. He had invited Genji when he had met him at the Palace only a few days before and was extremely annoyed when he did not appear. Feeling that the party would be a failure if Genji did not come, he sent his son Shii no Shosho to fetch him, with the poem: "Were my flowers as those of other gardens never should I have ventured to summon you." Genji was in attendance upon the Emperor and at once showed him the message. "He seems very pleased with himself and his flowers," said His Majesty with a smile; adding, "as he has sent for you like this, I think you had better go. After all, your half-sisters are being brought up at his house, and you ought not to treat him quite as a stranger." He went to his apartments and dressed. It was very late indeed when at last he made his appearance at the party. He was dressed in a cloak of thin Chinese fabric, white outside but lined with yellow. His robe was of a deep wine-red colour with a very long train. The dignity and grace with which he carried this fancifully regal attire in a company where all were dressed in plain official robes were indeed remarkable, and in the end his presence perhaps contributed more to the success of the party than did the fragrance of the Minister's boasted flowers. His entry was followed by some very agreeable music. It was already fairly late when Genji, on the plea that the wine had given him a headache, left his seat and went for a walk. He knew that his two stepsisters, the daughters of Kokiden, were in the inner apartments of the palace. He went to the eastern portico and rested there. It was on this side of the house that the wistaria grew. The wooden blinds were raised and a number of ladies were leaning out of the window to enjoy the blossoms. They had hung bright-coloured robes and shawls over the windowsill just as is done at the time of the New Year dancing and other gala days and were behaving with a freedom of allure which contrasted very oddly with the sober decorum of Fujitsubo's household. "I am feeling rather overpowered by all the noise and bustle of the flower-party," Genji explained. "I am very sorry to disturb my sisters, but I can think of nowhere else to seek refuge . . ." and advancing towards the main door of the women's apartments, he pushed back the curtain with his shoulder. "Refuge indeed!" cried one of the ladies, laughing at him. "You ought to know by now that it is only poor relations who come to seek refuge with the more successful members of their family. What pray have you come to bother us for?" "Impertinent creatures!" he thought, but nevertheless there was something in their manner which convinced him they were persons of some consequence in the house and not, as he at first supposed, mere waiting-women. A scent of costly perfumes pervaded the room; silken skirts rustled in the darkness. There could be little doubt that these were Kokiden's sisters and their friends. Deeply absorbed, as indeed was the whole of his family, in the fashionable gaieties of the moment, they had flouted decorum and posted themselves at the window that they might see what little they could of the banquet which was proceeding outside. Little thinking that his plan could succeed, yet led on by delightful recollections of his previous encounter, he advanced towards them chanting in a careless undertone the song:

At Ishikawa, Ishikawa
A man from Koma [Korea] took my belt away . . .

But for "belt" he substituted "fan" and by this means he sought to discover which of the ladies was his friend. "Why, you have got it wrong! I never heard of *that* Korean," one of them cried. Certainly it was not she. But there was another who though she remained silent seemed to him to be sighing softly to herself. He stole towards the curtain-of-state behind which she was sitting and taking her hand in his at a venture he whispered the poem: "If on this day of shooting my arrow went astray, 'twas that in dim morning twilight only the mark had glimmered in my view." And she, unable any longer to hide that she knew him, answered with the verse: "Had it been with the arrows of the heart that you had shot, though from the moon's slim bow no brightness came, would you have missed your mark?" Yes, it was her voice. He was delighted, and yet . . .

CHAPTER ELEVEN

Islamic Civilization

35. THE KORAN:
35.1. SCRIPTURE AND LITERATURE

James Kritzeck

The following is an introduction to the Koran by a leading modern inter-
preter of Islam. What is the Koran? How was it written? Why is it so
difficult to understand in translation? What were the main elements of
Muhammad's religion? What was appealing, and unappealing, to those
who heard Muhammad's message? What changes were occasioned by
Muhammad's move from Mecca to Medina?

"That inimitable symphony, the very sounds of which move men to tears
and ecstasy," wrote Marmaduke Pickthall, describing the Koran. "As
tedious a piece of reading as I ever undertook, a wearisome, confused
jumble, crude, incondite—nothing but a sense of duty could carry any
European through the Koran," was Thomas Carlyle's verdict. How could
two sensitive and intelligent men of very similar backgrounds differ so
markedly concerning a book which everyone knows is a world classic?
The answer is complicated, but it can be made simple: Pickthall read
Arabic and Carlyle did not.

For all of the world's Moslems, the Koran is the greatest work of
literature. For almost everyone else it is, literally, a closed book. One
would be hard pressed to find a single non-Moslem friend who has
actually read it from cover to cover. Why is that? The Koran is not a long
book; it is shorter than the New Testament. It is readily available in a
variety of translations which are accurate enough, some of which have
been issued in inexpensive editions. Is the Koran worth reading? To start
with, what is it?

The Koran is the collection of formal utterances of Mohammed [Mu-
hammad] the prophet of Islam. He was born in Mecca about 570 and was
orphaned soon after his birth. The family into which he was born was
part of a prominent tribe, but indications are that it was in straitened
circumstances. Little reliable information has come down to us concerning Mohammed's youth. He became a trader, perhaps participated in

caravans to Syria, and when he was about twenty-five, married a wealthy merchant's widow some years his senior.

Mecca at that time, it is important to note, was no mere desert oasis, but a bustling and prosperous center for commerce on the major north-south caravan route, and its sanctuaries were places of religious pilgrimage for many neighboring tribes. Mohammed began by following the beliefs and customs which were commonly adhered to by his tribe and by most Arabians. However, he soon became disgusted with polytheism and the morality which went along with it and gave careful (but probably concealed) audience to the worship and disputation of Jews and Christians, who lived in Arabia in considerable numbers. He seems to have accepted their general religious tradition and pattern without feeling inclined to embrace either Judaism or Christianity. When he was about forty years old he experienced his first "revelation" and a call to prophethood. These revelations, which continued to occur at intervals during the rest of his life, constitute the Koran.

Mohammed proved himself a prophet in an important sense of the Hebrew term: he was not a man who *foretold*, but a man who *told forth*. He did not claim to be divine; that is the very last thing he would ever have claimed and the very last claim he would ever have recognized. Rather he claimed to be the reciter of a "recitation" (*qur'ān*, or Koran, means "recitation") unmistakably within the tradition of the Hebrew prophets. Mohammed preached; he did not write. Indeed, one of the principal bits of evidence adduced by Moslems for the divine origin of the Koran is the doubtful fact, and even more doubtful compliment, that their prophet was illiterate.

The Koran was not put together in written form until well after Mohammed's death. A special point must be made of the form in which it was put together, since that helps to explain why even well-meaning non-Moslems never get very far in reading it. Its one hundred fourteen chapters, except for the first, are arranged roughly in order of length; many of the chapters must themselves have been compilations. There was no good reason, apart from a rare rabbinical custom, for doing such a thing—and every reason for doing otherwise. The chapters vary in length from thousands of words to only a line or two, and generally speaking the longer ones are of a later period than the shorter ones. One is reading the Koran, therefore, in roughly the reverse order of that in which it was composed. This is a serious obstacle for any book to have to overcome.

For the Moslems, on the other hand, it is no obstacle at all, only a trivial complaint characteristic of infidels. The nature of their claim for the Koran (which is the Koran's claim for itself) fully accounts for this attitude. There is absolutely no doctrine of inspiration in Islam. The Koran must be believed to have no human author at all, but rather to be, syllable for syllable, the very dictation of God. That dictation, through an angel customarily identified as Gabriel, was "taken" by Mohammed's memory and then confidently set adrift in other men's memories. From the evidence of the final text, it must be granted that those memories were excellent. Nevertheless, by comparison with the claims advanced for the Koran, those advanced by Jews and Christians for the books of the Bible seem very modest.

When the Moslem legists forbade translations of the Koran, they recognized something important for us to recognize. The most difficult things to translate from any language are those captivating little nuances, lying somewhere between prose and poetry, which catch perfectly the beauty of that language. The Koran was composed entirely of such prose-poetry, in a form called *saj'*. Moslem sages contend that it is untranslatable, and they have no idea how right they are. It is regarded as a foolish cliché to say of a work that "it loses everything in translation." In the case of the Koran, this is true. No translation can convey more than the barest suggestion of what it is in the Koran that can "move men to tears and ecstasy."

So much for that. The Koran is still a book which can be read, if one is dogged enough, in a single day. One is likely to get further along with it, for the reason already given, if one starts at the back. Above all, one must bear in mind constantly while reading it that it is supposed to have been "spoken" by God to mankind through Mohammed. The *saj'* and many individual features, which will be noted in due course, are common to the book as a whole. However, among the chapters a distinction can be made between those composed at Mecca and those composed later at Medina. The distinction has sometimes been exaggerated by commentators but holds up well enough for the novice.

At Mecca, for some twelve years, Mohammed preached a religion which was quite simple and easy for anyone familiar with the Judeo-Christian tradition to understand. For his polytheistic countrymen, of course, it was neither so simple nor so easy to understand. It was a religion of one God who created man, subsidized him with the goods of this world, revealed himself through the prophets and "messengers," and intends to judge him, rewarding good and punishing evil, in a life hereafter. Through Islam, this God wished to re-emphasize the fundamentals of what had become, in man's hands, a confused and contentious religious structure.

The themes and forms of the Meccan chapters are, from a literary standpoint, probably the most attractive in the book. The first chapter to be revealed, according to Islamic tradition, was "The Clot" (Koran 96). Each chapter has a title, usually taken from some striking reference within it, and all but one begin with the invocation, "In the name of God, the Merciful, the Compassionate":

Recite: In the name of your Lord who created,
created man from a clot.
Recite: And your Lord is most generous,
who taught by the pen,
taught man what he did not know.

No, but man is rebellious
because he sees himself grown rich.
Indeed, the return is to your Lord.

Have you seen him who forbids a servant to pray?
Have you seen if he was rightly guided or ordered piety?
Did he know that God sees?

No, if he does not desist, we shall seize him by the forelock,
a lying, sinful forelock!
So let him call his council.
We shall call the guards of hell.

No, do not obey him,
but fall down and draw near.

This chapter is obviously a conglomeration of editorial layers, and requires a great deal of explanation. It is more than likely that everything after the first five lines was added later, and everything after the first eight was aimed against a particular enemy. Most of the early Meccan chapters are simpler. Usually they begin with an interesting but harmless oath ("by the daylight," "by the fig and the olive," "by the city"), go on to indict some form of evil-doing, warn of judgment, frighteningly describe hell, and call men to repentance. "The Chargers" (100) is one of the most beautiful of them, though it, also, is difficult:

By the snorting chargers,
    the fire-strikers,
    the plunder-raiders at daybreak,
    the dust-raisers
    centering in it all together!

Man is indeed ungrateful to his Lord,
and he himself is a witness to that:
he is strong in his love of goods.

Does he not know that when
    what is in the graves will be torn out
    and what is in the breasts will be made to appear,
on that day their Lord will be an expert on them?

That chapter was chosen because it is an especially brilliant example of the rhythmic _saj'._ It sounds, insofar as its sound can be represented by the Roman alphabet, something like this:

> Waal aadiYAATi DAB-han,
> faal mooriYAATi KAD-han,
> faal mogheeRAATi SUB-han,
> fa atharna beehee NAK-an
> fa wasatna beehee JAM-an!

> Innal inSAANa lee rubbeehee la-kaNOOD,
> wa innahoo ala THAAlika la-shaHEED:
> wa innahoo lee hobbil khair la-shaDEED.

> Afalaa yalamoo itha
> bothira maa fill koBOOR
> wa hossila maa fis soDOOR,
> inna rubbahom beehim yawma-ithin la-khaBEER?

Such clever combinations of repetition and variation of sound give these chapters their special lilt. They are brief, lively, menacing, full of crisp and startling imagery. Some of them are built entirely around strange words, presumably as strange to their first audiences as they are to us. It has been shown that in this respect they resemble the oracular pronouncements of the Arabian soothsayers, although Mohammed took an extremely harsh stand against them—and, indeed, against all mere poets. "The Striking" (101) is an example:

> The "Striking"!—what is the "Striking"?
> What could convey to you what the "Striking" is?
> It is the day when people will be like scattered moths
> and the mountains will be like carded wool!

> Then, as for him whose scales [of merit] are heavy,
> he will be in a pleasing life.
> But as for him whose scales are light,
> he will be a son of—"Bereft"!
> And what could convey to you what "Bereft" is?—
> Raging fire!

During this period, Mohammed liked to appeal, though somewhat vaguely, to the authority of the Bible for his teachings: "All this is written in earlier scriptures, of Abraham and Moses" (87.18). As he then saw it, his was mainly a confirming scripture for the Arabs, who were without a scripture: "Before [the Koran], the book of Moses was revealed, a guide and blessing to all men. This book confirms it. It is revealed in the Arabic tongue" (46.12). Later, when Jews and Christians proved unwilling to accept his claim in sufficient numbers, he emphasized that they had deformed God's pure religion and that the Koran invalidated their scriptures, which had been corrupted. He represented Ishmael, the father of the Arabs according to Jewish lore, as coheir with Isaac to God's covenant with Abraham.

The chapters of the later Meccan period already betray something of this conflict. They also tend to be somewhat longer and to take on more ambitious substance. Entire stories from the Old Testament (such as that of Joseph) are narrated in general conformity with the Hebrew versions. Although there is only one indisputable quotation from the Bible in the Koran (that of Psalm 37.29 in 21.105), the Bible is paraphrased in almost every chapter after the early Meccan period. Some of the more trenchant chapters, for example "Unity" (112), bespeak Islam's disassociation from Christianity:

> Say: He is God—One!
>> God—the eternally sought after!
> He did not have a son
> and was no one's son.
> And there is no one equal to Him.

In Mecca, Mohammed's message was first met with indifference, then countered with opposition. The Meccans, and in particular Mohammed's wealthier relatives who profited from the pilgrimage trade to the pagan shrine of the Ka'bah, took his monotheistic warning very much to heart, but not in the manner he intended. They planned the elimination of his small sect. Some new material, aimed at coming to terms with these opponents, was introduced into the Koran. Three pagan goddesses, for instance, were acknowledged to be "daughters of God," whose cults might therefore be expected to continue. But such devices neither convinced nor placated the Meccans, and Mohammed himself soon regretted these "Satanic suggestions" and repudiated them. Ultimately a good many verses of the Koran were abrogated in this fashion. "The Unbelievers" (109) is said to have been revealed at this time:

> Say: O unbelievers!
>> I do not worship what you worship
>> and you do not worship what I worship;
>> and I shall not worship what you worship
>> and you will not worship what I worship.
> You have your religion and I have mine.

By 621, Islam's prospects seemed bleak. Mohammed had sent about eighty of his followers to Abyssinia, and indications are that some differences of opinion within his community, as well as the Meccan persecution, prompted that action. He had lost the encouraging presence of his first wife and the protective presence of his guardian, who, as chief of the Hashimite clan, had prevented violent steps being taken against him. Just as the situation was growing desperate, a miracle happened. Two of the principal tribes in Medina, a city some distance north of Mecca, had been feuding for years. Some of their members had heard Mohammed preach and sought him as mediator to end the feud. The Moslems left Mecca unobtrusively in small groups, and finally Mohammed himself fled.

The year of that "emigration" (*al-Hijrah*, or Hegira), 622, was later chosen as the commencement of the Islamic era. Although it might appear strange that it was selected in preference to the year of Mohammed's birth or that of his first revelation, it was actually an appropriate choice. For it was at Medina that Islam became a state—and ultimately a world empire and a world religion. That transformation did not, of course, take place overnight, but it took place rapidly. Mohammed proved himself a clever and farsighted statesman, as well as a religious leader. His conciliation was successful, and the expansion of his community began.

The style of the Meccan chapters of the Koran had been fitting for the blunt warnings and succinct preaching which were necessary there. At Medina, however, Mohammed became a lawgiver. The basic *saj'* form did not change in the Medinan chapters, but it was stretched tight to accommodate the lengthy and detailed prescriptions which now came forth. Certainly any legal portion of a typical Medinan chapter, such as the following from "Women" (4.11–12), provides a sharp contrast with any early Meccan chapter:

> God enjoins you [as follows] concerning [inheritance for] your children: A male shall get twice as much as a female. If there are more than two females, then they shall get two thirds of the estate; but if there is only one, then she shall get half. Parents shall get a sixth each, provided the deceased has a child; if he has no child and his parents are his only heirs, then his mother shall get a third. If he has more than one brother, then his mother shall get a sixth—after payment of legacies and debts.

It is really unfair to choose a passage like this one, but it was not chosen to typify the content of all the Medinan chapters.

Mohammed tried to secure the support of Jewish communities in the vicinity of Medina by incorporating into Islam many elements of Jewish law and ritual. Those which remained within it (for example, the prohibition of pork, the regulations concerning fasting and circumcision) are too numerous to list. It is more important to note that at some point Mohammed broke violently with the past. Islam assumed its own direction of prayer, Mecca (previously it had been Jerusalem), and its own "sabbath," Friday.

Some authorities have professed to sense in this period a greater appreciation of Christianity on Mohammed's part. He regarded the Gospel (in the singular) as a book revealed to Christ, which would indicate that he knew very little about it. The position that he had taken concerning Christ seems to have prevented him from inquiring into the New Testament. He denied original sin, so the incarnation became, in his eyes, the most wicked of blasphemies. Why he kept referring to Jesus as "the Messiah" is therefore something of a mystery, unless (as is quite possible) he had no idea of everything that title implied. Surprisingly enough, he affirmed the virgin birth (19.17–26) in words very similar to St. Luke's. According to one tradition, he even asserted the immaculate conception. What is most surprising of all, perhaps, is that he believed in the ascension of Jesus, while denying his crucifixion:

> [The Jews] declared: "We have put to death the Messiah, Jesus the son of Mary, the apostle of God." But they did not kill him, nor did they crucify him. They only thought they did. . . . But God took him up to himself (4.156–158).

A clearer indication of greater friendliness toward Christians would be the following verse:

> You will discover that those who are most implacable in their hatred of the [Moslems] are the Jews and the pagans, while those nearest to them in affection are those who profess to be Christians. That is because there are priests and monks among them, and they are free of pride (5.85).

Ultimately, however, both the Jews and the Christians, as "people of the Book" (i.e., the Bible), were accorded a status as privileged minorities within the Islamic state, or, more accurately, "protected" minorities, in return for payment of special taxes.

Against other non-Moslems the Koran ordered warfare, a holy warfare (jihād) against unbelievers. Mohammed spent much of the rest of his life in directing military campaigns against trading caravans and neighboring tribes, all with the general goals of consolidating and extending his community and of forcing the Meccans, his most formidable enemies, into submission. Not all of these expeditions ended in victory, and many of the victories were hard won. Tribal alliances gradually emerged as almost as effective a means of attaining the goals as warfare.

Mohammed's actions during these later years are usually regarded by non-Moslems as, at best, unbecoming to him. In Islamic terms, on the other hand, they appear both necessary and consistent. The fire of warning had simply been translated, by Koranic direction, into the fire of action. Toward the end, Mohammed was assured of final victory in "The Assistance" (110):

> When God's assistance comes, and victory,
> and you see the people entering God's religion in droves,
> then glorify your Lord with praise and ask His forgiveness.
> Indeed, He is a forgiver.

In 631, Mecca capitulated and the way was prepared for further expansion. A few months later, in 632, Mohammed died in the arms of his favorite wife, Aishah, whose father succeeded him as his first "successor" (*khalīfah*, hence caliph). Within a century, after one of the most remarkable series of military conquests in history, Moslems had carried the Koran into the valleys of France and the steppes of Central Asia.

The Koran stands at the beginning of Islamic literature, but it stands apart, preeminent without being dominant. All but a few [Moslems] would agree that it represents divine truth as well as superlative literary style—the personal style of God.

For Moslems the Koran is no more literature because it is scripture, than it is scripture because it is literature. It is both scripture and literature at the same time, in a manner absolutely unique to itself. The classical legists formulated it in the concept of "inimitability" (*i'jāz*), a formulation which in time found its way into several of the Islamic creeds. The important thing, however, was not so much its "inimitability" (its style was in fact consciously imitated by such poets as Abu Nuwas and Al-Maarri and was even, upon occasion, criticized by Moslems) as its singular claim, so unhesitatingly accepted by so many persons. For them, first and foremost, the Koran is God's word.

By the same token, the literary style of the Koran has seldom engaged Moslem thinkers except in illustration of its divine nature or for ancillary purposes. For the Koran is everything to the devout Moslem: It is history, sacred and profane; it is prayer; it is a code of civil and religious law; it is a guide to conduct and meditation. "Everything is in a clear book" (11.6). When the first tortuous theological debates were over, the Koran was formally declared the "uncreated" Word of God, on a par with the divine presence itself. The non-Moslem may be captivated by its beauty, may discern its sharply characterized styles and manifold literary subtleties, but he can never fully understand or appreciate how the Koran has superintended all genuine Moslem thought and fashioned the Moslem soul.

35.2. SELECTIONS

As James Kritzeck pointed out in the previous reading, the Koran is a closed book for those who are unfamiliar with Islam or Arabic. Much is lost in translation. There is more poetic repetition and less direct statement than Westerners are used to. Chapters are titled after key words (like "clot") that seem better designed to jog the memory than reveal a meaning. Then they are arranged according to length.

Because of these difficulties for the Western reader, we have taken passages out of their original context and organized them according to more familiar categories. Numbers indicating original chapter and verse appear at the end of each selection.

What are some of the main messages contained in these selections? In what ways does the Koran continue the teachings of Judaism and Christianity, and to what extent does it depart from these? What kind of society would these teachings create?

THE OPENING

In the name of God, the Mercy-giving, the Merciful!

Praise to God, Lord of the Universe, the Mercy-giving, the
   Merciful!
Ruler on the Day for Repayment!
You alone do we worship and You alone do we call on for help.
Guide us along the Straight Road, the road of those whom You
have favoured, with whom You are not angry, nor who are lost! (1:1–7)

MUHAMMED'S FIRST CALL

In the name of God, the Mercy-giving, the Merciful!

Read in the name of your Lord Who creates,
creates man from a clot!
Read, for your Lord is most Generous;
Who teaches by means of the pen,
teaches man what he does not know.   (96:1–5)

THE WARNING

In the name of God, the Mercy-giving, the Merciful!

You who are wearing a cloak,
stand up and warn!

Magnify your Lord,
purify your clothing
and steer clear of filth.
Do not give so much away
in order to receive more;
be patient with your Lord!
For when the bugle is sounded on that day
it will be such a harsh day,
anything but easy on disbelievers.   (74:1–9)

THE MESSAGE

The Day for Sorting has been announced,
the day when the trumpet shall be blown
and you shall come in droves
and the sky will open up
as if it had gates,
and the mountains will travel along
like a mirage.

He will lurk in ambush to receive
home the arrogant.
They will linger there for ages;
They will taste nothing cool nor any drink . . .

The heedful will have their scene of triumph with parks
and vineyards as well as buxom
maidens their own age
and a brimming cup.   (78:17–34)

BELIEFS

Say: "We believe in God and what has been sent down to us, and what
was sent down to Abraham, Ishmael, Isaac, Jacob, and their descendents,
and what was given Moses, Jesus, and the prophets by their Lord. We do
not differentiate between any one of them, and are committed to [live at]
peace with Him."   (3:84)

Say: God has spoken truly, so
follow the sect of Abraham, the Seeker;
he was not one to associate
[others with God].   (3:95)

Some People of the Book
form an upright community;
they recite God's verses through
the small hours of the night
as they fall down on their knees.   (3:113)

They believe in God and the Last Day;
they command decency and forbid dishonor,
and compete in doing good deeds.
These are honorable men.   (3:114)

THE WOMEN'S OATH

O Prophet, whenever believing women come to swear allegiance to you, saying they will not associate anything with God, nor steal or misbehave sexually, nor kill their children, nor give any [cause for] slander they may invent between their hands and legs, nor disobey you in any decent matter; then accept their allegiance and seek forgiveness from God for them. God is forgiving, merciful (60:12).

THE MESSIAH IS NOT GOD

Those who say that God is Christ the son of Mary have disbelieved. Christ [himself] said: "Children of Israel, serve God [Who is] my Lord as well as your Lord." God will ban the Garden to anyone who associates anything else with God; his lodging will be Fire.

Wrongdoers have no supporters. Those who say: "God is the third of three," have disbelieved! There is no deity except God alone. If they do not stop saying what they say, painful torment will afflict those of them who disbelieve. Why do they not turn towards God and seek His forgiveness? God is forgiving, merciful (5:72–74).

WAR (JIHĀD)

Fight against those who fight against you along God's way, yet do not initiate hostilities. God loves not aggressors. Kill them wherever you may catch them and expel them out from anywhere they may have expelled you. Sedition is more serious than killing! But do not fight them at the Hallowed Mosque unless they fight you there. If they should fight you, then fight them back; such is the reward for those disbelievers! However, if they stop, surely God will be forgiving, merciful. Fight them until there is no more subversion and [all] religion belongs to God alone. If they stop, let there be no [more] hostility except towards wrongdoers (2:190–193).

Do not reckon those who are killed for God's sake as dead, but rather, they are living; they will be provided for by their Lord and are provided for. So happy they will be with whatever God has given them out of His bounty, and rejoicing for those they left behind who have not yet overtaken them. No fear will fall on them nor will they be saddened; they will rejoice because of favor and bounty from God, since God does not deprive believers of their wages (3:169–171).

36. THE CIVILIZATION OF MEDIEVAL ISLAM

J. J. Saunders

In this selection the author, a modern historian, suggests answers to three important questions. First, he asks why the Arab invasions of the seventh century brought about a cultural flowering while the German invasions of Western Europe in the fifth century had the opposite effect. What, in other words, were the causes of this rise of Arabic civilization? Next, he asks about the nature of that civilization. What were its notable features? Finally, he asks about its decline after the thirteenth century. How was such a vigorous civilization overcome by the previously backward West?

What are the author's answers to these questions? Which answers do you find most convincing? Why?

For some centuries (roughly between A.D. 800 and 1200) the lands conquered by the Arabs were the soil from which grew and blossomed one of the most brilliant civilizations in the history of humanity. To give it a suitable name is a matter of some difficulty. It has been variously styled Arab, Muslim, Islamic and Arabic. The first is clearly a misnomer, implying as it does that this culture was created or dominated by men of Arab race, which was by no means the case; the second and third define it too narrowly in religious terms, whereas many of its most distinguished figures were Christians, Jews or pagans, and not Muslims at all. "Arabic" seems open to the least objection, since it draws attention to the fact that the literature of this particular civilization was written almost wholly in the Arabic language and acquired its characteristic unity largely from this circumstance.

The causes of the rise and fall of civilizations are often hidden from us, and the questions which start to mind are more easily framed than answered. Why were the German invasions of Western Europe in the fifth century followed by a long "dark age" of barbarism and ignorance, while the Arab invasions of the seventh century were followed by a general rise in the cultural level of the countries affected by them? So startling a contrast demands explanation, which must take the form of showing that certain conditions favourable to the growth of the arts and sciences were present in one case and absent in the other.

1. The Arab conquests politically unified a huge segment of the globe from Spain to India, a unity which remained unbroken until the fall of the Omayyads in 750. The disappearance of so many dividing frontiers, above all the one which had so long separated Rome and Persia, was a useful preliminary to the building of a new civilization.

2. As the Arabs overran one country after another, they carried their language with them. But that language possessed a unique status: to every Muslim it was not just one form of human speech among others, but the vehicle through which God had chosen to deliver his final revelation to men. Arabic was "God's tongue," and as such enjoyed a prestige which Latin and Greek and Hebrew had never known. The Koran could not, must not be translated: the believer must hear and understand and if possible read the divine book in the original, even though Arabic were not his mother tongue. To study, illustrate and elucidate the text became a pious duty: the earliest branch of science developed by Muslims was Arabic philology, traditionally founded at Basra in the late Omayyad age. The further Islam spread among non-Arabs, the further a knowledge of Arabic spread with it. A century or so after the conquests even Christians, Jews and Zoroastrians within the Caliphate found it convenient to speak and write Arabic. Thus to political unity was added the widespread use of a common language, which immensely facilitated the exchange of ideas.

3. The first conquests of the Arabs were made in lands which had been the home of settled, urban civilizations for thousands of years, that is, the river valleys of the Nile and the Tigris-Euphrates. The fighting here was relatively brief (Syria was conquered in six or seven years, Egypt and Iraq in two or three), and the physical destruction was light. The native population was akin to the Arabs in race and speech, and stood aside from a struggle which was essentially between the invaders and the Byzantine or Sassanid [Persian dynasty ruling just before the Arab invasion] ruling class. The local officials often stayed at their posts, and administrative continuity, at least at the lower levels, remained unbroken. From motives of policy, the Caliphs cultivated friendly relations with the Jacobite and Nestorian Christians, who constituted the bulk of the people, and who during the long period of Roman rule had learnt a good deal of the science and philosophy of the Greeks. This learning, translated into

Syriac, a Semitic tongue closely related to Arabic, was at the disposal of the newcomers, who were impressed by the rich and ancient culture of the region, and it was this region, and not Arabia proper, which was the birthplace of the Arabic civilization.

4. Once invasion and resettlement were over, the lands brought under the sovereignty of the Caliphs enjoyed immunity from serious external attack for three or four centuries. There was plenty of fighting on the frontiers and many internal revolts and disturbances, but no prolonged and ruinous barbarian assaults such as the Latin Christian West had to endure from the Vikings and Magyars. Under the shield of the *Pax Islamica,* which may be compared with the Augustan and Antonine Peace of the early Roman Empire, the arts and sciences rose to a new and flourishing life. Not until about 1050 did this peace begin to break down: Islam was then exposed to a series of attacks from the nomads of the steppes and deserts, culminating in the dreadful Mongol explosion of the thirteenth century.

5. The creation of the vast Arab Empire, besides levelling barriers and abolishing frontiers, brought into existence a great free-trade area, promoted safe and rapid travel, and gave a tremendous stimulus to commerce. During these four centuries (800–1200) international trade was more vigorous than at any time since the heyday of imperial Rome. Merchants from the Caliphate were found in places as far apart as Senegal and Canton. The hoards of Arabic coins dug up in Scandinavia reveal the brisk exchange of goods between Northern Europe and the cities of Iraq and Persia via the great rivers of Russia. The negro lands south of the Sahara were drawn into the stream of world commerce. The ancient Silk Road through the oases of Central Asia which carried the products of China to the West had never been so frequented. Cities expanded, fortunes were made, a wealthy middle-class of traders, shippers, bankers, manufacturers and professional men came into being, and a rich and sophisticated society gave increasing employment and patronage to scholars, artists, teachers, physicians and craftsmen.

6. The pursuit of knowledge was quickened by the use of paper and the so-called "Arabic" numerals. Neither originated in the Islamic world, but both were widely employed there by the ninth century. The manufacture of paper from hemp, rags and tree-bark seems to have been invented in China about A.D. 100, but it remained unknown outside that country until some Chinese prisoners of war skilled in the art were brought to Samarkand in 751. In 793 a paper manufactory was set up in Baghdad; by 900 the commodity was being produced in Egypt, and by 950 in Spain. The Arabic numerals, despite their name, are probably Hindu, and may have reached Islam through the translation of the *Siddhanta,* a Sanskrit astronomical treatise, made by order of the Caliph Mansur in 773. The oldest Muslim documents employing these signs date from 870–890: the zero is represented by a dot, as has always been

the case in Arabic. These innovations multiplied books and facilitated calculation, and the rich scientific literature of the next few centuries undoubtedly owes much to them.

Such are some of the possible causes of the rise of the Arabic civilization. To attempt a detailed description and analysis of that civilization would be impossible, but certain notable features or peculiarities of it may be considered:—

1. It was not specifically Muslim. Islam provided it with a framework and a universal language, but its only creations which possess a definitely Muslim character are Arabic grammar, law and theology. All else came from non-Muslim sources, even Arabic poetry and belles-lettres, which were based on a literary tradition going back to pre-Islamic times, the "days of ignorance" of the sixth century.

2. The biggest single influence which helped to shape it was Greek science and philosophy, but this reached it indirectly, chiefly through the medium of Syriac. Of course, the great days of Hellenism were long over by the time of the Arab conquests: Greek science went out with Ptolemy in the second century, and the noble line of Greek thinkers ended when Justinian closed the schools of Athens in 529. But if nothing new was being created or discovered, the work of preserving and transmitting what had already been accomplished went on among the Byzantine Greeks and their Syriac-speaking pupils in Syria, Egypt and Iraq, and when the Arabs broke into these lands most of the leading works of Greek medicine and metaphysics had been translated into Syriac by scholars of the Oriental Christian communities. Established in an educated society, the invaders grew ashamed of their ignorance, and the Caliphs encouraged learned Christians and Jews to turn these books into the dominant language of the Empire. This translating went on for some two centuries (800–1000), at the close of which educated Muslims could read the masters of Hellenic thought in Arabic versions of Syriac translations of the Greek originals.

3. As the Syriac-speaking Christians spread through the Islamic world a knowledge of Greek thought, so the Persians introduced to it much of the lore of Sanskrit India. Hindu influences had travelled west in late Sassanid times: the game of chess and Sanskrit medical writings are said to have reached Ctesiphon in the reign of Khusrau Nushirvan. When the Abbasids moved the metropolis of Islam to Iraq, Persian scholars were given every facility to pursue this quest. At the command of Mansur, Fazari translated the *Siddhanta;* Ibn al-Mukaffa turned into Arabic the famous *Fables of Bidpai,* an Indian collection of animal stories which has gone round the world; and the celebrated mathematician al-Khwarizmi, from whose name the European word "algorism" (the old term for arithmetic) was derived, founded the science of algebra (Arabic *al-jabr,* a restoring, literally, setting a bone) on the basis of Hindu mathematical

achievement. Translation from Sanskrit into Arabic went on till the time of the great Persian scientist al-Biruni (973–1048), who among numerous learned works left an admirable sociological description of India. The double and simultaneous impact of Greece and India provided a powerful stimulus to the building of the Arabic civilization.

4. The centre of Arabic intellectual life was long fixed in Iraq, the ancient home of culture, "a palimpsest (as it has been styled) on which every civilization from the time of the Sumerians had left its trace." A meeting-place of Hellenic and Iranian culture, it had been the heart of the old Persian monarchy and was the seat of the Caliphate from 750 to 1258. Baghdad became a greater Ctesiphon, the capital not simply of a State but of a world civilization. Perhaps in no other region of its size could such an extraordinary variety of belief and speech have been found. Jews and Zoroastrians, Nestorian, Monophysite and Greek Orthodox Christians, Gnostics and Manichaeans, the pagans of Harran and the strange baptist sect of the Mandeans, all mingled in the same province. In the Arab camp settlements of Basra and Kufa the Muslims first found leisure to devote themselves to things of the mind: here was inaugurated the study of Arabic philology and Islamic law. In Baghdad the Caliph Ma'mun, the son of a Persian mother, founded and endowed as a centre of research the Bait al-Hikma, or House of Wisdom, which was at once a library, an observatory and a scientific academy. Men of many races and faiths contributed to the fame of Baghdad as a home of scholarship, and Arabic civilization never recovered from the sack of the city by the Mongols in 1258.

5. The culture of medieval Islam was multiracial. Arabs, Syrians, Jews, Persians, Turks, Egyptians, Berbers, Spaniards, all contributed to it. One of its leading philosophers, al-Kindi, was an Arab of the tribe of Kinda (as his name implies), al-Farabi, a Neo-Platonist and commentator on Aristotle, a Turk from Transoxiana, Ibn Sina or Avicenna, perhaps the finest scientific thinker of Islam, a Persian from Bukhara, and Ibn Rushd, best known under his Europeanized name Averroës, a Spanish Moor from Cordova. A remarkable feature of Arabic philosophical literature is that much of it was written by Jews. As the Jewish religion, like the Christian, was a tolerated one among Muslims, Jews were found settled in almost all the great cities of Islam, where they learnt to write Arabic and to share in the vigorous intellectual life around them. In Spain they acted as mediators between the Muslim and Christian Spanish culture, helping Christian scholars to translate Arabic works into Latin and so making them available to the then backward West. Spain was also the birthplace of Maimonides, "the second Moses," perhaps the acutest Jewish thinker before Spinoza, who was born in Cordova in 1135 and died in Cairo in 1204, and whose *Guide for the Perplexed*, a bold attempt to reconcile reason and religious faith, finds readers to this day.

6. By far the biggest share in the construction of the Arabic civilization

was taken by the Persians, a people whose recorded history was already more than a thousand years old when the Arabs broke into their land, and who found in their cultural superiority compensation for their political servitude. Persia has been described as "the principal channel irrigating the somewhat arid field of Islam with the rich alluvial flood of ancient culture": Sufism was virtually a Persian creation, and the Persian al-Ghazali was the greatest of Muslim theologians. In secular learning the Persians were predominant. "If knowledge were attached to the ends of the sky, some amongst the Persians would have reached it," was a traditional saying. Among the famous men of the age sprung from this gifted race were Razi (Rhazes), the great physician who first distinguished small-pox from measles, Tabari (died 923), the Arabic Livy, whose *Annals of Apostles and Kings* provided us with our chief source of information on early Muslim history, Ibn Sina, whose medical writings instructed the world for centuries, Biruni, a many-sided genius whose fame now rests chiefly on his description of medieval India, Omar Khayyám (died 1123), more celebrated in the East for his mathematical achievements than for his poetry, Shahrastani (died 1153), whose *Book of Religion and Sects* is really a pioneering study in comparative religion, Nasir al-Din al-Tusi (died 1274), a distinguished astronomer who collected valuable data at his observatory at Maragha in Azerbaijan, and Rashid al-Din Fadl Allad (died 1318), author of the first world history worthy of that name. If to these scholars and scientists we add the poets (Firdawsi, Sa'di, Rumi, etc.), who shone lustre on their country's literature, the picture is even brighter.

7. The core of the scientific studies of medieval Islam was medicine. Socially, the medical profession had always stood high in the East: whereas in the Greco-Roman world doctors were often freed slaves, in Persia and Babylonia they could rise to be the prime ministers of kings. At the time of the Arab conquests the classical medicine of Hippocrates and Galen was being studied by Egyptian Greeks in Alexandria and Nestorian Christians at Jundi-Shapur, in southwest Persia. The Caliphs employed graduates of these schools as their personal physicians: members of one Nestorian family, the Bakht-yashu (a name meaning "happiness of Jesus") served in this capacity at the court of Baghdad for several generations. Nestorian medical professors translated most of Galen and other authorities into Arabic, and by 900 the science of medicine was being assiduously cultivated by Muslims all over Islam. Razi was the first of their faith to acquire world fame through his vast medical encyclopedia, the *Hawi* (best known under its Latin title *Continens*), which was filled with long extracts from Greek and Hindu writers and displayed a knowledge of chemistry most unusual in that age. A similar work by Ibn Sina, the *Canon*, attained even greater celebrity and was treated for centuries as a kind of medical Bible. The branch of medicine most successively investigated was ophthalmology, eye diseases being sadly common in the East, and the *Optics* of Ibn al-Haitham, court physician to the Fatimids in

Cairo where he died in 1039, remained the standard authority on its subject till early modern times, being studied with profit by the astronomer Kepler in the seventeenth century. It was through the medical schools that many of the natural sciences found their way into Muslim education, the curricula including instruction in physics, chemistry and botany as well as in anatomy and pathology, and it was in this field that the Arabic writers made their greatest contribution to human knowledge. They added substantially to the achievement of the Greeks in the theory and art of healing disease; they founded hospitals and invented new drugs, and they filled libraries of books with detailed and accurate clinical observations. Their long superiority is proved by the fact that most of the Arabic works translated into Latin in the twelfth and thirteenth centuries were medical writings and that these were among the first to be printed at the time of the Renaissance. Razi, Ibn Sina and Ibn al-Haitham in their Latinized form continued to be "set books" in the medical schools of Europe till as late as the mid-seventeenth century.

8. Like all civilizations, the Arabic was highly selective in its borrowings from outside. Human societies take over only those elements which seem well suited to fill a conscious gap, and disregard those which conflict with their fundamental values; thus in modern times Russia has appropriated the science rather than the humanism of the West, and China has borrowed Marxism and rejected almost all else of European origin. Islam drew extensively on Hindu mathematics and medicine, but took small notice of Hindu philosophy, which being the reflection of a polytheistic society and of belief in the world as *maya* or illusion, was wholly repugnant to the teachings of the Koran. It helped itself to a good deal of Greek (chiefly Aristotelian) logic and metaphysics, in order to clothe its religious doctrines in a form more acceptable to a sophisticated society and enable it to defend them against philosophically trained opponents, but though it knew Aristotle's *Poetics* and *Rhetoric*, it ignored the Greek poets, dramatists and historians as spokesmen of a pagan past it had no desire to investigate. In architecture it was ready to use Byzantine and Persian models, but painting and sculpture were virtually banned because the Prophet [Mohammed] was alleged to have pronounced representational art a temptation to idolatry. Of classical Latin literature it knew nothing: the only Latin work ever translated into Arabic is said to have been the *History* of Orosius.

That the Arabic culture was merely imitative, that it copied and transmitted what it learnt at secondhand from the Greeks, and lacked the ability to strike out on independent lines of its own, is a judgment no longer accepted. It certainly borrowed freely from the Greeks—so did the West later—but what it built on these foundations was truly original and creative, and one of the great achievements of the human spirit. For more than four hundred years the most fruitful work in mathematics, astronomy, botany, chemistry, medicine, history and geography, was produced in the world of Islam by Muslims and Christians, Jews and Zoroastrians, pagans and Manichaeans. Neither the collapse of the Caliphate nor the Isma'ilian schism checked the process, for the local dynasties which sprang up on the ruins of the old Arab Empire competed with one another to attract scholars and artists to their courts, and the possession of a common language far outweighed the loss of political unity. Yet this brilliant culture, which shone so brightly in contrast to the darkness of the Latin West and the stagnation of Byzantium, began to fade from the thirteenth century onwards. Arabic philosophy was dead by 1200, Arabic science by 1500. The nations of Western Europe, once sunk in barbarism, caught up and overtook the peoples of Islam. How did this come about? The question has hardly yet received a complete and satisfactory answer, but some tentative suggestions may be offered:—

1. The collapse of the *Pax Islamica* after about 1050. The end of the long peace was marked by wave after wave of nomadic invasion, the Banu-Hilal in North Africa, the Turkomans and Seljuks in Western Asia, and the mighty Mongol devastations which inflicted such irreparable damage on so many Muslim lands between 1220 and 1260. Cities were sacked and burnt, wealth dissipated, libraries destroyed and teachers dispersed. The loss to culture in the fall of Baghdad alone is incalculable. The Christian West escaped all this, since after the Northmen and Magyars had been tamed and converted around 1000, it had nothing more to fear from barbarian attack, and the Mongols never got farther west than Hungary and Silesia.

2. The decay of city life and economic prosperity. The Arabic civilization was essentially urban, and its material basis was the vigorous commercial activity which once covered an area extending as far as Scandinavia, China and the Sudan. This activity was much diminished when nomad raids and invasions threatened the security of the caravan routes. From the eleventh century onwards the volume of international trade contracted, urban wealth declined, and social and economic conditions in the Muslim world underwent drastic change. Princes, finding their revenues falling, were obliged to pay their civil and military officers out of the rents and produce of landed estates: hence the growth of the *ikta* system, which has been compared, rather loosely, to Western feudalism. Owing presumably to the prevalence of slavery, which assured a plentiful supply of labour, there was no stimulus to technological progress and invention, which might have provided some compensation for the loss of distant markets. Nor did the cities of Islam ever develop self-governing institutions or combine in defence of their interests like the Lombard League or the Hansa in contemporary Europe: it was not that civic patriotism was wholly lacking (Arabic literature contains many town histories and biographical dictionaries of famous citizens), but that in this society the primary loyalty of a man was to his religious community, and in cities where Muslims, Christians and Jews lived together in separate

quarters, it was not easy for the inhabitants to feel and act as a united body. Thus the middle classes (merchants, traders, shippers, shopkeepers and craftsmen) had little defence when the economic basis of their position weakened, and the decline of the town was almost certainly related to the falling off of intellectual capacity and output.

3. The loss of linguistic and cultural unity. In the days of its widest expansion, Arabic was written and understood wherever Islam prevailed, but its intellectual monopoly was threatened and finally broken by the revival of Persian in the lands east of the Tigris. The fall of the Sassanid Empire reduced the native tongue to the level of Anglo-Saxon in England after the Norman conquest, but under the Abbasids it began to reemerge in an altered form, its vocabulary swollen with Arabic words and the old Pahlawi script replaced by the Arabic. With the rise of native dynasties after the disintegration of the Caliphate, Persia experienced a literary renaissance; the Samanids and Ghaznavids in particular were generous patrons of poets and scholars, and Firdawsi's great epic, the *Shah-nama,* or Book of Kings, finished in 1010, gave the new Persian a position in world literature it has never since lost. Fewer and fewer Persians wrote in Arabic, though the sacred language of the Koran continued to be used for works of theology, law and devotion. When the Turks entered Islam *en masse* with the Seljuks, it was the Persianized provinces that they first occupied, and it was on Persian officials that they relied for the administration of their Empire. Deeply affected in consequence by Persian culture, the Turks carried it with them westwards into Asia Minor and eastwards into northern India: by contrast, they set little store by Arabic, except for purely religious purposes. The Mongol invasions, the fall of Baghdad and the destruction of the Caliphate dealt a fatal blow to Arabic in eastern Islam, where in the field of secular learning and literature it was steadily overshadowed by Persian and Turkish. Never again was the Muslim world to be dominated by a single language.

4. Probably the biggest factor was the strongly religious character of Islam itself and the absence of a vigorous pre-Islamic secular tradition. Behind Christian Europe lay the science and rationalism of classical Greece: behind Islam lay nothing save the cultural poverty of "the days of ignorance." The Muslims did, as we have seen, borrow a good deal from Greece, but in a limited and indirect fashion: the Greek past never *belonged* to them in the sense in which it did to Christendom, and there was never a joyous acceptance or recovery of it as took place in the West at the time of the Renaissance. The spirit of Islam was not rational in the Greek sense of the term, in that God is beyond reason and his ordering of the universe is to be accepted rather than explained. True knowledge is that of God and his Law, and the Law embraces all human activity: secular learning for its own sake is to be strongly discouraged, and intellectual pursuits are permissible only insofar as they further a deeper piety and understanding of religious truth. Such an attitude was implicit in Islamic thinking from the

onset, but it became explicit only at a later stage, largely in consequence of the reaction against the Isma'ilian heresy and of a fuller realisation of the dangers to orthodoxy lurking in Greek philosophy. The shift in outlook became noticeable in the Seljuk age. The great Ghazali devoted his life to the defence of Koranic truth against what he regarded as the insidious encroachments of unbelief. Islamic dogma was linked with Sufi mysticism. Muslim education was geared to the new orthodoxy by the founding of *madrasas*, where the religious sciences alone received intensive study. The Shari'a came to dominate Muslim life as the Torah had dominated post-exilic Judaism. The door was closed against further borrowings from outside: philosophy was repudiated as a danger to the Faith, because it was alleged to deny a personal God, creation *ex nihilo*, and the resurrection of the body. The attempt of Ibn Rushd (Averroës) in Spain to answer Ghazali and defend the pursuit of secular science fell on deaf ears and exposed him to the charge of teaching atheism. How far the reaction went can be seen from the attitude of Ibn Khaldun (1337–1406), often regarded as Islam's profoundest thinker, who dismissed all knowledge unconnected with religion as useless. Plato (he says) admitted that no certainty about God could be attained by the reason: why then waste our time on such futile inquiries? Truth is to be sought only in divine revelation. The profane sciences, which had always operated on the fringe and had never been free from the suspicion of impiety, were largely and quietly dropped as "un-Muslim."

37. *DELIVERANCE FROM ERROR*

al-Ghazzâlî

Abû Hâmid Muhammad al-Ghazzâlî (1058–1111) was a great Muslim philosopher, jurist, and teacher. He wrote something like seventy books on legal, political, philosophical, and religious subjects. This selection is taken from his autobiography, Deliverance from Error. *He tells us here of his early doubts and his struggles to gain certain knowledge.*

What is the reason for Ghazzâlî's doubt? Why does he reject sense perceptions? Why does he reject intellect as well? Why did Sufi mysticism have greater appeal for Ghazzâlî than philosophy?

The different religious observances and religious communities of the human race, and likewise the different theological systems of the religious leaders, with all the multiplicity of sects and variety of practices, constitute ocean depths in which the majority drown and only a minority reach safety. From my early youth, since I attained the age of puberty before I was twenty, until the present time when I am over fifty, I have ever recklessly launched out into the midst of these ocean depths; I have ever bravely embarked on this open sea, throwing aside all craven caution; I have poked into every dark recess; I have made an assault on every problem; I have plunged into every abyss; I have scrutinized the creed of every sect; I have tried to lay bare the inmost doctrines of every community. All this have I done that I might distinguish between true and false, between sound tradition and heretical innovation.

To thirst after a comprehension of things as they really are was my habit and custom from a very early age. It was instinctive with me, a part of my God-given nature, a matter of temperament and not of my choice or contriving. Consequently as I drew near the age of adolescence the bonds of mere authority (*taqlīd*) ceased to hold me, and inherited beliefs lost their grip upon me, for I saw that Christian youths always grew up to be Christians, Jewish youths to be Jews, and Muslim youths to be Muslims.

I therefore said within myself: "To begin with, what I am looking for is knowledge of what things really are, so I must undoubtedly try to find what knowledge really is." It was plain to me that sure and certain knowledge is that knowledge in which the object is disclosed in such a fashion that no doubt remains along with it, that no possibility of error or illusion accompanies it, and that the mind cannot even entertain such a supposition. Certain knowledge must also be infallible; and this infallibility or security from error is such that no attempt to show the falsity of the knowledge can occasion doubt or denial, even though the attempt is made by someone who turns stones into gold or a rod into a serpent. Thus I know that ten is more than three. Let us suppose that someone says to me: "No, three is more than ten, and in proof of that I shall change this rod into a serpent"; and let us suppose that he actually changes the rod into a serpent and that I witness him doing so. No doubts about what I know are raised in me because of this. The only result is that I wonder precisely how he is able to produce this change. Of doubt about my knowledge there is no trace.

After these reflections I knew that whatever I do not know in this fashion and with this mode of certainty is not reliable and infallible knowledge; and knowledge that is not infallible is not certain knowledge.

Thereupon I investigated the various kinds of knowledge I had, and found myself destitute of all knowledge with this characteristic of infallibility except in the case of sense-perception and necessary truths. So I said: "Now that despair has come over me, there is no point in studying any problems except on the basis of what is self-evident, namely, necessary truths and the affirmations of the senses. I must first bring these to be judged in order that I may be certain on this matter. Is my reliance on sense-perception and my trust in the soundness of necessary truths of the same kind as my previous trust in the beliefs I had merely taken over from others, and as the trust most men have in the results of thinking? Or is it a justified trust that is in no danger of being betrayed or destroyed?"

I proceeded therefore with extreme earnestness to reflect on sense-perception and on necessary truths, to see whether I could make myself doubt them. The outcome of this protracted effort to induce doubt was that I could no longer trust sense-perception either. Doubt began to spread here and say: "From where does this reliance on sense-perception come? The most powerful sense is that of sight. Yet when it looks at the shadow (e.g., of a stick or the gnomon of a sundial), it sees it standing still, and judges that there is no motion. Then by experiment and observation, after an hour it knows that the shadow is moving and, moreover, that it is moving not by fits and starts but gradually and steadily by infinitely small distances in such a way that it is never in a state of rest. Again, it looks at the heavenly body (*sc.* the sun) and sees it small, the size of a shilling;[1] yet geometrical computations show that it is greater than the earth in size."

In this and similar cases of sense-perception the sense as judge forms his judgments, but another judge, the intellect, shows him repeatedly to be wrong; and the charge of falsity cannot be rebutted.

To this I said: "My reliance on sense-perception also has been destroyed. Perhaps only those intellectual truths which are first principles (or derived from first principles) are to be relied upon, such as the assertion that ten are more than three, that the same thing cannot be both affirmed and denied at one time, that one thing is not both generated in time and eternal, nor both existent and nonexistent, nor both necessary and impossible."

Sense-perception replied: "Do you not expect that your reliance on intellectual truths will fare like your reliance on sense-perception? You used to trust in me; then along came the intellect-judge and proved me wrong; if it were not for the intellect-judge you would have continued to regard me as true. Perhaps behind intellectual apprehension there is another judge who, if he manifests himself, will show the falsity of intellect in its judging, just as, when intellect manifested itself, it showed the falsity of sense in its judging. The fact that such a supraintellectual apprehension has not manifested itself is no proof that it is impossible."

My ego hesitated a little about the reply to that, and sense-perception heightened the difficulty by referring to dreams. "Do you not see," it said, "how, when you are asleep, you believe things and imagine circumstances, holding them to be stable and enduring, and, so long as you are in that dream-condition, have no doubts about them? And is it not the case that when you awake you know that all you have imagined and believed is unfounded and ineffectual? Why then are you confident that all your waking

1. Literally *dīnār.*

beliefs, whether from sense or intellect, are genuine? They are true in respect of your present state; but it is possible that a state will come upon you whose relation to your waking consciousness is analogous to the relation of the latter to dreaming. In comparison with this state your waking consciousness would be like dreaming! When you have entered into this state, you will be certain that all the suppositions of your intellect are empty imaginings. It may be that that state is what the Sufis claim as their special 'state' (*sc.* mystical union or ecstasy), for they consider that in their 'states' (or ecstasies), which occur when they have withdrawn into themselves and are absent from their senses, they witness states (or circumstances) which do not tally with these principles of the intellect. Perhaps that 'state' is death; for the Messenger of God (God bless and preserve him) says: 'The people are dreaming; when they die, they become awake.' So perhaps life in this world is a dream by comparison with the world to come; and when a man dies, things come to appear differently to him from what he now beholds, and at the same time the words are addressed to him: 'We have taken off thee thy covering, and thy sight today is sharp (Koran 50:21).' "

When these thoughts had occurred to me and penetrated my being, I tried to find some way of treating my unhealthy condition; but it was not easy. Such ideas can only be repelled by demonstration; but a demonstration requires a knowledge of first principles; since this is not admitted, however, it is impossible to make the demonstration. The disease was baffling, and lasted almost two months, during which I was a sceptic in fact though not in theory nor in outward expression. At length God cured me of the malady; my being was restored to health and an even balance; the necessary truths of the intellect became once more accepted, as I regained confidence in their certain and trustworthy character.

This did not come about by systematic demonstration or marshalled argument, but by a light which God most high cast into my breast. That light is the key to the greater part of knowledge. Whoever thinks that the understanding of things divine rests upon strict proofs has in his thought narrowed down the wideness of God's mercy.

38. *THE RUBÁIYÁT*

Umar Khayyám

To English readers, some of the following poems are the most known of all Islamic literature. The popularity of The Rubáiyát *(rubáiyát means quatrain, a four-line stanza or poem) in English is due to the translation by Edward FitzGerald published in 1859. FitzGerald took an Arabic line that might be literally translated as "If hand should give of the pith, of the wheat a loaf, and of wine a two-maunder jug, of sheep a thigh, with a little sweetheart . . ." and transformed it into*

A Book of Verses underneath the Bough,
A Jug of Wine, A Loaf of Bread—and Thou

FitzGerald thought that the quatrains were written by Omar (or Umar) Khayyám, a Persian scientist and mathematician who lived at the end of the eleventh and the beginning of the twelfth century. FitzGerald selected from a large number of poems by Umar Khayyám (and perhaps others). While many of the poems were joyous, many are more somber and grave. Joyous or grave, by Khayyám or others, the poems provide a window on Persian life and a reminder of a sensibility that is timeless. What do they tell you about their author, his ideas, and his world? Would you call these poems religious or secular?

I

Wake! For the Sun, who scatter'd into flight
The Stars before him from the Field of Night,
 Drives Night along with them from Heav'n, and strikes
The Sultán's Turret with a Shaft of Light.

II

Before the phantom of False morning died,
Methought a Voice within the Tavern cried,
 "When all the Temple is prepared within,
Why nods the drowsy Worshipper outside?"

IV

Now the New Year reviving old Desires,
The thoughtful Soul to Solitude retires,
 Where the WHITE HAND OF MOSES on the Bough
Puts out, and Jesus from the Ground suspires.

VII

Come, fill the Cup, and in the fire of Spring
Your Winter-garment of Repentance fling:

The Bird of Time has but a little way
To flutter—and the Bird is on the Wing.

VIII

Whether at Naishápúr or Babylon,
Whether the Cup with sweet or bitter run,
    The Wine of Life keeps oozing drop by drop,
The Leaves of Life keep falling one by one.

IX

Each Morn a thousand Roses brings, you say;
Yes, but where leaves the Rose of Yesterday?
    And this first Summer month that brings the Rose
Shall take Jamshýd and Kaikobád away.

XI

With me along the strip of Herbage strown
That just divides the desert from the sown,
    Where name of Slave and Sultán is forgot—
And Peace to Mahmúd on his golden Throne!

XII

A Book of Verses underneath the Bough,
A Jug of Wine, a Loaf of Bread—and Thou
    Beside me singing in the Wilderness—
Oh, Wilderness were Paradise enow!

XIII

Some for the Glories of This World; and some
Sigh for the Prophet's Paradise to come;
    Ah, take the Cash, and let the Credit go,
Nor heed the rumble of a distant Drum!

XVI

The Worldly Hope men set their Hearts upon
Turns Ashes—or it prospers; and anon,

Like Snow upon the Desert's dusty Face,
Lighting a little hour or two—is gone.

XVII

Think, in this batter'd Caravanserai
Whose Portals are alternate Night and Day,
    How Sultán after Sultán with his Pomp
Abode his destined Hour, and went his way.

XXIV

Ah, make the most of what we yet may spend,
Before we too into the Dust descend;
    Dust into Dust, and under Dust to lie
Sans Wine, sans Song, sans Singer, and—sans End!

XXV

Alike for those who for To-DAY prepare,
And those that after some To-MORROW stare,
    A Muezzín from the Tower of Darkness cries
"Fools! your Reward is neither Here nor There."

XXXII

There was the Door to which I found no Key;
There was the Veil through which I might not see:
    Some little talk awhile of ME and THEE
There was—and then no more of THEE and ME.

XXXVII

For I remember stopping by the way
To watch a Potter thumping his wet Clay:
    And with its all-obliterated Tongue
It murmur'd—"Gently, Brother, gently, pray!"

XXXVIII

And has not such a Story from of Old
Down Man's successive generations roll'd
　Of such a clod of saturated Earth
Cast by the Maker into Human mould?

XLII

And if the Wine you drink, the Lip you press
End in what All begins and ends in—Yes;
　Think then you are TO-DAY what YESTERDAY
You were—TO-MORROW you shall not be less.

LV

You know, my Friends, with what a brave Carouse
I made a Second Marriage in my house;
　Divorced old barren Reason from my Bed
And took the Daughter of the Vine to Spouse.

LX

The mighty Mahmúd, Allah-breathing Lord
That all the misbelieving and black Horde
　Of Fears and Sorrows that infest the Soul
Scatters before him with his whirlwind Sword.

LXIV

Strange, is it not? that of the myriads who
Before us pass'd the door of Darkness through,
　Not one returns to tell us of the Road,
Which to discover we must travel too.

LXVI

I sent my Soul through the Invisible,
Some letter of that After-life to spell:

And by and by my Soul return'd to me,
And answer'd "I Myself am Heav'n and Hell."

LXVII

Heav'n but the Vision of fulfill'd Desire,
And Hell the Shadow from a Soul on fire,
   Cast on the Darkness into which Ourselves,
So late emerged from, shall so soon expire.

LXIX

But helpless Pieces of the Game He plays
Upon this Chequer-board of Nights and Days;
   Hither and thither moves, and checks, and slays,
And one by one back in the Closet lays.

LXXI

The Moving Finger writes; and, having writ,
Moves on: nor all your Piety nor Wit
   Shall lure it back to cancel half a Line,
Nor all your Tears wash out a Word of it.

LXXIII

With Earth's first Clay They did the Last Man knead;
And there of the Last Harvest sow'd the Seed:
   And the first Morning of Creation wrote
What the Last Dawn of Reckoning shall read.

LXXXVII

Whereat some one of the loquacious Lot—
I think a Súfi pipkin—waxing hot—
   "All this of Pot and Potter—Tell me then,
Who is the Potter, pray, and who the Pot?"

CHAPTER TWELVE

Byzantine Civilization

39. BYZANTIUM AND ITS SPHERE

J. M. Roberts

In this selection a modern historian introduces Byzantine civilization. In what ways was Byzantine civilization different from the Western Roman? What were the Byzantine empire's sources of strength? What were its weaknesses?

In 1453, nine hundred years after Justinian [the emperor who codified Roman law and built the great St. Sophia church—Ed.], Constantinople fell to an infidel army. "There has never been and there never will be a more dreadful happening," wrote one Greek scribe. It was indeed a great event. No one in the West was prepared; the whole Christian world was shocked. More than a state, Rome itself was at an end. The direct descent from the classical Mediterranean civilization had been shaped at last; if few saw this in quite so deep a perspective as the literary enthusiasts who detected in it retribution for the Greek sack of Troy, it was still the end of two thousand years' tradition. And if the pagan world of Hellenistic culture and ancient Greece were set aside, a thousand years of Christian empire at Byzantium itself was impressive enough for its passing to seem an earthquake.

This is one of those subjects where it helps to know the end of the story before beginning it. Even in their decline Byzantine prestige and traditions had amazed strangers who felt through them the weight of an imperial past. To the end its emperors were *augusti* and its citizens called themselves "Romans." For centuries, St. Sophia had been the greatest of Christian churches, the orthodox religion it enshrined needing to make even fewer concessions to religious pluralism as previously troublesome provinces were swallowed by the Moslems. Though in retrospect it is easy to see the inevitability of decline and fall, therefore, this was not how the men who lived under it saw the Eastern empire. They knew, consciously or unconsciously, that it had great powers of evolution. It was a great conservative *tour de force* which had survived many extremities and its archaic style was almost to the end able to cloak important changes.

Nonetheless, a thousand years brought great upheavals in both East and West; history played upon Byzantium, modifying some elements in its heritage, stressing others, obliterating others, so that the empire was in the end very different from Justinian's while never becoming wholly distinct from it. There is no clear dividing line between antiquity and Byzantium. The centre of gravity of the empire had begun to shift eastward before Constantine and when his city became the seat of the world empire it was the inheritor of the pretensions of Rome. The office of the emperors showed particularly sharply how evolution and conservatism could combine. Until 800 there was no formal challenge to the theory that the emperor was the secular ruler of all mankind. With the coronation of a western emperor in that year, whatever might be said of the exact relationship of his power to that of the East, the uniqueness of the imperial purple had gone. Yet Byzantium continued to cherish the fantasy of universal empire; there would be emperors right to the end and their office was one of awe-inspiring grandeur. Still theoretically chosen by Senate, army and people, they had nonetheless an absolute authority. While the realities of his accession might determine for any particular emperor the actual extent of his power— and sometimes the dynastic succession broke under the strain—he was *autocrat* as a western emperor never was. Respect for legal principle and the vested interests of bureaucracy might muffle the emperor's will in action, but it was always supreme in theory. The heads of all the great departments of state were responsible to no one but him. This authority explains the intensity with which Byzantine politics focused at the imperial court, for it was there, and not through corporate and representative institutions such as evolved slowly in the West, that authority could be influenced.

This autocratic power had its harsh side. The *curiosi* or secret police informers who swarmed through the empire were not there for nothing. But the nature of the imperial office also laid obligations on the emperor. Crowned by the Patriarch of Constantinople, the emperor had the enormous authority, but also the responsibilities, of God's representative upon earth. The line between lay and ecclesiastical was always more blurred in the East than in the West. Though this meant that there was in the East nothing like the western opposition of Church and State there was a continuing pressure upon God's vice-regent to act appropriately, to show *philanthropia*, a love of mankind, in his acts. The purpose of the autocratic power was the preservation of mankind and of the conduits by which it drew the water of life—orthodoxy and the Church. Appropriately most of the early Christian emperors were canonized—just as pagan emperors had been deified. Other traditions than the Christian also affected the office, as this suggested. Byzantine emperors were to receive the ritual prostrations of oriental tradition and the images of them which look down from their mosaics show their heads surrounded by the nimbus in which the last pre-Christian emperors were depicted, for it was

part of the cult of the sun god. (Some representations of Sassanid[1] rulers
have it, too.) It was, nonetheless, above all as a Christian ruler that the
emperor justified his authority.

The imperial office itself thus embodied much of the Christian heritage of Byzantium. That heritage also marked the eastern empire off
sharply from the West at many other levels. There were, in the first
place, the ecclesiastical peculiarities of what came to be called the Orthodox Church. Islam, for example, was sometimes seen by the eastern
clergy less as a pagan religion than a heresy. Other differences lay in the
Orthodox view of the relationship of clergy to society; the coalescence of
spiritual and lay was important at many levels below the throne. One
symbol of it was the retention of a married clergy; the Orthodox priest,
for all his reputed holiness, was never to be quite the man apart his
western Catholic colleague became. This suggests the great rôle of the
Orthodox Church as a cementing force in society down to modern times.
Above all, no sacerdotal authority as great as that of the papacy would
emerge. The focus of authority was the emperor, whose office and responsibility towered above the equally ranked bishops. Of course, so far
as social regulation went, this did not mean that Orthodoxy was more
tolerant than the Church of the medieval West. Bad times were always
liable to be interpreted as evidence that the emperor had not been doing
his Christian duty—which included the harrying of such familiar scape-
goats as Jews, heretics and homosexuals.

Distinction from the West was in part a product of political history, of
the gradual loosening of contact after the division of the empires, in part
a matter of an original distinction of style. The Catholic and Orthodox
traditions were on divergent courses from early times, even if at first the
divergence was only slight. At an early date Latin Christianity was somewhat estranged by the concessions the Greeks had to make to Syrian and
Egyptian practice. Yet such concessions had also kept alive a certain
polycentrism within Christendom. When Jerusalem, Antioch and Alexandria, the other three great patriarchates of the East, fell into Arab
hands, the polarization of Rome and Constantinople was accentuated.
Gradually, the Christian world was ceasing to be bilingual; a Latin West
came to face a Greek East. It was at the beginning of the seventh century
that Latin finally ceased to be the official language of the army and of
justice, the two departments where it had longest resisted Greek. That
the bureaucracy was Greek-speaking was to be very important. When the
eastern Church failed among Moslems, it opened a new missionary field
and won much ground among the pagans to the north. Eventually, southeastern Europe and Russia owed their evangelizing to Constantinople.
The outcome—among many other things—was that the Slav peoples
would owe to their teachers not only the creation of a literature and

1. Persian dynasty (c. 224–640) before the Arab invasion.—Ed.

written language based on Greek, but many of their most fundamental political ideas. And because the West was Catholic, its relations with the Slav world were sometimes hostile, so that the Slav peoples came to view the western half of Christendom with deep reservations. This lay far in the future and takes us further afield than we need go for the present.

The distinctiveness of the eastern Christian tradition could be illustrated in many ways. Monasticism, for example, remained closer to its original forms in the East and the importance of the Holy Man has always been greater there than in the more hierarchically aware Roman Church. The Greeks, too, seem to have been more disputatious than Latins; the Hellenistic background of the early Church had always favoured speculation and the eastern Churches were open to oriental trends, always susceptible to the pressures of many traditional influences. Yet this did not prevent the imposition of dogmatic solutions to religious quarrels.

Some of these were about issues which now seem trivial or even meaningless. Inevitably, a secular age such as our own finds even the greatest of them difficult to fathom simply because we lack a sense of the mental world lying behind them. It requires an effort to recall that behind the exquisite definitions and logic-chopping of the Fathers lay a concern of appalling importance, nothing less than that mankind should be saved from damnation.

One major source of division and difficulty for the empire in the earlier part of this period was, as so often before, religion. This plagued the empire and held back its recovery because it was so often tangled with political and local issues. The outstanding example was a controversy which embittered feelings for over a century, the campaign of the iconoclasts.

The depicting of the saints, the Blessed Virgin and God Himself had come to be one of the great devices of Orthodox Christianity for focusing devotion and teaching. In late antiquity such images, or icons, had a place in the West, too, but to this day they occupy a special place in Orthodox churches where they are displayed in shrines and on special screens to be venerated and contemplated by the believer. They are much more than mere decoration, for their arrangement conveys the teachings of the Church and (as one authority has said) provides "a point of meeting between heaven and earth," for the faithful amid the icons can feel surrounded by the whole invisible Church, by the departed, the saints and angels, and Christ and His mother themselves. It is hardly surprising that something concentrating religious emotion so intensely should have led in paint or mosaic to some of the highest achievements of Byzantine (and, later, Slav) art.

Icons had become prominent in eastern churches by the sixth century. There followed two centuries of respect for them and in many places growing popular devotion to them, but then their use came to be questioned. Interestingly, this happened just after the caliphate had mounted a campaign against the use of images in Islam, but it cannot be inferred that the iconoclasts took their ideas from Moslems. The critics of the icons claimed that they were idols, perverting the worship due to God to the creations of men. They demanded their destruction or expunging and set to work with a will with whitewash, brush and hammer.

Leo III favoured such men. There is still much that is mysterious about the reason why imperial authority was thrown behind the iconoclasts, but he acted on the advice of bishops, and Arab invasions and volcanic eruptions were no doubt held to indicate God's disfavour. In 730, therefore, an edict forbade the use of images in public worship. A persecution of those who resisted followed; enforcement was always more marked at Constantinople than in the provinces. The movement reached its peak under Constantine V and was ratified by a council of bishops in 754. Persecution became fiercer, and there were martyrs, particularly among monks, who usually defended icons more vigorously than did the secular clergy. But iconoclasm was always dependent on imperial support and there were ebbings and flowings in the next century. Under Leo IV and Irene, his widow, persecution was relaxed and the "iconophiles" (lovers of icons) recovered ground, though this was followed by renewed persecution. Only in 843, on the first Sunday of Lent, a day still celebrated as a feast of Orthodoxy in the eastern Church, were the icons finally restored.

What was the meaning of this strange episode? There was a practical justification, in that the conversion of Jews and Moslems was said to be made more difficult by Christian respect for images, but this does not take us very far. Once again, a religious dispute cannot be separated from factors external to religion, but the ultimate explanation probably lies in a sense of religious precaution, and given the passion often shown in theological controversy in the eastern empire, it is easy to understand how the debate became embittered. No question of art or artistic merit arose: Byzantium was not like that. What was at stake was the feeling of reformers that the Greeks were falling into idolatry in the extremity of their (relatively recent) devotion to icons and that the Arab disasters were the first rumblings of God's thunder; a pious king, as in the Israel of the Old Testament, could yet save the people from the consequences of sin by breaking the idols. This was easier in that the process suited the mentalities of a faith which felt itself at bay. It was notable that iconoclasm was particularly strong in the army. Another fact which is suggestive is that icons had often represented local saints and holy men; they were replaced by the uniting, simplifying symbols of eucharist and cross, and this says something about a new, monolithic quality in Byzantine religion and society from the eighth century onwards. Finally, iconoclasm was also in part an angry response to a tide which had long flowed in favour of the monks who gave such prominence to icons in their teaching. As well as a prudent step towards placating an angry God, therefore, iconoclasm represented a reaction of centralized authority, that of emperor and bishops, against local pieties, the independence of cities and monasteries, and the cult of holy men.

Iconoclasm offended many in the western Church but it showed more clearly than anything yet how far Orthodoxy now was from Latin Christianity. The western Church had been moving, too; as Latin culture was taken over by the Germanic peoples, it drifted away in spirit from the churches of the Greek East. The iconoclast synod of bishops had been an affront to the papacy, which had already condemned Leo's supporters. Rome viewed with alarm the emperor's pretensions to act in spiritual matters. Thus iconoclasms drove deeper the division between the two halves of Christendom. Cultural differentiation had now gone very far— not surprisingly when it could take two months by sea to go from Byzantium to Italy and by land a wedge of Slav peoples soon stood between two languages.

Contact between East and West could not be altogether extinguished at the official level. But here, too, history created new divisions. The appearance of an empire in the West, where a Frankish king was crowned "emperor" by the Pope of Rome in 800, was a challenge to the Byzantine claim to be the legatee of Rome. Distinctions within the western world did not much matter in Constantinople; the Byzantine officials identified a challenger in the Frankish realm and thereafter indiscriminately called all westerners "Franks," a usage which was to spread as far as China. The two states failed to cooperate against the Arab and offended one another's susceptibilities. The Roman coronation was in part a response to the assumption of the title of emperor at Constantinople by a woman, Irene, an unattractive mother who had blinded her own son. But the Frankish title was only briefly recognized in Byzantium; later emperors in the West were regarded only as kings. Italy divided the two Christian empires, too, for the remaining Byzantine lands there came to be threatened by Frank and Saxon as much as they had ever been by Lombards. In the tenth century the manipulation of the papacy by Saxon emperors made matters worse.

Of course the two Christian worlds could not altogether lose touch. One German emperor of the tenth century had a Byzantine bride and German art of the tenth century was much influenced by Byzantine themes and techniques. But it was just the difference of two cultural worlds that made such contacts fruitful, and as the centuries went by, the difference became more and more palpable. The old aristocratic families of Byzantium were replaced gradually by others drawn from Anatolian and Armenian stocks. Above all, there was the unique splendour and complication of the life of the imperial city itself, where religious and secular worlds seemed completely to interpenetrate one another. The calendar of the Christian year was inseparable from that of the court; together they set the rhythms of an immense theatrical spectacle in which the rituals of both Church and State displayed to the people the majesty of the empire. There was some secular art, but the art constantly before men's eyes was overwhelmingly religious. Even in the worst times it had a continuing vigour, expressing the greatness and omnipresence of God, whose vice-regent was the emperor. Ritualism sustained the rigid etiquette of the court about which there proliferated the characteristic evils of intrigue and conspiracy. The public appearance of even the Christian emperor could be like that of the deity in a mystery cult, preceded by the raising of several curtains from behind which he dramatically emerged. This was the apex of an astonishing civilization which showed half the world for perhaps half a millennium what true empire was. When a mission of pagan Russians came to Byzantium in the tenth century to examine its form of the Christian religion as they had examined others, they could only report that what they had seen in Hagia Sophia [St. Sophia] had amazed them. "There God dwells among men," they said.

40.   SAINTS AND SINNERS:
40.1. THEODORA

Procopius

The reign of the Byzantine emperor Justinian, from 527 to 565, is remembered as an age of restored imperial greatness. His generals recovered northern Africa from the Vandals and Italy from the Ostrogoths. He codified Roman law and embarked on an extensive building program that included the church of Hagia Sofia. His wife, the Empress Theodora, crushed a religious rebellion in 532 and helped shape Byzantine control of religion by the emperor. Procopius wrote of the achievements of Justinian and Theodora in other books. In what has been called his Secret History *(because he did not publish it while the emperor was alive), he evidently wanted to show the seamy and brutal side of the world of Justinian and Theodora. In this selection from the* Secret History *Procopius describes the world of circuses, taverns, theaters, and back-street brothels where Theodora grew up. This decidedly hostile account of Theodora's checkered past gives as an unusual look into the world of popular entertainment and sexuality. What does it tell you about the life*

of the urban poor in sixth-century Byzantium? How were their lives similar
to, and different from, our own? What does Procopius's account suggest
about the history of morality or sexuality?

In Byzantium there was a man called Acacius, a keeper of the circus
animals, belonging to the Green faction [or political party] and entitled
the Bearward. This man died of sickness while Anastasius occupied the
imperial throne, leaving three daughters, Comito, Theodora, and Anas-
tasia, of whom the eldest had not yet completed her seventh year. The
widow married again, hoping that her new husband would from then on
share with her the management of her house and the care of the animals
[including the dancing bears]. But the Greens' Dancing-master, a man
called Asterius, was offered a bribe to remove these two from their
office, in which he installed his Paymaster without any difficulty, for the
Dancing-masters were allowed to arrange such matters just as they chose.
But when the wife saw the whole populace congregated in the circus, she
put wreaths on the heads of the little girls and in both their hands, and
made them sit down as suppliants. The Greens refused absolutely to
admit the supplication; but the Blues [faction or party] gave them a
similar office, as their Bearward too had died.

When the children were old enough, they were at once put on the
stage there by their mother, as their appearance was very attractive; not
all at the same time, however, but as each one seemed to her to be mature
enough for this profession. The eldest one, Comito, was already one of
the most popular harlots of the day. Theodora, who came next, clad in a
little tunic with long sleeves, the usual dress of a slave girl, used to assist
her in various ways, following her about and invariably carrying on her
shoulders the bench on which her sister habitually sat at public meetings.
For the time being Theodora was still too undeveloped to be capable of
sharing a man's bed or having intercourse like a woman; but she acted as
a sort of male prostitute to satisfy customers of the lowest type, and slaves
at that, who when accompanying their owners to the theatre seized their
opportunity to divert themselves in this revolting manner; and for some
considerable time she remained in a brothel, given up to this unnatural
bodily commerce. But as soon as she was old enough and fully developed, she joined the women on the stage and promptly became a courte-
san, of the type our ancestors called 'the dregs of the army'. For she was
not a flautist or harpist; she was not even qualified to join the corps of
dancers; but she merely sold her attractions to anyone who came along,
putting her whole body at his disposal.

Later she joined the actors in all the business of the theatre and played
a regular part in their stage performances, making herself the butt of
their ribald buffoonery. She was extremely clever and had a biting wit,
and quickly became popular as a result. There was not a particle of
modesty in the little hussy, and no one ever saw her taken aback: she

complied with the most outrageous demands without the slightest hesitation, and she was the sort of girl who if somebody walloped her or boxed her ears would make a jest of it and roar with laughter; and she would throw off her clothes and exhibit naked to all and sundry those regions, both in front and behind, which the rules of decency require to be kept veiled and hidden from masculine eyes.

She used to tease her lovers by keeping them waiting, and by constantly playing about with novel methods of intercourse she could always bring the lascivious to her feet; so far from waiting to be invited by anyone she encountered, she herself by cracking dirty jokes and wiggling her hips suggestively would invite all who came her way, especially if they were still in their teens. Never was anyone so completely given up to unlimited self-indulgence. Often she would go to a bring-your-own-food dinner-party with ten young men or more, all at the peak of their physical powers and with fornication as their chief object in life, and would lie with all her fellow-diners in turn the whole night long: when she had reduced them all to a state of exhaustion she would go to their menials, as many as thirty on occasions, and copulate with every one of them; but not even so could she satisfy her lust.

One night she went into the house of a distinguished citizen during the drinking, and, it is said, before the eyes of all the guests she stood up on the end of the couch near their feet, pulled up her dress in the most disgusting manner as she stood there, and brazenly displayed her lasciviousness. And though she brought three openings into service, she often found fault with Nature, grumbling because Nature had not made the openings in her nipples wider than is normal, so that she could devise another variety of intercourse in that region. Naturally she was frequently pregnant, but by using pretty well all the tricks of the trade she was able to induce immediate abortion.

Often in the theatre, too, in full view of all the people she would throw off her clothes and stand naked in their midst, having only a girdle about her private parts and her groins—not, however, because she was ashamed to expose these also to the public, but because no one is allowed to appear there absolutely naked: a girdle round the groins is compulsory. With this minimum covering she would spread herself out and lie face upwards on the floor. Servants on whom this task had been imposed would sprinkle barley grains over her private parts, and geese trained for the purpose used to pick them off one by one with their bills and swallow them. Theodora, so far from blushing when she stood up again, actually seemed to be proud of this performance. For she was not only shameless herself, but did more than anyone else to encourage shamelessness.

Many times she threw off her clothes and stood in the middle of the actors on the stage, leaning over backwards or pushing out her behind to invite both those who had already enjoyed her and those who had not been intimate as yet, parading her own special brand of gymnastics. With such lasciviousness did she misuse her own body that she appeared to have her private parts not like other women in the place intended by nature, but in her face! And again, those who were intimate with her showed by so doing that they were not having intercourse in accordance with the laws of nature; and every person of any decency who happened to meet her in the forum would swing round and beat a hasty retreat, for fear he might come in contact with any of the hussy's garments and so appear tainted with this pollution. For to those who saw her, especially in the early hours of the day, she was a bird of ill omen. As for her fellow-actresses, she habitually and constantly stormed at them like a fury; for she was malicious in the extreme.

40.2.   MONASTICISM

Theodore of Studius

Monasticism was an important force in Byzantine society. Some monks chose to live alone as hermits. Others joined monastic communities. Theodore of Studius (d. 826) took the more social route, joining the monastic order of St. Basil (d. 379). In this letter to a pupil, Theodore shows how severe even the social form of monasticism could be. What advice does he give his pupil? What seems to be his greatest concern? Compare this document with that of Procopius. Are the two writers living in the same world?

Since, by the good pleasure of God, you have been promoted, my spiritual child Nicolas, to the dignity of abbot, it is needful for you to keep all the injunctions in this letter. Do not alter without necessity the type and rule that you have received from your spiritual home, the monastery. Do not acquire any of this world's goods, nor hoard up privately for yourself to the value of one piece of silver. Be without distraction in heart and soul in your care and your thought for those who have been entrusted to you by God, and have become your spiritual sons and brothers;—and do not look aside to those formerly belonging to you according to the flesh, whether kinsfolk, or friends, or companions. Do not spend the property of your monastery, in life or death, by way of gift or legacy, to any such kinsfolk or friends. For you are not of the world, neither have you part in the world. Except that if any of your people come out of ordinary life to join our rule, you must care for them according to the example of the Holy Fathers. Do not obtain any slave nor use in your private service or in that of the monastery over which you preside, or in the fields, man who was made in the image of God. For such an indulgence is only for those who live in the world. For you should yourself be as a servant to the brethren like-minded with you, at least in intention, even if in outward appearance you are reckoned to be master and teacher. Have no animal of the female sex in domestic use, seeing that you have renounced the female sex altogether, whether in house or fields, since none of the Holy Fathers had such, nor does nature require them. Do not be driven by horses and mules without necessity, but go on foot in imitation of Christ. But if there is need, let your beast be the foal of an ass.

Use all care that all things in the brotherhood be common and not distributed, and let nothing, not even a needle, belong to any one in particular. Let your body and your spirit, to say nothing of your goods, be ever divided in equality of love among all your spiritual children and brethren. Use no authority over the two brothers of yours who are my sons. Do nothing, by way of command or of ordination, beyond the injunctions of the Fathers. Do not join in brotherhood or close relation with secular persons, seeing that you have fled from the world and from marriage. Such relations are not found in the Fathers, or but here and there, and not according to rule. Do not sit at a feast with women, except with your mother according to the flesh, and your sister, or possibly with others in case of necessity, as the Holy Fathers enjoin. Do not go out often, nor range around, leaving your fold without necessity. For even if you remain always there, it is hard to keep safe your human sheep, so apt are they to stray and wander.

By all means keep to the instruction three times a week in the evening, since that is traditional and salutary. Do not give what they call the little habit [of novice or postulant?] and then, some time later, another as the larger. For there is one habit, as there is one baptism, and this is the practice of the Holy Fathers. Depart not from the rules and canons of the Fathers, especially of the Holy Father Basil; but whatever you do or say, be as one who has his witness in the Holy Scriptures, or in the custom of the Fathers, so as not to transgress the commandments of God. Do not leave your fold or remove to another, or ascend to any higher dignity, except by the paternal decision. Do not make friends with any canoness, nor enter any women's monastery, nor have any private conversation with a nun, or with a secular woman, except in case of necessity; and then let it be so that two are present on either side. For one, as they say, is cause of offence. Do not open the door of the sheepfold to any manner of woman, without great necessity; if it is possible to receive such in silence, it is all the better. Do not procure a lodging for yourself, or a secular house for your spiritual children, in which there are women, for that were to run great risks; but provide yourself with what is necessary for journeys and other occasions from men of piety. Do not take as pupil into your cell a youth for whom you have a fancy; but use the services of some one above suspicion, and of various brothers.

Do not have any choice or costly garment, except for priestly functions. But follow the Fathers in being shod and clad in humility. Be not delicate in food, in private expenditure, or in hospitality; for this belongs to the portion of those who take their joy in the present life. Do not lay up money in your monastery; but things of all kinds, beyond what is needed, give to the poor at the entrance of your court; for so did the Holy Fathers. Do not keep a safe place, nor have a care for wealth. But let all your care be the guardianship of souls. As to the money, and various necessaries, entrust them to the steward, the cellarer, or to whosesoever charge it falls; but so that you keep for yourself the whole authority, and change offices among persons from time to time as you see fit, receiving account as you may demand, of the tasks entrusted to each. Do nothing, carry out nothing, according to your own judgment, in any matter whatever, in journeying, buying or selling, receiving or rejecting a brother, or in any change of office or in anything material, or in regard to spiritual failings, without the counsel of those who stand first in knowledge and in piety, one, two, three or more, according to circumstances, as the Fathers have directed. These commands, and all others that you have received, keep and maintain, that it may be well with you, and that you may have prosperity in the Lord all the days of your life. But let anything to the contrary be far from you in speech and in thought.

41. *THE ALEXIAD*

Anna Comnena

The Alexiad *is a history of the reign of the Byzantine Emperor Alexius I from 1081 to 1118, written by his daughter, Anna Comnena. If the Princess shows an expected loyalty to her father, she was also independent, intelligent, and insightful. When her father died, he was replaced by Anna's younger brother. She schemed for the throne on behalf of her husband instead but was defeated. She retired to a convent and wrote the history, originally as a long poem.*

The section here concerns the attack on Byzantium by the Christian crusaders. Alexius had asked Pope Urban of Rome in 1095 for aid. He was being pressured by the Normans in the South and the Seljuk Turks in the East and asked for mercenaries. This was a significant request since relations between Byzantium and Rome had been ruptured in 1054. Pope Urban saw the request as an opportunity for a general mobilization of Christian forces that might regain the Holy Land from the Saracens as well.

The resulting army of pilgrims, priests, families, and the forces of indepen-
dent princes was not easily controlled. They even included Bohemund of
Sicily, the Norman leader who had already attacked Byzantine outposts.
Anna Comnena writes of her father's reaction. How did she and her father
view these "Frankish," or European, armies? Were the Europeans "barbari-
ans," as she says, or were she and her father merely ungrateful?

Before he had enjoyed even a short rest, he heard a report of the approach of innumerable Frankish armies. Now he dreaded their arrival for
he knew their irresistible manner of attack, their unstable and mobile
character and all the peculiar natural and concomitant characteristics
which the Frank retains throughout; and he also knew that they were
always agape for money, and seemed to disregard their truces readily for
any reason that cropped up. For he had always heard this reported of
them, and found it very true. However, he did not lose heart, but prepared himself in every way so that, when the occasion called, he would be
ready for battle. And indeed the actual facts were far greater and more
terrible than rumour made them. For the whole of the West and all the
barbarian tribes which dwell between the further side of the Adriatic and
the pillars of Heracles, had all migrated in a body and were marching into
Asia through the intervening Europe, and were making the journey with
all their household. The reason of this upheaval was more or less the
following. A certain Frank, Peter by name, nicknamed Cucupeter, had
gone to worship at the Holy Sepulchre and after suffering many things at
the hands of the Turks and Saracens who were ravaging Asia, he got back
to his own country with difficulty. But he was angry at having failed in his
object, and wanted to undertake the same journey again. However, he saw
that he ought not to make the journey to the Holy Sepulchre alone again,
lest worse things befall him, so he worked out a cunning plan. This was to
preach in all the Latin countries that "the voice of God bids me announce
to all the Counts in France" that they should all leave their homes and set
out to worship at the Holy Sepulchre, and to endeavour wholeheartedly
with hand and mind to deliver Jerusalem from the hand of Hagarenes.*
And he really succeeded. For after inspiring the souls of all with this
quasi-divine command he contrived to assemble the Franks from all sides,
one after the other, with arms, horses and all the other paraphernalia of
war. And they were all so zealous and eager that every highroad was full
of them. And those Frankish soldiers were accompanied by an unarmed
host more numerous than the sand or the stars, carrying palms and
crosses on their shoulders, women and children, too, came away from
their countries and the sight of them was like many rivers streaming from
all sides, and they were advancing towards us through Dacia generally
with all their hosts. Now the coming of these many peoples was preceded

*Saracens, who were considered "children of Hagar" (cf. Genesis 16).—Ed.

by a locust which did not touch the wheat, but made a terrible attack on the vines. This was really a presage as the diviners of the time interpreted it, and meant that this enormous Frankish army would, when it came, refrain from interference in Christian affairs, but fall very heavily upon the barbarian Ishmaelites who were slaves to drunkenness, wine, and Dionysus.[1] For this race is under the sway of Dionysus and Eros,[2] rushes headlong into all kind of sexual intercourse, and is not circumcised either in the flesh or in their passions. It is nothing but a slave, nay triply enslaved, to the ills wrought by Aphrodite. For this reason they worship and adore Astarte and Ashtaroth[3] too and value above all the image of the moon, and the golden figure of Hobar[4] in their country. Now in these symbols Christianity was taken to be the corn because of its wineless and very nutritive qualities; in this manner the diviners interpreted the vines and the wheat. However let the matter of the prophecy rest.

The incidents of the barbarians' approach followed in the order I have described, and persons of intelligence could feel that they were witnessing a strange occurrence. The arrival of these multitudes did not take place at the same time nor by the same road (for how indeed could such masses starting from different places have crossed the straits of Lombardy all together?). Some first, some next, others after them and thus successively all accomplished the transit, and then marched through the Continent. Each army was preceded, as we said, by an unspeakable number of locusts; and all who saw this more than once recognized them as forerunners of the Frankish armies. When the first of them began crossing the straits of Lombardy sporadically the Emperor summoned certain leaders of the Roman forces, and sent them to the parts of Dyrrachium and Valona[5] with instructions to offer a courteous welcome to the Franks who had crossed, and to collect abundant supplies from all the countries along their route; then to follow and watch them covertly all the time, and if they saw them making any foraging-excursions, they were to come out from under cover and check them by light skirmishing. These captains were accompanied by some men who knew the Latin tongue, so that they might settle any disputes that arose between them.

Let me, however, give an account of this subject more clearly and in due order. According to universal rumour Godfrey,[6] who sold his country, was

---

1. Anna's account of the beliefs of the Muslims was highly biased. Muhammad forbade his followers to drink intoxicating liquors.

2. Dionysus was the Greek god associated with wine and revelry; Eros was the patron of lovers, and son of Aphrodite, goddess of love.

3. Names of the Semitic goddess of fertility.

4. I.e., Hathor, the Egyptian goddess of love, usually depicted with the head of a cow. (N.B. Idol worship was strictly forbidden by Islamic law.)

5. Ports on the Adriatic, directly opposite the heel of Italy in modern Albania.

6. Godfrey of Bouillon, the duke of Lower Lorraine (c. 1060–1100). To raise money for the Crusade, he sold two of his estates, and pledged his castle at Bouillon to the bishop of Liège.

the first to start on the appointed road; this man was very rich and very proud of his bravery, courage and conspicuous lineage; for every Frank is anxious to outdo the others. And such an upheaval of both men and women took place then as had never occurred within human memory, the simpler-minded were urged on by the real desire of worshipping at our Lord's Sepulchre, and visiting the sacred places; but the more astute, especially men like Bohemund and those of like mind, had another secret reason, namely, the hope that while on their travels they might by some means be able to seize the capital itself, looking upon this as a kind of corollary. And Bohemund disturbed the minds of many nobler men by thus cherishing his old grudge against the Emperor. Meanwhile Peter, after he had delivered his message, crossed the straits of Lombardy before anybody else with eighty thousand men on foot, and one hundred thousand on horseback, and reached the capital by way of Hungary.[7] For the Frankish race, as one may conjecture, is always very hotheaded and eager, but when once it has espoused a cause, it is uncontrollable.

The Emperor, knowing what Peter had suffered before from the Turks, advised him to wait for the arrival of the other Counts, but Peter would not listen for he trusted to the multitude of his followers, so crossed and pitched his camp near a small town called Helenopolis.[8] After him followed the Normans numbering ten thousand, who separated themselves from the rest of the army and devastated the country round Nicaea, and behaved most cruelly to all. For they dismembered some of the children and fixed others on wooden spits and roasted them at the fire, and on persons advanced in age they inflicted every kind of torture. But when the inhabitants of Nicaea became aware of these doings, they threw open their gates and marched out upon them, and after a violent conflict had taken place they had to dash back inside their citadel as the Normans fought so bravely. And thus the latter recovered all the booty and returned to Helenopolis. Then a dispute arose between them and the others who had not gone out with them, as is usual in such cases, for the minds of those who stayed behind were aflame with envy, and thus caused a skirmish after which the headstrong Normans drew apart again, marched to Xerigordus[9] and took it by assault. When the Sultan[10] heard what had happened, he dispatched Elchanes[11] against them with a substantial force. He came, and recaptured Xerigordus and sacrificed some of the Normans to the sword, and took others captive, at the same time laid plans to catch those who had remained behind with Cucupeter. He placed ambushes in suitable spots so that any coming from the camp in the direction of Nicaea would fall into them unexpectedly and be killed. Besides this, as he knew

7. Peter's contingent probably numbered about 20,000 including noncombatants.
8. I.e., Peter moved his forces across the Bosphorus and into Asia Minor.
9. A castle held by the Turks.
10. Qilij Arslan I, ruled 1092–1106.
11. An important Turkish military commander.

the Franks' love of money, he sent for two active-minded men and ordered them to go to Cucupeter's camp and proclaim there that the Normans had gained possession of Nicaea, and were now dividing everything in it. When this report was circulated among Peter's followers, it upset them terribly. Directly they heard the words "partition" and "money" they started in a disorderly crowd along the road to Nicaea, all but unmindful of their military experience and the discipline which is essential for those starting out to battle. For, as I remarked above, the Latin race is always very fond of money, but more especially when it is bent on raiding a country; it then loses its reason and gets beyond control. As they journeyed neither in ranks nor in squadrons, they fell foul of the Turkish ambuscades near the river Dracon and perished miserably. And such a large number of Franks and Normans were the victims of the Ishmaelite sword, that when they piled up the corpses of the slaughtered men which were lying on either side they formed, I say, not a very large hill or mound or a peak, but a high mountain as it were, of very considerable depth and breadth—so great was the pyramid of bones. And later men of the same tribe as the slaughtered barbarians built a wall and used the bones of the dead to fill the interstices as if they were pebbles, and thus made the city their tomb in a way. This fortified city is still standing today with its walls built of a mixture of stones and bones. When they had all in this way fallen a prey to the sword, Peter alone with a few others escaped and reentered Helenopolis,[12] and the Turks who wanted to capture him, set fresh ambushes for him. But when the Emperor received reliable information of all this, and the terrible massacre, he was very worried lest Peter should have been captured. He therefore summoned Constantine Catacalon Euphorbenus (who has already been mentioned many times in this history), and gave him a large force which was embarked on ships of war and sent him across the straits to Peter's succour. Directly the Turks saw him land they fled. Constantine, without the slightest delay, picked up Peter and his followers, who were but few, and brought them safe and sound to the Emperor. On the Emperor's reminding him of his original thoughtlessness and saying that it was due to his not having obeyed his, the Emperor's, advice that he had incurred such disasters, Peter, being a haughty Latin, would not admit that he himself was the cause of the trouble, but said it was the others who did not listen to him, but followed their own will, and he denounced them as robbers and plunderers who, for that reason, were not allowed by the Saviour to worship at His Holy Sepulchre. Others of the Latins, such as Bohemund and men of like mind, who had long cherished a desire for the Roman Empire, and wished to win it for themselves, found a pretext in Peter's preaching, as I have said, deceived the more single-minded, caused this great upheaval and were selling their own estates under the pretence that they were marching against the Turks to redeem the Holy Sepulchre.

12. According to other accounts of the battle, Peter was in Constantinople at the time.

CHAPTER THIRTEEN

Western European Civilization

42. FEUDALISM AND MANORIALISM:

42.1. A FEUDAL OATH OF HOMAGE

This document details the mutual obligations of a feudal lord and his vassal. In this case, the lord is a religious institution, the monastery of St. Mary of Grasse, in France. The vassal who swears homage and fealty in this document is Bernard Atton, viscount of Carcassonne. The year is 1110. What does the Viscount of Carcassonne promise to do? What does Leo the Abbot promise as the lord of the monastery? What else does this document tell you about the relationship of lords and vassals?

In the name of the Lord, I, Bernard Atton, Viscount of Carcassonne, in the presence of my sons, Roger and Trencavel, and of Peter Roger of Barbazan, and William Hugo, and Raymond Mantellini, and Peter de Vietry, nobles, and of many other honorable men, who had come to the monastery of St. Mary of Grasse, to the honor of the festival of the august St. Mary; since lord Leo, abbot of the said monastery, has asked me, in the presence of all those above mentioned, to acknowledge to him the fealty and homage for the castles, manors, and places which the patrons, my ancestors, held from him and his predecessors and from the said monastery as a fief, and which I ought to hold as they held, I have made to the lord abbot Leo acknowledgment and homage as I ought to do.

Therefore, let all present and to come know that I the said Bernard Atton, lord and viscount of Carcassonne, acknowledge verily to thee my lord Leo, by the grace of God, abbot of St. Mary of Grasse, and to thy successors that I hold and ought to hold as a fief, in Carcassonne, the following: ... Moreover, I acknowledge that I hold from thee and from the said monastery as a fief the castle of Termes in Narbonne; and in Minerve the castle of Ventaion, and the manors of Cassanolles, and of Ferral and Aiohars; and in Le Rogès, the little village of Longville; for each and all of which I make homage and fealty with hands and with mouth to thee my said lord abbot Leo and to thy successors, and I swear upon these four gospels of God that I will always be a faithful vassal to thee and to thy successors and to St. Mary of Grasse in all things in which a vassal is required to be faithful to his lord, and I will defend thee, my lord, and all thy successors, and the said monastery and the monks present and to come and the castles and manors and all your men and their possessions against all malefactors and invaders, at my request and that of my successors at my own cost; and I will give to thee power over all the castles and manors above described, in peace and in war, whenever they shall be claimed by thee or by thy successors.

Moreover I acknowledge that, as a recognition of the above fiefs, I and my successors ought to come to the said monastery, at our own expense, as often as a new abbot shall have been made, and there do homage and return to him the power over all the fiefs described above. And when the abbot shall mount his horse I and my heirs, viscounts of Carcassonne, and our successors ought to hold the stirrup for the honor of the dominion of St. Mary of Grasse; and to him and all who come with him, to as many as two hundred beasts, we should make the abbot's purveyance in the borough of St. Michael of Carcassonne, the first time he enters Carcassonne, with the best fish and meat and with eggs and cheese, honorably according to his will, and pay the expense of the shoeing of the horses, and for straw and fodder as the season shall require.

And if I or my sons or their successors do not observe to thee or to thy successors each and all the things declared above, and should come against these things, we wish that all the aforesaid fiefs should by that very fact be handed over to thee and to the said monastery of St. Mary of Grasse and to thy successors.

I, therefore, the aforesaid lord Leo, by the grace of God, abbot of St. Mary of Grasse, receive thy homage and fealty for all the fiefs of castles and manors and places which are described above; in the way and with the agreements and understandings written above; and likewise I concede to thee and thy heirs and their successors, the viscounts of Carcassonne, all the castles and manors and places aforesaid, as a fief, along with this present charter, divided through the alphabet. And I promise to thee and thy heirs and successors, viscounts of Carcassonne, under the religion of my order, that I will be good and faithful lord concerning all those things described above.

Moreover, I, the aforesaid viscount, acknowledge that the little villages of [twelve are listed] with the farmhouse of Mathus and the chateaux of Villalauro and Claromont, with the little villages of St. Stephen of Surlac, and of Upper and Lower Agrifolio, ought to belong to the said monastery, and whoever holds anything there holds from the same monastery, as we have seen and have heard read in the privileges and charters of the monastery, and as was there written.

Made in the year of the Incarnation of the Lord 1110, in the reign of Louis. Seal of [the witnesses named in paragraph one, Bernard Atton and abbot Leo] who has accepted this acknowledgment of the homage of the said viscount.

And I, the monk John, have written this charter at the command of the said lord Bernard Atton, viscount of Carcassonne and of his sons, on the day and year given above, in the presence and witness of all those named above.

42.2.   DUTIES OF A VILLEIN

This document from England in 1307 delineates the duties required of a villein, John of Cayworth, to the lord of the manor, Battle Abbey. What duties does the abbey require of John of Cayworth? What does he get in return? A villein was one of the class of serfs. How is the status of this villein different from that of the vassal in the previous document? What similar and different purposes do the two documents serve?

They say that John of Cayworth holds one house and thirty acres of land, and he owes 2 *s.* a year at Easter and Michaelmas, and he owes one cock and two hens at Christmas worth 4 *s.*

And he ought to harrow for two days at the sowing at Lent with one man and his own horse and harrow, the value of the work is 4 *d.*; and he receives from the lord on each day three meals worth 3 *d.*; and the lord will thus lose 1 *d.*; and so this harrowing is worth nothing to the service of the lord.

And he ought to carry the manure of the lord for two days with one cart using his own two oxen, the work to value 8 *s.*, and he receives from the lord three meals of the above value each day; and so the work is worth 3 *d.* clear.

And he should find one man for two days to mow the meadow of the lord, who can mow an estimated one acre and a half: the value of mowing one acre is 6 *d.*; and the total is 9 *d.*; and he receives for each day three meals of the above value, and thus the mowing is worth 4 *d.* clear.

And he ought to collect and carry that same hay which he has mowed, the value of the work is 3 *d.* And he has from the lord two meals for one man worth 1½ *d.*; thus the work is worth 1½ *d.* clear.

And he ought to carry the hay of the lord for one day with one cart and three animals of his own, the price of the work is 6 *d.*; and he has from the lord three meals worth 2½ *d.*; and thus the work has a value of 3½ *d.* clear.

And he ought to carry in the autumn beans or oats for two days with one cart and three of his own animals, the price of the work is 12 *d.*; and he has from the lord three meals of the above price for each day, and thus the work is worth 7 *d*. clear.

And he ought to carry wood from the woods of the lord to the manor house for two days in summer with one cart and three of his own animals, the price of the work is 9 *d*.; and he receives from the lord for each day three meals of the above price. And so the work is worth 4 *d*. clear.

And he ought to find one man for two days to cut heath, the price of the work is 4 [*d*.]; and he will have three meals for each day of the above price; and so the lord loses if he receives the work 1 *d*.; and thus that cutting is worth nothing to the work of the lord.

And he ought to carry the heath that that he has cut, the price of the work is 5 *d*.; and he receives from the lord three meals of the price of 2½ *d*.; and thus the work is worth 2½ *d*. clear.

And he ought to carry to Battle [Abbey] two times in the summer half a load of grain each time, the price of the work is 4 *d*.; and he will receive in the manor each time one meal worth 2 *d*.; and thus the work is worth 2 *d*. clear.

The sum of the rents, with the price of the chickens is 2 *s*. 4 *d*.; the sum of the value of the work is 2 *s*. 3½ *d*.; owed from the said John per year. . . .

And it must be noted that all the aforesaid villeins may not marry their daughters nor have their sons tonsured, nor can they cut down timber growing on the lands they hold, without the personal approval of the bailiff or servant of the lord, and then for building and no other purpose.

And after the death of any one of the aforesaid villeins the lord will have as a heriot the best animal that he had; if, however, he had no living beast, the lord will have no heriot, as they say.

The sons or daughters of the aforesaid villeins will give to enter the tenement after the death of their ancestors as much as they gave in rent per year.

43.   THE ART OF COURTLY LOVE

Andreas Capellanus

The complex of feelings called romantic love began to be recognized in the "courtly love" tradition of European courts in the eleventh and twelfth centuries. A description of this "new" kind of love was written by Andreas

*the Chaplain sometime between 1174 and 1186. Do these ideas seem very
different from or similar to our own? How do such ideas affect the status
of women? Do these ideas encourage better social relations?*

INTRODUCTION TO THE TREATISE ON LOVE

We must first consider what love is, whence it gets its name, what the
effect of love is, between what persons love may exist, how it may be
acquired, retained, increased, decreased, and ended, what are the signs
that one's love is returned, and what one of the lovers ought to do if the
other is unfaithful.

What Love Is

Love is a certain inborn suffering derived from the sight of and excessive
meditation upon the beauty of the opposite sex, which causes each one to
wish above all things the embraces of the other and by common desire to
carry out all of love's precepts in the other's embrace.

That love is suffering is easy to see, for before the love becomes
equally balanced on both sides there is no torment greater, since the
lover is always in fear that his love may not gain its desire and that he is
wasting his efforts. He fears, too, that rumors of it may get abroad, and
he fears everything that might harm it in any way, for before things are
perfected a slight disturbance often spoils them. If he is a poor man, he
also fears that the woman may scorn his poverty; if he is ugly, he fears
that she may despise his lack of beauty or may give her love to a more
handsome man; if he is rich, he fears that his parsimony in the past may
stand in his way. To tell the truth, no one can number the fears of one
single lover. This kind of love, then, is a suffering which is felt by only
one of the persons and may be called "single love." But even after both
are in love the fears that arise are just as great, for each of the lovers
fears that what he has acquired with so much effort may be lost through
the effort of someone else, which is certainly much worse for a man than
if, having no hope, he sees that his efforts are accomplishing nothing, for
it is worse to lose the things you are seeking than to be deprived of a gain
you merely hope for. The lover fears, too, that he may offend his loved
one in some way; indeed he fears so many things that it would be difficult to tell them.

That this suffering is inborn I shall show you clearly, because if you
will look at the truth and distinguish carefully you will see that it does not
arise out of any action; only from the reflection of the mind upon what it
sees does this suffering come. For when a man sees some woman fit for
love and shaped according to his taste, he begins at once to lust after her

in his heart; then the more he thinks about her the more he burns with love, until he comes to a fuller meditation. Presently he begins to think about the fashioning of the woman and to differentiate her limbs, to think about what she does, and to pry into the secrets of her body, and he desires to put each part of it to the fullest use. Then after he has come to this complete meditation, love cannot hold the reins, but he proceeds at once to action; straightway he strives to get a helper to find an intermediary. He begins to plan how he may find favor with her, and he begins to seek a place and a time opportune for talking; he looks upon a brief hour as a very long year, because he cannot do anything fast enough to suit his eager mind. It is well known that many things happen to him in this manner. This inborn suffering comes, therefore, from seeing and meditating. Not every kind of meditation can be the cause of love, an excessive one is required; for a restrained thought does not, as a rule, return to the mind, and so love cannot arise from it.

Between What Persons Love May Exist

Now, in love you should note first of all that love cannot exist except between persons of opposite sexes. Between two men or two women love can find no place, for we see that two persons of the same sex are not at all fitted for giving each other the exchanges of love or for practicing the acts natural to it. Whatever nature forbids, love is ashamed to accept.

What the Effect of Love Is

Now it is the effect of love that a true lover cannot be degraded with any avarice. Love causes a rough and uncouth man to be distinguished for his handsomeness; it can endow a man even of the humblest birth with nobility of character; it blesses the proud with humility; and the man in love becomes accustomed to performing many services gracefully for everyone. O what a wonderful thing is love, which makes a man shine with so many virtues and teaches everyone, no matter who he is, so many good traits of character! There is another thing about love that we should not praise in few words: it adorns a man, so to speak, with the virtue of chastity, because he who shines with the light of one love can hardly think of embracing another woman, even a beautiful one. For when he thinks deeply of his beloved the sight of any other woman seems to his mind rough and rude.

If One of the Lovers Is Unfaithful to the Other

If one of the lovers should be unfaithful to the other, and the offender is the man, and he has an eye to a new love affair, he renders himself wholly unworthy of his former love, and she ought to deprive him completely of her embraces.

But what if he should be unfaithful to his beloved,—not with the idea of finding a new love, but because he has been driven to it by an irresistible passion for another woman? What, for instance, if chance should present to him an unknown woman in a convenient place or what if at a time when Venus is urging him on to that which I am talking about he should meet with a little strumpet or somebody's servant girl? Should he, just because he played with her in the grass, lose the love of his beloved? We can say without fear of contradiction that just for this a lover is not considered unworthy of the love of his beloved unless he indulges in so many excesses with a number of women that we may conclude that he is overpassionate. But if whenever he becomes acquainted with a woman he pesters her to gain his end, or if he attains his object as a result of his efforts, then rightly he does deserve to be deprived of his former love, because there is strong presumption that he has acted in this way with an eye toward a new one, especially where he has strayed with a woman of the nobility or otherwise of an honorable estate.

I know that once when I sought advice I got the answer that a true lover can never desire a new love unless he knows that for some definite and sufficient reason the old love is dead; we know from our own experience that this rule is very true. We have fallen in love with a woman of the most admirable character, although we have never had, or hope to have, any fruit of this love. For we are compelled to pine away for love of a woman of such lofty station that we dare not say one word about it, nor dare we throw ourself upon her mercy, and so at length we are forced to find our body shipwrecked. But although rashly and without foresight we have fallen into such great waves in this tempest, still we cannot think about a new love or look for any other way to free ourself.

But since you are making a special study of the subject of love, you may well ask whether a man can have a pure love for one woman and a mixed or common love with another. We will show you, by an unanswerable argument, that no one can feel affection for two women in this fashion. For although pure love and mixed love may seem to be very different things, if you will look at the matter properly you will see that pure love, so far as its substance goes, is the same as mixed love and comes from the same feeling of the heart. The substance of the love is the same in each case, and only the manner and form of loving are different, as this illustration will make clear to you. Sometimes we see a man with a desire to drink his wine unmixed, and at another time his appetite prompts him to drink only water or wine and water mixed; although his appetite manifests itself differently, the substance of it is the same and unchanged. So likewise when two people have long been united by pure love and afterwards desire to practice mixed love, the substance of the love remains the same in them, although the manner and form and the way of practicing it are different.

Various Decisions in Love Cases

Now then, let us come to various decisions in cases of love:

I. A certain knight loved his lady beyond all measure and enjoyed her full embrace, but she did not love him with equal ardor. He sought to leave her, but she, desiring to retain him in his former status, opposed his wish. In this affair the Countess of Champagne gave this response: "It is considered very unseemly for a woman to seek to be loved and yet to refuse to love. It is silly for anybody disrespectfully to ask of others what she herself wholly refuses to give to others."

II. A certain man asked the Lady Ermengarde of Narbonne to make clear where there was the greater affection—between lovers or between married people. The lady gave him a logical answer. She said: "We consider that marital affection and the true love of lovers are wholly different and arise from entirely different sources, and so the ambiguous nature of the word prevents the comparison of the things and we have to place them in different classes. Comparisons of more or less are not valid when things are grouped together under an ambiguous heading and the comparision is made in regard to that ambiguous term. It is no true comparison to say that a name is simpler than a body or that the outline of a speech is better arranged than the delivery."

III. The same man asked the same lady this question. A certain woman had been married, but was now separated from her husband by a divorce, and her former husband sought eagerly for her love. In this case the lady replied: "If any two people have been married and afterwards separate in any way, we consider love between them wholly wicked."

IV. A certain knight was in love with a woman who had given her love to another man, but he got from her this much hope of her love—that if it should ever happen that she lost the love of her beloved, then without a doubt her love would go to this man. A little while after this the woman married her lover. The other knight then demanded that she give him the fruit of the hope she had granted him, but this she absolutely refused to do, saying that she had not lost the love of her lover. In this affair the Queen gave her decision as follows: "We dare not oppose the opinion of the Countess of Champagne, who ruled that love can exert no power between husband and wife. Therefore we recommend that the lady should grant the love she has promised."

V. The Queen was also asked which was preferable: the love of a young man or of one advanced in years. She answered this question with wonderful subtlety by saying, "We distinguish between a good and a better love by the man's knowledge and his character and his praiseworthy manners, not by his age. But as regards that natural instinct of passion, young men are usually more eager to gratify it with older women than with young ones of their own age; those who are older prefer to receive the embraces and kisses of young women rather than of the older ones. But on the other hand a woman whether young or somewhat older likes the embraces and solaces of young men better than those of older ones. The explanation of this fact seems to be a physiological one. . . ."

The Rules of Love

Let us come now to the rules of love, and I shall try to present to you very briefly those rules which the King of Love is said to have proclaimed with his own mouth and to have given in writing to all lovers.

     I. Marriage is no real excuse for not loving.

     II. He who is not jealous cannot love.

    III. No one can be bound by a double love.

    IV. It is well known that love is always increasing or decreasing.

     V. That which a lover takes against the will of his beloved has no relish.

    VI. Boys do not love until they arrive at the age of maturity.

   VII. When one lover dies, a widowhood of two years is required of the survivor.

  VIII. No one should be deprived of love without the very best of reasons.

    IX. No one can love unless he is impelled by the persuasion of love.

     X. Love is always a stranger in the home of avarice.

    XI. It is not proper to love any woman whom one should be ashamed to seek to marry.

   XII. A true lover does not desire to embrace in love anyone except his beloved.

  XIII. When made public love rarely endures.

  XIV. The easy attainment of love makes it of little value; difficulty of attainment makes it prized.

   XV. Every lover regularly turns pale in the presence of his beloved.

  XVI. When a lover suddenly catches sight of his beloved his heart palpitates.

 XVII. A new love puts to flight an old one.

XVIII. Good character alone makes any man worthy of love.

  XIX. If love diminishes, it quickly fails and rarely revives.

   XX. A man in love is always apprehensive.

  XXI. Real jealousy always increases the feeling of love.

 XXII. Jealousy, and therefore love, are increased when one suspects his beloved.

XXIII. He whom the thought of love vexes, eats and sleeps very little.

XXIV. Every act of a lover ends in the thought of his beloved.

XXV. A true lover considers nothing good except what he thinks will please his beloved.

XXVI. Love can deny nothing to love.

XXVII. A lover can never have enough of the solaces of his beloved.

XXVIII. A slight presumption causes a lover to suspect his beloved.

XXIX. A man who is vexed by too much passion usually does not love.

XXX. A true lover is constantly and without intermission possessed by the thought of his beloved.

XXXI. Nothing forbids one woman being loved by two men or one man by two women.

44. GENOA, VENICE, AND THE CRUSADES

Janet Abu-Lughod

In this modern historical study of two important Italian merchant cities— Genoa and Venice—and the Crusades, the author asks about the origins and successes of each city. She also asks what impact the Crusades had on each city. In what ways were the histories of Genoa and Venice similar? In what ways were their histories different? How did Christians and Muslims view each other at the time of the Crusades? What was the impact of the Crusades on these Italian cities?

William McNeill gave his book on Venice the subtitle, "The Hinge of Europe"; the awkwardness of the term is compensated for by its precision. He may, however, be accused of pro-Venetian bias (a prejudice not uncommon in the literature on Italian cities) since Genoa could lay equal claim to that key position as link between Europe and the Orient.

Both cities played pivotal roles in joining Europe to the ongoing world economy of the east. Both became great naval and merchant powers, struggling for supremacy over the Mediterranean, hitherto an "Arab Sea," and for exclusive and/or preferential trading concessions in the Black Sea areas, along the coast of Palestine, and in Egypt, which guarded the gateway to India and beyond. And from the eleventh to the end of the fourteenth century when Genoa finally capitulated, both were locked in a deadly battle to preserve their own sea lanes and destroy those of their rival.

Each was a vanguard. Geographically, each tried to reach as far as possible in Asia. Institutionally, each tried to devise better ways to do business, to accumulate larger amounts of less risky capital, to administer companies, and to monopolize the markets for commodities and money. Technologically, both developed impressive sophistication in navigation, shipbuilding, and armaments. Either could have accomplished the task of connecting the cultural islands of the thirteenth-century world system. Tragically, these two giants proved one too many, for they spent as much energy fighting one another as they did conquering the East. Both were fated to take to the sea, being insulated by politics, water, or high terrain from strong land-based hinterlands.

Origins of the Two Port Cities

Genoa, a superb harbor town huddled at the base of a mountainous escarpment that insulated [it] from the mainland behind, was from earliest times a port and, from time to time, a victim of invasions. Settled as early as the fifth century B.C., virtually destroyed by the Carthaginians in the Second Punic War, rebuilt by the Romans who encircled it with new walls in the fourth century A.D., it fell to the Ostrogoths and then the Lombards who occupied it until it was retaken by the Byzantines in 588. It remained under the nominal rule of Constantinople between the sixth and tenth centuries, but only as a modest fishing and agricultural town whose inhabitants lived at subsistence levels; trade was only beginning.

It could be said that the Crusades actually commenced in the tenth century, for by then Genoa was already "at war" with the Muslim states of the western Mediterranean. In 934–935 a Fatimid fleet stormed and sacked the city. Only much later did the Genoese, assisted by the Pisans, counterattack, sending expeditions in 1061 against the Muslims in Sardinia and Corsica, and later even against the former North African capital of the Fatimids, Mahdiya; they captured that town briefly in 1087, exacting tribute and the first, but not last, trade concession from its Muslim rulers—an exemption from the tolls.

By the end of the eleventh century, the Genoese had gained de facto independence from the Eastern Roman Empire and had established a self-ruled *compagna,* an association of citizens under the authority of six and later ten consuls elected for three-year terms. Appetites whetted and abilities tested by prior sea battles and seeking to expand their horizon from the western basin of the Mediterranean to the eastern, the Genoese enthusiastically answered the call of the Pope for the first foray of that bloody and eventually unsuccessful venture—the conquest of Palestine. Begun in 1095 and not abandoned until the last Crusader foothold in

Acre fell to the Mamluks in 1291, the Crusades brought West and East into admittedly antagonistic but nevertheless permanent involvement with one another.

Venice was less eager than Genoa to enter that struggle, however, for [it] had a very different and earlier link to the east that [it] was reluctant to disturb. In spite of Edith Ennen's generally true contention that Italy, unlike the regions of northern Europe, had an unbroken continuity of urban settlement throughout the so-called "Dark Ages," Venice must be counted, unlike venerable Genoa, as a "new town," albeit one with urban roots. It was founded in about 568 (at a preexisting fishing village) when a stream of migrant mainlanders fled the invading Lombards to seek refuge at the lagoons off shore. Venice remained firmly attached to Byzantium, even after the Lombards had conquered all of the Italian mainland, including Ravenna, which had been the Italian capital of the Byzantine Empire. And even after the Lombards were incorporated into Charlemagne's domains, the Venetians, with the help of a Byzantine fleet, were able to resist Charlemagne's attempt in 810 to include [it] as well. In the treaty of peace finally concluded between the Byzantine emperor and Charlemagne, Venice was explicitly protected, which thus "laid the foundations for the absolute primacy of Venice over the other Italo-Byzantine seaports in western trade."

Although Venice benefited from this allegiance, gaining certain trade privileges in Byzantine ports, [it] was not yet able to take full advantage of the commercial opportunities they made possible. Even though before 1000 A.D. "some Venetians were seamen expert enough to cross the Mediterranean, . . . Greeks, Syrians, and other Easterners carried most of the trade between Venice and the Levant," as indeed they did in other European ports. At that time, Venice could only offer for trade local supplies of salt, fish, and timber, as well as slaves captured primarily from [its] not-yet-Christianized neighbors across the Adriatic. As Braudel stresses, up to the time of the Crusades "Italy was still only a poor 'peripheral' region, intent on making her services acceptable to others as a purveyor of timber, grain, linen cloth, salt and slaves from the European interior."

But Venice had already begun to play a more active role in commerce, even before the Crusades began. In 1080 [it] finally broke through the blockade of the Norman kingdom that controlled the lower waters of the Adriatic. Coming to the rescue of the Byzantine fleet, [it] assisted in freeing that crucial waterway, for which [it] was rewarded by the Byzantine Emperor Alexius I in 1082 with a special charter (the Golden Bull) granting [it] virtually full trading privileges and exemptions from tolls throughout the empire and most importantly in Constantinople, Christendom's largest and most prosperous city and the gateway to Central Asia. Having gained this concession and now able to expand [its] trade in the Levant, [it] was understandably reluctant to risk [its] ships and [its] reputation to follow the first Crusade.

At this point, Genoa and Venice still occupied relatively separate spheres. Genoa, on the west coast of Italy, commanded the western basin of the Mediterranean, gaining significant territorial or trading concessions from the Muslims of Spain, from the islands off [its] shore, and in littoral North Africa. The Venetians were similarly strenghtening *their* lines of communication in the eastern basin of the Mediterranean, having gained access to ports of call throughout the Aegean and at least some of its islands, as well as Constantinople and the Black Sea. [Its] reluctance to tamper with this status was matched by Genoa's eagerness to "break into" the richer markets of the East.

The Impact of the Crusades on Venice and Genoa

It was thus Genoese and Pisan ships that came to the rescue of the French, Flemish, and other European knights who had eagerly answered Pope Urban the Second's call in 1095 for a "reconquest" of the Holy Land from the Muslims who, ever since the second half of the seventh century—hardly a new threat—had converted most of the resident population to Islam. It is difficult today to comprehend the earnest zeal with which kings and counts gathered their retainers and headed for a place more fabled than known. Some cynics suggest that it was more eagerness for booty than for divine redemption that motivated the counts of Champagne, Brie, and Flanders and the kings of France and England, inter alia, to set off on so perilous a journey. Yet the documents of the time are both more naive and otherworldly than such an interpretation would predict.

Nevertheless, the relative levels of civilization in Europe and the Levant do suggest that the Crusaders were more akin to the barbarians who periodically preyed on the settled wealth of high cultures than to carriers of the *mission civilisatrice*. As Cipolla (1976: 206) puts it, "there is no doubt that from the fall of the Roman Empire to the beginning of the thirteenth century Europe was an underdeveloped area in relation to the major centers of civilization at the time . . . [—] clearly a land of barbarians." Archibald Lewis (1970: vii) uses this discrepancy to account for the asymmetrical interest East and West showed in each other. Although Europeans eagerly sought out Muslim lands and their wealth and "copied many facets of Muslim culture," their interest was not reciprocated. Not only did "the average upper-class Moslem [feel] superior to most Western Europeans," but the wide geographic lore of the Arabs never extended to western Europe, an area they considered had little to offer. Even after the Crusades thrust a European threat into their heartland,

Muslim attitudes remained condescending at best and aghast at worst, whereas their invaders were filled with a strange mixture of hatred and romantic (if reluctant) awe and admiration.

In the twelfth and thirteenth century the literature in both societies reflected this asymmetry. The best summary of European views is by Sylvia Thrupp, who points out that

> *Chansons de geste* and romances that bring their heroes into contact with Muslims are our best clues to the views of the various Muslim peoples prevailing among French nobles and probably among the upper bourgeoisie in the twelfth and thirteenth centuries. . . . The elements of the pattern are the cosmopolitanism of the world of Islam, its power and wealth, the splendor of its cities, the cleverness of its people. . . . The Muslims are openly envied because they know even better than the French how to live.

Such an exalted view of the enemy, however, was belied by the Crusaders' behavior toward them, which evoked revulsion in their Muslim victims. Muslims saw the "Franks"—as westerners were consistently referred to in Arab literature—"as beasts superior in courage and fighting ardour but in nothing else, just as animals are superior in strength and aggression."

This characterization was not totally unfounded. In 1098 Crusader destruction of the Syrian town of Ma'arra had been accompanied by acknowledged acts of Frankish cannibalism. Graphically described in the chronicle of Radulph of Caen (he admits that "In Ma'arra our troops boiled pagan adults in cooking pots; they impaled children on spits and devoured them grilled"), they were later "justified" in a letter sent to the Pope by the Christian commander, who blamed the lapse on extreme hunger. Needless to say, this excuse was dismissed by Arab historians who continued to describe their bloodthirsty enemies as eaters not only of people but, what was worse, even of dogs, considered the uncleanest of species.

The barbarians, however, met with some success in this first military incursion. The Genoese and Pisans, who had so eagerly supported the Crusaders in their attack on Palestine, reaped their promised reward. They were given one-third of the city and suburbs of Acre as well as similar portions in the other cities they helped to conquer. Once the Crusader state was set up, they also received, retroactively, one-quarter of Jerusalem and of Jaffa.

Venice held back until the operation looked as though it might succeed. Not until "1099, after the Frank armies had battered their way into Jerusalem, slaughtering every Muslim in the city and burning all the Jews alive in the main synagogue . . . did a Venetian fleet of 200 [leave] the Lido port." It finally arrived in the summer of 1100 just in time to assist in the recapture of Jaffa and other towns. As a reward the Venetians were also allotted one-third of the towns' land and environs and given special trading concessions in the new Crusader kingdom. Later, Venice received [its] usual third when the ports of Tyre and Ascalon were taken with [its] help. Venetians were allowed to form their own quarters and enjoyed a position privileged to exploit the commercial opportunities of expanding trade.

This direct entrée to the riches of the East changed the role of the Italian merchant mariner cities from passive to active. The revival of the Champagne fairs in the twelfth century can be explained convincingly by both the enhanced demand for eastern goods stimulated by the Crusades and, because of the strategic position of the Italians in coastal enclaves of the Levant, the increased supplies of such goods they could now deliver.

The Genoese and to a lesser extent the Venetians had begun the long process of tipping the fulcrum of the world system. By the thirteenth century "the center of gravity [of Europe at least] had definitely moved to the 'big four' of northern and central Italy (Venice, Milan, Genoa and Florence) whose powerful merchants had a firm grip on the routes towards the fertile and industrious European hinterland and endeavored to reach far beyond the declining Islamic facade into the depths of Asia and Africa" (Lopez, 1976: 99). But that process—aided not a little by the thrust into the Near Eastern heartland of "other barbarians" arriving from the east, the Mongols—would take all of the twelfth and most of the thirteenth century and would not be decisively achieved until the opening years of the sixteenth century, when the fruits would be gathered not by the Italians who planted them but by the Portuguese who succeeded (albeit with the help of Genoese capital and sailors) in outflanking them.

45. MAGNA CARTA

The Magna Carta was a contract between King John of England and his nobles (or "liegemen") in which the king agreed to recognize certain rights and liberties of the nobility. In return the nobles accepted certain obligations to the king. What were some of these rights and obligations? Can you tell from these provisions what some of the nobles' complaints had been? Did the signing of this agreement in 1215 improve the position of the common people, women, or foreigners? What does the document tell you about English society in the early thirteenth century?

John, by the grace of God, King of England, Lord of Ireland, Duke of Normandy and Aquitaine, and Count of Anjou: To the Archbishops, Bishops, Abbots, Earls, Barons, Justiciaries, Foresters, Sheriffs, Reeves, Ministers, and all Bailiffs and others, his faithful subjects, Greeting. Know ye that in the presence of God, and for the health of Our soul, and the souls of Our ancestors and heirs, to the honor of God, and the exaltation of Holy Church, and amendment of Our Kingdom, by the advice of Our reverend Fathers, Stephen, Archbishop of Canterbury, Primate of all England, and Cardinal of the Holy Roman Church; Henry, Archbishop of Dublin; William of London, Peter of Winchester, Jocelin of Bath and Glastonbury, Hugh of Lincoln, Walter of Worcester, William of Coventry, and Benedict of Rochester, Bishops; Master Pandulph, the Pope's subdeacon and familiar; Brother Aymeric, Master of the Knights of the Temple in England; and the noble persons, William Marshal, Earl of Pembroke; William, Earl of Salisbury; William, Earl of Warren; William, Earl of Arundel; Alan de Galloway, Constable of Scotland; Warin Fitz-Gerald, Peter Fitz-Herbert, Hubert de Burgh, Seneschal of Poitou, Hugh de Neville, Matthew Fitz-Herbert, Thomas Basset, Alan Basset, Philip Daubeny, Robert de Roppelay, John Marshal, John Fitz-Hugh, and others, Our liegemen:

1. We have, in the first place, granted to God, and by this Our present Charter confirmed for Us and Our heirs forever—That the English Church shall be free and enjoy her rights in their integrity and her liberties untouched. And that We will this so to be observed appears from the fact that We of Our own free will, before the outbreak of the dissensions between Us and Our barons, granted, confirmed, and procured to be confirmed by Pope Innocent III the freedom of elections, which if considered most important and necessary to the English Church, which Charter We will both keep Ourself and will it to be kept with good faith by Our heirs forever. We have also granted to all the free men of Our kingdom, for Us and Our heirs forever, all the liberties underwritten, to have and to hold to them and their heirs of Us and Our heirs.

2. If any of Our earls, barons, or others who hold of Us in chief by knight's service shall die, and at the time of his death his heir shall be of full age and owe a relief [a form of tax], he shall have his inheritance by ancient relief; to wit, the heir or heirs of an earl of an entire earl's barony, £100; the heir or heirs of a baron of an entire barony, £100; the heir or heirs of a knight of an entire knight's fee, 100s. at the most; and he that owes less shall give less, according to the ancient custom of fees.

3. If, however, any such heir shall be under age and in ward, he shall, when he comes of age, have his inheritance without relief or fine.

4. The guardian of the land of any heir thus under age shall take therefrom only reasonable issues, customs, and services, without destruc-

tion or waste of men or property; and if We shall have committed the wardship of any such land to the sheriff or any other person answerable to Us for the issues thereof, and he commit destruction or waste, We will take an amends from him, and the land shall be committed to two lawful and discreet men of that fee, who shall be answerable for the issues to Us or to whomsoever We shall have assigned them. And if We shall give or sell the wardship of any such land to anyone, and he commit destruction or waste upon it, he shall lose the wardship, which shall be committed to two lawful and discreet men of that fee, who shall, in like manner, be answerable unto Us as has been aforesaid.

5. The guardian, so long as he shall have the custody of the land, shall keep up and maintain the houses, parks, fishponds, pools, mills, and other things pertaining thereto, out of the issues of the same, and shall restore the whole to the heir when he comes of age, stocked with ploughs and tillage, according as the season may require and the issues of the land can reasonably bear.

6. Heirs shall be married without loss of station, and the marriage shall be made known to the heir's nearest of kin before it be contracted.

7. A widow, after the death of her husband, shall immediately and without difficulty have her marriage portion and inheritance. She shall not give anything for her marriage portion, dower, or inheritance which she and her husband held on the day of his death, and she may remain in her husband's house for forty days after his death, within which time her dower shall be assigned to her.

8. No widow shall be compelled to marry so long as she has a mind to live without a husband, provided, however, that she give security that she will not marry without Our assent, if she holds of Us, or that of the lord of whom she holds, if she holds of another.

9. Neither We nor Our bailiffs shall seize any land or rent for any debt so long as the debtor's chattels are sufficient to discharge the same; nor shall the debtor's sureties be distrained so long as the debtor is able to pay the debt. If the debtor fails to pay, not having the means to pay, then the sureties shall answer the debt, and, if they desire, they shall hold the debtor's lands and rents until they have received satisfaction of the debt which they have paid for him, unless the debtor can show that he has discharged his obligation to them.

10. If anyone who has borrowed from the Jews any sum of money, great or small, dies before the debt has been paid, the heir shall pay no interest on the debt so long as he remains under age, of whomsoever he may hold. If the debt shall fall into Our hands, We will take only the principal sum named in the bond. . . .

12. No scutage [a payment in place of a personal service] or aid shall be imposed in Our kingdom unless by common counsel thereof, except to ransom Our person, make Our eldest son a knight, and once to marry

Our eldest daughter, and for these only a reasonable aid shall be levied. So shall it be with regard to aids from the City of London.

13. The City of London shall have all her ancient liberties and free customs, both by land and water. Moreover, We will and grant that all other cities, boroughs, towns, and ports shall have their liberties and free customs.

14. For obtaining the common counsel of the kingdom concerning the assessment of aids (other than in the three cases aforesaid) or of scutage, We will cause to be summoned, severally by Our letters, the archbishops, bishops, abbots, earls, and great barons; We will also cause to be summoned, generally, by Our sheriffs and bailiffs, all those who hold lands directly of Us, to meet on a fixed day, but with at least forty days' notice, and at a fixed place. In all letters of such summons We will explain the cause thereof. The summons being thus made, the business shall proceed on the day appointed, according to the advice of those who shall be present, even though not all the persons summoned have come.

15. We will not in the future grant permission to any man to levy an aid upon his free men, except to ransom his person, make his eldest son a knight, and once to marry his eldest daughter, and on each of these occasions only a reasonable aid shall be levied.

16. No man shall be compelled to perform more service for a knight's fee or other free tenement than is due therefrom.

17. Common Pleas shall not follow Our Court, but shall be held in some certain place.

20. A free man shall be amerced [fined] for a small fault only according to the measure thereof, and for a great crime according to its magnitude, saving his position; and in like manner a merchant saving his trade, and a villein [serf] saving his tillage, if they should fall under Our mercy. None of these amercements shall be imposed except by the oath of honest men of the neighborhood.

21. Earls and barons shall be amerced only by their peers, and only in proportion to the measure of the offense.

22. No amercement shall be imposed upon a clerk's [clergyman's] lay property, except after the manner of the other persons aforesaid, and without regard to the value of his ecclesiastical benefice.

23. No village or person shall be compelled to build bridges over rivers except those bound by ancient custom and law to do so.

28. No constable or other of Our bailiffs shall take corn or other chattels of any man without immediate payment, unless the seller voluntarily consents to postponement of payment.

29. No constable shall compel any knight to give money in lieu of castle-guard when the knight is willing to perform it in person or (if reasonable

cause prevents him from performing it himself) by some other fit man. Further, if We lead or send him into military service, he shall be quit of castle-guard for the time he shall remain in service by Our command.

30. No sheriff or other of Our bailiffs, or any other man, shall take the horses or carts of any free man for carriage without the owner's consent.

31. Neither We nor Our bailiffs will take another man's wood for Our castles or for any other purpose without the owner's consent.

35. There shall be one measure of wine throughout Our kingdom, and one of ale, and one measure of corn, to wit, the London quarter, and one breadth of dyed cloth, russets, and haberjets [types of cloth—Ed.] to wit, two cells within the selvages. As with measures so shall it also be with weights.

38. In the future no bailiff shall upon his own unsupported accusation put any man to trial without producing credible witnesses to the truth of the accusation.

39. No free man shall be taken, imprisoned, disseised [dispossessed], outlawed, banished, or in any way destroyed, nor will We proceed against or prosecute him, except by the lawful judgment of his peers and by the law of the land.

40. To no one will We sell, to none will We deny or delay, right or justice.

41. All merchants shall have safe conduct to go and come out of and into England, and to stay in and travel through England by land and water for purposes of buying and selling, free of illegal tolls, in accordance with ancient and just customs, except, in time of war, such merchants as are of a country at war with Us. If any such be found in Our dominion at the outbreak of war, they shall be attached, without injury to their persons or goods, until it be known to Us or Our Chief Justiciary how Our merchants are being treated in the country at war with Us, and if Our merchants be safe there, then theirs shall be safe with Us.

42. In the future it shall be lawful (except for a short period in time of war, for the common benefit of the realm) for anyone to leave and return to Our kingdom safely and securely by land and water, saving his fealty to Us. Excepted are those who have been imprisoned or outlawed according to the law of the land, people of the country at war with Us, and merchants, who shall be dealt with as aforesaid.

52. If anyone has been disseised or deprived by Us, without the legal judgment of his peers, of lands, castles, liberties, or rights, We will immediately restore the same, and if any dispute shall arise thereupon, the matter shall be decided by judgment of the twenty-five barons mentioned below in the clause for securing the peace. With regard to all those things, however, of which any man was disseised or deprived,

without the legal judgment of his peers, by King Henry Our Father or Our Brother King Richard, and which remain in Our warranty, We shall have respite during the term commonly allowed to the Crusaders, except as to those matters on which a plea had arisen, or an inquisition had been taken by Our command, prior to Our taking the Cross. Immediately after Our return from Our pilgrimage, or if by chance We should remain behind from it, We will at once do full justice.

CHAPTER FOURTEEN

The Impact of the Mongols

46. THE IMPACT OF TURKISH AND MONGOL CONQUESTS, 1000–1500

William H. McNeill

The explosion of the Mongol and Turkish nomads from the grasslands of Eurasia after A.D. 1000 had a decisive effect on the Christian, Islamic, Indian, and Chinese civilizations of the continent. In this section, the modern historian William H. McNeill looks at some of the ways these invasions changed the balance of Eurasia.

What were the Mongol and Turkish invasions? What changes did they bring about across Eurasia? What effects did they have on Orthodox Christendom and traditional Chinese civilization?

Close ties between steppe nomads and the civilized world had been a prominent feature of the centuries before A.D. 1000. During the ensuing five hundred years, this led to a series of infiltrations and conquests that brought Turkish and Mongol rulers to China, the Middle East, India, and eastern Europe. Civilized victims and subjects reacted in different ways.

The Moslems altered the emphasis and internal balance of their society and civilization in a far-reaching and strikingly successful fashion. In effect, the Moslems captured the military energy of the steppe peoples for themselves. Turkish and (much less important) Mongol recruits gave Islam a new cutting edge that established it as the ruling faith in all of India and in eastern Europe. Simultaneously, merchants and wandering holy men carried the religion of Mohammed to southeast Asia and through east and west Africa as well, and even penetrated some of China's western provinces.

The Chinese found nothing to admire in the novelties brought to their attention by Mongol conquerors, and at the first propitious moment they rallied to cast off what was always felt to be an alien and barbarian yoke. Hence the episode of Mongol rule (the Yuan dynasty, 1260–1368) left remarkably few traces behind, unless the Ming dynasty's (1368–1644) enhanced determination to value old and authentically Chinese culture can be attributed to their reaction against Mongol rule.

The great majority of Indians and orthodox Christians who found themselves under the government of Islamized Turks remained faithful to their respective religious traditions. Nevertheless, prolonged geographical intermingling provoked a good deal of interchange between the rival religious communities, despite official efforts by guardians of the faith on each side to maintain the purity of their respective versions of theological truth.

THE TURKISH INFILTRATION

Before examining civilized reactions in more detail it will be well to recapitulate the course of world events. In A.D. 1000 Turkish-speaking tribes lived throughout the middle reaches of the steppe, from the Altai mountains as far west as southern Russia. In eastern Iran, extensive interpenetration between Moslem towns and cultivators and Turkish nomads had already occurred, and many Turkish tribes had accepted Islam, usually in a somewhat casual and superficial fashion. The Iranian barons who for so many centuries had held the steppe nomads at bay ceased to be effective after about A.D. 850 or 900. The reasons are obscure, but it seems possible that many moved into towns, acquired a far richer culture than their forefathers had known, and in the process lost their taste for war and hard knocks, leaving that role to Turkish mercenaries, who presently found themselves in a position to hold the Moslem heartlands of Iran, Iraq, and Syria up for ransom.

When, therefore, Turkish mercenaries and tribesmen started everywhere to dominate the political life of Islam (after about A.D. 900) the newcomers already knew a good deal about both Persian and Arab versions of Moslem culture. Yet the Turks maintained their own languages and a certain sense of military camaraderie against the rest of Islamic society. Their rule was disorderly. Detribalized military adventures competed with the unstable power of clan leaders, whose followers regularly deserted tribal discipline after a few years in a civilized environment. Rivalries and alliances among such precariously situated rulers were unusually fragile and created an endless political kaleidoscope throughout the heartland of Islam.

Nevertheless, the newcomers extended Moslem frontiers very substantially. Penetration deep into India began with massive raids launched by Mohammed of Ghazni in the year 1000. Within three centuries only the southern part of that sub-continent had escaped Moslem conquest; and in 1565 the south capitulated also when the empire of Vijayanager fell before a coalition of Moslem princes. Turkish successes against Christendom were also very great. After the battle of Manzikert (1071) the Byzantines lost control of the interior of Asia Minor to Seljuk Turks. Simultaneously other Turkish tribes (Kipchaks) pressed across what is now the Ukraine, where they cut off easy communication between Byzantium and freshly Christianized Russia. These heavy blows helped to precipitate the First Crusade (1096–99); but despite its dramatic success, this and later crusades failed to check the Turkish advance. On the contrary, when the Fourth Crusade actually attacked Constantinople and captured and sacked the city (1204), the weakness of the Byzantine state was advertised to all the world. Partial recovery—there was a Greek emperor again in Constantinople after 1261—was not sufficient to check the force of Italian commercial exploitation on the one hand and Turkish military assault on the other. The Ottoman Turks reaped the ultimate victory. They won their first foothold in Europe in 1354 by crossing the Dardanelles and seizing the peninsula of Gallipoli. After 1389, when they defeated the Serbians at the battle of Kossovo, the Turks won military supremacy in the Balkans. Not until 1453, however, when they conquered Constantinople and made it the capital of their empire, was the last trace of Byzantine power erased from the face of the earth.

THE MONGOL CONQUEST

This vast tide of Turkish advance into India and Europe was punctuated in the thirteenth century by a sudden storm emanating from Mongolia. The founder of Mongol greatness was Genghis Khan (ruled 1206–27). In his youth an all but helpless refugee from local enemies, Genghis succeeded in welding together a vast military confederacy among the peoples of the steppe. He then raided successfully in every direction—southward into China, westward against the Moslems of Iran and Iraq, and against the Christians of Russia as well. On his death the empire was divided among his four sons. They transformed the massive raiding of Genghis' time into a somewhat more stable form of political rule. For some time, there continued to be effective co-operation among the separate parts of the vast empire. Leadership rested, according to Mongol custom, with Genghis' youngest son and that son's heirs. They ruled Mongolia and China and commanded nearly the whole of the Mongol army.

In Genghis' time the Mongol tribesmen were pagan shamanists. They treated their human victims much as they treated their animals—tending or slaughtering them as convenience might dictate. But once encamped amid more cultivated peoples, the Mongols did what every other nomadic conqueror had done: they quickly took on the color of their subjects' civilization. In the Middle East and Russia this meant the acceptance of Islam. In China, matters were different, for the Mongol emperors could not afford to see the armed forces upon which their power depended dissolve into the Chinese mass. The effort to hold themselves aloof from the Chinese led the Mongols to accept Tibetan Lamaism as the preferred religion of state, although a grand mixture of faiths—Christian, Moslem, shamanist, and others—continued to be represented at court. Yet the penalty of remaining distinct from the Chinese was vulnerability to native reaction, which brought the Ming dynasty to power only a century and a half after Genghis had launched his raids.

Mongol rule therefore constituted no more than an episode in China's long history. In the Middle East and Russia almost the same was true, for after an initial anti-Moslem policy the Mongols not only accepted Islam (Russia, 1257; Persia, 1295) but rapidly assimilated themselves to the Turkish community, which was already dominant everywhere on the central and western steppe. There were too few Mongols and their culture was too crude to permit any other result. Hence in the fourteenth and fifteenth centuries Islamized Turkish warriors, often led by captains who claimed descent from Genghis Khan, again pressed forward against Christendom and Hindustan. The Moslem world had by then largely recovered from the setback wrought by the pagan Mongol conquest of the thirteenth century. Baghdad, however, and the irrigation system that made Iraq fertile, were not restored. Mongol destruction had been too great. As a result, the former seat of the caliphate remained in ruins until the twentieth century.

THE OTTOMAN EMPIRE

By far the most durable and important of the new states that arose in the course of this renewed Turkish offensive was the Ottoman empire. It originated as a small frontier principality in northwestern Asia Minor. Turkish warriors flocked to the service of the Ottoman sultan from all over the Moslem world, because his raids against Christian territory made religious merit and heroic exercise of violence coincide, as was true nowhere else in the Moslem world. Under these circumstances territorial advance became rapid, especially after 1354, when the Turks made their first permanent lodgment across the straits in Europe. Presently, the Sultan faced difficulty in commanding the loyalty and obedience of his followers, who had been assigned conquered lands on the usual feudal pattern. The Ottoman rulers met this difficulty by expanding their personal household into a standing army. This became the famous janissary (i.e. "new troops") corps. Its members, together with the officers who commanded them, were legally classed as slaves. So were the specially trained and selected men who went out into the provinces as agents of the Sultan and took command of local Moslem landowners and warriors when they were called up for active service with the Sultan in war. Since these special slave commanders were backed up by the janissary corps and by the Sultan himself, their commands were usually obeyed. The Ottoman state therefore had at its disposal both an effective standing army, the janissaries, and an obedient feudal army of Turkish warriors.

Personnel for the Sultan's slave family numbered several thousand. At first, war captives provided most of the needed manpower, supplemented by purchases from commercial slave dealers. But soon this method of recruitment proved inadequate. The Turkish Sultan therefore fell back upon rough-and-ready conscription among the Christian villages of the remote Balkans. Thus it happened that young men born as Serb, Greek, or Albanian peasants in the western mountain zone of the Balkan peninsula provided a strategically decisive element in the military and administrative cadres of the Ottoman empire.

No other Moslem state achieved such a remarkable and effective internal organization; and none played anything like the role in world affairs that the Ottoman empire was to do.

ORTHODOX CHRISTENDOM

The separation between Latin (Roman Catholic) and Greek (Orthodox) Christendom achieved formal and lasting definition in 1054, when the pope and the patriarch of Constantinople anathematized each other, thus creating a schism which has endured until the present. The occasion of the quarrel was a difference of opinion about the proper phrasing of the Apostles' Creed; but the distinction between the two halves of Christendom ran very deep, and the gap widened when a new and vigorous civilization began to arise in western Europe, in which the Greek Orthodox had no real share. Instead, as the Latin west increased in wealth, power, culture, and self-confidence, eastern Christendom became one of the victims of Latin expansive energy.

The Orthodox world's loss of Asia Minor and of southern Russia to Turkish invaders coincided with a similar double thrust from the west. Italian merchant traders came by sea; Norman knights seized southern Italy (by 1071) and Sicily (by 1091) from the Byzantines, and then crossed the Adriatic to march overland against Constantinople. Byzantine diplomacy was able to parry this first thrust from the west by diverting the formidable "Franks" to the Holy Land, where they could expend their ferocity on Byzantium's other dangerous enemy, the Turks. The result was the First Crusade, 1096–99. Later, however, the Greeks were less fortunate. The climax came in 1204 when the Fourth Crusade actually captured the city of Constantine, and left behind a short-lived Latin empire of the Levant.

From the point of view of Orthodox Christians, Moslem Turks were definitely preferable to Latin Christians. The Latins insisted on trying to force the Orthodox Christians to accept their version of Christian doctrine at the expense of the immutable truths of Orthodoxy. The Moslems, on the contrary, were prepared to allow Christians of whatever persuasion to continue to follow their accustomed rites. Moreover, the theologians of the church officially classified Islam as Christian heresy: hence Moslem error was really no worse theologically than Latin schism. In addition, the Ottoman Turks, when they first appeared in the Balkans, were much less oppressive tax gatherers than their Christian predecessors had been. The Turks, indeed, in accordance with the Sacred Law gave their Christian subjects far wider local autonomy than they were likely to enjoy under any Christian ruler. Every consideration, therefore, predisposed the Orthodox Christians to opt for Turkish Moslems against Latin Christians if and when choice between the two became necessary. The option expired in 1453 when Constantinople fell to the Turks. Nearly the same factors applied further north in the Russian forests, where such a ruler as Alexander Nevsky (d. 1263) resisted Latin conquest heroically and then tamely submitted to the Mongols.

The northern offshoot of Orthodox Christendom, Holy Russia, underwent a slow but very significant development during the period of Mongol rule (1240–1480). Agriculture crept deep into the forest, back from the river banks where the population had first congregated. Little by little great areas of ground were cleared for farming. This allowed a comparatively numerous, though extremely poor, peasantry to establish itself despite the inhospitable soil and severe climate.

Politically, the Mongols were content to farm out taxes, first to corporations of central Asian merchants and then to native Russian princes, of whom the Grand Duke of Moscow became the chief. As agent for a harsh though distant taskmaster, the Grand Duke of Moscow created an administrative bureaucracy of tax gatherers. The result was that in 1480, when Ivan III repudiated Mongol suzerainty, he had a ready-made administrative machine at his command. Moscow thus became the only great and independent Orthodox state. Russian churchmen soon developed the idea that Moscow was the Third Rome, succeeding to Constantinople as Constantinople had succeeded the first Rome on the Tiber, because only in Russia had Orthodoxy remained pure and undefiled. Ever since then the notion that Russia was uniquely chosen for the special mission of guarding the true faith on earth has never ceased to play a part in Russian public life, not least since the Communist revolution of 1917.

CHINA—THE TRIUMPH OF TRADITION

As already explained, the outward appearance of Chinese civilization was remarkably little affected by the episode of Mongol domination. Neo-Confucianism attained its full development under the later Sung, when the greatest philosopher of this school, Chu Hsi (1130–1200), flourished. But the whole effort of Chu Hsi and his fellow literati was to remain faithful to the ancients, as Confucius himself had tried to be. Hence innovation was never consciously admitted, whether in thought or in art, in manners or in government.

Nevertheless, during the Mongol period important socioeconomic changes put considerable strain upon the traditional frame of Chinese civilization. In the end, the old Confucian forms triumphed decisively, but this should not blind us to the importance of the forces which nearly transformed Chinese society. The late Sung and Mongol periods saw a great development in trade and commerce, based upon regional specialization within China upon far-ranging export and import up and down the coast. Fukien and adjacent parts of the south China coast were among the most active centers of this development.

Early in the Ming period (1368–1644) official organization was brought to the maritime enterprise of south China. Results were spectacular. Between 1405 and 1433 a court eunuch named Cheng-ho launched a series of expeditions into the Indian Ocean, in the course of which truly imperial fleets of several hundred vessels visited all the strategic gateways to the southern seas—Malacca, Ceylon, Calicut, and even Hormuz at the mouth of the Persian Gulf—and temporarily established Chinese control over most of these places. Then the Ming emperor ordered the expeditions stopped, and forbade Chinese subjects from building sea-going vessels or leaving the country. Court intrigues between rival cliques may have had something to do with this decision, so pregnant for the future commercial and imperial balance of power in Asia. But basically the Ming rulers, from their capital at Peking near the ever-dangerous Mongol border, felt that imperial resources should not be squandered on such distant enterprises when the need for protection against the nomads required all the strength the government could muster.

This deliberate abdication from an active role in the southern seas condemned Chinese overseas colonies to speedy decay. Mastery of the seas passed to Japanese and Malay pirates, who soon made the coasts of China unsafe for peaceable shipping. From time to time they even succeeded in interrupting transport on the Grand Canal by penetrating inland along China's numerous waterways.

Merchants had always, of course, ranked as social parasites in Confucian estimation, whereas Mongols and other steppe peoples accorded them a much more dignified place in society. The trading community, which had prospered under barbarian protection, was therefore particularly disadvantaged by the Ming restoration of Neo-Confucian orthodoxy. Yet the failure of the mercantile interest to hold its own after the really great advances made in Sung and Mongol times seems, at least to a Westerner, to require further explanation. The fact that Chinese agriculture also underwent a very great development may help to explain why the conservative Confucian ideal prevailed. About A.D. 1000 new varieties of rice were introduced that could ripen quickly enough to permit double cropping on well-watered land. Even more important, this early ripening rice could mature successfully on hilly ground where water was available for the paddy fields only during a short period of the spring run-off. The total agricultural productivity of China was thereby greatly enlarged, especially in the far south, where hilly ground, previously unsuited to rice growing, prevailed. Hence, as trade and commerce prospered, so did the landowning gentry. Their numbers and weight in society presumably increased more or less equally with the increase in the importance of merchants and artisans. Then, with the overthrow of the Mongol rulers who had been special patrons and protectors of merchants (witness Marco Polo), the stage was set for the native Ming dynasty first to organize and then officially to throttle China's overseas trade.

The social dominance of the gentry class meant that even such potentially disturbing inventions as gunpowder (reported in Chinese sources from about 1100), printing (invented 756), and the magnetic compass (first mentioned early twelfth century) were kept under control and used simply to strengthen the existing social order. Printing, for example, widened the circle of Confucian literati; it was not employed to bring unorthodox novelties to public attention, as happened so dramatically in Reformation Europe. Gunpowder, similarly, made suppression of local warlords easier than before and allowed the imperial government to maintain a more or less effective central control over all of China (with only a few brief periods of breakdown) from the time the Ming dynasty completed the expulsion of the Mongols until 1911. Nothing could be more traditional. The equally traditional, high-handed yet effective, fashion with which the Ming court warded off the distraction of sea-borne enterprise, which use of the compass and other navigational improvements permitted, has already been mentioned.

Chinese culture and institutions had, in short, attained such inner perfection and balance that nothing short of wholesale social breakdown, of a sort that did not occur in China until the twentieth century, sufficed to make more than a superficial, transitory impression upon the bearers of the Chinese learned tradition. The myth of immutability, so eagerly accepted by nineteenth-century Europeans, fed upon this fact, overlooking earlier times and aspects of Chinese society which continued to alter, even when the government and official culture remained frozen to the ideal of Confucian propriety.

47.   MARCO POLO TRAVELS TO KUBLAI KHAN

Marco Polo was born into a Venetian trading family around 1254. The family had already developed trading contacts with the Mongol Khans when Marco joined his father and uncle on a visit to China in 1271. Kublai [Kubilai] Khan, whom they visited at his capital Khan-balik (Beijing), was much more sophisticated than his ancestors, such as Genghis, who had conquered northern China. Kublai combined the vigor and simplicity of his fathers with the humanitarian spirit of Buddhism and a unique vision in administering the Chinese bureaucracy. It was equally characteristic of him to sow the wild grasses of Mongolia in his palace gardens to remind him of the freedom of his youth and to discuss the finer points of theology with invited missionaries from all over the world.

Notice how different the world of Kublai is from that of Genghis Khan. Judging from Marco Polo's description and comments, is the world of Kublai Khan more, or less, developed than the Venice he knew? In what ways was it different?

Emperors and kings, dukes and marquises, counts, knights, and townsfolk, and all people who wish to know the various races of men and the peculiarities of the various regions of the world, take this book and have it read to you. Here you will find all the great wonders and curiosities of Greater Armenia and Persia, of the Tartars and of India, and of many other territories. Our book will relate them to you plainly in due order, as they were related by Messer Marco Polo, a wise and noble citizen of Venice, who has seen them with his own eyes. There is also much here that he has not seen but has heard from men of credit and veracity. We will set down things seen as seen, things heard as heard, so that our book may be an accurate record, free from any sort of fabrication. And all who read the book or hear it may do so with full confidence, because it contains nothing but the truth. . . .

Let me tell you next of the personal appearance of the Great Lord of Lords whose name is Kubilai Khan. He is a man of good stature, neither short nor tall but of moderate height. His limbs are well fleshed out and modelled in due proportion. His complexion is fair and ruddy like a rose, the eyes black and handsome, the nose shapely and set squarely in place.

He has four consorts who are all accounted his lawful wives; and his eldest son by any of these four has a rightful claim to be emperor on the death of the present Khan. They are called empresses, each by her own name. Each of these ladies holds her own court. None of them has less than 300 ladies in waiting, all of great beauty and charm. They have many eunuchs and many other men and women in attendance, so that each one of these ladies has in her court 10,000 persons. When he wishes to lie with one of his four wives, he invites her to his chamber; or sometimes he goes to his wife's chamber.

He also has many concubines, about whom I will tell you. There is a province inhabited by Tartars who are called Kungurat, which is also the name of their city. They are a very good-looking race with fair complexions. Every two years or so, according to his pleasure, the Great Khan sends emissaries to this province to select for him out of the most beautiful maidens, according to the standard of beauty which he lays down for them, some four or five hundred, more or less as he may decide. This is how the selection is made. When the emissaries arrive, they summon to their presence all the maidens of the province. And there valuers are deputed for the task. After inspecting and surveying every girl feature by feature, her hair, her face, her eyebrows, her mouth, her lips, and every other feature, to see whether they are well-formed and in harmony with her person, the valuers award to some a score of sixteen marks, to others seventeen, eighteen, or twenty, or more or less according to the degree of their beauty. And, if the Great Khan has ordered them to bring him all who score twenty marks, or perhaps twenty-one, according to the number ordered, these are duly brought. When they have come to his presence, he has them assessed a second time by other valuers, and then the thirty or forty with the highest score are selected for his chamber. These are first allotted, one by one, to the barons' wives, who are instructed to observe them carefully at night in their chambers, to make sure that they are virgins and not blemished or defective in any member, that they sleep sweetly without snoring, and that their breath is sweet and they give out no unpleasant odour. Then those who are approved are divided into groups of six, who serve the Khan for three days and three nights at a time in his chamber and his bed, ministering to all his needs. And he uses them according to his pleasure. After three days and nights, in come the next six damsels. And so they continue in rotation throughout the year. While some of the group are in attendance in their lord's chamber, the others are waiting in an antechamber hard by. If he is in need of anything from outside, such as food or drink, the damsels inside the chamber pass word to those outside, who immediately get it ready. In this way the Khan is served by no one except these damsels. As for the other damsels, who are rated at a lower score, they remain with the Khan's other women in the palace, where they are instructed in needlework, glove-making, and other elegant accomplishments. When some nobleman is looking for a wife, the Great Khan gives him one of these damsels with a great dowry. And in this way he marries them all off honourably.

You must know that for three months in the year, December, January, and February, the Great Khan lives in the capital city of Cathay, whose name is Khan-balik. In this city he has his great palace, which I will now describe to you.

The palace is completely surrounded by a square wall, each side being a mile in length so that the whole circuit is four miles. It is a very thick wall and fully ten paces in height. It is all white-washed and battlemented. At each corner of this wall stands a large palace of great beauty and splendour, in which the Great Khan keeps his military stores. In the middle of each side is another palace resembling the corner palaces, so that round the whole circuit of the walls there are eight palaces, all serving as arsenals. Each is reserved for a particular type of munition. Thus, one contains saddles, bridles, stirrups, and other items of a horse's harness. In another are bows, bowstrings, quivers, arrows, and other requisites of archery. In a third are cuirasses, corselets, and other armour of boiled leather. And so with the rest.

In the southern front of this wall there are five gates. There is one great gate in the middle, which is never opened except when the Great Khan is leaving or entering. Next to this, one on either side, are two small gates, by which everyone else enters. There are also two more large gates, one near each corner, which are likewise used by other people.

Within this outer wall is another wall, somewhat greater in length than in breadth. In this also there are eight palaces, just like the others, and used in the same way to house military stores. It also has five gates in its southern front, corresponding to those in the outer wall. In each of the other sides it has one gate only; and so has the outer wall.

Within this wall is the Great Khan's palace, which I will now describe to you. It is the largest that was ever seen. It has no upper floor, but the basement on which it stands is raised ten palms above the level of the surrounding earth; and all round it there runs a marble wall level with the basement, two paces in thickness. The foundation of the palace lies within this wall, so that as much of the wall as projects beyond it forms a sort of terrace, on which men can walk right round and inspect the outside of the palace. At the outer edge of this wall is a fine gallery with columns, where men can meet and talk. At each face of the palace is a great marble staircase, ascending from ground level to the top of this marble wall, which affords an entry into the palace.

The palace itself has a very high roof. Inside, the walls of the halls and chambers are all covered with gold and silver and decorated with pictures of dragons and birds and horsemen and various breeds of beasts and scenes of battle. The ceiling is similarly adorned, so that there is nothing to be seen anywhere but gold and pictures. The hall is so vast and so wide that a meal might well be served there for more than 6,000 men. The number of chambers is quite bewildering. The whole building is at once so immense and so well constructed that no man in the world, granted that he had the power to effect it, could imagine any improvement in design or execution. The roof is all ablaze with scarlet and green and blue and yellow and all the colours that are, so brilliantly varnished that it glitters like crystal and the sparkle of it can be seen from far away. And this roof is so strong and so stoutly built as to last for many a long year.

In the rear part of the palace are extensive apartments, both chambers and halls, in which are kept the private possessions of the Khan. Here is stored his treasure: gold, and silver, precious stones and pearls, and his gold and silver vessels. And here too are his ladies and his concubines. In these apartments everything is arranged for his comfort and convenience, and outsiders are not admitted.

Between the inner and the outer walls, of which I have told you, are stretches of park-land with stately trees. The grass grows here in abundance, because all the paths are paved and built up fully two cubits above the level of the ground, so that no mud forms on them and no rain-water collects in puddles, but the moisture trickles over the lawns, enriching the soil and promoting a lush growth of herbage. In these parks there is a great variety of game, such as white harts, musk-deer, roebuck, stags, squirrels, and many other beautiful animals. All the area within the walls is full of these graceful creatures, except the paths that people walk on.

I assure you that the streets are so broad and straight that from the top of the wall above one gate you can see along the whole length of the road to the gate opposite. The city is full of fine mansions, inns, and dwelling-houses. All the way down the sides of every main street there are booths and shops of every sort. All the building sites throughout the city are square and measured by the rule; and on every site stand large and spacious mansions with ample courtyards and gardens. These sites are allotted to heads of households, so that one belongs to such-and-such a person, representing such-and-such a family, the next to a representative of another family, and so all the way along. Every site or block is surrounded by good public roads; and in this way the whole interior of the city is laid out in squares like a chessboard with such masterly precision that no description can do justice to it.

In this city there is such a multitude of houses and of people, both within the walls and without, that no one could count their number. Actually there are more people outside the walls in the suburbs than in the city itself. There is a suburb outside every gate, such that each one touches the neighbouring suburbs on either side. They extend in length for three or four miles. And in every suburb or ward, at about a mile's distance from the city, there are many fine hostels which provide lodging for merchants coming from different parts: a particular hostel is assigned to every nation, as we might say one for the Lombards, another for the Germans, another for the French. Merchants and others come here on business in great numbers, both because it is the Khan's residence and because it affords a profitable market. And the suburbs have as fine houses and mansions as the city, except of course for the Khan's palace.

You must know that no one who dies is buried in the city. If an idolater dies there, his body is taken to the place of cremation, which lies outside all the suburbs. And so with the others also; when they die they are taken right outside the suburbs for burial. Similarly, no act of violence is performed inside the city, but only outside the suburbs.

Let me tell you also that no sinful woman dares live within the city, unless it be in secret—no woman of the world, that is, who prostitutes her body for money. But they all live in the suburbs, and there are so many of them that no one could believe it. For I assure you that there are fully 20,000 of them, all serving the needs of men for money. They have a captain general, and there are chiefs of hundreds and of thousands responsible to the captain. This is because, whenever ambassadors come to the Great Khan on his business and are maintained at his expense, which is done on a lavish scale, the captain is called upon to provide one of these women every night for the ambassador and one for each of his attendants. They are changed every night and receive no payment; for this is the tax they pay to the Great Khan. From the number of these prostitutes you may infer the number of traders and other visitors who are daily coming and going here about their business.

You may take it for a fact that more precious and costly wares are imported into Khan-balik than into any other city in the world. Let me give you particulars. All the treasures that come from India—precious stones, pearls, and other rarities—are brought here. So too are the choicest and costliest products of Cathay itself and every other province. This is on account of the Great Khan himself, who lives here, and of the lords and ladies and the enormous multitude of hotel-keepers and other residents and of visitors who attend the courts held here by the Khan. That is why the volume and value of the imports and of the internal trade exceed those of any other city in the world. It is a fact that every day more than 1,000 cart-loads of silk enter the city; for much cloth of gold and silk is woven here. Furthermore, Khan-balik is surrounded by more than 200 other cities, near and far, from which traders come to it to sell and to buy. So it is not surprising that it is the centre of such a traffic as I have described.

In the centre of the city stands a huge palace in which is a great bell; in the evening this peals three times as a signal that no one may go about the town. Once this bell has sounded the due number of peals, no one ventures abroad in the city except in case of childbirth or illness; and those who are called out by such emergencies are obliged to carry lights. Every night there are guards riding about the city in troops of thirty or forty, to discover whether anyone is going about at an abnormal hour, that is after the third peal of the bell. If anyone is found, he is promptly arrested and clapped into prison. Next morning he is examined by the officials appointed for the purpose, and if he is found guilty of any offence, he is punished according to its gravity with a proportionate number of strokes of a rod, which sometimes cause death. They employ this mode of punishment in order to avoid bloodshed, because their *Bakhshi,* that is, the adepts in astrology, declare that it is wrong to shed human blood.

It is ordered that every gateway must be guarded by 1,000 men. You must not suppose that this guard is maintained out of mistrust of the inhabitants. It is there, in fact, partly as a mark of respect to the Great

Khan who lives in the city, partly as a check upon evil-doers—although, because of the prophecy of his astrologers, the Khan does harbour certain suspicions of the people of Cathay.

You must know that most of the inhabitants of the province of Cathay drink a wine such as I will describe to you. They make a drink of rice and an assortment of excellent spices, prepared in such a way that it is better to drink than any other wine. It is beautifully clear and it intoxicates more speedily than other wine, because it is very heating.

Let me tell you next of stones that burn like logs. It is a fact that throughout the province of Cathay there is a sort of black stone, which is dug out of veins in the hillsides and burns like logs. These stones keep a fire going better than wood. I assure you that, if you put them on the fire in the evening and see that they are well alight, they will continue to burn all night, so that you will find them still glowing in the morning. They do not give off flames, except a little when they are first kindled, just as charcoal does, and once they have caught fire they give out great heat. And you must know that these stones are burnt throughout the province of Cathay. It is true that they also have plenty of firewood. But the population is so enormous and there are so many bath-houses and baths continually being heated, that the wood could not possibly suffice, since there is no one who does not go to a bath-house at least three times a week and take a bath, and in winter every day, if he can manage it. And every man of rank or means has his own bathroom in his house, where he takes a bath. So it is clear that there could never be enough wood to maintain such a conflagration. So these stones, being very plentiful and very cheap, effect a great saving of wood.

To return to the provision of grain, you may take it for a fact that the Great Khan, when he sees that the harvests are plentiful and corn is cheap, accumulates vast quantities of it and stores it in huge granaries, where it is so carefully preserved that it remains unspoilt for three or four years. So he builds up a stock of every sort of grain—wheat, barley, millet, rice, panic [a cereal grass], and others—in great abundance. Then, when it happens that some crops fail and there is a dearth of grain, he draws on these stocks. If the price is running at a bezant for a measure of wheat, for instance, he supplies four measures for the same sum. And he releases enough for all, so that everyone has plenty of corn to meet his needs. In this way he sees to it that none of his subjects need ever go short. And this he does throughout all parts of his empire.

Let me now tell you how the Great Khan bestows charity on the poor people of Khan-balik. When he learns that some family of honest and respectable people have been impoverished by some misfortune or disabled from working by illness, so that they have no means of earning their daily bread, he sees to it that such families (which may consist of six to ten persons or more) are given enough to cover their expenses for the whole year. These families, at the time appointed, go to the officials whose task it is to superintend the Great Khan's expenditure and who live in a palatial building assigned to their office. And each one produces a certificate of the sum paid to him for his subsistence the year before, and provision is made for them at the same rate this year. This provision includes clothing inasmuch as the Great Khan receives a tithe of all the wool, silk, and hemp used for cloth-making. He has these materials woven into cloth in a specially appointed building in which they are stored. Since all the crafts are under obligation to devote one day a week to working on his behalf, he has this cloth made up into garments, which he gives to the poor families in accordance with their needs for winter and for summer wear. He also provides clothing for his armies by having woolen cloth woven in every city as a contribution towards the payment of its tithe.

You must understand that the Tartars according to their ancient customs, before they became familiar with the doctrines of the idolaters, never used to give any alms. Indeed, when a poor man came to them, they would drive him off with maledictions, saying: "Go with God's curse upon you! If he had loved you as he loves me, he would have blessed you with prosperity!" But since the sages of the idolaters, in particular the *Bakhshi* of whom I have spoken above, preached to the Great Khan that it was a good work to provide for the poor and that their idols would be greatly pleased by it, he was induced to make such provision as I have described. No one who cares to go to his court in quest of bread is ever turned away empty-handed. Everyone receives a portion. And not a day passes but twenty or thirty thousand bowls of rice, millet, and panic are doled out and given away by the officials appointed. And this goes on all the year round. For this amazing and stupendous munificence which the Great Khan exercises towards the poor, all the people hold him in such esteem that they revere him as a god.

48. THE GREAT ISLAMIC EMPIRES

C. E. Bosworth

The Mongol invasions of the thirteenth and fourteenth centuries not only reunified Asia, they also dramatically changed the character of the Muslim world, the previous unifier. After the defeat of the Abbasid Caliphate in 1258, there was no longer a single Muslim state. But as the West Asian

Mongol Khans adopted Islam, a new Muslim cultural unity spread from North Africa to India. By 1500 three Muslim states (Ottoman Turk, Persian, and Indian) dominated southern Asia. What were the strengths and weaknesses of these Islamic empires, according to this modern historian?

The Mongol invasions of the thirteenth and fourteenth centuries constituted a "time of troubles" for all the Islamic lands east of Egypt, out of which various powerful and comparatively long-lived empires emerged. The Mongols expanded from their homeland around Lake Baikal in eastern Siberia in one of those eras of expansion which population pressures and the emergence of forceful leaders seem regularly to have generated. Under an outstanding leader, Chingiz [Genghis] Khan, the Mongols irrupted both into China and into western Asia, the Islamic world. Within a few years of Chingiz's appearance on the Oxus River in 1219, the Muslim powers in Central Asia and eastern Persia had been overturned, and a trail of desolation left by the Mongol or Mongol-Turkish cavalrymen. Later, Mongol forces rode through the Siberian steppes into Russia, and defeated German-Polish and Hungarian armies in Central Europe. The impetus here was not maintained, but the Mongols remained in South Russia, and the Golden Horde, as this part of the Mongol empire was known, held the Russian princes tributary for one-and-a-half centuries. Within the Islamic world proper, Baghdad fell to Chingiz's grandson Hülegü in 1258. A line of *fainéant* Abbasid Caliphs was set up soon after this in Cairo under Mamlūk protection, but the medieval Caliphate, the symbol of orthodox, Sunnī Muslim unity, had gone for ever. The Mongols had originally been shamanists, i.e., pagan animists, but with some sympathies for other faiths of Inner Asia like Buddhism and Nestorian Christianity. The various branches of the Western Mongols gradually adopted Islam: the Khanate which was set up in Iraq and Persia, that of the Il-Khanids ("Subordinate Khans," i.e., subordinate to the Greek Khan in Mongolia), became Muslim in 1295.

Despite the fact that the name of the Mongols ranks in the popular mind with those of the Goths, Huns, and Vandals as perpetrators of mass destruction, this initial violence subsided and the age of the Mongols had its favourable aspect. Domination over such a great expanse of the Old World, from the Ukraine to Korea, opened up the possibility of East-West cultural exchanges on an unprecedented scale. Chinese artistic techniques and motifs began perceptibly to affect Islamic Persian art. People could move freely across Inner Asia as never before or since, unhampered by political boundaries. Impelled by the search for Prester John, the legendary Christian monarch who was tentatively identified with the Mongol Great Khan, many Europeans travelled to Mongolia and have left us fascinating accounts of life there.

That an alliance between the western Europe Papacy and the pagan Mongols against the Muslims of the Near East never really materialised in the thirteenth century was largely due to the vigour of a great imperial power in Egypt and Syria, that of the Mamlūks [Mamelukes]. As their name implies ("owned"), these were of slave status, gaining independent power in 1250 and retaining it till the Ottoman conquest of 1516–17. The earlier Mamlūk Sultans were predominantly Qipchāq Turks from the South Russian steppes, and so for about a century after 1250 the Mamlūks pursued a policy of friendly relations with Byzantium, the surviving Seljuk line in Anatolia, and the Golden Horde, in order to ensure replenishments of slaves. The Mamlūks won prestige in orthodox eyes by their defeats of the Mongols in Palestine and Syria, their ejection of the last Crusaders from the Levant coast, and the reduction of the Christian kingdom of Little Armenia. Their diplomatic and commercial policies embraced Christian Mediterranean powers like Aragon, Naples and Venice on the one hand, and the princes of the Indian Ocean coastlands on the other. They cultivated the support of the Sunnī 'ulamā or religious scholars, maintaining the line of puppet Caliphs but ignoring them for practical purposes. The Arabic scholarship of the Mamlūk period was outstanding in quantity and not infrequently in quality; the sheer volume of material extant makes it possible to reconstruct Mamlūk history in remarkable detail as compared with many other Islamic states.

The impressive achievement of the Mamlūks was founded upon a hierarchy of military slavery, from the Sultans downwards; free soldiers had only a subordinate, socially depressed position in the state. Thus we have the paradoxical situation, duplicated, as we shall see, in Ottoman Turkey, of slaves ruling over free men and being able to rise to the highest positions in the state without social stigma. This phenomenon seems to have been peculiar to the Islamic world; it is strange that Christian powers like the Byzantines, who must have been perfectly familiar with the military slavery system, never attempted to emulate it. The later Mamlūks were recruited from the Circassians of the Caucasus, and in the fifteenth century the state grew perceptibly poorer in resources and fighting manpower. The successive conquest of Syria and Egypt by the Ottomans in 1516–17 therefore occasioned no surprise. One factor in the Mamlūks' failure to withstand the Ottomans was their reluctance to use hand-guns, for wholesale adoption of these new weapons would have relegated the Mamlūk mounted archer to a position inferior to the infantryman and thus destroyed the whole basis of the state.

More than any other Muslim power of the late classical period, the Ottoman Turks struck terror into the hearts of Christian Europe, so that the Elizabethan historian of the Turks, Richard Knollys, described them as "the present Terror of the World." Backed by the Turkish military qualities of self-discipline and endurance, the Turkish invasions of Europe were indeed a potent threat, reaching on two occasions to Vienna itself. The Ottomans began as a group of *ghāzīs* (i.e., corps of mystically inspired warriors) in northwestern Anatolia, confronting the truncated Byzantine empire there, and eventually eclipsing other Turkish principalities by their superior *élan* and experience in war. In 1354 they crossed the Dardanelles into Europe, cutting off Constantinople in its rear, and expanded relentlessly into the Balkans. States like Serbia and Bulgaria were humbled, and for 500 years to come were to be nations without history. The Ottoman victory at Mohács in 1526 brought most of Hungary under Turkish rule for a century-and-a-half, providing a base from which to threaten Austria and the very heart of Christian Europe. The Balkan provinces came to form Rumelia, the European "twin" of Anatolia. Turks were settled there, and there were also converts from the indigenous peoples, giving a strongly Islamic impress to much of the Balkans down to the nineteenth century and after; in 1939 one-third of the Yugoslavian province of Bosnia was still Muslim and about half of Albania. Ottoman authority in Anatolia received a setback from the invasion of the Tatar military conqueror Timur (or Tamerlane) at the opening of the fifteenth century. Half a century later, it revived under a series of outstanding Sultans: Mehmed the Conqueror, who attained the glittering prize of Constantinople in 1453; Selīm the Grim, conqueror of Syria and Egypt and humbler of the Ottomans' rivals to the east, the Safavids of Persia; and Sulaymān the Magnificent (called by the Turks "the Lawgiver"), conqueror of Hungary and Iraq. Ottoman fleets and their allies, the corsairs of Barbary (i.e., North Africa), operated in the Mediterranean and beyond, terrorising the Christians and carrying off captives from as far afield as Ireland and Iceland; and in the late seventeenth century, the Ottomans enjoyed their last major success by capturing Crete from the Venetians.

Much of this Ottoman vigour sprang from the use of a system of military slavery analogous to that of the Mamlūks. The Janissaries or "New Troops," a crack corps of highly trained soldiers and officials, were recruited from the Christian populations of the Balkans and later, from those of Anatolia, from the late fourteenth down to the early eighteenth centuries. Like the Arabs in the first stages of their expansion, the Turks themselves were a military class comparatively thinly spread over what had grown to be a vast empire. Utilisation of the subject population was a brilliant device for tapping the manpower of the Balkans. Moreover, the lengthy and arduous training of a Janissary in a thoroughly Islamic atmosphere conduced to his adopting a soldierly type of Islam. It was the discipline and fire-power of these troops (the Ottoman army made use of artillery and hand-guns from the mid-fifteenth century onwards) which did much to create in Europe the image of Ottoman ferocity and invincibility.

Yet in its heyday, the Ottoman empire was the most powerful and lasting state known to the Islamic world since the early Arab Caliphate. It gave autocratic, but often good government to lands which had previously suffered internal chaos and dislocation, and only towards the end, when the political and economic pressure of the West contributed to administrative breakdown and internal economic decline, did the quality of Ottoman rule deteriorate.

The Safavids of Persia established the one late medieval empire which was Shī'ī* in faith. Somewhat remarkably, it arose from a local Azerbaijan Sūfī or dervish order which gradually became transformed into a militant Shī'ī propagandist movement. The Safavids came to power in an area where the ground had been prepared for Shī'ī heterodoxy, and consciously adopted Shī'ism as an affirmation of the Persian national identity against the pressures of adjoining, hostile Sunnī powers like the Ottomans on the west and the Özbeg states of central Asia on the northeast. In the opening years of the sixteenth century, Shāh Ismā'īl Safavī brought the whole of Persia under his control; later, the capital was moved first to Qazvīn and then to Isfahān, which was transformed into one of the finest cities of the Islamic world. The Safavids maintained their power for over two centuries, till in the early eighteenth century they were overthrown by the Afghans. Shāh 'Abbās I (1588–1629) cultivated relations with European powers such as England and Holland in an effort to obtain allies against his enemies, the Ottomans and the Portuguese; and we owe many valuable accounts of seventeenth-century Persia to the western diplomats, travellers, missionaries and traders who visited "the Grand Sophy." The title "Sophy" for the Shāhs almost certainly stems, of course, from Sūfī, and the Safavid state began as a theocracy, with the Shāhs claiming semi-divine status as emanations of the Godhead, with infallibility as representatives on earth of the Hidden Imām, thus the Shāhs demanded spiritual as well as political allegiance from their Turkish troops, the Qïzïl-bāsh or "Redheads" (from the red caps which they wore). In addition to these last, the Safavids followed prevailing military fashion by forming regiments of slave troops (ghulāms), comparable with the Ottoman Janissaries. The ghulāms were mainly of Christian origin, from such peoples of the Caucasus region as the Georgians and Armenians; by contrast with the Ottoman system, they were not levied on a regular basis.

The remaining great Muslim empire arose in northern India, where ubiquitous Turks and the Afghans founded military dynasties from the eleventh century onwards. Many of these stemmed from Turkish slave commanders, as the name of one dynasty of Delhi Sultans, the "Slave Kings" (1206–90) shows. Muslim rule was extended as far as Bengal (early thirteenth century), Lashmir (fourteenth century) and into the Deccan or South India, where several local dynasties of considerable cultural splendour arose. All through its existence, the dominant feature

*Shī'ī refers to the Shī'ah ('party of 'Alī') which is that group of Muslims who believed that leadership of the Muslim community ought to be held by descendants of Ali, the cousin and son-in-law of Muhammad, whether recognized by the majority or not. They are opposed to the Sunnīs, the majority of Muslims who accept the authority of the whole first generation of Muslims and the custom of the historical Muslim community.—Ed.

of Indian Islam has been its minority position, numerically speaking, within a non-Islamic, predominantly Hindu environment; hence Muslim princes often ruled over extensive non-Muslim populations and relied on them as officials or soldiers. The comparative isolation of Islam in India meant a perpetual struggle to preserve the faith from syncretism and from the characteristic absorptive influence of Hindu religion; thus Indian Muslim rulers and the 'ulamā usually identified themselves strongly with Sunnī Islam and the maintenance of orthodoxy.

The empire of the Mughals (this name being a form of "Mongols") arose out of the successful efforts of Bābur, a Turkish prince from Central Asia, to carve out a principality for himself in northern India in the early sixteenth century. Under a series of remarkable Sultans in the sixteenth and seventeenth centuries the Mughal empire expanded over the greater part of the subcontinent. Akbar the Great, a contemporary of Elizabeth I of England, in a dramatic divergence from traditional Indian Islamic thought, attempted a rapprochement with his Hindu subjects, toying with a new, monotheistic creed of his own, "the Divine Faith," which would transcend existing religions and bring about religious harmony in his dominions; such policies were, however, reversed by his successors, and Aurangzīb (d. 1707), the last great Mughal Emperor, reverted to strict enforcement of Muslim orthodoxy. A feature of these two centuries—one hardly noticed by the Muslim rulers of India, but portentous for the future—was the establishment of coastal trading stations or "factories" by European merchants, such as the Portuguese, English and French. The English settlements formed the bases for subsequent territorial expansion in the eighteenth and nineteenth centuries, and it was the British who, in the aftermath of the Indian Mutiny, in 1858 deposed the last feeble representative of the Mughal line in Delhi.

49. THE EMPEROR'S GIRAFFE

Samuel M. Wilson

The author, a modern anthropologist, writes about the great Chinese naval expeditions of the early fifteenth century. How far from China did Chinese sailors travel? What seems to have been their attitude to those they met? How does the "emperor's giraffe" serve as an effective symbol for these expeditions?

A huge fleet left port in 1414 and sailed westward on a voyage of trade and exploration. The undertaking far surpassed anything Columbus,

Isabella, and Ferdinand could have envisioned. The fleet included at least sixty-two massive trading galleons, any of which could have held Columbus's three small ships on its decks. The largest galleons were more than 400 feet long and 150 feet wide (the *Santa Maria*, Columbus's largest vessel, was about 90 by 30 feet), and each could carry about 1,500 tons (Columbus's ships combined could carry about 400 tons). More than one hundred smaller vessels accompanied the galleons. All told, 30,000 people went on the voyage, compared with Columbus's crew of 90-some.

The commander's name was Zheng He (Cheng Ho), the Grand Eunuch of the Three Treasures and the most acclaimed admiral of the Ming dynasty. He was sailing from the South China Sea across the Indian Ocean, heading for the Persian Gulf and Africa. As the historian Philip Snow notes in his wonderful book *The Star Raft* (1988), "Zheng He was the Chinese Columbus. He has become for China, as Columbus has for the West, the personification of maritime endeavour." The flotilla was called the star raft after the luminous presence of the emperor's ambassadors on board.

Zheng He did not really set out to explore unknown lands—neither did Columbus, for that matter—for the Chinese were aware of most of the countries surrounding the Indian Ocean. For centuries, China had been a principal producer and consumer of goods moving east and west from Mediterranean, African, and Middle Eastern trading centers. With this trade came cultural and ideological exchange. Zheng He, like many Chinese of his time, was a Muslim, and his father and his father before him had made the pilgrimage to Mecca. But in Zheng He's day, the trade routes were controlled by Arabian, Persian, and Indian merchants.

Private Chinese traders had been barred from traveling to the West for several centuries. China had been conquered by Genghis Khan and his descendants in the 1200s, and the Mongol emperors of the subsequent Yüan dynasty were the first to impose these constraints. In 1368 the Chinese expelled the Mongol rulers and established the Ming dynasty, which was destined to rule for the next 300 years. (Thus, in 1492 Columbus was searching for a "Gran Khan" who had been put out of business 124 years earlier.) After the period of Mongol rule, China became strongly isolationist, placing even more severe restrictions on Chinese traders.

In 1402 an outward-looking emperor named Yong'le (Yung-lo) came to power. Seeking to reassert a Chinese presence on the western seas and to enhance the prestige of his rule and dynasty, he began funding spectacular voyages by Zheng He. As sociologist Janet Abu-Lughod notes in *Before European Hegemony* (1989), "The impressive show of force that paraded around the Indian Ocean during the first three decades of the fifteenth century was intended to signal the 'barbarian nations' that China had reassumed her rightful place in the firmament of nations— had once again become the 'Middle Kingdom' of the world."

As Zheng He pressed westward in 1414, he sent part of the fleet north to Bengal, and there the Chinese travelers saw a wonderous creature. None like it had ever been seen in China, although it was not completely unheard of. In 1225 Zhao Rugua, a customs inspector at the city of Quanzhou, had recorded a secondhand description of such a beast in his strange and wonderful *Gazetteer of Foreigners*. He said it had a leopard's hide, a cow's hoofs, a ten-foot-tall body, and a nine-foot neck towering above that. He called it a *zula*, possibly a corruption of *zurafa*, the Arabic word for giraffe.

The giraffe the travelers saw in Bengal was already more than 5,000 miles from home. It had been brought there as a gift from the ruler of the prosperous African city-state of Malindi, one of several trading centers lining the east coast of Africa (Malindi is midway along modern Kenya's coast, three degrees south of the equator). Zheng He's diplomats persuaded the Bengal king to offer the animal as a gift to the Chinese emperor. They also persuaded the Malindi ambassadors to send home for another giraffe. When Zheng He returned to Beijing, he was able to present the emperor with two of the exotic beasts.

A pair of giraffes in Beijing in 1415 was well worth the cost of the expedition. In China they thought the giraffe (despite its having one horn too many) was a unicorn (*ch'i-lin*), whose arrival, according to Confucian tradition, meant that a sage of the utmost wisdom and benevolence was in their presence. It was a great gift, therefore, to bring to the ambitious ruler of a young dynasty. The giraffes were presented to the emperor Yong'le by exotic envoys from the kingdom of Malindi, whom the Chinese treated royally. They and their marvelous gift so excited China's curiosity about Africa that Zheng He sent word to the Kingdom of Mogadishu (then one of the most powerful trading states in East Africa and now the capital of modern Somalia) and to other African states, inviting them to send ambassadors to the Ming emperor.

The response of the African rulers was overwhelmingly generous, for China and Africa had been distant trading partners from the time of the Han dynasty (206 B.C. to A.D. 220). In the *Universal Christian Topography*, written about A.D. 525 by Kosmas, a Byzantine monk known as the Indian Traveler, Sri Lanka is described as a trading center frequented by both Chinese and Africans. Envoys from a place called Zengdan—the name translates as "Land of Blacks"—visited China several times in the eleventh century. And a Chinese map compiled in the early fourteenth century shows Madagascar and the southern tip of Africa in remarkable detail, nearly two centuries before the Portuguese "discovered" the Cape of Good Hope. Archaeologists find China (why the English word came to be synonymous with glazed pottery and porcelain instead of silk or spices is unclear) from the Han and later dynasties all along the east coast of Africa.

The African emissaries to the Ming throne came with fabulous gifts, including objects for which entrepreneurs had long before managed to create a market in the Far East—tortoiseshell, elephant ivory, and rhinoceros-horn medicine. On their many visits they also brought zebras, ostriches, and other exotica. In return, the Ming court sent gold, spices, silk, and other presents. Zheng He was sent with his fleet of great ships on yet another voyage across the Indian Ocean to accompany some of the foreign emissaries home. This escort was the first of several imperially supported trips to Africa. According to official records, they went to Mogadishu, Brava, and perhaps Malindi; Snow (in *The Star Raft*) suggests that these Chinese expeditions may have gone still farther—to Zanzibar, Madagascar, and southern Africa.

Meanwhile, as the Chinese were pushing down the east coast of Africa, Portuguese mariners were tentatively exploring the west coast. They had started the process in the early fifteenth century and were steadily working their way south. Bartolomeu Dias reached the Cape of Good Hope in 1488 and was the first of these mariners to see the Indian Ocean. Surely the Europeans and Chinese were poised to meet somewhere in southern Africa, where perhaps they would have set up trading depots for their mutual benefit.

This did not happen, however. Emperor Yong'le died in 1424, and by 1433 the Ming dynasty discontinued its efforts to secure tributary states and trading partners around the Indian Ocean. In Beijing, those favoring an isolationist foreign policy won out, and the massive funding needed to support Zheng He's fleet—difficult to sustain during what was a period of economic decline in China—was canceled. As Edwin Reischauer and John Fairbank note in *East Asia: The Great Tradition* (1960):

> The voyages must be regarded as a spectacular demonstration of the capacity of early Ming China for maritime expansion, made all the more dramatic by the fact that Chinese ideas of government and official policies were fundamentally indifferent, if not actually opposed, to such an expansion. This contrast between capacity and performance, as viewed in retrospect from the vantage point of our modern world of trade and overseas expansion, is truly striking.

The contrast also refutes the argument that as soon as a country possesses the technology of overseas trade and conquest it will use it. Zheng He's fleet was 250 times the size of Columbus's, and the Ming navy was many times larger and more powerful than the combined maritime strength of all of Europe. Yet China perceived her greatest challenges and opportunities to be internal ones, and Young'le's overseas agenda was forgotten. Restrictions on private trade were reimposed, and commercial and military ventures in the Indian Ocean and South China Sea in subsequent centuries were dominated by the Portuguese, Arabs, Indians, Spaniards, Japanese, Dutch, British, and Americans. Zheng He's magnificent ships finally rotted at their moorings.

CHAPTER FIFTEEN

African Civilizations

50. *SUNDIATA*

Sundiata is an epic from the medieval kingdom of Mali that has been told and retold for generations. The story is told by the griot (royal storyteller or historian). At the beginning of the thirteenth century, the great leader Sundiata united the Malinke clans and chiefdoms, which became the basis for an independent empire of Mali that dominated the Western Sudan of Africa.

The following is only a brief excerpt from the beginning of the Sundiata. In this early-twentieth-century version of the epic, we are introduced to the griot, Mamadou Kouyaté, who then tells the story of how Sundiata's father and mother met. What were the many functions of the griot? Here the griot goes to great lengths to tell us of the origins of Sundiata's mother and of the way in which his mother and father met. Why? What functions does this story serve? What does the story tell you about the society and culture of Mali or Sudanic Africa?

THE WORDS OF THE GRIOT MAMADOU KOUYATÉ

I am a griot. It is I, Djeli Mamadou Kouyaté, son of Bintou Kouyaté and Djeli Kedian Kouyaté, master in the art of eloquence. Since time immemorial the Kouyatés have been in the service of the Keita princes of Mali; we are vessels of speech, we are the repositories which harbour secrets many centuries old. The art of eloquence has no secrets for us; without us the names of kings would vanish into oblivion, we are the memory of mankind; by the spoken word we bring to life the deeds and exploits of kings for younger generations.

I derive my knowledge from my father Djeli Kedian, who also got it from his father; history holds no mystery for us; we teach to the vulgar just as much as we want to teach them, for it is we who keep the keys to the twelve doors of Mali.

I know the list of all the sovereigns who succeeded to the throne of Mali. I know how the black people divided into tribes, for my father bequeathed to me all his learning; I know why such and such is called Kamara, another Keita, and yet another Sibibé or Traoré; every name has a meaning, a secret import.

I teach kings the history of their ancestors so that the lives of the ancients might serve them as an example, for the world is old, but the future springs from the past.

My word is pure and free of all untruth; it is the word of my father; it is the word of my father's father. I will give you my father's words just as I received them; royal griots do not know what lying is. When a quarrel breaks out between tribes it is we who settle the difference, for we are the depositaries of oaths which the ancestors swore.

Listen to my word, you who want to know; by my mouth you will learn the history of Mali.

By my mouth you will get to know the story of the ancestor of great Mali, the story of him who, by his exploits, surpassed even Alexander the Great; he who, from the East, shed his rays upon all the countries of the West.

Listen to the story of the son of the Buffalo, the son of the Lion. I am going to tell you of Maghan Sundiata, of Mari-Djata, of Sogolon Djata, of Naré Maghan Djata; the man of many names against whom sorcery could avail nothing.

THE FIRST KINGS OF MALI

Listen then, sons of Mali, children of the black people, listen to my word, for I am going to tell you of Sundiata, the father of the Bright Country, of the savanna land, the ancestor of those who draw the bow, the master of a hundred vanquished kings.

I am going to talk of Sundiata, Manding Diara, Lion of Mali, Sogolon Djata, son of Sogolon, Naré Maghan Djata, son of Naré Maghan, Sogo Sogo Simbon Salaba, hero of many names.

I am going to tell you of Sundiata, he whose exploits will astonish men for a long time yet. He was great among kings, he was peerless among men; he was beloved of God because he was the last of the great conquerors.

Right at the beginning then, Mali was a province of the Bambara kings; those who are today called Mandingo, inhabitants of Mali, are not indigenous; they come from the East. Bilali Bounama, ancestor of the Keitas, was the faithful servant of the Prophet Muhammad (may the peace of God be upon him). Bilali Bounama had seven sons of whom the eldest, Lawalo, left the Holy City and came to settle in Mali; Lawalo had Latal Kalabi for a son, Latal Kalabi had Damul Kalabi who then had Lahilatoul Kalabi.

Lahilatoul Kalabi was the first black prince to make the Pilgrimage to Mecca. On his return he was robbed by brigands in the desert; his men were scattered and some died of thirst, but God saved Lahilatoul Kalabi, for he was a righteous man. He called upon the Almighty and jinn appeared and recognized him as king. After seven years' absence Lahilatoul was able to return, by the grace of Allah the Almighty, to Mali where none expected to see him any more.

Lahilatoul Kalabi had two sons, the elder being called Kalabi Bomba and the younger Kalabi Dauman; the elder chose royal power and reigned, while the younger preferred fortune and wealth and became the ancestor of those who go from country to country seeking their fortune. Kalabi Bomba had Mamadi Kani for a son. Mamadi Kani was a hunter king like the first kings of Mali. It was he who invented the hunter's whistle; he communicated with the jinn of the forest and bush. These spirits had no secrets from him and he was loved by Kondolon Ni Sané. His followers were so numerous that he formed them into an army which became formidable; he often gathered them together in the bush and taught them the art of hunting. It was he who revealed to hunters the medicinal leaves which heal wounds and cure diseases. Thanks to the strength of his followers, he became king of a vast country; with them Mamadi Kani conquered all the lands which stretch from the Sankarani to the Bouré. Mamadi Kani had four sons—Kani Simbon, Kamignogo Simbon, Kabala Simbon and Simbon Tagnogokelin. They were all initiated into the art of hunting and deserved the title of Simbon. It was the lineage of Bamari Tagnogokelin which held on to the power; his son was M'Bali Nènè whose son was Bello. Bello's son was called Bello Bakon and he had a son called Maghan Kon Fatta, also called Frako Maghan Keigu, Maghan the handsome.

Maghan Kon Fatta was the father of the great Sundiata and had three wives and six children—three boys and three girls. His first wife was called Sassouma Bérété, daughter of a great divine; she was the mother of King Dankaran Touman and Princess Nana Triban. The second wife, Sogolon Kedjou, was the mother of Sundiata and the two princesses Sogolon Kolonkan and Sogolon Djamarou. The third wife was one of the Kamaras and was called Namandjé; she was the mother of Manding Bory (or Manding Bakary), who was the best friend of his half-brother Sundiata.

THE BUFFALO WOMAN

Maghan Kon Fatta, the father of Sundiata, was renowned for his beauty in every land; but he was also a good king loved by all the people. In his capital of Nianiba he loved to sit often at the foot of the great silk-cotton tree which dominated his palace of Canco. Maghan Kon Fatta had been reigning a long time and his eldest son Dankaran Touman was already eight years old and often came to sit on the ox-hide beside his father.

Well now, one day when the king had taken up his usual position under the silk-cotton tree surrounded by his kinsmen he saw a man dressed like a hunter coming towards him; he wore the tight-fitting trousers of the favourites of Kondolon Ni Sané, and his blouse oversewn with cowries showed that he was a master of the hunting art. All present turned towards the unknown man whose bow, polished with frequent usage, shone in the sun. The man walked up in front of the king, whom he recognized in the midst of his courtiers. He bowed and said, "I salute you, king of Mali, greetings all you of Mali. I am a hunter chasing game and come from Sangaran; a fearless doe has guided me to the walls of Nianiba. By the grace of my master the great Simbon my arrows have hit her and now she lies not far from your walls. As is fitting, oh king, I have come to bring you your portion." He took a leg from his leather sack whereupon the king's griot, Gnankouman Doua, seized upon the leg and said, "Stranger, whoever you may be you will be the king's guest because you respect custom; come and take your place on the mat beside us. The king is pleased because he loves righteous men." The king nodded his approval and all the courtiers agreed. The griot continued in a more familiar tone, "Oh you who come from the Sangaran, land of the favourites of Kondolon Ni Sané, you who have doubtless had an expert master, will you open your pouch of knowledge for us and instruct us with your conversation, for you have no doubt visited several lands."

The king, still silent, gave a nod of approval and a courtier added, "The hunters of Sangaran are the best soothsayers; if the stranger wishes we could learn a lot from him."

The hunter came and sat down near Gnankouman Doua who vacated one end of the mat to him. Then he said, "Griot of the king, I am not one of these hunters whose tongues are more dexterous than their arms; I am no spinner of adventure yarns, nor do I like playing upon the credulity of worthy folk; but, thanks to the lore which my master has imparted to me, I can boast of being a seer among seers."

He took out of his hunter's bag twelve cowries which he threw on the mat. The king and all his entourage now turned towards the stranger who was jumbling up the twelve shiny shells with his bare hand. Gnankouman Doua discreetly brought to the king's notice that the soothsayer was left-handed. The left hand is the hand of evil, but in the divining art it is said that left-handed people are the best. The hunter muttered some incomprehensible words in a low voice while he shuffled and jumbled the twelve cowries into different positions which he mused on at length. All of a sudden he looked up at the king and said, "Oh king, the world is full of mystery, all is hidden and we know nothing but what we can see. The silk-cotton tree springs from a tiny seed—that which defies the tempest weighs in its germ no more than a grain of rice. Kingdoms are like trees; some will be silk-cotton trees, others will remain dwarf palms and the powerful silk-cotton tree will cover them with its shade. Oh, who can recognize in the little child the great king to come? The great comes from the small; truth and falsehood have both suckled at the same breast. Nothing is certain, but, sire, I can see two strangers over there coming towards your city."

He fell silent and looked in the direction of the city gates for a short while. All present silently turned towards the gates. The soothsayer returned to his cowries. He shook them in his palm with a skilled hand and then threw them out.

"King of Mali, destiny marches with great strides, Mali is about to emerge from the night. Nianiba is lighting up, but what is this light that comes from the east?"

"Hunter," said Gnankouman Doua, "your words are obscure. Make your speech comprehensible to us, speak in the clear language of your savanna."

"I am coming to that now, griot. Listen to my message. Listen, sire. You have ruled over the kingdom which your ancestors bequeathed to you and you have no other ambition but to pass on this realm, intact if not increased, to your descendants; but, fine king, your successor is not yet born. I see two hunters coming to your city; they have come from afar and a woman accompanies them. Oh, that woman! She is ugly, she is hideous, she bears on her back a disfiguring hump. Her monstrous eyes seem to have been merely laid on her face, but, mystery of mysteries, this is the woman you must marry, sire, for she will be the mother of him who will make the name of Mali immortal for ever. The child will be the seventh star, the seventh conqueror of the earth. He will be more mighty than Alexander. But, oh king, for destiny to lead this woman to you a sacrifice is necessary; you must offer up a red bull, for the bull is powerful. When its blood soaks into the ground nothing more will hinder the arrival of your wife. There, I have said what I had to say, but everything is in the hands of the Almighty."

The hunter picked up his cowries and put them away in his bag.

"I am only passing through, king of Mali, and now I return to Sangaran. Farewell."

The hunter disappeared but neither the king, Naré Maghan, nor his griot, Gnankouman Doua, forgot his prophetic words; soothsayers see far ahead, their words are not always for the immediate present; man is in a hurry but time is tardy and everything has its season.

Now one day the king and his suite were again seated under the great silk-cotton tree of Nianiba, chatting as was their wont. Suddenly their gaze was drawn by some strangers who came into the city. The small entourage of the king watched in silent surprise.

Two young hunters, handsome and of fine carriage, were walking along preceded by a young maid. They turned towards the Court. The two men were carrying shining bows of silver on their shoulders. The one who seemed the elder of the two walked with the assurance of a master hunter. When the strangers were a few steps from the king they bowed and the elder spoke thus:

"We greet King Naré Maghan Kon Fatta and his entourage. We come from the land of Do, but my brother and I belong to Mali and we are of the tribe of Traoré. Hunting and adventure led us as far as the distant land of Do where King Mansa Gnemo Diarra reigns. I am called Oulamba and my brother Oulani. The young girl is from Do and we bring her as a present to the king, for my brother and I deemed her worthy to be a king's wife."

The king and his suite tried in vain to get a look at the young girl, for she stayed kneeling, her head lowered, and had deliberately let her kerchief hang in front of her face. If the young girl succeeded in hiding her face, she did not, however, manage to cover up the hump which deformed her shoulders and back. She was ugly in a sturdy sort of way. You could see her muscular arms, and her bulging breasts pushing stoutly against the strong pagne of cotton fabric which was knotted just under her armpit. The king considered her for a moment, then the handsome Maghan turned his head away. He stared a long time at Gnankouman Doua then he lowered his head. The griot understood all the sovereign's embarrassment.

"You are the guests of the king; hunters, we wish you peace in Nianiba, for all the sons of Mali are but one. Come and sit down, slake your thirst and relate to the king by what adventure you left Do with this maiden."

The king nodded his approval. The two brothers looked at each other and, at a sign from the elder, the younger went up to the king and put down on the ground the calabash of cold water which a servant had brought him.

The hunter said: "After the great harvest my brother and I left our village to hunt. It was in this way that our pursuit of game led us as far as the approaches of the land of Do. We met two hunters, one of whom was wounded, and we learnt from them that an amazing buffalo was ravaging the countryside of Do. Every day it claimed some victims and nobody dared leave the village after sunset. The king, Do Mansa-Gnemo Diarra, had promised the finest rewards to the hunter who killed the buffalo. We decided to try our luck too and so we penetrated into the land of Do. We were advancing warily, our eyes well skinned, when we saw an old woman by the side of a river. She was weeping and lamenting, gnawed by hunger. Until then no passerby had deigned to stop by her. She beseeched us, in the name of the Almighty, to give her something to eat. Touched by her tears I approached and took some pieces of dried meat from my hunter's bag. When she had eaten well she said, 'Hunter, may God requite you with the charity you have given me.' We were making ready to leave when she stopped me. 'I know,' she said, 'that you are going to try your luck against the Buffalo of Do, but you should know that many others before you have met their death through their foolhardiness, for arrows are useless against the buffalo; but, young hunter, your heart is generous and it is you who will be the buffalo's vanquisher. I am the buffalo you are looking for, and your generosity has vanquished me. I am the buffalo that ravages Do. I have killed a hundred and seven

hunters and wounded seventy-seven; every day I kill an inhabitant of Do
and the king, Gnemo Diarra, is at his wit's end which jinn to sacrifice to.
Here, young man, take this distaff and this egg and go to the plain of
Ourantamba where I browse among the king's crops. Before using your
bow you must take aim at me three times with this distaff; then draw
your bow and I shall be vulnerable to your arrow. I shall fall but shall get
up and pursue you into a dry plain. Then throw the egg behind you and
a great mire will come into being where I shall be unable to advance and
then you will kill me. As a proof of your victory you must cut off the
buffalo's tail, which is of gold, and take it to the king, from whom you
will exact your due reward. As for me, I have run my course and punished the king of Do, my brother, for depriving me of my part of the
inheritance.' Crazy with joy, I seized the distaff and the egg, but the old
woman stopped me with a gesture and said, 'There is one condition,
hunter.' 'What condition?' I replied impatiently. 'The king promises the
hand of the most beautiful maiden of Do to the victor. When all the
people of Do are gathered and you are told to choose her whom you
want as a wife you must search in the crowd and you will find a very ugly
maid—uglier than you can imagine—sitting apart on an observation
platform; it is her you must choose. She is called Sogolon Kedjou, or
Sogolon Kondouto, because she is a hunchback. You will choose her for
she is my wraith. She will be an extraordinary woman if you manage to
possess her. Promise me you will choose her, hunter.' I swore to, sol-
emnly, between the hands of the old woman, and we continued on our
way. The plain of Ourantamba was half a day's journey from there. On
the way we saw hunters who were fleeing and who watched us quite
dumbfounded. The buffalo was at the other end of the plain but when it
saw us it charged with menacing horns. I did as the old woman had told
me and killed the buffalo. I cut off its tail and we went back to the town
of Do as night was falling, but we did not go before the king until
morning came. The king had the drums beaten and before midday all
the inhabitants of the country were gathered in the main square. The
mutilated carcass of the buffalo had been placed in the middle of the
square and the delirious crowd abused it, while our names were sung in a
thousand refrains. When the king appeared a deep silence settled on the
crowd. 'I promised the hand of the most beautiful maiden in Do to the
brave hunter who saved us from the scourge which overwhelmed us.
The buffalo of Do is dead and here is the hunter who has killed it. I am a
man of my word. Hunter, here are all the daughters of Do; take your
pick.' And the crowd showed its approval by a great cheer. On that day
all the daughters of Do wore their festive dress; gold shone in their hair
and fragile wrists bent under the weight of heavy silver bracelets. Never
did so much beauty come together in one place. Full of pride, my quiver
on my back, I swaggered before the beautiful girls of Do who were
smiling at me, with their teeth as white as the rice of Mali. But I remem-

bered the words of the old woman. I went round the great circle many times until at last I saw Sogolon Kedjou sitting apart on a raised platform. I elbowed my way through the crowd, took Sogolon by the hand and drew her into the middle of the circle. Showing her to the king, I said, 'Oh King Gnemo Diarra, here is the one I have chosen from among the young maids of Do; it is her I would like for a wife.' The choice was so paradoxical that the king could not help laughing, and then general laughter broke out and the people split their sides with mirth. They took me for a fool, and I became a ludicrous hero. 'You've got to belong to the tribe of Traoré to do things like that,' said somebody in the crowd, and it was thus that my brother and I left Do the very same day pursued by the mockery of the Kondés."

The hunter ended his story and the noble king Naré Maghan determined to solemnize his marriage with all the customary formalities so that nobody could dispute the rights of the son to be born to him. The two hunters were considered as being relatives of Sogolon and it was to them that Gnankouman Doua bore the traditional cola nuts. By agreement with the hunters the marriage was fixed for the first Wednesday of the new moon. The twelve villages of old Mali and all the peoples allied to them were acquainted with this and on the appointed day delegations flocked from all sides to Nianiba, the town of Maghan Kon Fatta.

51. A TRAVELER'S TALE OF AFRICA

Buzurg ibn Shahriyār

This Muslim traveler's tale from the tenth century describes the contacts between the center of the Islamic world and the east coast of Africa. In this case, we are told of an African King of the Zanj (modern Kenya) who was taken prisoner by Muslim traders and brought to the capital of the Abbasid Caliphate at Baghdad. He then went on the pilgrimage to Mecca, returning to his people by way of Egypt. (If you trace his route on a map, you will be following important Muslim trade routes.)

The tale suggests one of the ways Islam may have spread to East Africa. No doubt there were more systematic ways as well, including conquest. Often the traders, especially those who bought slaves, operated beyond the expanding sphere of the armies. Once a population had been converted to Islam, they could not be taken as slaves. By the

*end of the Abbasid Caliphate (A.D. 1250), the Muslim trading cities on
the East African coast were important centers of African Muslim learning
and culture.*

What does the tale suggest about the impact of Islam on East Africa?

Ismāʿīlūya and several sailors told me that he had sailed from ʿUmān on
board his ship bound for Qanbaluh in the year 310 [922–923], but the
ship was carried off course by a violent wind and taken to Sufāla in the
land of the Zanj. "When I had examined the place," said the ship's
captain, "I realized that we had come to the land of the man-eating Zanj
and that to land in this place was certain death. We therefore made our
ablution, repented of our sins to Almighty God, and recited the prayer
for the dead for one another. Canoes surrounded us and led us to an
anchorage, where we entered, cast anchor, and went ashore with these
people. They took us to their king. We found a young man, handsome
for a Zanji and well-built. He asked us about ourselves, and we told him
that our destination was his country. 'You lie,' he said, 'you were bound
for Qanbaluh and not here. The storm caught you and carried you to
our country.' 'It is so,' we said, 'but we spoke as we did only in order to
please you.' 'Unload your goods,' he said, 'and carry on your trade. You
have nothing to fear.' We therefore opened our bales and did very good
business. He imposed no tax on us, in kind or in cash, and when we gave
him some presents, he gave us presents of equal or greater value.

"We stayed in his country for several months, and when it was time to
go, we asked his permission, which he gave us. We therefore loaded our
goods and wound up our business, and when we decided to leave, we
informed him. Rising from his throne, he walked with us as far as the
shore with a group of his companions and his slaves, embarked on a
canoe, and came aboard our ship with us. He came on board with seven
of his chief slaves. When they were on board ship I said to myself, 'This
king would be worth 30 dinars at auction at ʿUmān and his seven slaves
160 dinars. They are wearing clothes worth 20 dinars, which would
bring us at least 3,000 dirhams—and this would do us no harm at all.' So
I shouted to the sailors, and they hoisted the sail and raised the anchors
while he was still expressing his friendship and goodwill and inviting us
to return and promising to treat us well when we did so.

"When the sails were hoisted and he saw that we were on our way, his
face changed. 'You are leaving,' he said. 'I bid you farewell,' and he rose
to go back to his canoe. But we cut the cable joining us to the canoe, and
we said to him, 'You will stay with us and we will take you to our country
and reward you for your kindness to us and repay you for what you have
done for us.' 'Good people,' he cried. 'When you came to me I could, as
my people desired, have let them eat you and take your goods, as they
did to others. But I treated you well; I took nothing from you and even
came to bid you farewell on your ship as a mark of esteem from me to

you. Therefore give me my due and take me home.' We paid no attention to what he said and took no notice of him. The wind was strong, and before very long his country disappeared from sight, and by nightfall we were in the open sea. The king and his companions were put with the other slaves, about 200 head, and we treated him in the same way as the other slaves. He kept aloof and neither answered nor spoke to us. He ignored us as if he did not know us, nor we him. When we got to 'Umān, we sold him and his companions along with the other slaves.

"In the year 31, we again left 'Umān bound for Qanbaluh, and the wind carried us away to Sufāla in the land of the Zanj, and without telling any lies, we arrived at the very same place. As soon as the people saw us, they came out and their canoes surrounded us. This time we really were convinced that we were lost, and we none of us said a word to one another, so great was our fear. We made our ablution, recited the prayer for the dead, and bade each other farewell.

"They came, seized us, brought us to the dwelling of their king and led us in—and there was the very same king, seated on his throne as if we had left him but a moment before. When we saw him, we fell prostrate and our strength left us, so that we could not move ourselves to stand up. 'You are my friends,' he said, 'no doubt about it.' None of us could speak, and all our limbs trembled. 'Look up,' he said. 'I give you my pledge of safety for your persons and your property.' Some of us looked up; others could not, through weakness and shame. But he spoke to us in a friendly way until we all raised our heads. We did not look at him, in our shame and fear.

"When, thanks to his promise of safety, we had recovered our composure, he said to us, 'Betrayers! I treated you as I did, and you repaid me by treating me as you did!' 'Despise us, O King,' we cried, 'and forgive us.' 'I have already forgiven you,' he replied. 'Carry on your trade as you did that time; there is nothing to stop you.'

"Our joy was such that we could not believe what we heard, and we thought that this was a trick to get our goods ashore. We brought them ashore, and we offered him a present of great value, but he refused it, and said, 'I have not enough regard for you to accept a present from you, nor do I wish to render my own possessions unlawful by taking anything from you, for all that you possess is tainted.'

"We therefore carried on our trade, and when it was time to go, we asked his permission to load the ship, which he gave us. When we had decided to set sail I said, 'O King, we have decided to sail.' And he replied, 'Go under the protection of God.' 'O King,' I said. 'You have treated us better than we could ever repay, and we betrayed and wronged you. But how did you manage to escape and return home?'

" 'When you had sold me in 'Umān,' he said, 'the man who bought me took me to a town called Basra' (which he described). 'There I learned prayer, fasting, and also a little of the Qur'ān. Then my master sold me to another who took me to the city of the king of the Arabs which is called Baghdad' (then he described Baghdad), 'where I learned to speak correct Arabic, learned the Qur'ān, and prayed with everybody in the mosques. I saw the Caliph who is called al-Muqtadir.[1] I stayed in Baghdad for a whole year and part of the next year. Then some people came from Khurāsān, mounted on camels. Seeing their great number, I asked who they were and why they had come, and they said they were on their way to Mecca. I then asked, "What is this Mecca?" And they said, "In it is the holy house of God, to which people go on pilgrimage," and they told me about this house. I said to myself, "I must follow these people to this house" and I told my master what I had heard, but I saw that he wished neither to go himself nor to let me go. I therefore pretended to think no more of it until the people had left, and when they did so I followed them and accompanied a group of travelers whom I served all the way. I ate with them, and they gave me two garments which I wore as the ritual dress of a pilgrim. They instructed me in the rites of the pilgrimage, and Almighty God helped me to complete my pilgrimage.

" 'Fearing to return to Baghdad, where my master would catch me and put me to death, I left with another caravan bound for Egypt. On the way I served some people, who took me with them and gave me a share in their provisions as far as Egypt.

" 'When I reached Egypt and saw this sea of sweet water which they call the Nile, I asked whence it came and they told me that its source lay in the land of the Zanj. "And in what part?" I asked. "In a part of Egypt," they said, "which is called Aswān, on the border of the land of the black people." So I followed the bank of the Nile, going from place to place, begging from people, and they fed me. Such was my way.

" 'Then I came among some black people who turned against me. They put me in chains and burdened me, along with other slaves, with more than I had the strength to bear. So I fled and fell into the hands of others who seized me and sold me. I fled again, and so I went on, from the time I left Egypt until I reached a certain place in the land of the Zanj.

" 'There I disguised and hid myself, for from the time when I left Egypt, in spite of all my terrifying experiences, I was never so much afraid as when I found myself now near to my own country. In my own country, I thought, another king would have gained the kingship and would be sitting in my place. The soldiers would obey him, and it would be hard to wrest the kingship from him. If I showed myself or if anyone got to know of me, I would be taken to him and he would put me to death, or else some loyal supporter would make bold to cut off my head and use it to show his loyalty.

" 'I was frightened beyond endurance. I began to hide by day and hurry by night in the direction of my country, until I reached the seashore. There I took passage in disguise on a ship to such and such a

---

1. Reigned 908–932.

place. Then I embarked again for another place, and the ship landed me at night on the shore of my own country. I made enquiries of an old woman, "Is your present reigning king just?" I asked. "By God, my son," she answered, "we have no king other than Almighty God." And she told me everything that had happened to their king. I expressed my astonishment as if I knew nothing about it and as if I were not myself that king. Then she said, "The people of the kingdom agreed among themselves that they would not have any king after him until they knew what had happened to him and until they despaired of his life, for their diviners had informed them that he was alive and well in the land of the Arabs."

" 'The next morning I came to this my town and entered this my palace and found my family just as I had left them, except they were full of sadness, as were also my subjects. I told them my story, and they marveled and rejoiced and joined with me in entering the religion of Islam. I became their king again one month before your arrival and am now full of joy and happiness that God has blessed me and my subjects with Islam and true faith and with the knowledge of prayer, fasting, and pilgrimage, of what is permitted and what is forbidden. I have thus attained what was never before attained by anyone in the land of the Zanj. Therefore, I forgive you, since you were the cause of my coming to the true religion. There is only one other matter which weighs on me, and I ask God to release me from the sin.' I asked him what it was, and he said, 'My master. I left Baghdad for the pilgrimage without his permission or his consent, and I did not return to him. If I could find a reliable man I would send him the price which he paid for me and ask him to accord me my liberty. If you had been honest and trustworthy men, I would have paid you my purchase price and asked you to remit it to him, and I would have given him ten times more as a gift in return for the patience which he showed me. But you are men of treachery and cunning.'

"We bade him farewell, and he said, 'Go. And if you come again, I will treat you in the same way and even more generously. Tell the Muslims to come to us, for now we are their brothers, Muslims as they are. As for accompanying you on board, I prefer not.' We bade him farewell and left."

52. TRAVELS IN MALI

Ibn Battuta

The gold of Mali held a strong attraction for Muslim traders from North Africa. A grueling trade developed across the Sahara Desert in which salt from the desert salt beds was traded for Sudanese gold. The great traveler Ibn Battuta gives us an idea of his trade. He made the trip in 1352. He also gives us an insight into both North African attitudes toward blacks and life in Mali. What kind of things impress him most? In what ways does he add to our understanding of Mali?

At Sijilmasa[1] I bought camels and a four month's supply of forage for them. Thereupon I set out on the 1st Muharram of the year seven hundred and fifty-three (18th February 1352) with a caravan including, amongst others, a number of the merchants of Sijilmasa. After twenty-five days we reached Taghaza,[2] an unattractive village, with the curious feature that its houses and mosques are built of blocks of salt, roofed with camel skins. There are no trees there, nothing but sand. In the sand is a salt mine; they dig for the salt, and find it in thick slabs, lying one on top of the other, as though they had been tool-squared and laid under the surface of the earth. A camel will carry two of these slabs. No one lives at Taghaza except the slaves of the Masufa tribe, who dig for the salt; they subsist on dates imported from Dara[3] and Sijilmasa, camel's flesh, and millet imported from the Negrolands. The Negroes come up from their country and take away the salt from there. At Walata a load of salt brings eight to ten *mithqals;* in the town of Mali it sells for twenty to thirty, and sometimes as much as forty. The Negroes use salt as a medium of exchange, just as gold and silver is used elsewhere; they cut it up into pieces, and buy and sell with it. The business done at Taghaza, for all its meanness, amounts to an enormous figure in terms of hundredweights of gold dust. . . .

Thus we reached the town of Walata after a journey of two months to a day. Walata is the northernmost province of the Negroes, and the sultan's representative there was one Farba Husayn, *farba* meaning deputy (in their language). When we arrived there, the merchants deposited their goods in an open square, where the blacks undertook to guard them, and went to the *farba.* He was sitting on a carpet under an archway, with his guards before him carrying lances and bows in their hands, and the headman of the Masufa behind him. The merchants remained standing in front of him while he spoke to them through an interpreter, although they were close to him, to show his contempt for them.[4] It was then that I repented of having come to their country, because of their lack of manners and their contempt for the whites. . . .

Later on the *mushrif* (inspector) of Walata, whose name was Mansa Ju, invited all those who had come with the caravan to partake of his hospital-

1. Principal trading station south of the Atlas, near modern Tafilelt.
2. Important outpost of the Negro empires.
3. The Wadi Dra which drains the southern slopes of the anti-Atlas mountains.
4. It was common practice in West Africa for rulers to communicate only through the medium of an official "interpreter," who relayed the speech backward and forward. There was a similar practice at the Ethiopian court.

ity. At first I refused to attend, but my companions urged me very strongly, so I went with the rest. The repast was served—some pounded millet mixed with a little honey and milk, put in a half calabash shaped like a large bowl. The guests drank and retired, I said to them, "Was it for this that the black invited us?" They answered, "Yes; and it is in their opinion the highest form of hospitality." This convinced me that there was no good to be hoped for from these people, and I made up my mind to travel back to Morocco at once with the pilgrim caravan from Walata. Afterwards, however, I thought it best to go to see the capital of their king (at Mali). My stay at Walata lasted about fifty days; and I was shown honor and entertained by its inhabitants. It is an excessively hot place, and boasts a few small date-palms, in the shade of which they sow watermelons. Its water comes from underground water beds at that point, and there is plenty of mutton to be had. The garments of the inhabitants, most of whom belong to the Masufa tribe, are of fine Egyptian fabrics. Their women are of surpassing beauty, and are shown more respect than the men. The state of affairs amongst these people is indeed extraordinary. Their men show no sign of jealousy whatever; no one claims descent from his father, but on the contrary from his mother's brother. A person's heirs are his sister's sons, not his own sons. This is a thing which I have seen nowhere in the world except among the Indians of Malabar. But those are heathens; *these* people are Muslims, punctilious in observing the hours of prayer, studying books of law, and memorizing the Koran. Yet their women show no bashfulness before men and do not veil themselves, though they are assiduous in attending prayers. Any man who wishes to marry one of them may do so, but they do not travel with their husbands, and, even if one desired to do so, her family would not allow her to go.

The women have their "friends" and "companions" amongst the men outside their own families, and the men in the same way have "companions" amongst the women of other families. A man may go into his house and find his wife entertaining her "companion" but he takes no objection to it. One day at Walata I went into the qadi's[5] house, after asking his permission to enter, and found with him a young woman of remarkable beauty. When I saw her I was shocked and turned to go out, but she laughed at me, instead of being overcome by shame, and the qadi said to me, "Why are you going out? She is my companion." I was amazed at their conduct, for he was a theologian and a pilgrim to boot. I was told that he had asked the sultan's permission to make the pilgrimage that year with his "companion" (whether this one or not I cannot say) but the sultan would not grant it.

When I decided to make the journey to Mali, which is reached in twenty-four days from Walata if the traveler pushes on rapidly, I hired a

---

5. Qadi: a Muslim judge.

guide from the Masufa (for there is no necessity to travel in company on account of the safety of that road), and set out with three of my companions. On the way there are many trees, and these trees are of great age and girth; a whole caravan may shelter in the shade of one of them. There are trees[6] which have neither branches nor leaves, yet the shade cast by their trunks is sufficient to shelter a man. Some of these trees are rotted in the interior and the rain water collects in them, so that they serve as wells, and the people drink of the water inside them. In others there are bees and honey, which is collected by the people. I was surprised to find inside one tree, by which I passed, a man, a weaver, who had set up his loom in it and was actually weaving.

A traveler in this country carries no provisions, whether plain food or seasonings, and neither gold nor silver. He takes nothing but pieces of salt and glass ornaments, which the people call beads, and some aromatic goods. When he comes to a village the women-folk of the blacks bring out millet, milk, chickens, pulped lotus fruit, rice, *funi* (a grain resembling mustard seed, from which *kuskusu*[7] and gruel are made), and pounded haricot beans. The traveler buys what of these he wants, but their rice causes sickness to whites when it is eaten, and the *funi* is preferable to it. . . .

Ten days after leaving Walata we came to the village of Zaghari, a large village, inhabited by Negro traders called *wanjarati,*[8] along with whom live a community of whites of the Ibadite sect. It is from this village that the millet is carried to Walata. After leaving Zaghari we came to the great river that is the Nile,[9] on which stands the town of Karsakhu. The Nile flows from there down to Kabara, and thence to Zagha. In both Kabara and Zagha there are sultans who owe allegiance to the king of Mali. The inhabitants of Zagha are of old standing in Islam; they show a great devotion and zeal for study. Thence the Nile descends to Timbuktu and Gao, both of which will be described later; then to the town of Muli in the land of the Limis, which is the frontier province of (the kingdom of) Mali; thence to Nupe, one of the largest towns of the Negroes, whose ruler is one of the most considerable of the Negro rulers. It cannot be visited by any white man because they would kill him before he got there. . . .

I saw a crocodile in this part of the Nile, close to the bank; it looked just like a small boat. One day I went down to the river to satisfy a need, and lo, one of the blacks came and stood between me and the river. I was amazed at such lack of manners and decency on his part, and spoke of it to someone or other. He answered, "His purpose in doing that was solely to protect you from the crocodile, by placing himself between you and it."

6. Baobab trees.
7. Cereal dish of Northwest Africa made from coarsely ground flour.
8. Wangara traders from Mali.
9. It was, of course, not the Nile but the Niger.

We set out thereafter from Karsakhu and came to the river of Sansara, which is about ten miles from Mali. It is their custom that no persons except those who have obtained permission are allowed to enter the city. I had already written to the white community (there) requesting them to hire a house for me, so when I arrived at the river, I crossed by the ferry without interference. Thus I reached the city of Mali, the capital of the king of the blacks. . . .

The sultan of Mali is Mansa Sulayman, *mansa* meaning (in Mande) sultan, and Sulayman being his proper name. He is a miserly king, not a man from who one might hope for a rich present. . . .

On certain days the sultan holds audiences in the palace yard, where there is a platform under a tree, with three steps; this they call the *pempi*. It is carpeted with silk, and has cushions placed on it. (Over it) is raised the umbrella, which is a sort of pavilion made of silk, surmounted by a bird of gold, about the size of a falcon. The sultan comes out of a door in a corner of the palace, carrying a bow in his hand and a quiver on his back. On his head he has a golden skullcap, bound with a gold band which has narrow ends shaped like knives, more than a span in length. His usual dress is a velvety red tunic, made of the European fabrics called *mutanfas*. The sultan is preceded by his musicians, who carry gold and silver *gumbris* (two-stringed guitars), and behind him come three hundred armed slaves. He walks in a leisurely fashion, affecting a very slow movement, and even stops from time to time. On reaching the *pempi* he stops and looks round the assembly, then ascends it in the sedate manner of a preacher ascending a mosque pulpit. As he takes his seat the drums, trumpets, and bugles are sounded. Three slaves go out at a run to summon the sovereign's deputy and the military commanders, who enter and sit down. Two saddled and bridled horses are brought, along with two goats, which they hold to serve as a protection against the evil eye. Dugha stands at the gate, and the rest of the people remain in the street under the trees.

The Negroes are, of all people, the most submissive to their king and the most abject in their behavior before him. They swear by his name, saying, "Mansa Sulayman ki."[10] If he summons any of them while he is holding an audience in the pavilion, the person summoned takes off his clothes and puts on worn garments, removes his turban and dons a dirty skullcap, and enters with his garments and trousers raised knee-high. He goes forward in an attitude of humility and dejection, and knocks the ground hard with his elbows, then stands with bowed head and bent back listening to what he says. If anyone addresses the king and receives a reply from him, he uncovers his back and throws dust over his head and back, for all the world like a bather splashing himself with water. I used to wonder how it was they did not blind themselves. If the sultan delivers any remarks during his audience, those present take off their turbans

10. "The Emperor Sulayman has commanded," in Mandingo.

and put them down, and listen to what he says. Sometimes one of them stands up before him and recalls his deeds in the sultan's service, saying "I did so-and-so on such a day," or, "I killed so-and-so on such a day." Those who have knowledge of this confirm his words, which they do by plucking the cord of the bow and releasing it with a twang, just as an archer does when shooting an arrow. If the sultan says, "Truly spoken," or thanks him, he removes his clothes and "dusts." That is their idea of good manners. . . .

I was at Mali during the two festivals of the sacrifice and the fast-breaking. On these days the sultan takes his seat on the *pempi* after the mid-afternoon prayer. The armor-bearers bring in magnificent arms— quivers of gold and silver, swords ornamented with gold and with golden scabbards, gold and silver lances, and crystal maces. At his head stand four *amirs* driving off the flies, having in their hands silver ornaments resembling saddle stirrups. The commanders, qadi, and preacher sit in their usual places. The interpreter Dugha comes with his four wives and his slave-girls, who are about a hundred in number. They are wearing beautiful robes, and on their heads they have gold and silver fillets, with gold and silver balls attached. A chair is placed for Dugha to sit on. He plays on an instrument made of reeds, with some small calabashes at its lower end, and chants a poem in praise of the sultan, recalling his battles and deeds of valor. The women and girls sing along with him and play with bows. Accompanying them are about thirty youths, wearing red woolen tunics and white skullcaps; each of them has a drum slung from his shoulder and beats it. Afterward come his boy pupils who play and turn wheels in the air, like the natives of Sind. They show a marvelous nimbleness and agility in these exercises, and play most cleverly with swords. Dugha makes a fine play with the sword. Thereupon the sultan orders a gift to be presented to Dugha and he is given a purse containing two hundred *mithqals* of gold dust, and is informed of the contents of the purse before all the people. The commanders rise and twang their bows in thanks to the sultan. The next day each one of them gives Dugha a gift, every man according to his rank. Every Friday after the *'asr* prayer, Dugha carries out a similar ceremony to this that we have described.

On feast-days, after Dugha has finished his display, the poets come in. Each of them is inside a figure resembling a thrush, made of feathers, and provided with a wooden head with a red beak, to look like a thrush's head. They stand in front of the sultan in this ridiculous make-up and recite their poems. I was told that their poetry is a kind of sermonizing in which they say to the sultan: "This *pempi* which you occupy was that whereon sat this king and that king, and such were this one's noble actions and such and such the other's. So do you too do good deeds whose memory will outlive you." After that the chief of the poets mounts the steps of the *pempi* and lays his head on the sultan's lap, then climbs to the top of the *pempi* and lays his head first on the sultan's right shoulder and then on his left, speaking all the while in their tongue, and finally he comes down again. I was told that this practice is a very old custom amongst them, prior to the introduction of Islam, and that they have kept it up.

The Negroes disliked Mansa Sulayman because of his avarice. His predecessor was Mansa Magha, and before him reigned Mansa Musa, a generous and virtuous prince, who loved the whites and made gifts to them. It was he who gave Ibn Ishaq as-Sahili four thousand *mithqals* in the course of a single day. I heard from a truthworthy source that he gave three thousand *mithqals* on one day to Mudrik ibn Faqqus, by whose grandfather his own grandfather, Saraq Jata, had been converted to Islam.

The Negroes possess some admirable qualities. They are seldom unjust, and have a greater abhorrence of injustice than any other people. The sultan shows no mercy to anyone who is guilty of the least act of it. There is complete security in their country. Neither traveler nor inhabitant in it has anything to fear from robbers or men of violence. They do not confiscate the property of any white man who dies in their country, even if it be accounted wealth. On the contrary, they give it into the charge of some trustworthy person among the whites, until the rightful heir takes possession of it. They are careful to observe the hours of prayer, and assiduous in attending them in congregations, and in bringing up their children to them. On Fridays, if a man does not go early to the mosque, he cannot find a corner to pray in, on account of the crowd. It is a custom of theirs to send each man his boy (to the mosque) with his prayer-mat; the boy spreads it out for his master in a place befitting him and remains on it (until his master comes to the mosque). The prayer-mats are made of the leaves of a tree resembling a date-palm, but without fruit.

Another of their good qualities is their habit of wearing clean white garments on Fridays. Even if a man has nothing but an old worn shirt, he washes it and cleans it, and wears it at the Friday service. Yet another is their zeal for learning the Koran by heart. They put their children in chains if they show any backwardness in memorizing it, and they are not set free until they have it by heart. I visited the qadi in his house on the day of the festival. His children were chained up, so I said to him, "Will you not let them loose?" He replied, "I shall not do so until they learn the Koran by heart." Among their bad qualities are the following. The women servants, slave-girls, and young girls go about in front of everyone naked, without a stitch of clothing on them. Women go into the sultan's presence naked and without coverings, and his daughters also go about naked. Then there is the custom of their putting dust and ashes on their heads as a mark of respect, and the grotesque ceremonies we have described when the poets recite their verses. Another reprehensible practice among many of them is the eating of carrion, dogs, and asses.

53. AFRICAN LAW

Paul Bohannan and Philip Curtin

Traditional Africa contained wealthy centralized states like Mali, Ghana, and Songhai. It also contained stateless societies in which clans and villages were largely self-governing. In this modern account by Paul Bohannan, an anthropologist, and Philip Curtin, a historian, we get a sense of how traditional African law worked in stateless societies as well as states. How are stateless societies different from states in their law and courts? What are the relative advantages of each?

Although many references to warfare among African societies are found in travel books, in historical source materials, and even in ethnographic accounts, there is no study of warfare in Africa that pretends to tie that information together. With law, that other primary political function, the situation is far different. The written material on African law is extensive; although much of it written by Europeans is uncomprehending restatement of substantive norms as legal rules—the pigeonholes of common law filled with exotic fauna—there is nevertheless a substantial body of knowledge about African law.

Indeed, Africa is one of the homes of advanced legal institutions. Perhaps the most famous of these institutions are the courts still found among the Bantu states of the southern third of the continent. Here the local or provincial chief was one of a number of judges on a large and inclusive bench. The bench included representatives of all the important social groups of the community, whether in any particular case they were seen as territorial segments and communities, as kinship units such as clans, or even as age-sets. The judges formed a regular and pronounced hierarchy, and were seated in a row or an arc. The provincial chief sat in the middle; at his immediate right was the second most senior person (however seniority might be computed locally) and at his left the third most senior. To his right, but farther removed, the fourth most senior, and so on, right and left, until the whole court was deployed more or less in a row.

There were, then, certain areas in which the litigants were to stand or, more often, sit on the ground. There were assigned places for witnesses, for the nobility, for the followers and backers of the litigants, and for the community as an audience. These court sessions were often held out of doors, but there might be a building for them—colonial governments preferred them inside so that regular schedules, based on clock and calendar time, could be maintained even in the face of hostile weather.

There was, in all cases, also a known, and demanded, decorum and order of proceedings. The plaintiff (to use an English term with only a 90 percent fit) made his plea—usually without counsel—and was usually allowed to finish his whole complaint, so long as he spoke well and to the point. The defendant (another translation that does not fit precisely) then made a reply and told his version of the story. Witnesses were called—including what we would call expert witnesses and character witnesses. Then, after the principals had each told his side of the dispute, and after witnesses had been heard, the most junior member of the bench, down at the far end, pronounced sentence. His statements probably included moral lectures, statements of the proper kind of behavior that should have been carried out in the situation, and he may have cited precedent. His judgment would be followed by that of the man at the other end of the line, his immediate senior, who might disagree, and who added new views and new opinions. The third most junior man followed, and so on until they arrived at the middle where the head chief pronounced the final sentence. He had heard everything that the representatives of the community had to say. He had a chance to weigh the evidence, the judgments, and the opinions of his junior judges. His word on the decision became final.

In the southern Bantu states, there were also well-known and highly effective means for carrying out the decisions of the court. The community, having been represented in the audience as well as on the bench, brought both sacred and mundane sanctions to bear. The decisions of such courts were obeyed. Indeed, such communities might be reasonably said to have a "body of law" or *corpus juris* in the lawyer's sense—a body of law and adjudged precedent against which to try each succeeding case:

Law in a stateless society was almost as effective but worked differently. Each case became a treaty-making process. The difference between the two is vital, because in the treaty-making process, the role of precedent is far less commanding and the application of sanction far more diffuse. Indeed, the fact that a solution has been used before may be the very thing about it that a case sets out to overcome.

The difference can best be seen from an examination of our own family law. The norms of family living in modern America are fairly well known and fairly circumscribed. The institutionalization of families is such that these norms are fairly well maintained. A very few of these norms are *restated* for legal purposes: the grounds for divorce, the laws against beating children, and perhaps some others. The large range of family activity is not in any wise made part of a body of *law*, in the narrow sense. The mistake of assuming a body of law in an African stateless society is precisely the same mistake as would be the error of reporting all of the norms for living displayed by the American family as if those norms were part of the law of the land.

In order to comprehend African legal systems fully, then, it becomes necessary to have a new theoretical framework: one which is inclusive of both the law of a state system and that of stateless societies. Such a framework is particularly necessary when we investigate the ways in which the stateless societies are changing on the demand first of the colonial governments and now of the independent governments. These people, who are adapting to state forms on demand, often experience severe difficulty because they see law based on precedent as always and necessarily tyrannous.

There is seldom if ever a special body constituted in order to hear and settle disputes in stateless societies. Rather these disputes are settled by meetings that can be profitably compared with the old New England town meetings, except that in the case of the African stateless societies, there are always two factions and the actual size of the unit may change from case to case depending on the closeness of the relationship of the principals to the dispute.

There is, in Old English, a precise and accurate word to describe these "town meetings" or settlement of disputes by the important members of the village. This word is "moot." Well into the twelfth and thirteenth centuries Anglo-Saxon communities settled their disputes by meeting outside, under the shade of a tree, in whole communities, in order to discover correct and just solutions to disputes. Such is, in a sense, the origin of the "common law."

Courts, unlike moots, are special organs and require some sort of state organization from which they derive their power. While moots are a mode of the community, courts are special arms of politically organized states.

Moots and courts can, and in Africa often do, exist side by side within the same society. The jurisdiction of the courts may be limited to certain types of cases or to disputes of people of different villages or something of the sort. Vansina has given an extremely cogent example from the Luba of the Congo. The Luba state has a very complex court system, the personnel of which changes with the nature of the dispute or offense; at the same time, however, many Luba cases are settled by moots rather than by courts.

During the colonial era, and undoubtedly down to the present day, such stateless societies as that of the Tiv had a full-blown system of moots which ran side by side with the system of courts that had been introduced by the colonial government. Among these people it was considered to be totally immoral to call one's close kinsman before a government court. However, disputes obviously did occur between close kinsmen. These disputes were always and necessarily settled in moots. In colonial Nigeria charges of witchcraft could not be brought before courts, since "proof" had to be adduced or else the accused could sue the accuser for slander. Since witchcraft is difficult to "prove" in a court, witchcraft disputes had throughout the country to be settled either in moots or in kangaroo courts.

There were devices other than courts and moots by which Africans sometimes settled disputes. Ordeals and recourse to seers and diviners were both fairly widely spread throughout the continent. An ordeal is a means for settling a dispute in the absence of any kind of evidence which can prove or disprove the charge, either because there are no witnesses or because (as in the case of witchcraft) empirical proof is impossible.

Probably no people claims that oracles and ordeals have anything to do with justice. However, they do settle the dispute. Ordeals ran all the way from taking oaths on shrines through the deliberate administration of poisonous substances either to animals or to human beings themselves. These substances were not necessarily lethal, and if the animals or the person did not die, the party was usually considered innocent. Some tribes such as the Azande of the Sudan checked and counterchecked their oracular mechanisms by requiring corroboration by a second oracle before they would act on them. Ordeals have all but disappeared from modern Euro-American courts. However, the divine sanctions in which ordeals deal are still a part of such courts because it is still necessary for both witnesses and the principals to take oaths on entering the witness stand.

Africans sometimes resorted to contests to settle disputes. This "game" solution to a dispute is one in which the disputants are either forced to or agree to reduce the field of relevance, and determine a winner; they reopen the field and declare the winner in the game to be the winner of the real-life situation. In the early history of Roman law and others, gladiatorial contests to settle disputes were not unknown.

Perhaps the most important of the sanctions, particularly in the stateless societies, was the institutionalized use of self-help (an example of which is the man who takes a goat from another man who legitimately owes him one). Some degree of self-help is either condoned or required in all legal systems. It becomes even more important in non-state organizations than it is in states because the major sanction, and the power behind it, is to be found in the right and ability of the groups concerned to carry out the decisions made by the elders.

If self-help gets out of hand it becomes, of course, akin to lawlessness— in any sort of society. The boundaries have to be fixed and the use of self-help contained if it is to be an adequate judicial mechanism. In states, such limitations can be defined by legislation or by precedent. In non-states, self-help is controlled, but controlled somewhat differently. In our example of the man taking the goat, his own group will come to his defense if the others try to retaliate. However, if he takes the goat irrationally, and in a way that they believe the moot would not approve of—if he has a "bad case," or if he is a criminal—his kinfolk will not risk their hides and their reputation for him. Limitation is achieved by balance of power and of organizational principles.

Africans in every part of the continent have proved themselves capable of running complex modern governments. The basic ideas behind the political thinking of many of their citizens, however, are still to be found in the type of situation that has been described here.

On the surface, African institutions are changing very rapidly, but the quickening ideas, molded by experience and language, have deep roots in African tradition and history. Because the deep roots of both African and European tradition tap the same prehistoric reserves, and because Africans have passed through most of the cultural revolutions which have, perhaps in other terms, also been the experience of the West, their adaptation has been fast and successful. For all that, however, the distinct idiom in many instances remains. Whatever trouble Africans and Europeans may have in discussing matters with one another in the postcolonial world, much at least is attributable to the fact that they make different political assumptions.

CHAPTER SIXTEEN

American Civilizations

54. THE SECRETS OF THE MAYA DECODED

Erik Eckholm

The elaborate picture writing of the Maya is finally being translated, and it reveals a darker side to Maya culture than had previously been imagined. This is the subject of the following article from the New York Times.

What is the "darker side" of Maya culture revealed in the translation of the writings? Why was the decoding of Maya script so difficult? What were some of the achievements of Maya culture? What were some of its less attractive features? What questions about the Maya still remain?

Cascading advances in the interpretation of ancient Maya hieroglyphs have extended the written history of the New World back more than 2,000 years, creating the Americas' first written record from the age before the European invasions.

With the Maya script deciphered, the bare, often faulty sketch of their culture drawn from the study of pyramids and temples can finally be fleshed out with real people and real events. Long placed on a mist-shrouded pedestal as austere, peaceful stargazers, the Maya elites are now known to have been the rulers of populous, aggressive city-states. They had a penchant for self-mutilation, warfare and protracted torture of captives.

If their new image is less romantic, it is also more human, scholars are quick to assert. The Maya displayed the full range of human propensities, brilliant and dark.

"The written history of the Americas began in 50 B.C., and from that moment on it resounds with the names and lives of individuals: Pacal of Palenque, Bird Jaguar of Yaxchilán, Yax-Pac of Copán, among many others," according to Linda Schele of the University of Texas and Mary Ellen Miller of Yale University.

The Maya, whose civilization arose in steamy jungles of Mexico and Central America after 300 B.C. and then flowered from the second to the ninth centuries, are now joining the Egyptians and Assyrians as ancient civilizations who speak to modern society through written text as well as mute artifacts.

"I look forward to the day when third-graders will learn Pacal's name along with that of Tutankhamen or Alexander the Great," Dr. Schele, an art historian and hieroglyphic expert, added in an interview.

The otherworldly stone monuments, the intricate script and drawings and the astonishing astronomical feats of the Maya have mesmerized generations of scholars and amateur Maya buffs alike. But in the absence of historical accounts, the pictures drawn of Maya culture mirrored the souls of the observers as much as those of the ancients.

Today, Maya studies are in the throes of a revolutionary change in perspective. The messages left by Maya rulers in the form of elegant symbols and images on stone slabs and temple walls have been decoded at an escalating pace in recent years.

"Before, it was a one-sided conversation with rocks and dirt," said David Freidel, an anthropologist at Southern Methodist University in Dallas. "While sweating and swatting at mosquitoes we glared at rocks, trying to give them some humanity."

"Now," Dr. Freidel went on, "the Maya can talk back, telling us about their families, their politics, their wars. Human beings are there."

The new history has debunked many myths. Until recently, many scholars thought the great clusters of pyramids and temples housed peaceful students of the stars and the calendar, who served as aloof priests to scattered populations of primitive farmers. Now it is clear that the temples were built to the glory of kings and sometimes queens who ruled bustling cities of tens of thousands.

Warfare with rival cities was frequent, in large part to capture aristocrats for torture and sacrifice. If the Maya sacrificed humans in lesser numbers than the Aztecs, against whom they have often been held up as superior, they tortured their victims more viciously. Ancient ball games, like Roman gladiatorial contests, pitted captives against one another for their lives; the heads of losers were sometimes used for balls.

"Blood was the mortar of ancient Maya ritual life," Dr. Schele and Dr. Miller wrote in "The Blood of Kings." On important occasions, Maya aristocrats drew their own blood in rituals, designed to nourish the gods or to inspire hallucinations of serpents through which they contacted the gods and the dead. Before going to war, for example, the king would puncture his penis with a stingray spine, while his wife drew a thorn-barbed rope through her tongue. The Maya believed such activities were vital for sustaining the universe.

Evidence of these darker practices has been available for decades in the Maya's stone reliefs and paintings, observed Dr. Miller, an art historian, but scholars "seemed to blind themselves to it." A picture of a man squirming under the foot of another may have been interpreted as religious symbolism rather than the suffering of a war captive, for example.

"It's almost as if people were trying to protect Maya history from itself," Dr. Miller said.

Although the earliest known written document from the Maya, of a king's accession, was carved onto stone in 50 B.C., the culture's golden era dates from around A.D. 200, just as the Barbarian invasions of the Roman Empire in Europe were beginning. In an extraordinary, unexplained efflorescence, the Maya built graceful stone pyramids and temples in at least 40 cities of more than 20,000 people each. They practiced advanced irrigation methods, honed their astronomy and mathematics and elaborated their script. Then, just as mysteriously, the civilization collapsed around A.D. 900.

Estimates of the peak Maya population range from one million to three million. In the 16th century, the Spaniards conquered a smaller, less-advanced populace. Today, about two million descendants speak assorted Mayan languages in Mexico and Guatemala. Although some still practice ancient rites, essential details of the classical society lay buried in jungle ruins for a thousand years.

With the uncoding of hieroglyphs, "Maya civilization has crossed the threshold from prehistory to history," said Robert J. Sharer, an archeologist at the University of Pennsylvania. "The study of the ancient Maya is undergoing the same profound change that occurred in Egyptian and Mesopotamian studies with the decipherments of hieroglyphic and cuneiform scripts in the 19th century."

The Maya script is one of only five basic writing systems ever developed. The others are Chinese, Harappan, Egyptian and Sumerian, from which the script now used for Western languages was derived.

SYMBOLS FOR SOUNDS AND IDEAS

The Maya hieroglyphs are a mixed system of phonetic symbols, standing for units of sound, and ideographs, standing for words. Some of the ideographs, such as the ones for bat, fish, hand and certain birds, are recognizable renderings, according to Christopher Jones, a hieroglyph specialist at the University of Pennsylvania. Most [hieroglyphs] are more stylized and baffling.

The same word could be written phonetically or with an ideograph. Hence the name of Pacal, a great 7th-century king of Palenque, was sometimes written with the ideograph for shield, pronounced "pacal" in Mayan, and sometimes with a combination of the three syllables "pa," "ca" and "la." (The last vowel of the last syllable is dropped.)

Interpreters of Maya hieroglyphs have not enjoyed the benefit of a Rosetta Stone. While the sketchy notes of a 16th-century Spanish friar gave scholars a start, the notes also had incorrect information. Three surviving astrological texts written on bark paper, called codices, aided decipherment of numbers and dates.

But progress was slow. Through the 1950's, according to Dr. Jones, scholars debated such basic questions as whether any symbols were phonetic and whether they described actual events or were observations about religion and astronomy.

The breakthrough came in a 1960 paper by Tatiana Proskouriakoff of the Carnegie Institute. She demonstrated that the hieroglyphs documented, in predictable sequences, the life histories of Maya rulers.

This opened the floodgates. The existence of phonetic symbols, for example, was proved when a name such as Pacal was written phonetically at points where it was clear his name should appear. More and more ideographs could be deciphered through their context.

By now, perhaps 80 percent of the hundreds of hieroglyphs have been interpreted, but more important, observed Dr. Freidel, "we have a methodology for translation."

"EXPONENTIAL" PROGRESS

"We have the syntax," he said. "We know where the verbs, the objects, the subjects are, and we know the punctuation."

"Every day now we're making new translations," Dr. Freidel added. "The progress is exponential."

The discovery that real people were depicted in the artwork meant that biographical information could also be derived from the poses, costuming and events. Image and text could be connected and historians could "read" the art.

Together with archeological data, the writings and art provide enough details to evoke with some richness the yearnings, triumphs and tragedies of individuals, Dr. Freidel said. Inscriptions show that in the 8th century Kan-Xul (Precious Animal) assumed the kingship of Palenque after the death of his brother Chan-Bahlum (Snake Jaguar), who had succeeded their father, Pacal. Kan-Xul built a temple for his brother, committing his soul to heaven and also sealing off his monuments.

Kan-Xul began constructing a palace extolling his own achievements but when he was in his 70s, before it was finished, he was captured by the rival polity of Toniná. The narrative on his own monument ends with the coronation of another brother. And inscriptions in Toniná show a bent, broken Kan-Xul being sacrificed.

Palace intrigue, too, is evident in some records. A tablet from a house in Palenque shows a Kan-Xul descendant being ordained in a subordinate role while his younger brother took the kingship. "How did this younger brother maneuver his older brother out of his rightful position?" Dr. Freidel asked.

KINGSHIP AND SACRIFICE

The lessons from inscriptions have been bolstered through a new archeological approach that examines the periphery as well as the core of sites, and small as well as large sites. With these broader studies, Dr. Sharer said that "for the first time, a great deal of information about the non-elite portions of society has become available," showing dense settlements and sophisticated agricultural methods.

Although the stone writings discuss only royalty, evidence indicates a cooperative, sacred relationship between the elites and the commoners, according to Dr. Freidel. "To be king was to be the living sacrifice for your people," he said. The elites were expected to bleed and mutilate themselves for the gods and to capture and sacrifice royalty from other cities while constantly risking the same fate themselves.

If the new history has robbed Maya gazers of some cherished myths and mysteries, the scholars point out that plenty of tantalizing enigmas remain: What spurred the transition from scattered villages to magnificent city-states? What relations did the Maya have with other civilizations? And what political, economic or ecological crises knocked this powerful culture into a tailspin?

Although their writing has been decoded, the Maya still give a long leash to the modern imagination.

55. THE AZTEC CIVILIZATION OF MEXICO

Bernal Diaz

Aztec civilization was the last of a long line of native American civilizations that had sprung up in the central highlands of Mexico. In this selection it is described by Bernal Diaz, a conquistador who accompanied Cortes to Mexico in 1519. In what ways was the Aztec civilization like that of Spain? In what ways was it different?

When it was announced to Cortes that Motecusuma [Montezuma] himself was approaching, he alighted from his horse and advanced to meet him. Many compliments were now passed on both sides. Motecusuma bid Cortes welcome, who, through Marina, said, in return, he hoped his majesty was in good health. If I still remember rightly, Cortes, who had Marina next to him, wished to concede the place of honor to the monarch, who, however, would not accept of it, but conceded it to Cortes, who now brought forth a necklace of precious stones, of the most beautiful colours and shapes, strung upon gold wire, and perfumed with musk, which he hung about the neck of Motecusuma. Our commander was then going to embrace him, but the grandees by whom he was surrounded held back his arms, as they considered it improper. Our general then desired Marina to tell the monarch how exceedingly he congratulated himself upon his good fortune of having seen such a powerful monarch face to face, and of the honour he had done us by coming out to meet us himself. To all this Motecusuma answered in very appropriate terms, and ordered his two nephews, the princes of Tetzuco and Cohohuacan, to conduct us to our quarters. He himself returned to the city, accompanied by his two other relatives, the princes of Cuitlahuac and Tlacupa, with the other grandees of his numerous suite. As they passed by, we perceived how all those who composed his majesty's retinue held their heads bent forward, no one daring to lift up his eyes in his presence; and altogether what deep veneration was paid him.

The road before us now became less crowded, and yet who would have been able to count the vast numbers of men, women, and children who filled the streets, crowded the balconies, and the canoes in the canals, merely to gaze upon us? . . .

We were quartered in a large building where there was room enough for us all, and which had been occupied by Axayacatl, father of Motecusuma, during his lifetime. Here the latter had likewise a secret room full of treasures, and where the gold he had inherited from his father was hid, which he had never touched up to this moment. The apartments and halls were very spacious, and those set apart for our general were furnished with carpets. There were separate beds for each of us, which could not have been better fitted up for a gentleman of the first rank! Every place was swept clean, and the walls had been newly plastered and decorated.

When we had arrived in the great courtyard adjoining this palace, Motecusuma came up to Cortes, and taking him by the hand, conducted him himself into the apartments where he was to lodge, which had been beautifully decorated after the fashion of the country. He then hung about his neck a chaste necklace of gold, most curiously worked with figures all representing crabs. The Mexican grandees were greatly astonished at all these uncommon favours which their monarch bestowed upon our general.

Cortes returned the monarch many thanks for so much kindness, and the latter took leave of him with these words: "Malinche, you and your brothers must now do as if you were at home, and take some rest after the fatigues of the journey," then returned to his own palace, which was close at hand.

We allotted the apartments according to the several companies, placed our cannon in an advantageous position, and made such arrangements that our cavalry, as well as the infantry, might be ready at a moment's notice. We then sat down to a plentiful repast, which had been previously spread out for us, and made a sumptuous meal.

This our bold and memorable entry into the large city of Temixtitlan, Mexico took place on the 8th of November, 1519. Praise be to the Lord Jesus Christ for all this. . . .

The mighty Motecusuma may have been about this time in the fortieth year of his age. He was tall of stature, of slender make, and rather thin, but the symmetry of his body was beautiful. His complexion was not very brown, merely approaching to that of the inhabitants in general. The hair of his head was not very long, excepting where it hung thickly down over his ears, which were quite hidden by it. His black beard, though thin, looked handsome. His countenance was rather of an elongated form, but cheerful; and his fine eyes had the expression of love or severity, at the proper moments. He was particularly clean in his person, and took a bath every evening. Besides a number of concubines, who were all daughters of persons of rank and quality, he had two lawful wives of royal extraction, whom, however, he visited secretly without any one daring to observe it, save his most confidential servants. He was perfectly innocent of any unnatural crimes. The dress he had on one day was not worn again until four days had elapsed. In the halls adjoining his own private apartments there was always a guard of 2000 men of quality, in waiting: with whom, however, he never held any conversation unless to give them orders or to receive some intelligence from them. Whenever for this purpose they entered his apartment, they had first to take off their rich costumes and put on meaner garments, though these were always neat and clean; and were only allowed to enter into his presence barefooted, with eyes cast down. No person durst look at him full in the face, and during the three prostrations which they were obliged to make before they could approach him, they pronounced these words: "Lord! my Lord! sublime Lord!" Everything that was communicated to him was to be said in few words, the eyes of the speaker being constantly cast down, and on leaving the monarch's presence he walked backwards out of the room. I also remarked that even princes and other great personages who come to Mexico respecting lawsuits, or on other business from the interior of the country, always took off their shoes and changed their whole dress for one of a meaner appearance when they entered his palace. Neither were they allowed to enter the palace straightway, but had to show themselves for a considerable time outside the doors; as it would have been considered want of respect to the monarch if this had been omitted.

Above 300 kinds of dishes were served up for Motecusuma's dinner from his kitchen, underneath which were placed pans of porcelain filled with fire, to keep them warm. Three hundred dishes of various kinds were served up for him alone, and above 1000 for the persons in waiting. He sometimes, but very seldom, accompanied by the chief officers of his household, ordered the dinner himself, and desired that the best dishes and various kinds of birds should be called over to him. We were told that the flesh of young children, as a very dainty bit, were also set before him sometimes by way of a relish. Whether there was any truth in this we could not possibly discover; on account of the great variety of dishes, consisting in fowls, turkeys, pheasants, partridges, quails, tame and wild geese, venison, musk swine, pigeons, hares, rabbits, and of numerous other birds and beasts; besides which there were various other kinds of provisions, indeed it would have been no easy task to call them all over by name.

I had almost forgotten to mention, that during dinnertime, two other young women of great beauty brought the monarch small cakes, as white as snow, made of eggs and other very nourishing ingredients, on plates covered with clean napkins, also a kind of long-shaped bread, likewise made of very substantial things, and some pachol, which is a kind of wafer-cake. They then presented him with three beautifully painted and gilt tubes, which were filled with liquid amber, and a herb called by the Indians tabaco. After the dinner had been cleared away and the singing and dancing done, one of these tubes was lighted, and the monarch took the smoke into his mouth, and after he had done this a short time, he fell asleep.

About this time a celebrated cazique [or cacique, a native Indian chief], whom we called Tapia, was Motecusuma's chief steward: he kept an account of the whole of Motecusuma's revenue, in large books of paper which the Mexicans call *Amatl*. A whole house was filled with such large books of accounts.

Motecusuma had also two arsenals filled with arms of every description, of which many were ornamented with gold and precious stones. These arms consisted in shields of different sizes, sabres, and a species of broadsword, which is wielded with both hands, the edge furnished with flint stones, so extremely sharp that they cut much better than our Spanish swords: further, lances of greater length than ours, with spikes at their end, full one fathom in length, likewise furnished with several sharp flint stones. The pikes are so very sharp and hard that they will pierce the strongest shield, and cut like a razor; so that the Mexicans even shave themselves with these stones. Then there were excellent bows and arrows, pikes with single and double points, and the proper thongs to throw them with; slings with round stones purposely made for them; also a species of large shield, so ingeniously constructed that it could be rolled up when not wanted: they are only unrolled on the field of battle, and completely cover the whole body from the head to the feet. Further, we saw here a great variety of cuirasses made of quilted cotton, which were outwardly adorned with soft feathers of different colours, and looked like uniforms. . . .

I will now, however, turn to another subject, and rather acquaint my readers with the skilful arts practised among the Mexicans: among which I will first mention the sculptors, and the gold and silversmiths, who were clever in working and smelting gold, and would have astonished the most celebrated of our Spanish goldsmiths: the number of these was very great, and the most skilful lived at a place called Ezcapuzalco, about four miles from Mexico. After these came the very skilful masters in cutting and polishing precious stones, and the calchihuis, which resemble the emerald. Then follow the great masters in painting, and decorators in feathers, and the wonderful sculptors. Even at this day there are living in Mexico three Indian artists, named Marcos de Aguino, Juan de la Cruz, and El Crespello, who have severally reached to such great proficiency in the art of painting and sculpture, that they may be compared to an Apelles, or our contemporaries Michael Angelo and Berruguete. . . .

The powerful Motecusuma had also a number of dancers and clowns: some danced in stilts, tumbled, and performed a variety of other antics for the monarch's entertainment: a whole quarter of the city was inhabited by these performers, and their only occupation consisted in such like performances. Last, Motecusuma had in his service great numbers of stone-cutters, masons, and carpenters who were solely employed in the royal palaces. Above all, I must not forget to mention here his gardens for the culture of flowers, trees, and vegetables, of which there were various kinds. In these gardens were also numerous baths, wells, basins, and ponds full of limpid water, which regularly ebbed and flowed. All this was enlivened by endless varieties of small birds, which sang among the trees. Also, the plantations of medical plants and vegetables are well worthy of our notice: these were kept in proper order by a large body of gardeners. All the baths, wells, ponds, and buildings were substantially constructed of stonework, as also the theaters where the singers and dancers performed. There were upon the whole so many remarkable things for my observation in these gardens and throughout the whole town, that I scarcely find words to express the astonishment I felt at the pomp and splendour of the Mexican monarch. . . .

We had already been four days in the city of Mexico, and neither our commander nor any of us had, during that time, left our quarters, excepting to visit the gardens and buildings adjoining the palace. Cortes now, therefore, determined to view the city, and visit the great market, and the chief temple of Huitzilopochtli. . . . The moment we arrived in this immense market, we were perfectly astonished at the vast numbers of people, the profusion of merchandise, which was there exposed for sale, and at the good police and order that reigned throughout. The grandees who accompanied us drew our attention to the smallest circumstance, and gave us full explanation of all we saw. Every species of merchandise had a separate spot for its sale. We first of all visited those divisions of the market appropriated for the sale of gold and silver wares, of jewels, of cloths interwoven with feathers, and of other manufactured goods; besides slaves of both sexes. This slave market was upon as great a scale as the Portuguese market for negro slaves at Guinea. To prevent these from running away, they were fastened with halters about their neck, though some were allowed to walk at large. Next to these came the dealers in coarser wares—cotton, twisted thread, and cacao. In short, every species of goods which New Spain produces were here to be found and everything put me in mind of my native town Medino del Campo during fair time, where every merchandise had a separate street assigned for its sale. In one place were sold the stuffs manufactured of nequen; ropes, and sandals; in another place, the sweet maguey root, ready cooked and various other things made from this plant. In another division of the market were exposed the skins of tigers, lions, jackals, otters, red deer, wild cats, and of other beasts of prey, some of which were tanned. In another place were sold beans and sage, with other herbs and vegetables. A particular market was assigned for the merchants in fowls, turkeys, ducks, rabbits, hares, deer, and dogs; also for fruit-sellers, pastry-cooks, and tripe-sellers. Not far from these were exposed all manner of earthenware, from the large earthen cauldron to the smallest pitchers. Then came the dealers in honey and honey-cakes, and other sweetmeats. Next to these, the timber-merchants, furniture-dealers, with their stores of tables, benches, cradles, and all sorts of wooden implements, all separately arranged. What can I further add? If I am to note everything down, I must also mention human excrements, which are exposed for sale in canoes lying in the canals near this square, and is used for the tanning of leather; for, according to the assurances of the Mexicans, it is impossible to tan well without it. I can easily imagine that many of my readers will laugh at this; however, what I have stated is a fact, and, as further proof of this, I must acquaint the reader that along every road accommodations were built of reeds, straw, or grass, by which those who made use of them were hidden from the view of the passers-by, so that great care was taken that none of the last mentioned treasures should be lost. But why should I so minutely detail every article exposed for sale in this great market? If I had to enumerate everything singly, I should not so easily get to the end. And yet I have not mentioned the paper, which in this country is called amatl; the tubes filled with liquid amber and tobacco; the various sweet-scented salves, and similar things; nor the various seeds which were exposed for sale in the porticoes of this market, nor the medicinal herbs.

In this marketplace there were also courts of justice, to which three judges and several constables were appointed, who inspected the goods exposed for sale. I had almost forgotten to mention the salt, and those who made the flint knives; also the fish, and a species of bread made of a kind of mud or slime collected from the surface of this lake, and eaten in that form, and has a similar taste to our cheese. Further, instruments of brass, copper, and tin; cups, and painted pitchers of wood; indeed, I wish I had completed the enumeration of all this profusion of merchandize. The variety was so great that it would occupy more space than I can well spare to note them down in; besides which, the market was so crowded with people, and the thronging so excessive in the porticoes, that it was quite impossible to see all in one day. . . .

On quitting the market, we entered the spacious yards which surrounded the chief temple. These appeared to encompass more ground than the marketplace at Salamanca, and were surrounded by a double wall, constructed of stone and lime: these yards were paved with large white flagstones, extremely smooth; and where these were wanting, a kind of brown plaster had been used instead, and all was kept so very clean that there was not the smallest particle of dust or straw to be seen anywhere.

Before we mounted the steps of the great temple, Motecusuma, who was sacrificing on the top to his idols, sent six papas and two of his principal officers to conduct Cortes up the steps. There were 114 steps to the summit. . . . Indeed, this infernal temple, from its great height, commanded a view of the whole surrounding neighbourhood. From this place we could likewise see the three causeways which led into Mexico—that from Iztapalapan, by which we had entered the city four days ago; that from Tlacupa, along which we took our flight eight months after, when we were beaten out of the city by the new monarch Cuitlahuatzin; the third was that of Tepeaquilla. We also observed the aqueduct which ran from Chapultepec, and provided the whole town with sweet water. We could also distinctly see the bridges across the openings, by which these causeways were intersected, and through which the waters of the lake ebbed and flowed. The lake itself was crowded with canoes, which were bringing provisions, manufacturers, and other merchandize to the city. From here we also discovered that the only communication of the houses in this city, and of all the other towns built in the lake, was by means of drawbridges or canoes. In all these towns the beautiful white plastered temples rose above the smaller ones, like so many towers and castles in our Spanish towns, and this, it may be imagined, was a splendid sight.

After we had sufficiently gazed upon this magnificent picture, we again turned our eyes toward the great market, and beheld the vast numbers of buyers and sellers who thronged there. The bustle and noise occasioned by this multitude of human beings was so great that it could be heard at a distance of more than four miles. Some of our men, who had been at Constantinople and Rome, and travelled through the whole of Italy, said that they never had seen a marketplace of such large dimensions, or which was so well regulated, or so crowded with people as this one at Mexico.

On this occasion Cortes said to father Olmedo, who had accompanied us: "I have just been thinking that we should take this opportunity, and apply to Motecusuma for permission to build a church here."

To which father Olmedo replied, that it would, no doubt, be an excellent thing if the monarch would grant this; but that it would be acting overhasty to make a proposition of that nature to him now, whose consent would not easily be gained at any time.

Cortes then turned to Motecusuma, and said to him, by means of our interpretress, Doña Marina: "Your majesty is, indeed, a great monarch, and you merit to be still greater! It has been a real delight to us to view all your cities. I have now one favour to beg of you, that you would allow us to see your gods and *Teules*."

To which Motecusuma answered, that he must first consult the chief papas, to whom he then addressed a few words. Upon this, we were led into a kind of small tower, with one room, in which we saw two basements resembling altars, decked with coverings of extreme beauty. On each of these basements stood a gigantic, fat-looking figure, of which the one on the right hand represented the god of war Huitzilopochtli. This idol had a very broad face, with distorted and furious-looking eyes, and was covered all over with jewels, gold, and pearls, which were stuck to it by means of a species of paste, which, in this country, is prepared from a certain root. Large serpents, likewise, covered with gold and precious stones, wound round the body of this monster, which held in one hand a bow, and in the other a bunch of arrows. Another small idol which stood by its side, representing its page, carried this monster's short spear, and its golden shield studded with precious stones. Around Huitzilopochtli's neck were figures representing human faces and hearts made of gold and silver, and decorated with blue stones. In front of him stood several perfuming pans with copal, the incense of the country; also the hearts of three Indians, who had that day been slaughtered, were now consuming before him as a burnt-offering. Every wall of this chapel and the whole floor had become almost black with human blood, and the stench was abominable.

Respecting the abominable human sacrifices of these people, the following was communicated to us: The breast of the unhappy victim destined to be sacrificed was ripped open with a knife made of sharp flint; the throbbing heart was then torn out, and immediately offered to the idol-god in whose honour the sacrifice had been instituted. After this, the head, arms and legs were cut off and eaten at their banquets, with the exception of the head, which was saved, and hung to a beam appropriated for that purpose. No other part of the body was eaten, but the remainder was thrown to the beasts which were kept in those abominable dens, in which there were also vipers and other poisonous serpents, and, among the latter in particular, a species at the end of whose tail there was a kind of rattle. This last mentioned serpent, which is the most dangerous, was kept in a cabin of a diversified form, in which a quantity of feathers had been strewed: here it laid its eggs, and it was fed with the flesh of dogs and human beings who had been sacrificed. We were positively told that, after we had been beaten out of the city of Mexico, and had lost 850 of our men, these horrible beasts were fed for many successive days with the bodies of our unfortunate countrymen. Indeed, when all the tigers and lions roared together, with the howlings of the jackals and foxes, and hissing of the serpents, it was quite fearful, and you could not suppose otherwise than that you were in hell.

Our commander here said smilingly, to Motecusuma: "I cannot imagine that such a powerful and wise monarch as you are should not have yourself discovered by this time that these idols are not divinities, but evil spirits, called devils. In order that you may be convinced of this, and that your papas may satisfy themselves of this truth, allow me to erect a cross on the summit of this temple; and, in the chapel, where stand your Huitzilopochtli and Tetzcatlipuca, give us a small space that I may place there the image of the holy Virgin; then you will see that terror will seize these idols by which you have been so long deluded."

Motecusuma knew what the image of the Virgin Mary was, yet he was very much displeased with Cortes' offer, and replied, in presence of two papas, whose anger was not less conspicuous, "Malinche, could I have conjectured that you would have used such reviling language as you have just done, I would certainly not have shown you my gods. In our eyes these are good divinities: they preserve our lives, give us nourishment, water, and good harvests, healthy and growing weather, and victory whenever we pray to them for it. Therefore we offer up our prayers to them, and make them sacrifices, I earnestly beg of you not to say another word to insult the profound veneration in which we hold these gods."

As soon as Cortes heard these words and perceived the great excitement under which they were pronounced, he said nothing in return, but merely remarked to the monarch with a cheerful smile: "It is time for us both to depart hence." To which Motecusuma answered, that he would not detain him any longer, but he himself was now obliged to stay some time to atone to his gods by prayer and sacrifice for having committed *gratlatlacol*, by allowing us to ascend the great temple, and thereby occasioning the affronts which we had offered them.

56.   THE INCA EMPIRE
William H. Prescott

William H. Prescott's The History of the Conquest of Peru *(published in 1847) is still one of the best introductions to the subject. In this brief selection we see the striking physical setting of the Inca empire and its capital at Cuzco, and we learn how the empire was governed.*

How did the geography of Peru affect the development of the Inca empire? How was the empire governed? What was it like to be a ruling Inca or a member of the nobility? If you could have been born a Maya or Inca ruler, which would you choose?

Of the numerous nations which occupied the great American continent at the time of its discovery by the Europeans, the two most advanced in power and refinement were undoubtedly those of Mexico and Peru. . . .

The empire of Peru, at the period of the Spanish invasion, stretched along the Pacific from about the second degree north to the thirty-seventh degree of south latitude; a line, also, which describes the western boundaries of the modern republics of Ecuador, Peru, Bolivia, and Chile. . . .

The topographical aspect of the country is very remarkable. A strip of land, rarely exceeding twenty leagues in width, runs along the coast, and is hemmed in through its whole extent by a colossal range of mountains, which, advancing from the Straits of Magellan, reaches its highest elevation—indeed, the highest on the American continent—about the seventeenth degree south, and, after crossing the line, gradually subsides into hills of inconsiderable magnitude, as it enters the Isthmus of Panamá. This is the famous Cordillera of the Andes, or "copper mountains," as termed by the natives, though they might with more reason have been called "mountains of gold." Arranged sometimes in a single line, though more frequently in two or three lines running parallel or obliquely to each other, they seem to the voyager on the ocean but one continuous chain; while the huge volcanoes, which to the inhabitants of the tableland look like solitary and independent masses, appear to him only like so many peaks of the same vast and magnificent range. So immense is the scale on which nature works in these regions that it is only when viewed from a great distance that the spectator can in any degree comprehend the relation of the several parts to the stupendous whole. Few of the works of nature, indeed, are calculated to produce impressions of higher sublimity than the aspect of this coast as it is gradually unfolded to the eye of the mariner sailing on the distant waters of the Pacific, where mountain is seen to rise above mountain, and Chimborazo, with its glorious canopy of snow, glittering far above the clouds, crowns the whole as with a celestial diadem.

The face of the country would appear to be peculiarly unfavorable to the purposes both of agriculture and of internal communication. The sandy strip along the coast, where rain rarely falls, is fed only by a few scanty streams, that furnish a remarkable contrast to the vast volumes of water which roll down the eastern sides of the Cordilleras into the Atlantic. The precipitous steeps of the sierra, with its splintered sides of porphyry and granite, and its higher regions wrapped in snows that never melt under the fierce sun of the equator, unless it be from the desolating action of its own volcanic fires, might seem equally unpropitious to the labors of the husbandman. And all communication between the parts of the long-extended territory might be thought to be precluded by the savage character of the region, broken up by precipices, furious torrents, and impassable *quebradas*—those hideous rents in the mountain chain, whose depths the eye of the terrified traveler, as he winds along his aerial pathway, vainly endeavors to fathom. Yet the industry, we might almost say the genius, of the Indian was sufficient to overcome all these impediments of nature.

By a judicious system of canals and subterraneous aqueducts, the waste places on the coast were refreshed by copious streams that clothed them in fertility and beauty. Terraces were raised upon the steep sides of the Cordillera, and as the different elevations had the effect of difference of latitude, they exhibited in regular gradation every variety of vegetable form, from the stimulated growth of the tropics to the temperate products of a northern clime, while flocks of *llamas*—the Peruvian sheep—wandered with their shepherds over the broad, snow-covered wastes on the crests of the sierra, which rose beyond the limits of cultivation. An industrious population settled along the lofty regions of the plateaus, and towns and hamlets, clustering amidst orchards and wide-spreading gardens, seemed suspended in the air far above the ordinary elevation of the clouds. Intercourse was maintained between these numerous settlements by means of the great roads which traversed the mountain-passes and opened an easy communication between the capital and the remotest extremities of the empire.

The ancient city of Cuzco . . . stood in a beautiful valley on an elevated region of the plateau, which among the Alps would have been buried in eternal snows, but which within the tropics enjoyed a genial and salubrious temperature. Towards the north it was defended by a lofty eminence, a spur of the great Cordillera; and the city was traversed by a river, or rather a small stream, over which bridges of timber, covered with heavy slabs of stone, furnished an easy means of communication with the opposite banks. The streets were long and narrow, the houses low, and those of the poorer sort built of clay and reeds. But Cuzco was the royal residence, and was adorned with the ample dwellings of the great nobility; and the massy fragments still incorporated in many of the modern edifices bear testimony to the size and solidity of the ancient.

The health of the city was promoted by spacious openings and squares, in which a numerous population from the capital and the distant country assembled to celebrate the high festivals of their religion. For Cuzco was the "Holy City"; and the great temple of the Sun, to which pilgrims resorted from the farthest borders of the empire, was the most magnificent structure in the New World, and unsurpassed, probably, in the costliness of its decorations by any building in the Old.

The government of Peru was a despotism, mild in its character, but in its form a pure and unmitigated despotism. The sovereign was placed at an immeasurable distance above his subjects. Even the proudest of the Inca nobility, claiming a descent from the same divine original as himself, could not venture into the royal presence unless barefoot, and bearing a light burden on his shoulders in token of homage. As the representative of the Sun, he stood at the head of the priesthood, and presided at the most important of the religious festivals. He raised armies, and usually commanded them in person. He imposed taxes, made laws, and provided for their execution by the appointment of judges, whom he removed at pleasure. He was the source from which everything flowed— all dignity, all power, all emolument. He was, in short, in the well-known phrase of the European despot, "himself the state."

The Inca asserted his claims as a superior being by assuming a pomp in his manner of living well calculated to impose on his people. His dress was of the finest wool of the vicuña [South American sheep], richly dyed, and ornamented with a profusion of gold and precious stones. Round his head was wreathed a turban of many-colored folds, called the *llautu*, with a tasseled fringe, like that worn by the prince, but of a scarlet color, while two feathers of a rare and curious bird, called the *corequenque*, placed upright in it, were the distinguishing insignia of royalty. The birds from which these feathers were obtained were found in a desert country among the mountains, and it was death to destroy or to take them, as they were reserved for the exclusive purpose of supplying the royal headgear. Every succeeding monarch was provided with a new pair of these plumes, and his credulous subjects fondly believed that only two individuals of the species had ever existed to furnish the simple ornament for the diadem of the Incas.

Although the Peruvian monarch was raised so far above the highest of his subjects, he condescended to mingle occasionally with them, and took great pains personally to inspect the condition of the humbler classes. He presided at some of the religious celebrations, and on these occasions entertained the great nobles at his table, when he complimented them, after the fashion of more civilized nations, by drinking the health of those whom he most delighted to honor.

But the most effectual means taken by the Incas for communicating with their people were their progresses through the empire. These were conducted, at intervals of several years, with great state, and magnificence. The sedan, or litter, in which they traveled, richly emblazoned with gold and emeralds, was guarded by a numerous escort. The men who bore it on their shoulders were provided by two cities, specially appointed for the purpose. It was a post to be coveted by no one if, as is asserted, a fall was punished with death. They traveled with ease and expedition, halting at the tambos, or inns, erected by the government along the route, and occasionally at the royal palaces, which in the great towns afforded ample accommodations to the whole of the monarch's retinue. The noble roads which traversed the tableland were lined with people, who swept away the stones and stubble from their surface, strewing them with sweet-scented flowers, and vying with each other in carrying forward the baggage from one village to another. The monarch halted from time to time to listen to the grievances of his subjects or to settle some points which had been referred to his decision by the regular tribunals. As the princely train wound its way along the mountain passes, every place was thronged with spectators eager to catch a glimpse of their sovereign; and when he raised the curtains of his litter and showed himself to their eyes, the air was rent with acclamations as they invoked blessings on his head. Tradition long commemorated the spots at which he halted, and the simple people of the country held them in reverence as places consecrated by the presence of an Inca.

The royal palaces were on a magnificent scale and, far from being confined to the capital or a few principal towns, were scattered over all the provinces of their vast empire. The buildings were low, but covered a wide extent of ground. Some of the apartments were spacious, but they were generally small, and had no communication with one another except that they opened into a common square or court. The walls were made of blocks of stone of various sizes, like those described in the fortress of Cuzco, rough-hewn but carefully wrought near the line of junction, which was scarcely visible to the eye. The roofs were of wood or rushes, which have perished under the rude touch of time, that has shown more respect for the walls of the edifices. The whole seems to have been characterized by solidity and strength, rather than by any attempt at architectural elegance.

But whatever want of elegance there may have been in the exterior of the imperial dwellings, it was amply compensated by the interior, in which all the opulence of the Peruvian princes was ostentatiously displayed. The sides of the apartments were thickly studded with gold and silver ornaments. Niches prepared in the walls were filled with images of animals and plants curiously wrought of the same costly materials; and even much of the domestic furniture, including the utensils devoted to the most ordinary menial services, displayed the like wanton magnificence! With these gorgeous decorations were mingled richly colored stuffs of the delicate manufacture of the Peruvian wool, which were of so beautiful a texture that the Spanish sovereigns, with all the luxuries of Europe and Asia at their command, did not disdain to use them. The royal household consisted of a throng of menials, supplied by the neighboring towns and villages, which, as in Mexico, were bound to furnish the monarch with fuel and other necessaries for the consumption of the palace.

But the favorite residence of the Incas was at Yucay, about four leagues distant from the capital. In this delicious valley, locked up within the friendly arms of the sierra, which sheltered it from the rude breezes of the east, and refreshed by gushing fountains and streams of running water, they built the most beautiful of their palaces. Here, when wearied with the dust and toil of the city, they loved to retreat and solace themselves with the society of their favorite concubines, wandering amidst groves and airy gardens that shed around their soft, intoxicating odors and lulled the senses to voluptuous repose. Here, too, they loved to indulge in the luxury of their baths, replenished by streams of crystal water which were conducted through subterraneous silver channels into basins of gold. The spacious gardens were stocked with numerous varieties of plants and flowers that grew without effort in this *temperate* region of the tropics, while parterres [ornamental gardens with paths between the beds—Ed.] of a more extraordinary kind were planted by their side, glowing with the various forms of vegetable life skillfully imitated in gold and silver! Among them the Indian corn, the most beautiful of American grains, is particularly commemorated, and the curious workmanship is noticed with which the golden ear was half disclosed amidst the broad leaves of silver, and the light tassel of the same material that floated gracefully from its top.

If this dazzling picture staggers the faith of the reader, he may reflect that the Peruvian mountains teemed with gold; that the natives understood the art of working the mines, to a considerable extent; that none of the ore, as we shall see hereafter, was converted into coin, and that the whole of it passed into the hands of the sovereign for his own exclusive benefit, whether for purposes of utility or ornament. Certain it is that no fact is better attested by the conquerors themselves, who had ample means of information, and no motive for misstatement. . . .

Our surprise, however, may reasonably be excited when we consider that the wealth displayed by the Peruvian princes was only that which each had amassed individually for himself. He owed nothing to inheritance from his predecessors. On the decease of an Inca, his palaces were abandoned; all his treasures, except what were employed in his obsequies, his furniture and apparel, were suffered to remain as he left them, and his mansions, save one, were closed up forever. The new sovereign was to provide himself with everything new for his royal state. The reason for this was the popular belief that the soul of the departed monarch would return after a time to reanimate his body on earth; and they wished that he should find everything to which he had been used in life prepared for his reception.

When an Inca died, or, to use his own language, "was called home to the mansions of his father, the Sun," his obsequies were celebrated with great pomp and solemnity. The bowels were taken from the body and deposited in the temple of Tampu, about five leagues from the capital. A quantity of his plate and jewels was buried with them, and a number of his attendants and favorite concubines, amounting sometimes, it is said, to a thousand, were immolated on this tomb. Some of them showed the natural repugnance to the sacrifice occasionally manifested by the victims of a similar superstition in India. But these were probably the menials and more humble attendants; since the women have been known, in more than one instance, to lay violent hands on themselves, when restrained from testifying their fidelity by this act of conjugal martyrdom. This melancholy ceremony was followed by a general mourning throughout the empire. At stated intervals, for a year, the people assembled to renew the expressions of their sorrow; processions were made, displaying the banner of the departed monarch; bards and minstrels were appointed to chronicle his achievements, and their songs continued to be rehearsed at high festivals in the presence of the reigning monarch—thus stimulating the living by the glorious example of the dead.

The body of the deceased Inca was skillfully embalmed and removed to the great temple of the Sun at Cuzco. There the Peruvian sovereign, on entering the awful sanctuary, might behold the effigies of his royal ancestors, ranged in opposite files—the men on the right, and their queens on the left, of the great luminary which blazed in refulgent gold on the walls of the temple. The bodies, clothed in the princely attire which they had been accustomed to wear, were placed on chairs of gold, and sat with their heads inclined downward, their hands placidly crossed over their bosoms, their countenances exhibiting their natural dusky hue—less liable to change than the fresher coloring of a European complexion—and their hair of raven black, or silvered over with age, according to the period at which they died! It seemed like a company of solemn worshipers fixed in devotion, so true were the forms and lineaments to life. The Peruvians were as successful as the Egyptians in the miserable attempt to perpetuate the existence of the body beyond the limits assigned to it by nature.

They cherished a still stranger illusion in the attentions which they continued to pay to these insensible remains, as if they were instinct with life. One of the houses belonging to a deceased Inca was kept open and occupied by his guard and attendants, with all the state appropriate to royalty. On certain festivals, the revered bodies of the sovereigns were brought out with great ceremony into the public square of the capital. Invitations were sent by the captains of the guard of the respective Incas to the different nobles and officers of the court; and entertainments were provided in the names of their masters, which displayed all the profuse magnificence of their treasures—and "such a display," says an ancient chronicler, "was there in the great square of Cuzco, on this occasion, of gold and silver plate and jewels, as no other city in the world ever witnessed." The banquet was served by the menials of the respective households, and the guests partook of the melan-

choly cheer in the presence of the royal phantom with the same attention to the forms of courtly etiquette as if the living monarch had
presided!

The nobility of Peru consisted of two orders, the first and by far the
most important of which was that of the Incas, who, boasting a common
descent with their sovereign, lived, as it were, in the reflected light of his
glory. As the Peruvian monarchs availed themselves of the right of polyg-
amy to a very liberal extent, leaving behind them families of one or even
two hundred children, the nobles of the blood royal, though compre-
hending only their descendants in the male line, came in the course of
years to be very numerous. They were divided into different lineages,
each of which traced its pedigree to a different member of the royal
dynasty, though all terminated in the divine founder of the empire.

They were distinguished by many exclusive and very important privileges; they wore a peculiar dress, spoke a dialect, if we may believe the
chronicler, peculiar to themselves, and had the choicest portion of the
public domain assigned for their support. They lived, most of them, at
court, near the person of the prince, sharing in his counsels, dining at his
board, or supplied from his table. They alone were admissible to the
great offices in the priesthood. They were invested with the command of
armies and of distant garrisons, were placed over the provinces, and, in
short, filled every station of high trust and emolument. Even the laws,
severe in their general tenor, seem not to have been framed with reference to them; and the people, investing the whole order with a portion of
the sacred character which belonged to the sovereign, held that an Inca
noble was incapable of crime.

The other order of nobility was the *Curacas*, the caciques [chiefs] of the
conquered nations, or their descendants. They were usually continued
by the government in their places, though they were required to visit the
capital occasionally, and to allow their sons to be educated there as the
pledges of their loyalty. It is not easy to define the nature or extent of
their privileges. They were possessed of more or less power, according to
the extent of their patrimony and the number of their vassals. Their
authority was usually transmitted from father to son, though sometimes
the successor was chosen by the people. They did not occupy the highest
posts of state, or those nearest the person of the sovereign, like the
nobles of the blood. Their authority seems to have been usually local,
and always in subordination to the territorial jurisdiction of the great
provincial governors, who were taken from the Incas.

It was the Inca nobility, indeed, who constituted the real strength of
the Peruvian monarchy. Attached to their prince by ties of consanguinity,
they had common sympathies and, to a considerable extent, common
interests with him. Distinguished by a peculiar dress and insignia, as well
as by language and blood, from the rest of the community, they were
never confounded with the other tribes and nations who were incorpo-

rated into the great Peruvian monarchy. After the lapse of centuries they still retained their individuality as a peculiar people. They were to the conquered races of the country what the Romans were to the barbarous hordes of the Empire, or the Normans to the ancient inhabitants of the British Isles. Clustering around the throne, they formed an invincible phalanx to shield it alike from secret conspiracy and open insurrection. Though living chiefly in the capital, they were also distributed throughout the country in all its high stations and strong military posts, thus establishing lines of communication with the court, which enabled the sovereign to act simultaneously and with effect on the most distant quarters of his empire.

57.   NORTH AMERICANS BEFORE 1492

Lynda Norene Shaffer

The author, a modern historian, calls our attention to the peoples of what is today the central and eastern United States from the Great Plains to the Appalachians, from the Great Lakes to the Gulf of Mexico. These "moundbuilders," she argues, were far more numerous than we have thought. They were also more powerful and successful than is usually believed. What evidence does she provide to support these claims? Do you agree with her assessment? What is the significance of her comparison of North American river systems with those of other parts of the world?

Only two hundred years ago, in the woodlands of Eastern North America, there were tens of thousands of large earthen mounds, all of which had been built by Native Americans. They were impressive structures. Visitors who saw them were amazed by the size of many, by their number, and by the intricacy of their design. Yet the significance of these earthworks, indeed, their very existence, is one of the best kept secrets of American history. Even the people who now live on or beside the mound sites are more likely to be familiar with the Native American past of Mexico, the Andes, or the U.S. Southwest than with the heritage of their own region.

Before 1492, moundbuilding centers in Eastern North America could be found from the Great Lakes region in the north to the Gulf of Mexico coast in the south, from the eastern portions of the Great Plains to the

Appalachian Mountains. They were built over a period of roughly four thousand years. Banana Bayou, one of the earliest earthen mound sites so far discovered, is located on Avery Island in Iberia Parish, on the Louisiana coast, and has been dated tentatively to 2490 B.C. The latest sites date from sometime around A.D. 1700.

Two hundred years ago almost all the mounds were still safely outside the bounds of the English-speaking settler colonies. Until about 1800, these colonies were generally confined to the Atlantic seaboard, east of the Appalachians. Thereafter, the number of mounds was reduced as waves of settlers from the east, continually reinforced by a flood of European immigrants, poured over the Appalachian Mountains and began plowing them down. In the twentieth century the mounds have been assaulted not only by farmers but also by vandals seeking valuable artifacts and highway-builders who have bulldozed their way through many, if not most sites. Nevertheless, a great many mounds still stand.

On occasion, the European-Americans who came upon the mounds and were amazed by them had the wisdom to ask the local Native American peoples about them. In Illinois in 1778, for example, Chief Baptist of the Kaskaskias was approached by a group of American Revolutionary War soldiers led by George Rogers Clark. They asked Chief Baptist about elaborate earthworks that they had seen near the Mississippi. The earthworks, he answered, were the outer fortifications of an old palace. It had belonged to the ancestors of the Native Americans when they had "covered the whole," when they had had large towns and been "as numerous as trees in the woods."

Many of the newcomers, however, were unwilling to believe that Native Americans could have built such imposing structures and felt it necessary to concoct fantastic theories about their origins. In the nineteenth century, various people argued that the mounds had been built by the Lost Tribes of Israel, or the Vikings, or sixteenth-century Spanish explorers. And in the twentieth century, Erich von Daniken's *Chariots of the Gods* has attributed the mounds to creatures from outer space.

But Chief Baptist knew whereof he spoke. Indeed, there had been a time when Native Americans towns and villages did cover many of the river valleys of Eastern North America. Although modern demographers might not agree that people were as numerous as the trees, one can say that the Native Americans numbered in the millions. Although for many years the pre-European contact population of North America north of the Rio Grande was said to be only about two million, recent scholarship indicates that this figure is a gross underestimate. In 1983 Henry F. Dobyns published an estimate of eighteen million, a figure that remains controversial. Nevertheless, the estimates of others do seem to be climbing upward toward this mark. Two important studies came out in 1987, one estimating more than seven million and another estimating a population of about twelve million. The latter, based upon settlement patterns revealed by archaeological explorations, tends to support Dobyns's assumptions and methods, even though its author concludes with a lower estimate.

Both archaeological evidence and explorers' accounts suggest that a large part of this population was concentrated within the moundbuilding region of Eastern North America. These sources also indicate that the mounds marked the centers of political and economic networks. Ceremonial goods and elite burials are concentrated at these sites, and so was military power. Archaeologists refer to the people who ruled from these centers as "paramount chiefs." They were the heads of alliance networks, possibly because of their prestige or control of scarce resources, or because of their superior military might. And through these networks they could command the loyalty and often the tribute of less powerful chiefs and the peoples they led. Paramount chiefs encountered by the Spanish and French were known as "Great Suns," and, just as Chief Baptist suggested, they lived in palaces—in large and elaborately decorated wooden structures—which were built on the top of high platform mounds. Specially designated groups known as "noble allies" and "honored people" also resided at these centers, and so did much larger numbers of "commoners"—farmers whose fields were nearby, hunters, traders, and artisans.

It is also clear from goods found in the graves of elite persons that moundbuilding centers participated in exchange networks that eventually grew to almost continental proportions. Products from far-off places can be found at many sites, but they tend to be concentrated at the largest centers. Some of the more notable items . . . that appear to have enjoyed wide circulation include Rocky Mountain stones used to make cutting edges, minerals from the upper reaches of the Mississippi used to make paint pigments, marine shells from Florida, copper from the Great Lakes, stone pipes from the Ohio River valley, and mica from southern Appalachia.

The construction of moundbuilding centers can be divided into three separate epochs. During the first epoch, which took place during the Late Archaic Period (ca. 1500–700 B.C.), such activity was confined to the Lower Mississippi River valley and adjacent areas. The largest center, a site that archaeologists call Poverty Point, was a few miles west of the Mississippi River in northeastern Louisiana. A second moundbuilding epoch took place during what is known either as the Woodlands Period or the Adena-Hopewell Period (ca. 500 B.C. to A.D. 400). It was during this epoch, when the most important centers were concentrated in southern Ohio on tributaries that flow south into the Ohio River, that construction of moundbuilding centers first spread throughout most of the Eastern Woodlands.

A third moundbuilding epoch (ca. A.D. 700–1700), which are

CHRONOLOGY OF THE MOUNDBUILDING REGION

Ice Age Hunters and Gatherers	12,0000–8000 B.C.*
Extinction of Ice Age animals (9000 B.C.)	
Early Archaic Period	8000–6000 B.C.
Localization, use of atlatl spear	
Middle Archaic Period	6000–3000 B.C.
Sedentary habits emerge	
Late Archaic Period	3000–500 B.C.
Population increase, long-distance exchange	
Domestication of indigenous plants	
Elite burials, copper in use in north	
Pottery in some southern locales	
First Moundbuilding Epoch (Late Archaic Period)	1500–700 B.C.
Poverty Point Cultural Area	
Lower Mississippi Valley	
Second Moundbuilding Epoch (Woodlands Period)	500 B.C.–A.D. 400
Adena-Hopewell Period	
Adena	500–100 B.C.
Ohio River valley	
Hopewell	200 B.C.–A.D. 400
Hopewellian sites throughout moundbuilding region	
Regionwide integration of exchange networks	
Pottery and corn found throughout region	
Increased use of indigenous domesticates	
Spread of bow and arrow (A.D. 300–600)	
Third Moundbuilding Epoch	A.D. 700–1731
The Mississippian Period	
Palisaded towns, hoes, ball courts	
Reliance upon corn, beans, and other crops	
Cahokia	A.D. 700–1250
Major Spanish invasions	A.D. 1513–1543
Postcontact survivals	A.D. 1550–1731
French defeat Natchez	A.D. 1731

*Most of the dates in this chronology are approximations. Especially with regard to the Archaic Period, many are based upon limited data and are subject to change as more data are analyzed and new findings reported. Although there is general agreement regarding this chronology, some scholars would use slightly different dates to define the various periods.

gists refer to as the Mississippian, witnessed the rise of Cahokia, a paramount center located on the Mississippi River, near what is now East St. Louis, Illinois. Between A.D. 900 and 1200, it was many times larger than any other center in Eastern North America. After its decline, a number of more modest centers flourished. Some survived the arrival of the Spanish, and at least one, that of the Natchez in what is now western Mississippi, survived into the eighteenth century.

Almost all of the moundbuilding centers were located within the Eastern Woodlands. This temperate, but relatively southern, forested region provided an ecological setting unlike any other in the world. There are no extensive forests in the temperate zone of the Southern Hemisphere, and all but one in the Northern Hemisphere are much further north. (Only the forests on the steep mountainsides of China's Yangzi River drainage share the Eastern Woodlands' southern temperate position.) Florida is at the same latitude as the Sahara Desert, and even Minnesota and Wisconsin, places usually thought of as northern, are, in fact, at the same latitude as Italy.

It should be emphasized, however, that the moundbuilding region was essentially a human creation—the result of cultural continuities that emerged from ceremonial and exchange networks—and that no single feature of the North American landscape, not even the Eastern Woodlands, shares with it exactly the same boundaries. The Woodlands, for example, extend north of the Great Lakes for a considerable distance and east of the Appalachian Mountains all the way to the Atlantic Ocean. But almost all moundbuilding centers were located south of the Great Lakes, and except in the Southeast (in the Carolinas, Georgia, Alabama, and Florida), almost all were located west of the Appalachian Mountains. It was only during the second epoch, when sites in southern Ohio were predominant, that centers could be found within the Lake Ontario drainage, in what is now New York State and the southeastern part of Ontario, Canada. On the other hand, during the third epoch when the largest center was at the mouth of the Missouri River, they extended westward along this river and its tributaries onto the Great Plains, well outside the bounds of the Woodlands.

Perhaps the best way to define the boundaries of the moundbuilding region would be to identify the four riverine drainage basins that it included. The largest part of the region was the eastern two-thirds of the Mississippi River drainage, from present-day Nebraska in the west to New York in the east, and from Minnesota in the north to Louisiana in the south. The region's second largest part was the Gulf Coast drainage basin from the Neches River in eastern Texas to the northern edge of the Everglades in Florida. These two basins were by far the largest and most important parts of the region. In addition, it included two adjacent areas. One was the southernmost part of the Atlantic Ocean drainage, from the Pee Dee River in North Carolina to southern Florida, and the other was the Lake Ontario drainage, which included much of New York and a small part of Ontario.

Unlike the ocean-linked networks of interaction that developed in Eastern North America after the Europeans came, those before 1492 faced inward toward the Mississippi River, and most of the eastern seaboard was a hinterland, on the far side of the Appalachians. West of the Woodlands, the Great Plains formed an ecological barrier, and except along the rivers that flowed into the Mississippi, the peoples there remained distinct from those of the moundbuilding region. Poverty Point in Louisiana, the largest center during the Late Archaic Moundbuilding Epoch, was located within sight of the Mississippi, and so was Cahokia in Illinois, the largest center during the third, Mississippian epoch. And during the second epoch when moundbuilding centers were concentrated in southern Ohio, they were near the Ohio River, a tributary of the Mississippi. Indeed, there is good reason to believe that at least some Native American peoples would have considered the Ohio centers to be near the Mississippi, since peoples in the western portion of present-day New York, for example, thought of the Allegheny, the Ohio, and the Mississippi below the Ohio as a single river.

The Mississippi River truly deserves its Indian name, *Missi* [Great] *Sippi* [River]. In the Western Hemisphere, it is the only major river that flows through a temperate zone. Its total drainage area is close to 1,250,000 square miles, an area equal in size to the country of India. Measured from its most distant headwaters in Montana, it flows for 3,741 miles before reaching the Gulf of Mexico. Thus its length is almost equal to that of the 4,000-mile-long Amazon River, which lies near the equator and flows through dense tropical forest.

Eastern North America's moundbuilding region is the only one in the hemisphere where the location of large centers was so closely related to a network of rivers. None of the great civilizations in Mesoamerica and the Andes was so closely identified with a large river basin. They generally had their origins in tropical or subtropical climes where the land rises steeply from coastal lowlands to high mountain plateaus, and much of the terrain is marked by numerous narrow and relatively steep drainage basins. In such locales, climate, growing conditions, and resources vary considerably from one elevation to another, and, in general, the earliest exchange networks and political structures brought about a vertical integration of lowland with highland.

Thus it is only the moundbuilding region of Eastern North America that resembles the pattern of the Eastern Hemisphere, where early civilizations were closely identified with rivers: the Tigris-Euphrates, the Nile, the Indus, and the Yellow River in China. Like the Mississippi, these rivers are located in the temperate latitudes, between 30 and 40 degrees north of the equator. There are, however, significant differences between the locales of these early riverine civilizations of Africa and Asia and Eastern North America's moundbuilding region. One of the most important is that a relatively steady and moderate amount of rain reliably falls over the Eastern Woodlands, whereas the Tigris-Euphrates, the Nile, the Indus, and the Yellow rivers flow for most of their courses through arid lands, in some cases through deserts and in others through what were once grasslands. Most of their water supply comes from the mountains where their headwaters are located, far from the coasts.

The ample rainfall in Eastern North America also accounts for another unique feature of the moundbuilding region. The Mississippi has a truly remarkable network of tributaries arrayed around it. A map of its trunkline and all the waterways that flow into it resembles a huge shrub, densely branched all the way out to the twigs. The Eastern Hemisphere rivers famous for the civilizations that grew up along them are not enhanced by any such array of tributaries. Because of the arid conditions over most of their drainage areas, they have few, if any, important tributaries, and most provide only a single trunk-line from the mountains to a distant coast.

The tributaries of the Mississippi are like the spokes of a wheel. The Missouri flows from Montana, from the northern end of the Rocky Mountains and all the way across the Great Plains before it enters the Mississippi. Further south, the Arkanses River links the Mississippi with Colorado. The Red River flows from what is now the New Mexico–Texas border to Arkansas, and down through Louisiana to the Mississippi. From the north the upper reaches of the Mississippi and the Illinois rivers link the Mississippi to Lake Superior and Lake Michigan. From the northeast, the Ohio River and its tributaries flow all the way from western New York and Pennsylvania, and from the southeast, the Tennessee River forms a waterway from western Virginia and the southern Appalachian highlands to the Ohio River, shortly before it enters the Mississippi.

Ample amounts of rain sustain the Woodlands, and its relatively southern position provides a considerably longer frost-free season than is typical of temperate forests. As a result, it is a uniquely hospitable environment for both plants and animals, and before 1492 it provided a much more diverse and rich array of resources for the people who lived there than did the more common temperate forests of Eurasia. Food was plentiful, even before A.D. 700, when peoples of the moundbuilding region began to depend upon corn and other domesticated plants for a large part of their food supply. Wild plants provided numerous edible seeds and highly nutritious nuts and berries, and wild animals and fish provided an ample source of meat. When people from the Eastern Hemisphere first arrived, deer were still so numerous that they roamed in great herds. The supply of bear meat and wild turkey was abundant. Early European travelers reported that the rivers were filled with monstrous fish, some so large that they threatened to overturn their canoes. And during those seasons when birds were migrating, flocks flew overhead that were so large that they darkened the sky. As late as 1810, a traveler remarked upon a flock of passenger pigeons (now extinct) that had come to rest in a willow grove near where the Ohio River flows into the Mississippi. They blanketed a forty-acre area, and were so densely perched that branches broke off from the trees and saplings bent to a ground covered with dung and feathers.

Thus in terms of such basic human needs as water, food, and shelter, this region was an abundant provider. It is, therefore, not surprising that prior to 1492 it was the most populous place north of the Valley of Mexico. Nor is it surprising that such a network of waterways, in combination with important overland trails, linked together one of the Western Hemisphere's earliest and largest exchange networks.

Nevertheless, most Americans are unaware of this past and of the mounds in their midst. We learn, instead, that soon after the Spaniards came to the Western Hemisphere, they seized the centers of the Aztec and Inca realms and thereby facilitated their conquests of Mexico and Peru. Few realize that there was one place, at least, where the Native Americans defeated the Spanish—this moundbuilding region of Eastern North America. Between 1513 and 1574, the Spanish launched a series of expeditions into what they called "Florida," the entire southeastern portion of what is now the United States. The expeditions of Juan Ponce de León (1513 and 1521), Pánfilo de Narváez (1528–1536), and Hernando de Soto (1539–1543) are well known, but what is not always made clear in our history books is that these three, as well as many of the others, ended in disaster for the Spaniards.

Both of Ponce de León's expeditions were forced to retreat to Cuba, where, after the second one, de León died of a wound. The Narváez expedition, with its five ships carrying about 600 men, was quite comparable in size to those that took Mexico and Peru. But it succumbed to storms, illness, mismanagement, and sustained Native American resistance. After the Spaniards had to abandon their position on the mainland, many of the men were lost at sea; on land, only four survived to make a retreat into the Spanish-held portion of Mexico.

De Soto's forces (which numbered 600 soldiers and 220 horses at the beginning) also suffered heavy losses. After de Soto's death from a fever on the Mississippi in 1542, only about 300 of his men were able to make a successful retreat by sea and find their way to Spanish territory in Mexico. It was not until 1574 that the Spaniards had a secure position even on the Florida peninsula. Thereafter they abandoned their efforts to conquer the rest of "Florida" and concentrated on maintaining the security of the Bahama Channel.

No doubt, there were many reasons why the expeditions of de León, de Narváez, and de Soto did not turn out like those of Cortés and Pizarro. Among them, one of the most important was that in Eastern North America there was no single center which the Spaniards could capture and thereby seize an empire, as they did in Mexico and in the Andes. Nor were there peoples recently subjugated by a single center, who would willingly ally with an outsider for an assault upon the hated conqueror. While it is true that Cahokia had been preeminent some three hundred years before, even at the peak of its influence it had been one of several important centers. In any case its power was gone long before the sixteenth century. At the time of the Spanish incursions, the moundbuilding region was home to a number of contending powers, and although a few of its rulers entertained hopes of enlisting the Europeans against their rivals, the Spaniards were unable to sustain any alliances for long.

The absence of an all-conquering power, however, did not mean that the region was lacking in military might. Its peoples did, after all, defeat the Spaniards, sometimes acting alone and sometimes in concert, and the Spaniards were impressed by the number and the skill of the warriors who mobilized against them. When the de Soto expedition was on the Mississippi River, for example, it encountered a fleet of two hundred large dugout canoes, each filled with many men. The warriors stood with their bows and arrows at the ready, while others sheltered the oarsmen with feathered shields. The leader of the expedition sat under an awning, on a raised platform at the rear of a barge, and from this perch gave orders to the rest of the force. According to one of the expedition's chroniclers, the fleet "appeared like a famous armada of galleys."

Had the Spaniards been able to conquer a significant portion of the moundbuilding region, the later history of Eastern North America would certainly have been different. To understand why the Native American peoples from this region were able to defeat them, it is necessary to know something about their precontact customs and organization. It was their past that influenced the manner in which they approached the newcomers, and it contributed to the outcome of those encounters as well. Events that transpired before 1492 thus had an impact on those after the arrival of peoples from the Eastern Hemisphere, when American history is usually deemed to begin. But even if this were not the case, and the peoples of the moundbuilding region had not played an important role in shaping postcontact events in this and many other ways, their story would still be important. It reveals the uniqueness of this land, the ingenuity of its peoples, and the diversity of the human experience. It deserves to be told, as a part of both American and world history. Without it, our history is incomplete.

2. The Urban Revolution in the Near East and North Africa

5. From *The West and the World: A History of Civilization*, second edition, by Kevin Reilly. New York: Harper & Row, 1989. Copyright © 1989 by Kevin Reilly. Reprinted by permission of Kevin Reilly.

6. From "Inventors and Technologists of Pharaonic Egypt" by Rashid el-Nadoury with the collaboration of Jean Vercoutter, from *Unesco Courier*, August/September 1979.

7. From *The Epic of Gilgamesh*, translated by N. K. Sanders (Penguin Classics, 1960, revised 1964, 1972). Copyright © 1960, 1964, 1972 N. K. Sanders. Reproduced by permission of Penguin Books, Ltd., London.

8. Reprinted with the permission of Charles Scribner's Sons, an imprint of Macmillan Publishing Company from *Babylonian and Assyrian Laws* by C. H. W. Johns. Copyright 1904 Charles Scribner's Sons; copyright renewed.

3. The Ancient Civilizations of Asia

9. From *India: A Concise History* by Francis Watson. Copyright © 1979 Francis Watson. Reprinted by permission of Thames and Hudson.

10.1. From *Sources of Indian Tradition* by William Theodore De Bary. Copyright © 1964 Columbia University Press, NY. Reprinted with permission of the publisher.

10.2. From *The Upanishads* (Penguin Classics, 1965), translated by Juan Mascaro. Copyright © 1965 by Juan Mascaro. Reproduced by permission of Viking Penguin.

10.3. From *The Thirteen Principal Upanishads*, second edition (Bombay: Oxford University Press, 1931), translated by R. E. Hume from *Brihad Aranyaka*, IV:4:5–6, pp. 140–1; and from *Chandogya*, V:10:7, p. 233.

11. From *The Shorter Science and Civilization in China*, Volume 1, by Colin A. Ronan. Copyright © 1978 Cambridge University Press. Reprinted with the permission of Cambridge University Press.

4. Greek Civilization

12. From *A World History*, second edition, by William H. McNeill. Copyright © 1971 by Oxford University Press, Inc. Reprinted by permission of the author.

13. From "The Athenian Constitution" by Aristotle, in *Aristotle, Politics, and the Athenian Constitution*, translated by John Warrington, 1959, Everyman's Library, David Campbell Publishers, UK.

14. From *The History of Thucydides*, Book II, translated by Benjamin Jowett. New York: Tandy-Thomas, 1909.

15. From *The Republic of Plato*, translated by F. M. Cornford (London: Oxford University Press, 1941).

5. Hellenistic and Roman Civilization

16. From *Asclepius*, Volume 1, by Emma J. and Ludwig Edelstein (reprinted in *Hellenistic Religions* edited by Frederick C. Grant). Copyright © 1988. Permission granted by Ayer Company Publishers, N. Stratford, NH.

17.1. From Mary R. Lefkowitz, *Women's Life in Greece and Rome: A Source Book in Translation*, 2nd ed. The Johns Hopkins University Press, Baltimore/London, 1992, pp. 135–139.

17.2. From Mary R. Lefkowitz, *Women's Life in Greece and Rome: A Source Book in Translation*, 2nd ed. The Johns Hopkins University Press, Baltimore/London, 1992, pp. 147–149.

18. "The Year One" (Chapter 15) from *Aspects of Antiquity* by M. I. Finley. Copyright © 1960, 1962, 1964, 1965, 1966, 1967, 1968 by M. I. Finley. Reprinted by permission of Viking Penguin, Inc.

6. Judeo-Christian Tradition

19. All biblical selections are from the King James Version.

20. S. G. Brandon, "Paul and His Opponents," in William L. Langer, ed., *Perspectives in Western Civilization*, Vol. I. New York: American Heritage Publishing Company, 1972. First published in *Horizon*, Winter 1968. Copyright by the author.

21. From *Psycho-Myth, Psycho-History*, Vol. II, by Ernest Jones. New York: Hillstone, 1974.

7. Indian Civilization

22. From The *Bhagavad-Gita*, translated by Barbara Stoler Miller. Translation copyright © 1986 by Barbara Stoler Miller. Used by permission of Bantam Books, a division of Bantam Doubleday Dell Publishing Group, Inc.

23.1. From *The Life of Gotama the Buddha*, translated by E. H. Brewster, as quoted in *Buddhism* by Clarence H. Hamilton (New York: 1952). London: Routledge & Kegan Paul, reprint of 1926 edition.

23.2. From *The Buddhist Tradition in India, China and Japan*, edited by William Theodore De Bary. Copyright © 1969 by Random House, Inc.

23.3. From *Ballads of Early Buddhist Nuns in Zero*, Volume V, translated from the *Pali Therigatha* by Barbara Stoler Miller.

8. Chinese Civilization

24. From *Analects of Confucius*, translated by Arthur Waley. London: George Allen & Unwin, 1958. Reprinted by permission.

25. From *Mencius*, translated by D. C. Lau. London: Penguin Classics, 1970. Copyright © D. C. Lau 1970. Reproduced by permission of Penguin Books, Ltd.

26. From *The Way & Its Power: A Study of the Tao Te Ching*, translated by Arthur Waley, 1934. Reprinted by permission of HarperCollins Publishers Limited, UK.

9. Hindu-Buddhist Civilization

27. From *Southeast Asia: Its Historical Development* by John Cady. New York: McGraw-Hill, Inc., 1964. Reprinted by permission of McGraw-Hill, Inc.

28. From *The Asians: Their Heritage and Their Destiny* by Paul Thomas Welty. Copyright © 1953, 1966, 1970, 1973, 1976 by Harper & Row, Publishers, Inc. Reprinted by permission of HarperCollins Publishers, Inc.

29. From *Nihongi: Chronicles of Japan from the Earliest Times*, Volume II, translated by W. G. Aston. London: George Allen & Unwin, 1896, 1956. Reprinted by permission.

10. East Asian Civilizations

30. From *China's Examination Hell* by Ichisada Miyazaki, translated by Conrad Schirokauer. Published by Weatherhill, Inc., of New York and Tokyo with editorial offices at 420 Madison Avenue, 15th Floor, New York, NY 10017.

31. Reprinted by permission of the publishers from *Remembrances: The Experience of the Past in Classical Chinese Literature* by Stephen Owen. Cambridge, Mass: Harvard University Press. Copyright © 1986 by the President and Fellows of Harvard College.

32. From Jacques Gernet, *Daily Life in China: On the Eve of the Mongol Invasion, 1250–1276*, translated from the French by H. M. Wright, Stanford, CA 1962. Copyright © 1959, Hachette. English translation copyright © 1962 by George Allen & Unwin, Ltd.

33. From the *World History Bulletin* (a publication of the World History Association, Drexel University, Philadelphia, PA), Fall/Winter 1986–7, volume 4, number 1. Permission granted by Lynda Norene Shaffer.

34. Excerpt from *The Tale of Genji* by Lady Murasaki, translated by Arthur Waley. Published by George Allen & Unwin, Ltd. and Houghton Mifflin Company. Copyright © 1929, Houghton Mifflin.

11. Islamic Civilization

35.1 From *Anthology of Islamic Literature*, selected, edited and introduced by James Kritzeck. Copyright © 1964 by James Kritzeck. Reprinted by permission of Henry Holt and Company, Inc.

35.2. From *The Qur'an: Selections from the Noble Reading*, third revised edition, translated by T. B. Irving. Copyright © 1991 by T. B. Irving. Published by the Mother Mosque Foundation, Cedar Rapids, Iowa.

36. From "The Civilization of Medieval Islam" by J. J. Saunders, in *A History of Medieval Islam* by J. J. Saunders. Copyright © 1978. Reprinted by permission of Routledge UK.

37. From *Anthology of Islamic Literature*, selected, edited and introduced by James Kritzeck. Copyright © 1964 by James Kritzeck. Reprinted by permission of Henry Holt and Company, Inc.

38. From *The Rubáiyát of Omar Khayyam*, Fitzgerald translation, fifth edition.

12. Byzantine Civilization

39. From *History of the World* by J. M. Roberts. Copyright © 1976 by J. M. Roberts. Reprinted by permission of Alfred A. Knopf, Inc.

40.1. From *The Secret History* by Procopius, translated by G. A. Williamson, pp. 82–86. Published by Penguin Classics, 1966. Copyright © 1966 G. A. Williamson. Reproduced by permission of Penguin Books Ltd., UK.

40.2. From *Theodore of Studium(s): His Life and Times*, translated by A. Gardner. London: Edward Arnold, 1905.

41. From *The Alexiad of the Princess Anna Comnena*, translated by Elizabeth A. S. Dawes. Copyright © 1967. Permission granted by Barnes & Nobles Books, Totowa, New Jersey 07512.

13. Western European Civilization

42.1. From "Charter of Homage and Fealty of the Viscount of Carcassone, 1110," D. C. Munro, *Translations and Reprints from the Original Sources of European History* (Philadelphia: University of Pennsylvania Press).

42.2. From "Services Due from a Villein, 1307," S. R. Scargill-Bird, ed., *Customals of Battle Abbey* (The Camden Society, 1887).

43. From *The Art of Courtly Love* by A. Capellanus, translated by John J. Parry. Copyright © 1990 Columbia University Press, New York. Reprinted with permission of the publisher.

44. From *Before European Hegemony: The World System A.D. 1250–1350* by Janet L. Abu-Lughod. Copyright © 1989 by Oxford University Press, Inc. Reprinted by permission.

45. From *Magna Carta*, translated by A. E. Dick Howard (Charlottesville: Virginia, 1964). Copyright © 1964 by The University Press of Virginia. Reprinted by permission.

14. The Impact of the Mongols

46. From *A World History*, second edition, by William H. McNeill. Copyright © 1971 by Oxford University Press, Inc. Reprinted by permission of the author.

47. From *Marco Polo: The Travels*, translated by Ronald Latham (Penguin Classics, 1958). Reproduced by permission of Penguin Books, Ltd., London.

48. From *Introduction to Islamic Civilization* by C. E. Bosworth, edited by Roger M. Savory. Copyright © 1976 Cambridge University Press. Reprinted with the permission of Cambridge University Press.

49. From "The Emperor's Giraffe" by Samuel M. Wilson. With permission from *Natural History*, December 1992. Copyright © the American Museum of Natural History, 1992.

15. African Civilizations

50. From *Sundiata: An Epic of Old Mali* by D. T. Niane, translated by G. E. Pickett, 1965. Reprinted by permission of Presence Africaine, Paris, France.

51. From *Ajaib-i Hind, talif-i Nakhuda Buzurg Shahriyar Ramhurmuzi* by al-Ram-Hurmuzi Buzurg ibn Shahriyar, pp. 50–60. Tihran, Iran: Bunyad-i Farhang-i Iran, 1969.

52. From *Travels of Ibn Battuta in Asia and Africa*, written and translated by H. A. R. Gibb. London: Routledge Kegan & Paul, 1927.

53. From *Africa and Africans* by Paul Bohannan. Copyright © 1964 by Paul Bohannan and 1971 by Paul Bohannan and Philip Curtin. Reprinted by permission of Waveland Press, Inc.

16. American Civilizations

54. "Secrets of the Maya Decoded at Last," by Erik Eckholm, May 13, 1986. Copyright © 1986 by The New York Times Company. Reprinted by permission.

55. From *The Memoirs of the Conquistador Bernal Diaz de Castillo*, translated by I. I. Lockhard. London: J. Hatchard, 1844.

56. From William H. Prescott, *The History of the Conquest of Peru*. New York: Harper, 1847.

57. From *Native Americans before 1492: The Moundbuilding Centers of the Eastern Woodlands*, by Lynda Norene Shaffer, pp. 3–15. Reprinted by permission of M. E. Sharpe, Inc., Armonk, New York 10504.